The Wretched Atom

THE WRETCHED ATOM
America's Global Gamble with Peaceful Nuclear Technology

Jacob Darwin Hamblin

OXFORD
UNIVERSITY PRESS

Oxford University Press is a department of the University of Oxford. It furthers
the University's objective of excellence in research, scholarship, and education
by publishing worldwide. Oxford is a registered trade mark of Oxford University
Press in the UK and certain other countries.

Published in the United States of America by Oxford University Press
198 Madison Avenue, New York, NY 10016, United States of America.

© Oxford University Press 2021

All rights reserved. No part of this publication may be reproduced, stored in
a retrieval system, or transmitted, in any form or by any means, without the
prior permission in writing of Oxford University Press, or as expressly permitted
by law, by license, or under terms agreed with the appropriate reproduction
rights organization. Inquiries concerning reproduction outside the scope of the
above should be sent to the Rights Department, Oxford University Press, at the
address above.

You must not circulate this work in any other form
and you must impose this same condition on any acquirer.

Library of Congress Cataloging-in-Publication Data
Names: Hamblin, Jacob Darwin, author.
Title: The wretched atom : America's global gamble with peaceful nuclear
technology / Jacob Darwin Hamblin.
Description: New York, NY : Oxford University Press, [2021] |
Includes index.
Identifiers: LCCN 2020039419 (print) | LCCN 2020039420 (ebook) |
ISBN 9780197526903 (hardback) | ISBN 9780197526927 (epub) | ISBN 9780197526934
Subjects: LCSH: Nuclear industry—United States—History—20th century. |
Nuclear energy—Government policy—United States. | Nuclear energy—
Economic aspects—United States. | Nuclear nonproliferation—
International cooperation. | United States—Foreign relations—
20th century. | United States—Foreign economic relations.
Classification: LCC HD9698.U52 H25 2021 (print) |
LCC HD9698.U52 (ebook) | DDC 338.4/762345119097309045—dc23
LC record available at https://lccn.loc.gov/2020039419
LC ebook record available at https://lccn.loc.gov/2020039420

DOI: 10.1093/oso/9780197526903.001.0001

9 8 7 6 5 4 3 2 1

Printed by Sheridan Books, Inc., United States of America

Dedicated to my sister
Sara Elizabeth Hamblin

CONTENTS

Acknowledgments   ix

Introduction   1

PART I: Atomic Promises

1. The Have-Nots   13

2. A Thousand Years into One   38

PART II: Atomic Propaganda

3. Forgetting the Bad Dreams of the Past   63

4. Colored and White Atoms   92

5. Turf Wars and Green Revolutions   123

PART III: Atomic Prohibition

6. Water, Blood, and the Nuclear Club   165

7. Nuclear Mosques and Monuments   189

8. The Era of Distrust   217

Conclusion: The Cornucopian Illusion   249

Notes   257
Index   305

ACKNOWLEDGMENTS

This is my fourth book based on original research, and it is no easy task to identify all the people who should be thanked. I began thinking about international dimensions of science and technology as a PhD student in the 1990s, and I even considered writing a history of the International Atomic Energy Agency as a dissertation. I'm glad I didn't. My PhD advisor, Lawrence Badash (1934–2010), didn't like the idea, and for good reason. The available archives were thin, the topic was vast, and besides, who wants to read an institutional history? I headed to other waters, choosing to write instead about oceanographers and the Cold War. Since that time, I have been helped in my work by scholars, students, archivists, and many others, as I have published on international cooperation in science, radioactive waste in the oceans, and the connections between military research and environmental science. Although the idea for this book came while I was looking through files at the archives of the Food and Agriculture Organization in Rome, I owe a debt to many others as I have researched and thought about these issues over the past two decades.

Some specific thanks are in order. Oxford University Press editor Susan Ferber has been a patient listener, and I continue to be awed by her capacity to read carefully and thoughtfully on such a wide range of subjects. The faculty and students at my home institution, Oregon State University, continuously shape my views about the past. Several scholars have been generous with feedback or other assistance over the years of researching, thinking about, and writing aspects of this book. They include Lisa Brady, Kate Brown, Angela Creager, John DiMoia, Toshihiro Higuchi, Paul Josephson, David Kaiser, Stuart W. Leslie, Gisela Mateos, Patrick McCray, Erika Milam, Ingrid Ockert, Jahnavi Phalkey, Maria Rentetzi, Linda Richards, Asif Siddiqi, Edna Suárez-Díaz, Aaron T. Wolf, Masakatsu Yamazaki, and Karin Zachmann. I especially wish to acknowledge Christine Keiner, Jayita

Sarkar, Robynne Mellor, and Jonathan Hunt for circulating drafts of their own manuscripts to me, prior to their publication.

I would like to thank the archivists and staff at all the institutions I consulted. I especially wish to thank those at the Food and Agriculture Organization (Rome) and the International Atomic Energy Agency (Vienna). At the IAEA, I was told that I was the first historian to use their archive for serious historical research. I remember my first 2008 visit to Vienna well; they did not quite know where to put me, so they cleared off someone's desk. The amount of material they released was sparse, even for documents more than forty years old. In 2014 I wrote an essay in *The Conversation* that criticized the agency for finding excuses to keep embarrassing material from the public eye. When I returned in 2016, the archivists were more experienced in receiving scholars and had been working to open up more. There is a long way to go for the agency as a whole, but I appreciate individual efforts to act in good faith within the wheels of bureaucracy.

Special thanks go to my family: my wife Sara and my children Sophia and Harper. I write these words several months into the COVID-19 pandemic, when we are confined together in strange circumstances. It is a reminder of how much patience and support are required from loved ones when a writer is trying to finish a book about one thing while worrying about so much else. My network of support includes my in-laws Paul and Cathy Goldberg, who amaze me in their capacity to provide encouragement. I especially want to thank my "first" family—my parents Les and Sharon Hamblin and my sister Sara. My father's long career in the Air Force working in strategic analysis and nuclear missiles shaped all our lives as we moved constantly from one place to another, and clearly influenced my own interests. I have admired my father's willingness to think critically and historically, just as I have appreciated my mother's wit, tenacity, and humility. As I have aged and seen my own children grow, I am reminded of how important those first relationships were to me. I also see how formative our own siblings are in the ways we see the world. Surely my life, my ideas, and my writing would be dramatically different without my sister, my first companion and friend. This book is dedicated to her.

The Wretched Atom

Introduction

When Iran's economic minister Hushang Ansari entered the Oval Office on March 4, 1975, he had ambitious dreams of a nuclear Iran. Though rich in oil, Iran planned to invest heavily in nuclear power, collaborating with Americans and Europeans on reactors, training, scientific surveys, and fuel production. It was part of a strategy to pump $180 billion of Iran's oil wealth into the country's economy, in the hope of improving the lives of every Iranian. US Secretary of State Henry Kissinger, who had been to Tehran just months before, encouraged these ambitions and noted to Ansari and President Gerald Ford that by 1983 Iranians could reach the European standard of living. Iran would focus not only on conventional economic measures, such as gross national product and per capita income, but on other markers of civilization, such as ownership of television sets, telephones, refrigerators, and cars. Iran would step up trade with the United States, invest in industries at home, and embark on massive infrastructure projects.[1] In return for oil, the United States promised billions of dollars in military equipment and a $12.5 billion civilian trade deal over five years, about half of which was for the development of Iran's civil nuclear program. The world seemed to be running out of oil, and even oil-rich nations would need to have a long-term energy plan. To escape the shortfalls looming on the horizon and to provide a future of abundance, Iran's future would be nuclear.[2]

Ansari was mildly apprehensive that Iran would not be able to acquire the technical know-how to build facilities to fabricate fuel for the reactors. During the previous summer, India had detonated a fission device, sparking worldwide outcry that nuclear weapons capability had spread to yet another country. Ansari wondered, should Iran be worried? If it invested in a nuclear power grid, would it one day be unable to acquire the technology to produce fuel for it? "There are technical obstacles," Kissinger acknowledged affably, "but we hope they can be worked out."[3]

Earlier that morning, Kissinger had a different sort of meeting with the president. "I don't think they realize what they are doing," Kissinger crowed, referring to "the Iranian stuff." The most important issue was not *proliferation*, but *petroleum*. Soon the Iranians would have so many financial commitments that they would lose their ability to cut oil production. "We may have broken OPEC, or will have if we can make one more deal like this."[4] In 1975, civilian nuclear technology was part of a worldwide strategy to bring the Organization of Petroleum-Exporting Countries (OPEC) to heel. That body's power seemed unprecedented, given that most of its countries were historically impoverished or "backward" peoples. Working with other big oil consumers in Europe, the United States secretly was "pushing the producers into big development programs, for which they will need the additional oil production." It would convince countries like Iran and Saudi Arabia to invest in expensive projects, like nuclear technology, so they would have so many bills to pay that they would have to sell their oil.[5]

By the time of the 1975 discussions with Iran, the United States had three decades of experience incorporating civilian nuclear technology into its relations with other countries. Atomic energy—to use the phrase most widely used at the time—had powerful appeal and seemed destined to lift up the poorest people on earth and deliver a future of abundance. Electricity generation was supposed to become "too cheap to meter," as one American political operator, Lewis Strauss, predicted in the 1950s.[6] Though civilian nuclear technology is most commonly associated with electricity, the promises extended beyond that. By exposing plants to the ionizing radiation from fission byproducts, it seemed possible to produce high-protein mutant strains of wheat and rice, staving off the kinds of cruel population corrections famously predicted by Thomas Malthus in 1798. As geneticist Diter von Wettstein imagined in the 1950s, "By radiation we can get almost anything out of a plant we really want. . . . We now have an instrument with which we can rebuild all the food plants in the world."[7] In addition, the irradiation of grain silos and packaged food could kill insects and bacteria, extending the shelf lives of the world's staple commodities. Exposing male flies to radioactive sources made them sterile, and females mating with them produced no offspring, thus reducing the population of major vectors of disease. Radioisotope tracers could be used to study ecosystems, fertilizers, or human metabolism. New sources of electrical power could be paired with desalination plants in coastal areas, and the water could be pumped into new irrigation systems—allowing deserts to bloom. Even nuclear detonations could be put to use, enabling enormous feats of engineering to rearrange natural landscapes. Atomic energy seemed to put the world on fast-forward: as American scientist Lloyd Berkner once remarked about mutation plant breeding, "It is as though, for evolutionary purposes, we had collapsed a thousand years into one."[8]

On the strength of such promises, atomic energy spread throughout the globe in the second half of the twentieth century, not only to the Soviet Union and to Europeans but also to the countries of the so-called developing world, with more fragile economies and often with newly independent governments grasping for stability. The United States' "Atoms for Peace" initiative was among the most famous of the Cold War era, launched by President Dwight Eisenhower in late 1953. It led to revisions of US legislation to allow more sharing of atomic technology, and it encouraged the notion that superpowers would disarm while the rest of the world would benefit from the civilian dimensions of the atom. The president offered to put sizable amounts of uranium fuel into the custody of a new international organization, to be used for the benefit of all. Dozens of nations joined the new International Atomic Energy Agency (IAEA), headquartered in Vienna. Atomic energy had a lot going for it: state sponsorship, diplomatic backing, and no shortage of scientists trying to imagine its bountiful future. Half a century after the historic speech, one could still visit the IAEA's Vienna headquarters and see images of a smiling Dwight Eisenhower and his "Atoms for Peace" slogan.[9]

By the century's end, the atom's utopian path had taken a decidedly dystopian turn. Atomic energy was as much a story of disenchantment and political opposition as it was of technological marvels. The nuclear sector suffered from high profile reactor accidents, waste disposal controversies, radiation exposure to people, the rise of anti-nuclear activist groups, and a decline in public trust in government institutions.[10] Many developing countries did adopt nuclear technologies, often with crucial parts of their national infrastructures relying on American and European expertise, equipment, and fuel. Rather than seeing liberation from nature, such countries faced renewed forms of dependence. Iran certainly never gained reliable access to uranium and did not become the economic miracle envisioned by Ansari back in 1975. Instead of lifting up the poorer nations of the world, the global nuclear order seemed structured in ways reminiscent of the colonial era. The most heated debates within the IAEA pitted the nuclear weapons states against the so-called LDCs—less developed countries. The agency never became a storehouse for fission products. Instead, one of its primary functions was to monitor an arms control treaty—the Treaty on the Non-Proliferation of Nuclear Weapons. By the end of the century, the IAEA was referred to as a "watchdog," known for its cadre of inspectors. In 2003, IAEA inspections were crucial talking points in public debates about the invasion of Iraq by the United States. What an extraordinary irony: exactly fifty years after Eisenhower's speech, evidence gathered over the years by the agency created for the peaceful atom was being interpreted by the United States government as justification for military intervention. Moreover, it was a war that pitted a technologically advanced superpower, fighting a limited war in a faraway land, against a formerly colonized, non-white, non-industrialized nation known for an important natural resource, battling to the death in its own total war.

What accounts for such a dystopian turn in the global nuclear order? One culprit typically springs to mind, namely, the steady rise of nuclear weapons programs from an original group comprised of the United States, the Soviet Union, and Britain. Nuclear states struck a "grand bargain" with the rest of the world, promising to share civilian nuclear technology with others in return for their oath to forgo nuclear weapons, and the promise that the nuclear states would reduce their own arms. Voluminous scholarship exists on the history and politics of proliferation, often framed as a story of arms control, with the United States and other nuclear states trying to meet their commitments while also attempting to prevent new bomb programs. Some countries, like India, balked at the notion of haves and have-nots in nuclear programs and refused to sign non-proliferation agreements. New countries joined the nuclear club in the 1960s and 1970s: first came France in 1960, China in 1964, India in 1974, and then others attempted to follow—Israel, South Africa, Pakistan, North Korea, Iraq, and Iran. Worries about proliferation dramatically altered the nuclear trade in the 1970s and 1980s and dampened the utopian prospects of the atom. The promise remained, but countries that once thought they would have access to commercial technologies came to face strict inspections and "safeguards" rules about how to use their equipment and fuel. Those countries in breach of such agreements faced the prospect of crippling economic sanctions or even war.[11]

While an arms control perspective is valuable in understanding the politics of weapons proliferation, it tells us little about the historical motivations for encouraging civilian nuclear programs in the first place. Focusing only on arms control glosses over the domestic politics of nuclear programs, particularly the role of high technology as symbols of state power and legitimacy.[12] But it also does not square with what scholars of the Cold War have been pointing out for decades—that governments, especially the United States, deployed science and technology as diplomatic tools, to achieve feats of prestige, to shape business arrangements, to conduct clandestine surveillance, or to bind countries together with technical assistance programs. Poorer countries' dreams of modernization, of using advanced technology to escape hunger, poverty, and the constraints of nature—these were the stock-in-trade of US diplomacy.[13] Why, then, should we imagine that the promises connected to peaceful uses of atomic energy were any less saturated with geopolitical maneuvers and manipulation? Indeed some historians have implicated the peaceful atom as one of the most important and overlooked political tools of the United States from the 1950s onward.[14] After all, it seemed to be the epitome of power and modernity at a crucial epoch of history: when the post–World War II political order was built; when dozens of countries around the world, especially in Asia and Africa, freed themselves from colonial masters; and when the balance of global natural resource wealth—especially petroleum—seemed to tilt away from the United States and Europe for the first time. Rather than ask what stopped the utopia from happening, we should be scrutinizing the promise of the atom, to understand how the United States and other governments used it as a tool to maneuver in such a world.

The Wretched Atom is the first historical study of efforts to promote nuclear technologies globally from the Second World War to the close of the twentieth century. It focuses on countries that seemed to live at the knife's edge of human existence—those with subsistence economies or resource shortfalls, or where peoples routinely were threatened by famine, drought, and disease. Such countries were comprised largely of non-white peoples, many of them former colonies or recently under military occupation. In the past, these would have been classed as belonging to the Third World, developing world, less developed countries—or even less charitably, as "backward" countries. Included are countries that today might seem out of place in such categories, such as Israel or Japan. The book explores the experiences of large and populous former colonies, such as India and Brazil, but also smaller ones, such as Ghana and other African states that gained independence in the 1960s. The term "wretched" is inspired by Frantz Fanon's 1961 book, *Les Damnés de la Terre*, published in English as *The Wretched of the Earth*. Written amid the war in Algeria by a black man attuned to colonial conflict, Fanon's book reflected on the bitter ironies of formerly brutalized and marginalized people being offered technological solutions. "They are wooed," he wrote. "They are given bouquets of flowers. Invitations. To be frank, everyone wants a piece of them."[15] To Fanon, the shortcut offered by technology was little more than a sales pitch, at best playing on naïve dreams that hundreds of years of economic evolution could be skipped and at worst providing an in-road to other forms of paternalistic influence, leaving such countries forever "wretched" or "damned" to continue the structures of colonialism.

To understand the origins of the global nuclear dystopia at the dawn of the twenty-first century requires paying attention to those who tried to convince the world—and especially those in the poorer regions of the world—that they should commit to atomic energy. By necessity that begins with the United States government, the promiser-in-chief, but it also extends to other nuclear states and to international organizations where bitter disputes arose. It includes those trying to build up nuclear infrastructure in countries such as Japan, Ghana, South Africa, India, Pakistan, Iraq, and Iran. By focusing on these historical actors, a past emerges in which the so-called peaceful atom is implicated in the exercise of state power, the attainment of personal ambitions, the cynical wielding of technological promises for political or diplomatic purposes, the manipulation of global trade, and even the reinforcement of racism and colonialism. The promise of civilian atomic energy was a formidable tool of state power in the late twentieth century because it took advantage of social aspirations, anxieties, and environmental vulnerabilities, especially in the developing world. Ironically, atomic energy rarely had to deliver on its promise to be effective. Further, the deployment of rhetoric to promote atomic energy was inseparable from geopolitics writ large and has rarely been entirely peaceful. Instead it has been embedded in stories of conventional warfare, racial and neocolonial divisiveness, struggles to assert control over the earth's natural resources, and the abetting of nuclear weapons programs both old and new.

In making this argument, *The Wretched Atom* highlights several themes that recurred from the dawn of the nuclear age to the close of the twentieth century—and even beyond. One was the manipulation of perceptions about atomic energy's technological potential, in order to achieve or maintain control of the world's natural resources. For example, American officials in the late 1940s and early 1950s were very worried that commercial nuclear power would siphon off supplies of uranium and monazite needed for the weapons arsenal. So they explicitly played down the possibility of electricity generation from atomic energy and instead played up the importance of radioisotopes for medicine and agriculture—because such radioisotopes were byproducts of the US weapons arsenal and did not compete with it. The kinds of technologies promoted in the developing world by the United States, the USSR, and Europeans thus seemed neocolonial, keeping the former colonies as sites of resource extraction—a fact noticed, and resented, by government officials in India, Brazil, and elsewhere. Mutation plant breeding, irradiation for insect control or food sterilization, and radioisotope studies in fertilizer—these were oriented toward food and export commodities and public health, problems indistinguishable from those of the colonial era. These were not the same kinds of technologies embraced by the global North, which focused on electricity generation through nuclear reactors, often as a hedge against the rising political power of petroleum-producing states in the Middle East. By the mid-1960s and 1970s, the United States and Europe did offer nuclear reactors even to some of the most politically volatile nations, as part of an effort to ensure access to oil. Convincing petroleum suppliers of their dire future need for nuclear reactors was part of a strategy to regain geopolitical leverage. Despite the moniker "peaceful atom," these technologies were often bundled in trade deals with fighter jets, tanks, and other military hardware.

Another key theme was the reliance by governments on a cornucopian vision that presented atomic energy as a savior to those peoples of the earth constantly threatened by disease, drought, famine, and poverty. Just as the fabled horn of plenty (cornucopia) in classical antiquity overflowed with fruits and grains, so too would atomic energy provide a future of abundance. Advocates of atomic energy spoke of "quickening the pulse" of nature, a nod to the conceit of modernization and its notion of quickly putting nations on an equal footing with the global North. With the atom, nature's constraints could be overcome; nature's pulse could be quickened; nature's scourges could be outrun. This discourse of overabundance did not belong solely to the United States and other industrialized countries. It also was adopted by governments attempting to build, justify, and protect their own nuclear energy programs—whether they were genuinely bent toward peaceful uses or not. Because of these rhetorical connections to nature, atomic energy's relationship to environmental issues was complicated and paradoxical. On the one hand, atomic energy advocates in the postwar decades were alive to environmental challenges, invoking threats such as Malthusian population pressure, water security, Rachel Carson's warning about indiscriminate use of insecticides, and even the relationship between carbon emissions and global climate change. And yet these same historical actors—backed by government agencies—often dismissed concerns of ecologists and environmental activists as irrational and emotional when they questioned atomic energy. By the close of the century, two competing environmental narratives were plainly in use. One was critical of atomic energy, drawing on scientific disputes about the public health effects of radiation, the experience of nuclear accidents such as Three Mile Island (1979) and Chernobyl (1986), or the egregious stories of public health injustice—including negligence in protecting uranium miners or the wanton destruction and contamination of indigenous peoples' homelands. In contrast was the narrative favored by most governments, depicting nuclear technology in a messianic role, promising not only abundant food, water, and electricity, but also an end to atmospheric pollution and climate change.

A third theme is that government promotion of atomic energy to solve social and environmental problems frequently was insincere, overstated, or speculative. Certainly there were historical actors who genuinely believed in the power of atomic energy to uplift the peoples of the world. But it should be stated at the outset that many of the technologies were promoted cynically—defended by government boosters for reasons having little to do with solving genuine problems. Many were designed instead to bolster the credibility of programs oriented toward nuclear weapons or to offer plausible peaceful applications to countries in return for forswearing weapons programs. Time and again, what mattered was not the problem to be solved but the solution to be offered. For example, when President Lyndon Johnson offered desalination plants to Israel in the 1960s as part of his "Water for Peace" plan, neither he nor his Israeli counterparts were interested in providing water in the most economical or technically feasible way; they wanted nuclear plants or nothing at all. Similarly, the IAEA's forays into solving problems of food security and public health, which put it into direct conflict with other international agencies such as the Food and Agriculture Organization and the World Health Organization, were designed to secure credible achievements in the nuclear realm. The agency was like a hammer in search of nails. It did not matter what the problem was as long as the solution was nuclear.

A final theme is the political use of international forums for the peaceful atom, especially the IAEA. As other scholars have noted, the IAEA tried to maintain a reputation of being primarily a technical body, devoid of politics. But it had numerous political uses. For example, it was a forum for intelligence gathering, as routinely noted by American Central Intelligence Agency (CIA) documents. It also outmaneuvered the World Health Organization and Food and Agriculture Organization in the early 1960s and was able to assert an authoritative voice playing down public health dangers from atomic energy. Further, it provided a vehicle for countries to stay engaged in atomic energy affairs even if they did not sign on to the non-proliferation treaty—India, Pakistan, and Israel most notably. It provided apartheid-era South Africa with a means of participating in international affairs when other bodies ousted it because of its blatantly racist policies.[16] By the same token, it gave the Americans and Europeans political cover for continuing to engage with South Africa, an important uranium supplier. The IAEA provided a public face to several countries' clandestine bomb programs, even as it purported to act as an instrument of non-proliferation. The United States and Europeans tried to defend the agency as purely technical, offering economic and social uplift to the formerly colonized world, a powerful rhetorical move that enabled turning the agency into a monitoring and surveillance organization.

This book is structured in three parts, reflecting historical shifts in the use of atomic energy as a tool of state power by the United States and other governments. The first part, Atomic Promises, focuses on the immediate postwar decade, in which atomic bombs were new and ideas for civilian applications were abundant—some based on science and others on science fiction. The chapters emphasize how the global search for uranium and monazite shaped the US government's changing position on sharing technology in the years before Eisenhower's iconic 1953 speech, and they highlight the powerful attraction of promising the atom to "backward" countries. What we find in these chapters are myriad attempts to imagine what could be promised to other nations in return for loyalty, minerals, or political acquiescence in American nuclear weapons tests. The second part, Atomic Propaganda, explores the consequences of such promises in the 1950s and 1960s, as the United States confronted the limits of its own rhetoric, particularly in Asia and Africa. These chapters focus on the heyday of "Atoms for Peace" when American presidents feared the language of race, colonialism, and neocolonialism, and hoped to supplant it with hopes of technological marvels or rapid economic development. India, Japan, Ghana, and South Africa all launched efforts to adopt atomic energy as symbols of modernity and prosperity, and the new International Atomic Energy Agency cast itself as a partner in domains ranging from electricity to agriculture, disease control, and medicine. Finally, Part III, Atomic Prohibition, underscores how the peaceful atom changed after the first "colored" Bombs appeared—in China in 1964 and India in 1974—and after control of a key energy resource, petroleum, shifted away from the United States and Europe and toward less industrialized countries, especially in the Middle East. The politics of non-proliferation and peaceful atomic energy went hand in hand, and nuclear technologies became embedded more than ever in strategies to achieve political and economic leverage. These chapters stress how indispensable the cornucopian promise of the atom was to the American exercise of global power by the end of the century.

Despite *The Wretched Atom* being framed as a story of manipulation and control, the United States, European nations, and the Soviet Union clearly did not always succeed in their efforts. Even in the late 1940s, many Americans feared that encouraging the worldwide adoption of atomic technologies was an immense gamble with unpredictable consequences. Much of what transpired in subsequent decades can be interpreted as struggles for agency in deciding the future of one's own country or in leveraging opportunities amid swiftly changing geopolitical circumstances. Many of the most surprising and interesting stories are of individuals within developing countries trying to make the promise of atomic energy serve national ambitions. For example, Japanese newspapers attempted to turn the atom into a friend, collaborating with American intelligence agents, less than a decade after the devastation of Hiroshima and Nagasaki. Atomic energy was used as a tool of pan-Africanism in newly independent sub-Saharan states in the 1960s and of pan-Arabism during the oil crisis of the 1970s. The nuclear sector became a national point of pride in India, Pakistan, and Iran. Many of these impulses are in the distant past but others are still with us, including the use of peaceful programs to hide or distract from bomb programs, the continued downplaying of environmental harm by the International Atomic Energy Agency, and the role of nuclear power's vision of plenty in propping up the Treaty on the Nonproliferation of Nuclear Weapons.

A careful reader may wonder at the outset whether the perspectives in *The Wretched Atom* are pro-nuclear or anti-nuclear. They are neither. The perspectives here are historical. What should be clear by the end of this book is that the promise of the peaceful atom has been used, abused, and exploited for decades, certainly by industry boosters but most powerfully by governments—led by the United States and including many others—often leveraging the greatest fears and highest ambitions of peoples around the world. It has been in the national interest of certain states to protect the integrity of their nuclear weapons programs and their energy strategies from critics. The peaceful atom has been an instrument to do so, just as it has been an instrument for shaping the control of natural resources and global energy supplies. Adopting nuclear power has never been a mere technical choice. It may be natural to imagine a nuclear solution to present and future crises, as we do when considering how to mitigate threats from a changing planetary climate. Nevertheless, it would be folly to imagine that this promise—a future of abundance and avoiding environmental disaster—is new or that it is not an irrevocable part of the global nuclear order.

PART I
Atomic Promises

CHAPTER 1

The Have-Nots

When Boris Davidovitch first saw the white sand beaches of Brazil, he knew they held a secret. The stretch of spectacular coastline in the state of Espírito Santo, long favored by tourists and beach lovers, was unusually radioactive. The Russian-born businessman came there in the 1930s as director and part owner of a French firm, Société Minière, after participating in several mining and commercial concerns trafficking in radioactive substances since the 1920s. He knew the radioactivity in Espírito Santo's beaches meant the presence of monazite, a precious and profitable commodity. By extracting the sand, he could sell the monazite abroad to chemical refineries that isolated "rare earths" such as cerium and lanthanum, as well as a mysterious radioactive element called thorium.

After the fall of France to Nazi Germany in 1940, Davidovitch became a personal ally of the United States in its quest to secure strategic minerals around the world. In a move that would later invite unsuccessful criminal prosecution in France, he sold the French company and used his proceeds to form a new one owned by himself, Monazita Ilmenita do Brasil (MIBRA), with its major mining operations on the beaches of the coastal town of Guarapari.[1] Most of the world's supply of monazite thus far had come from India. Davidovitch became the "monazite baron" after convincing the Chicago-based Lindsay Light and Chemical Company to open up a new source in Brazil as a hedge against the British losing control of its Indian colony during the war. Brazil's share of Lindsay's wartime supply climbed to some 30 percent. The monazite was then broken down into products crucial for US military technology. Mischmetal, an alloy of cerium, lanthanum, and other rare earths, was used in the manufacture of jet propulsion plane motors, for example, while a mixture called rare earth fluoride was used to make hard carbons, needed in aerial searchlights (as well as making motion pictures). At first, the thorium seemed innocent compared to the other rare earths, being used primarily to make incandescent bags (mantles) within gas lanterns.[2]

The acquisition of that monazite, along with the uranium sources of the world, became a high priority for the United States and other aspiring nuclear powers. The scientists of the wartime Manhattan Project believed thorium had a destiny far more consequential than lantern bags—that it, like uranium, could be used to build atomic bombs. On the day of the first detonation of an atomic bomb in the New Mexico desert—the so-called Trinity Test of July 16, 1945—the United States also negotiated a secret agreement with Brazil to ensure the US purchase of 3,000 tons of monazite sands per year. Soon the US State Department made thorium's relevance abundantly clear in its *Report on the International Control of Atomic Energy* (the so-called Acheson-Lilienthal Report), which highlighted thorium's role in chain reactions with uranium and its role in producing other fissile material. The report was released publicly in March 1946, just half a year after the first bombs were dropped on Japan, alerting the whole world to the strategic importance of monazite sands.

At the end of the war, the United States seemed to possess awesome power across a range of atomic technologies. Some were real, such as the bomb itself, and others were imagined future peaceful applications in agriculture, medicine, and other domains such as electricity generation. The United States was positioned as a technological leader, holding secrets to be shared with allies or perhaps given for peaceful purposes to the rest of the world. If there were "haves" and "have-nots," the United States was surely a "have." And yet such a perspective, while it accorded with the image fashioned by the US State Department, ignored an important vulnerability. The nation's intense focus on fuel sources for the atomic bomb made it immensely dependent on colonial holdings of allies or on other countries Americans deemed to be "backward." In this respect the Americans—and like them, the Soviets, British, and French—were not "haves" but "have-nots," exerting their considerable diplomatic, trade, and military power to find and extract strategic materials all around the world. One strategy for doing so was to encourage the notion that peaceful applications of the atom in such countries should focus on subsistence, raw materials commodities, and basic sanitation and medicine—the same areas of focus under colonialism. Such attitudes were deeply resented, and resisted, by independent former colonial states such as India, Argentina, and Brazil. But US diplomats persisted, keen to shape conversations about what constituted feasible peaceful atomic energy technologies. They did so to prevent commercial competition for uranium and monazite. In the late 1940s, when uranium seemed scarce, the US government made it policy to cast doubt on commercial uses of atomic energy and instead to trumpet the use of radioisotopes, which had potential applications in agricultural and medical research. These were created after the use of uranium in weapons production and could even be considered waste products. In practice, in their quest for strategic resources to secure the weapons arsenal, US officials narrowed the state-sanctioned meaning of the peaceful atom—deemphasizing industrial power and instead playing up the ability of the atom to provide plentiful food and to improve human health.

* * *

In a top secret briefing to Congress's Joint Committee on Atomic Energy in 1947, Under Secretary of State Dean Acheson pointed out that "practically none of the raw materials [for the atomic bomb] lie in territories under the direct control of the United States."[3] The uranium for the first bombs had come from Africa, in Belgium-controlled Congo, and supplies elsewhere appeared scarce. British-controlled India had extensive beaches of monazite sands and accounted for most of the American supply during the war. The Brazilian source was meant as a backup, in case Britain lost India to the Axis Powers. Although Britain did not lose India during the war, India did gain independence soon after. Among India's first acts as an independent state was to halt exports of monazite. When Secretary of State George Marshall went to the Inter-American Conference for the Maintenance of Continental Peace and Security in late August 1947, he made the negotiation of monazite trade a high priority, hoping for increased imports from Brazil, for atomic energy uses.[4] By the end of 1949, the US embassy made it crystal clear to the Brazilian government that the nation wanted to buy "Brazil's entire exportable surplus" of monazite, and if Brazil ever acquired the ability to extract thorium from monazite, it wanted to buy all of it.[5]

American anxieties about uranium and monazite had a direct impact on the state-sanctioned view of the future of peaceful atomic energy. Secretary of State Marshall routinely downplayed the importance of atomic reactors to meet electricity demands. The last thing he wanted was for uranium to be perceived as a valuable civilian commodity. Instead of highlighting electricity generation, American diplomats began to stress other peaceful uses of the atom, ones that conceivably could help countries develop light industries while combating the scourges of nature such as drought and disease. This could be done most effectively not through electricity production, they would argue, but by the use of the radioisotopes produced in reactors and in cyclotrons. Such radioisotopes were not rare fissionable elements like uranium and thorium but instead were the more common elements such as carbon and iodine, made radioactive by exposure to intense, ionizing radiation in the reactors within weapons facilities. Because these radioisotopes, dubbed radiocarbon or radioiodine, were easily detectable with a Geiger counter, they made ideal research materials for working with human and animal metabolism, fertilizer studies, and ecology—any subject in which tracking flows was important. They were products of the nuclear arsenal but could be bent toward civilian use.

The Americans and the British had already begun promoting the uses of radioisotopes, but demand for them was low. The distribution of radioisotopes from Oak Ridge National Laboratory (the principal site of uranium enrichment for bomb materials), managed by corporate contractors such as Monsanto and Union Carbide, began in 1946. Paul C. Aebersold, who headed the "Isotopes Branch" at Oak Ridge from 1946, was an enthusiastic booster of civilian uses and expected a wide market for them. However, even though the laboratory kept costs low, at times it could not even give radioisotopes away. Like many of his colleagues, Aebersold had bought into the idea that in cancer research and other applications, radioisotopes held the key to redeeming the atom and solving real problems in the world. But there were just not enough people who agreed, who were highly trained, who had appropriate facilities, and who had matching research agendas. The radioisotope program overestimated the number of requests, and the industrial-scale production by 1947 far surpassed demand. As historian Angela Creager has written, the Isotopes Branch at Oak Ridge consequently developed "a culture of promotion" to convince users that the future of peaceful atomic energy lay in radioisotopes.[6]

In the late 1940s, the Americans and British engaged in an extensive effort to focus attention on radioisotopes as the principal means of connecting atomic energy to social progress. Radioisotopes were not new; they could be produced in the cyclotrons developed in the 1930s. But they also were waste products of nuclear reactors, and consequently the American and British bomb programs were awash in them. The UK's Atomic Energy Research Establishment at Harwell, led by John Cockcroft, was eager to produce radioisotopes for export. Cockcroft had participated in the wartime Anglo-Canadian program at Chalk River, Canada, where a reactor was used to produce plutonium and other radioactive isotopes. For him, it seemed like the most natural thing to do, upon returning to England, to focus on radioisotope production and create alliances with the British Medical Research Council to promote their use in hospital and biomedical research settings. Then Atomic Energy Research Establishment marketed them to Western European institutions. Harwell's Isotope Division, created in 1948, was modeled after the one at Oak Ridge, but by 1949 its export of radioisotopes exceeded that of the United States. Like Paul Aebersold, German-born British scientist Henry Seligman imagined a large market in radioisotopes and to develop this market he worked hard to provide training, public health manuals, and plenty of publicity.[7]

In the United States, many within the Truman administration and his Atomic Energy Commission (AEC) initially resisted approving shipments of radioisotopes abroad. Aebersold and others at Oak Ridge—sitting on an enormous supply and hoping for access to European users in particular—complained bitterly against the legal constraints, saying that the AEC's reluctance to share "goes as far as to class us in somewhat the same light as Russia on scientific and political matters." After President Truman announced the plan for European economic recovery in 1947, widely known as the Marshall Plan, the AEC agreed to open up a much larger market for distribution of the radioisotopes. The president announced the availability of radioisotopes to foreigners on September 3, 1947, at the International Cancer Research Congress in St. Louis, thus stamping it as an action that could save lives. After that, Oak Ridge made not only rhetorical but also infrastructural commitments to these international markets. In 1949 it started building facilities to reflect its status as a permanent national laboratory (a designation made in 1948) rather than a holdover from a wartime operation. This included ten buildings devoted to processing, packaging, and shipping radioisotopes—known locally as Isotope Alley—which would be expanded over time.[8]

Sharing anything atomic, radioisotopes or not, was a foreign notion to many in the US government, and at the time, the political cost of the radioisotope program was high. Opponents mistrusted it as a giveaway program of a sensitive military technology. For example, Lewis Strauss, one of the AEC commissioners, tried in vain to stop shipments, saying that distribution should be linked to an agreement on international control of atomic energy. Strauss and other Republicans characterized the radioisotope distribution program as handing over American secrets to the communists. It was one of several points used by Republican politicians to implicate AEC chairman David Lilienthal as inattentive to security concerns. Strauss pored over shipment reports with a fine-toothed comb, and when he saw that radioactive iron had been sent to the Norwegian Defense Establishment, he brought it to Congress as an example of the AEC's leaky security procedures. He also disliked Finland as a recipient, given its proximity to, and close relationship with, the Soviet Union. Worse perhaps, in

Strauss's estimation, was that the French also received radioisotopes, even though the head of France's atomic energy establishment, Frédéric Joliot-Curie, was an avowed communist.[9]

Although Strauss imagined anything radioactive as an American commodity to be kept under lock and key, the truth was more complicated. The United States already had begun to leverage the peaceful atom to consolidate relations with countries that had important strategic resources. The US radioisotope distribution program targeted European colonial powers in particular (about 70 percent of shipments in the first year went to Europe or to British Commonwealth countries such as Australia). No one had built a commercial nuclear reactor, and the State Department hoped to keep it that way. Radioisotopes were easy to promise because they were plentiful. By contrast, the United States was noticeably unwilling to help with other kinds of atomic development. For example, Brazil offered diplomatic backing to American proposals about international control of atomic energy but wanted price guarantees on the raw materials it would supply, representation on any future international atomic energy body, and preferential treatment in building nuclear power plants. American negotiators stalled, not wanting to hint at a future of commercial power plants.[10]

Focusing on radioisotopes helped the United States to appear willing to share, focusing on the life sciences, agriculture, or medicine, and avoiding physics. As former Manhattan Project scientist Henry DeWolf Smyth pointed out in 1950, "The isotope distribution program is enormously valuable because it reveals the Atomic Energy Commission as more than just a weapons organization. This is true not only in this country, but abroad where the foreign distribution of isotopes has had a very good effect on our foreign relations." Argentina's National Academy of Medicine was one of the first recipients of American radioisotopes in late 1947, and Peru and South Africa also received shipments. The vast majority of foreign shipments went to biomedical research, with a small portion to agriculture.[11] The AEC held back on the physics side, avoiding connections to bombs and civilian reactors, while pushing uses for health and food.

Promoting anything "atomic" in South America was anathema to American officials in the first few years after the war. Both Brazil and Argentina had been centers of operations for Nazi intelligence agents, and the United States clashed with Argentina about the repatriation of Nazis to Germany. After the war, under pro-fascist leader Juan Perón, Argentina became a haven for many ex-Nazis and harbored several indicted war criminals, such as Auschwitz physician Joseph Mengele, Adolf Eichmann, and (the Americans suspected) Martin Bormann.[12] In 1946, Secretary of State James Byrnes wrote to the Argentine embassy that German influence had penetrated the highest levels of the Argentine Foreign Office.[13] He issued a "Blue Book on Argentina" (its cover bore the words "Argentina Exposed!"), a compendium of information enumerating ways that Argentina had collaborated with the Nazis and still posed a threat to its neighbors. It warned: "The industries essential to warfare in which experimentation in the weapons of future wars may take place and in which prototypes may be developed exist in Argentina and are controlled by Germans."[14]

Argentina was a leading example of a country determined to avoid being treated as a subordinate nation. Early on, it viewed the United States' asymmetrical atomic sharing (heavy on agriculture and medicine, light on physics) as a quasi-colonial power move. Argentina's government and scientists were quite interested in nuclear physics. In fact, Perón tried to construct a nuclear program with help from some of Hitler's best physicists. During the war, Enrique Gaviola, director of the National Observatory of Córdoba, had recruited to Argentina the Austrian physicist Guido Beck, who arrived in 1943 after working directly with Werner Heisenberg, the scientific head of the Nazi atomic bomb project. Gaviola hoped to repeat this kind of recruitment in the postwar years, attracting top scientists away from dismal conditions in war-torn Europe in order to build up expertise in Argentina. "Such a favorable situation to convert Argentina into a civilized and educated country," he wrote, "might not take place again for the next hundred years." Gaviola dreamed of recruiting Heisenberg and invited him to visit campus. The prospect of having a Nobel prize-winning physicist visit the new University of Buenos Aires would have been a boon to local prestige, but was far from what the United States hoped would transpire with radioisotopes in Latin America.[15] The American magazine *New Republic* published an essay called "Perón's Atomic Plans," directly stating that a military research project was under way, citing the Heisenberg invitation and the discovery of uranium ores in Argentina. Gaviola never did get Heisenberg to come to Argentina, since British occupation authorities informed Heisenberg that he would unlikely be granted permission to leave, "for obvious reasons."[16]

For Gaviola, British interference over Heisenberg struck a nerve—it was not interpreted as a security measure for occupied Germany but instead as a way of keeping Argentina in its place. It smacked of just the kind of paternalistic, imperialistic attitude that he expected of the British. It reminded Gaviola of Britain's shabby treatment of Argentina during the 1932 Ottawa conference, when Britain gave economic preference to its colonies. Several subsequent, lopsided pacts with Argentina—ones that guaranteed British access to beef, for example—made Argentina look like an informal colony.[17] Gaviola saw interference in the nuclear domain similarly, and he complained to a high-ranking Argentine naval officer, "Is it that Argentina is still an English 'Honorific Dominion'?"[18]

The brain hunting of German talent by Argentina turned out to be a bold yet infamous misstep. Perón invested his confidence in German expatriate Ronald Richter, who made promises of energy from controlled fusion (rather than fission). Perón created the Comisión Nacional de Energía Atómica to support his goals and delegated to Richter extraordinary authority over a secretive, island laboratory away from the public eye and far from Buenos Aires. Richter showed little interest in collaborating with scientists from metropolitan areas, and ultimately in 1952 he was denounced as a fraud. He had made an attractive promise, namely, that Argentina would be a leader rather than a follower. It allowed Perón to offer his people a tool to "provide light, cook food, and heat the iron." Fusion power would be unique, and Argentina would not be forced to play the child any longer to American and British paternalism. While the Richter fiasco was an embarrassment, the impulse to remain defiant and pragmatic would continue to guide atomic energy in Argentina.[19]

So why did the United States warm to Argentina in 1947, even agreeing to send radioactive isotopes there at a time when David Lilienthal was in hot water for sending them to Norway? It was not as if the Nazi problem had been resolved. The Federal Bureau of Investigation, which maintained staff in foreign countries under its Special Intelligence Service (SIS) Division, stated in 1947 that "most of the really dangerous agents are still in Argentina, although negotiations for their repatriation are still being carried on."[20] Still, the Truman administration was reorienting its focus toward anti-communism rather than denazification, showing support to governments willing to resist external influences and totalitarian regimes. In asking Congress for aid to Greece and Turkey in March 1947, President Truman explicitly mentioned the communist threat and noted that "totalitarian regimes are nurtured by misery and want." In what became known as the Truman Doctrine, US presidential policy was to support governments fending off communist influences. Secretary of State George Marshall, appointed in January 1947, hoped to discourage states in the Western Hemisphere from shipping goods to Eastern Europe and the Soviet Union and also to discourage arms purchases from non-US sources. The primary lever he had for accomplishing this was to offer favorable terms for military equipment procured from the United States.[21] So the rationale went in Argentina, especially after the country began to flirt with the Soviet Union. When Perón recognized the Soviet regime in 1946, the Federal Bureau of Investigation (FBI) warned that "the Soviet Union was intensely interested in developing influence in Argentina, which it considered one of the most important posts in the Western Hemisphere for counteracting United States power."[22]

Shifting gears to imagine Argentina and Brazil as partners rather than unreliable dictatorships was not simply a matter of containing communist influence but was specifically related to the strategic minerals available in both countries. The FBI was already working closely with Boris Davidovitch's mining company in Brazil to secure access to monazite. At the time, the thorium in those sands seemed like fuel for the weapons of the future, because thorium was fissionable. The two bombs used in war thus far had been made from uranium and plutonium. In a discussion of strategic minerals, mineralogists Jack DeMent and H. C. Drake wrote in 1947, "It is quite probable that we may be shortly aware of the existence of still another type, the 'thorium bomb.' If this proves to be the case, the ores of thorium will immediately assume vast importance." The race for mineral reserves typically included both thorium and uranium, and sometimes beryl (used in atomic reactors). They put the situation bluntly in 1947: "Politically, the nation which has large reserves of radioactive ore assumes a stature far out of proportion to mere size or population or wealth."[23] By mid-1948 Argentina was even receiving military equipment from the United States and Britain.[24] Just as American officials wanted the thorium from Brazil and eyed that country's promising uranium deposits, they knew that Argentinian mining companies in late 1946 had found deposits of uranium.[25] In subsequent years those bonds would tighten, and by 1953 Perón was negotiating with Americans for technical assistance in mining the untapped uranium and beryl deposits in the country—in return for a promise to sell it all to the United States.[26]

The US State Department devoted extraordinary efforts to finding more bomb fuel while also redirecting any interest in electricity generation toward radioisotopes instead. For example, Secretary of State Marshall tried to develop uranium and thorium sources in China in 1947 and 1948. At the time, China was engaged in a civil war between the existing nationalist government led by Chiang Kai-shek and the communist forces led by Mao Zedong. Wen-hao Wong, Chiang Kai-shek's main advisor on atomic energy matters, promised a Sino-American survey of uranium and monazite in return for cash and technical assistance for a laboratory and the training of physicists. The United States would have exclusive rights to the resources.[27] Secretary Marshall balked at the idea that his government would promise to train the Chinese in physics or help it develop peaceful atomic energy. It would be far better, in Marshall's view, to focus on agricultural uses. The Chinese plan "seems to strike too optimistic a note with respect to imminence of peaceful uses of atomic energy," Marshall wrote to the ambassador.

"Except for some research uses, these seem to be still remote, and require vast capital and industrial plant [sic] to realize."[28] Wong protested that he would be criticized by Chinese physicists and other scientists for giving too much away and missing the opportunity to develop atomic energy in China. He was making some headway with Marshall by October 1948—getting agreements for some laboratory facilities and promises to help find placements for Chinese students in American universities—when the war in China turned in favor of the communists. The US ambassador called off the uranium survey negotiations, and Wong instructed all the uranium-related papers to be sent to Taiwan.[29]

Similarly, American diplomats downplayed the commercial significance of uranium to the Belgians, whose Congo colony continued to be crucial to the US arsenal. Belgian diplomats had asked the Americans to share information related to peaceful atomic energy. Fortunately for Marshall, he could claim that US legislation prevented it. The restrictions of the 1946 Atomic Energy Act (sometimes called the McMahon Act) prevented the kind of sharing that Belgium wanted, namely, help in building reactors. Meeting with the Belgian ambassador in 1947, Marshall suggested that American scientists might be able to provide appraisals of Belgium's power program or of obstacles facing them in a broad sense, but the details would not be forthcoming. Instead he suggested that the radioisotope program might prove extremely useful; and he "commented in passing that it might very well one day prove to be true that the most useful peacetime application of atomic energy would lay [sic] in this field."[30] In conversation with the Belgian ambassador and others, Assistant Secretary of State George Perkins "pointed out that uranium was a unique commodity which had no present significant commercial use and from which the United States derived no economic benefit, since it was being entirely used for military purposes in strengthening the defenses of the Western world." It was the Belgian commissioner for Atomic Energy (and former governor-general of the Belgian Congo), Pierre Ryckmans, who argued to the contrary that commercial applications might arise in the near future. The Belgians disclosed that their own atomic energy program was well under way, modeled after the British experimental reactor program. At the time, State Department official Gordon Arneson noted to Ryckmans that "there were conflicting opinions as to when atomic energy could be used for power purposes but that the general body of expert opinion was that it would not be for some time."[31]

Like the State Department, the newly created Atomic Energy Commission maintained that uranium offered little to no economic benefits. Commissioners visited other countries to convince governments to explore for uranium and to sell whatever they found to the United States. They offered to pay for uranium prospecting and to work with American companies such as Westinghouse to get the job done. Commissioner Thomas Murray, who visited Portugal and Spain in 1951, offered intangible benefits to accrue in the future—free exchanges of scientific personnel and eventual cooperation in the use of uranium for power, medicine, and industrial purposes. Reporting on his conversation with Spain's dictator Francisco Franco, Murray said, "Several times I stated that uranium should not be considered in the same category as other metals such as copper, tin, zinc, lead, et cetera. . . . Uranium has no real vital importance today except for military purposes." [32]

Like the "Scramble for Africa" among European colonial powers in the late nineteenth and early twentieth centuries, the late 1940s and early 1950s saw a global scramble for uranium and thorium, fueled by guaranteed purchases. France was building reactors and sought uranium primarily within its colonial territories in Africa but was also negotiating with India for its monazite sands. Fuel for the American wartime arsenal had been acquired from the Belgian Congo, in western Africa. That supply was dwindling. The United States and United Kingdom partnered during the war to create the Combined Development Trust to find and secure such strategic minerals, and after the war this arrangement continued. The two countries worked with other governments to secure exclusive access, then became reliable buyers for the corporations that operated mines or dredged sand. The two allies planned to purchase all the uranium mined in the Belgian Congo by the Union Minière of Belgium. The British also looked to its Commonwealth allies, Canada and Australia, for future prospecting. Canada's existing mines during wartime were government owned, but it began to permit private prospecting in 1947; Australia offered tax incentives to prospectors in 1948. Both countries experienced uranium booms by the 1950s, much of it on lands occupied by indigenous people.[33]

The Soviet Union, eager to build its first bomb, exploited mines in the zones it occupied after World War II, especially the fabled "ore mountains" (Erzgebirge) on the border of Germany and Czechoslovakia, the source of the radium first isolated by Marie Curie at the turn of the century. Scholars of occupied Germany note that prisoners and day laborers, drawn from the recently defeated German and Czech populations, worked in these mines without much medical attention or protective gear, and thousands suffered injury or death. Soviet impatience with geologists' sluggishness in identifying new uranium sources even contributed to the arrest in 1949 of hundreds of geologists and other mining specialists, some of whom stood accused of covering up knowledge of rich ores. The Soviet government knew the United States was trying to deny it access to uranium and was desperate to find domestic sources of it. Like the Americans, the Soviets were "have-nots" in terms of uranium and had to rely on foreign sources.[34]

The uranium scramble pushed US officials to make decisions aligning themselves not only with colonialism but also with explicitly white supremacist political leaders. Under chairman Gordon Dean, the AEC entered into negotiations with the Union of South Africa, which in the late 1940s had moved from informal racial segregation toward a formal, legal system of separating whites from blacks—the system known as apartheid. There were several promising sources of uranium in South Africa, to be worked by black laborers, and Dean guessed that soon its production would be as important as production in the Congo. Unlike other strategic minerals in India, Brazil, and Congo—each considered the source of "raw materials" to be processed in the United States or Belgium—the uranium ore in South Africa would be processed domestically, in a factory outside Johannesburg. Several US atomic energy commissioners met with South Africans in 1951, emphasizing the importance of maintaining good relations. The South Africans said they would wish something more—not to be perceived as a source of raw materials, like the Congo, but instead to have "some kind of special position in atomic energy matters in recognition of the new status of that country as a uranium supplier." South Africans did not wish to be treated like a colonial, colored people, and the Americans did not treat them as such.[35]

American politicians crafted foreign policies with sharp distinctions between the industrialized world of Europe and North America—plus Australia and South Africa—and the primarily agricultural and extractive regions of the world. In Europe under the Marshall Plan, American rhetoric focused on rehabilitation and industry; elsewhere it focused on liberation from natural challenges and the provision of basic sustenance. President Truman noted that Americans should utilize their leadership in science and industry to assist the "free peoples of the world, through their own efforts, to produce more food, more clothing, more materials for housing, and more mechanical power to lighten their burdens."[36] Truman first introduced the idea in the fourth point of his 1949 inaugural address after winning reelection, and thus the programs took on the label "Point Four." These goals were designed to utilize American material and technological advantages to help other nations while binding them closer to the United States. Point Four and the Marshall Plan were qualitatively distinct, oriented toward different peoples of the world.

Truman attempted to justify this difference by characterizing Point Four as the positive replacement for colonialism. "Point Four is a successor to the old colonialism idea, the exploiting idea of the middle seventeenth, eighteenth and nineteenth centuries," he said in a 1950 speech to the American Newspaper Guild. "We want to have a prosperous world that will be interested in buying the immense amount of surplus things that we are going to have to sell. And now to do that they have got to have something to give back to us in order that they can buy our goods. I want to keep this factory organization of ours going at full tilt. In order to do that we must help these people to help themselves."[37] Truman often stated that peoples in such conditions were vulnerable to the influence of communism—and thus the United States should strengthen them, lest they fall prey to the Kremlin. "Famine, disease, and poverty are the scourge of vast areas of the globe. . . . Animal plagues and plant pests carry away their crops and their livestock. Misuse of natural resources exposes their land to flood and drought." He mentioned several success stories: spraying DDT in India to allow farming on mosquito-infested lands; training Iranians how to dig deep wells and use water filters; surveying mineral and timber resources in Liberia. Future plans included the eradication of rinderpest in East Asia and the development of high-yielding hybrid rice strains.[38] Truman did not mention the atom—except by allusion, to say Point Four would "bring about a chain reaction in economic development"—but others speculated that the atom would address precisely the kinds of problems that kept so much of the world at the edge of existence.[39]

In practice, Point Four incorporated atomic energy in an oblique way, namely, in securing uranium for the United States. Belgium saw opportunity in Point Four to consolidate its hold on Congo while adopting the notion of science and technology as the great liberator. Pierre Wigny, Belgium's colonial minister, proclaimed in 1949 his desire to "fight with all our strength against the color bar" and to contribute to the social and economic well-being of non-white Africans. He tried to fit his colonial plan of farm projects into Point Four, and he said he would combine American and Belgian money and expertise to address the plight of such people, suffering under racism and a segregated economy. The agricultural program would be "for medium-sized farms run by white colonizers . . . [and] is expected to attract the natives out of the bush and induce them to settle down." It also was supposed to encourage light industries. In reality the plan was not aimed at educating the Congolese. It was designed to encourage white Belgians to emigrate to the Congo—as Sydney Gruson wrote in the *New York Times*, to encourage these "efficient, hard-working groups prepared to sink their roots in the Congo soil" and inspire Africans by their example.[40] In addition, it was explicitly aimed at bringing more Africans into the cities for work. "Some 90 per cent of the natives still live in the bush," the *New York Times* reported in 1950, "existing in the most meager fashion on primitive agriculture and roaming from one place to another in the attempt to make a bare living."[41]

Major news outlets glossed over the racist divisions in Congo that made the US arsenal possible. Columnist William S. White in the *New York Times* wrote: "In this permanent holiday from the highest responsibilities, that of making some political accommodation between whites and Negroes, the Congo's Belgian administrators are making a land of good living for whites and fairly tolerable living for Negroes." He noted approvingly that black Africans earned decent pay compared to other Africans, and that 10,000 of them earned more than $120 per month "and are paying income taxes in some instances while still praying to heathen gods." He reassured his readers that the Belgians were not white supremacists like the South Africans. "The leaders here are not 'kind' to the native in a sentimental sense, but in a pragmatic sense they are developing magnificent hospitals for his care and in Leopoldville they are building a 72,000-seat stadium for his recreation." According to White, the Belgians in Congo thought the South Africans were senselessly inflaming a continent in which whites were outnumbered. They hoped the United States would favor central Africa, where NATO allies such as France, Britain, Belgium, and Portugal still maintained "enlightened" colonial regimes.[42]

The United States did strengthen the Belgian colonial government in Congo. It did so openly under the rubric of Point Four, and this could be framed as aid to Africans. Secretly, it propped up the colonial regime even more. Although it insisted that providing benefits to the colony would be a matter for Belgium to deal with and that Congress would not be asked to provide special funds for this purpose, the United States took discreet measures to ensure the steady flow of uranium from the Shinkolobwe mine in Congo. The US Joint Chiefs of Staff explicitly highlighted "the natives of the area," rather than a foreign power, as the main threat to the mine. The Joint Chiefs recommended that the United States advise Belgium to provide more troops and strengthen its intelligence forces, to pay careful attention to morale among Congolese living near or working in the mines, and to counteract anything smacking of communism. In addition, it recommended that Allen Dulles, director of the Central Intelligence Agency (CIA), initiate as soon as possible some covert plans for military security in the Belgian Congo.[43]

Although it was relatively simple for the United States to make such arrangements with military allies that held colonies—such as the Netherlands, Belgium, or the United Kingdom—negotiations were more delicate with independent countries with histories of colonialism.

Politicians in both India and Brazil resented the familiar arrangement of being treated purely as a source of raw materials to serve the profitable manufacturing enterprises in the United States and Europe. The extent to which India should adopt industrial technologies had been a serious point of discord in Indian politics during the independence movement, dividing prominent figures such as Mohandas Gandhi from Jawaharlal Nehru. Both men saw technology as instruments of past colonial exploitation, but Nehru, unlike Gandhi, believed intensive industrialization was the best course to keep India from being exploited anew by powerful European or North American powers. As prime minister when India gained independence in 1947, Nehru did not wish to see India perceived solely as a site of resource extraction.[44] Similarly, when an American delegation led by John Abbink, president of the McGraw-Hill International Corporation, came to Brazil in 1948 as part of a joint Brazil-US Technical Commission to discuss Brazil's economic future, local newspapers referred to him as "Viceroy Abbink" and "H. M. Dom João Abbink," unsubtle allusions to the kinds of representatives sent from Portugal in the colonial era.[45] Brazilian president Getúlio Dornelles Vargas, like Indian prime minister Jawaharlal Nehru, favored the development of domestic manufacturing rather than a continuation of time-honored extractive practices.[46]

Despite the official position of the US government, electricity generation—not agricultural applications—was the technology everyone seemed to associate with helping pull the world out of want and "backwardness." Optimistic predictions appeared from numerous sources, perhaps best encapsulated by British physicist Patrick Blackett, winner of the 1949 Nobel Prize in Physics, in his book *Fear, War and the Bomb*. The work was controversial because of Blackett's sympathetic treatment of the Soviet Union on the question of international control of atomic energy. Blackett also routinely cast the atomic future as two extremes of either destruction or paradise. In predicting the role of atomic power in ending the misery of the world, he specifically identified India as a country most likely to benefit from the rapid development of this new source of electrical power.[47] Blackett's suggestion made intuitive sense but there was one serious problem: there was little genuine information about atomic energy, since no one had ever built a commercial atomic reactor.

One of the first attempts to calculate the potential of atomic energy in what many experts called "backward areas" of the world—meaning Japan, China, India, and the countries of South America—was authored by Herbert A. Simon, a future Nobel Laureate. He did so as part of a study by the Cowles Commission, a research institute based at the University of Chicago. Simon later recalled that "the atomic energy project was my real baptism in economic analysis."[48] He asked a simple question: could the atom do something to speed up the process of industrialization? He defined "backward areas" as those characterized by subsistence economies made up of agriculture and local handicraft, or cash crop economies relying heavily on imports. The major dividing line between the backward and other areas of the world was the presence of manufacturing industries intended to produce goods for domestic use and export. To Simon, and many others before and since, the "industrialized" distinction helped to segregate countries conceptually. Would the availability of atomic power—leaving aside other potential applications—have much of an effect on helping a country to leap from a backward state into an industrialized one? [49]

At that time, discussions about industrialization focused not just on increased productivity but also on the possibility of achieving the so-called demographic transition. The term expressed a widespread notion that making a change from pre-industrial to industrial was not just a kind of modernization but instead was the ultimate escape from population pressure. One adherent of this view, American sociologist Kingsley Davis, noted in 1950 that the demographic transition had a peculiar relationship with global political struggles. He alluded not only to colonialism but also to the Cold War. "The archaic agricultural regions of the world are now the battleground," he said. "Because they are weak and poor, because they are industrial vacuums, because they embrace huge areas and large populations, they are important pawns in the struggle." Without industrialization, they would forever be subjugated by more powerful nations and remain pawns in perpetuity. "The governments themselves realize this," Davis argued in 1950. "Although an occasional Gandhi may wish to turn back the clock and retrieve the traditional culture, all governments now favor higher economic productivity."[50]

Hebert Simon's calculations marked the first serious attempt to assess atomic power as an economically viable enterprise in the so-called developing world. He too framed it in terms of making the demographic transition. Simon believed the highly urban Europeans "appear to have definitely escaped the dilemma posed by the pressure of population against resources." Not so in the "backward" countries. He warned that some countries might never escape population pressure and would be subjected frequently to nature's corrections: famines, wars, diseases. Yet he was optimistic that, compared to coal and hydroelectric power, atomic power could reduce the amount of capital required for industrialization. "This is particularly significant since it is only by means of a rather rapid industrialization that these countries can hope to escape the pressure of a growing population against limited agricultural resources." Atomic energy might hold the key to rapid change in society and escape from nature's stresses.[51]

Some experts scoffed at such faith in atomic power. A leading critic, Harvard economist Walter Isard, was skeptical about cost estimates and offered his own monograph on the subject, co-authored with sociologist Vincent Whitney. Together they did not believe the "backward areas" would jump at the chance to industrialize with the atom. Whitney in particular criticized Blackett's book for naïvely imagining that the mere availability of a technology would lead to its use. Instead, Whitney stated, there were scores of reasons that cultures had resisted innovations ranging from steam engines to the horse and carriage.[52] He and Isard dismissed the physicist's notion that low-cost atomic power "will somehow produce the cornucopia of plenty even for the most backward regions of the earth." They deployed stereotypes, such as intrinsically submissive cultures, to play down the atom's potential. "Mexico and most of the countries of Central and South America are examples of such submissive culture types," they argued. Some of those countries had rich yet undeveloped resources, and an economist would say that the main barrier was lack of capital or transportation infrastructure. "But these are surface manifestations of cultures which display political instability, unbalanced and unintegrated economies, a widespread disinterest in universal education, and so on. Poverty, illiteracy, and in general a set of customs and values which are not favorable to industrialization are widespread." It was a "serious miscalculation" to think that knowledge of the atom could cause economic and social development in such countries.[53]

Isard and Whitney pointed specifically to India and Brazil as places that might seem ripe for atomic development but that would fail to make the transition. India—with some 425 million people at the time, including Pakistan and Burma—seemed to be "a striking example of the operation of Malthusian principles." Yet they were also victims of cultural inertia, the scholars argued. One could not assume that most cultures would adapt to innovation like the people in a country inured to the idea of technological change, such as the United States. "Over large areas of the earth, cultural premises which are centuries old and stubbornly rooted must be destroyed or greatly modified if atomic power is to be greeted with something other than a combination of inertia and hostility." Brazil was another case in point. Its population was some 48 million, about half of all South America's people; yet its territory was huge and had plenty of untapped resources, so it could not be called overpopulated. Its people were not at the ragged edge of their existence, and (to the authors) Brazilians seemed complacent and unmotivated, for reasons they attributed to climate, culture, and long-standing inability to change one's lot in life. Atomic power was unlikely to alter these conditions. Isard and Whitney wished to debunk the myth that atomic power was a miraculous cure and concluded that "atomic power will not, after all, lead to world equality of economic opportunity."[54]

While scholars debated whether they could do it, both India and Brazil attempted to treat the US need for strategic minerals as leverage for domestic industrial development. It is tempting to interpret India's post-independence embargo of monazite exports as an attempt to hamper British and American military efforts. But in reality the Indian government continued to trade in strategic resources—for example, when it negotiated a secret agreement with the United States to supply beryl, typically used to strengthen metal alloys but also thought to be an effective moderator of neutrons in nuclear reactors. Even with monazite sand, Indian politicians argued that they simply wished to process the sand in India, producing thorium and other materials themselves and building some kind of industry. India claimed it wished to hold on to the thorium for its own future atomic energy uses, such as building reactors for electricity. The rest of the rare earths in the sand could be sold, as long as the chemical plant to produce them from monazite was located in India.[55] Brazil's attitude was very similar, and in 1951 Brazil joined India's embargo of monazite. To them, it was a question of industrial development, not of preventing the United States from acquiring strategic resources. After the announcement of the embargo, Brazil's foreign minister João Neves da Fontoura privately stated to American diplomats that, if the United States needed the monazite, Brazil would find a way to furnish it.[56]

Some American politicians and business owners considered leveraging the misery of people in countries such as India to get better terms for strategic minerals, but not with promises of nuclear power. In 1951, the United States was considering a massive aid package to India of 2 million tons of wheat to help forestall a major shortfall of food. The person to initiate conversation about leveraging famine to secure strategic minerals was Charles R. Lindsay III, the president of Lindsay Light and Chemical Company—the US's largest importer of monazite. He lobbied several members of Congress about the strategic importance of the monazite sands, noting that thorium was one of only two elements (with uranium) mentioned as source materials for atomic energy. He reminded Congress that India had embargoed the export of monazite since April 1946. Lindsay said that he heartily endorsed giving aid to friendly countries, whether for political reasons or humanitarian ones. But in light of the proposed shipment of grain, he stated, "We feel that our Government has lost sight of the very potential bargaining power that it holds to obtain raw materials." Lindsay wanted a quid pro quo with India—a gift of wheat in exchange for the right to purchase monazite. He warned that in the event of war, should the Soviet Union invade India it would have access to vast stores of thorium and rare earths, crucial materials for atomic and conventional arms.[57]

A few American politicians feared the United States, despite its dominant atomic weapons arsenal, was losing in the "scramble" for strategic resources to better negotiators—ones who knew better how to make promises of industrial development to poor countries. A French company, La Société des Terres Rares, had convinced the Indian government that a facility to process monazite sand could be built (by the French) within India.[58] That would have served Nehru's goal of building industrial infrastructure. Instead of being a source for "raw materials" only, India would be in a position to extract thorium and then sell the rest of the strategic minerals needed by the United States. The American firm, Lindsay, had refused, citing the cost of shipping the processing chemicals to India. In the meantime, the owners of a French firm "were pretty foxy and went down there and got in a combination with the Indians," as Senator Brien McMahon put it, to do exactly as the Nehru government suggested. Then "this French crook" went to Brazil and convinced the government there to embargo it too, leaving the United States with no source of monazite.[59] William D. Pawley, the former ambassador to Brazil and recent builder of a fertilizer plant in India, pointed out in his testimony that the French had been "extremely shrewd and smart in their negotiations." The French seemed to give both India and Brazil what was wanted—a vision of the future that included industrial prosperity. Reflecting on his experience as ambassador, Pawley said, "The Brazilians, as an example, on many, many occasions, stated 'What we want to do, Pawley, is develop an industry of our own. We do not want to be always the supplier of raw materials.'" Pawley understood too that tying the monazite to wheat might court trouble, citing the "touchy situation" of recent colonial rule in India, "and they are just desperately afraid that we may be maneuvering ourselves into a position where we will have some political control over them."[60]

As Congress debated the food aid, American radio commentator H. V. Kaltenborn framed the discussion as if India were unfairly keeping thorium from the United States: "We need the monazite to defend the world against communism. India needs the wheat to effect a reduction in the always-appalling death rate of her undernourished millions. I submit that our cause is as good as hers. We would be sentimental fools if we did not seek to serve humanity by getting some Indian monazite in exchange for our American wheat. There is no sound reason why India refuses to let us buy it. Hers is a dog-in-the-manger attitude."[61] Kaltenborn was referring to the ancient fable of the dog that does not itself eat grain, but nonetheless prevents the horse from eating it. Why, Kaltenborn wondered, should a country like India be able to keep the United States from its crucial strategic resources?

Gordon Dean, chairman of the Atomic Energy Commission at the end of the Truman administration, also was eager to ensure that access to the monazite sands would not be forgotten amid discussion of the humanitarian crisis about wheat. He was savvy enough not to insist that wheat be used explicitly as leverage for getting the monazite. In a letter to Dean Acheson—secretary of state in Truman's second term—he mentioned the discussion of wheat briefly before reminding him of the Atomic Energy Commission's desire for India's thorium and beryl. "It is our hope," he wrote, " that equitable arrangements could be arrived at now or in the near future which would secure monazite and larger quantities of beryl for the United States, and uranium if it becomes available, and in doing so, assist in providing the Commission with those crucial raw materials necessary for its program." [62]

Officially, Acheson's State Department did not tie the wheat directly to strategic materials.[63] "What I should like to stress at this moment," he stated before Congress, "is that the matter of fundamental and outstanding importance is that the grain should go, otherwise people will starve to death." The shortage had come from "drought, floods, and locust pests" and affected some 120 to 130 million people on government rations.[64] The United States was the one with the dog-in-the-manger attitude, as Acheson's comments on thorium made clear. It did not absolutely need the thorium. "So far as the thorium is concerned, we have a preclusive interest in it. I do not think we have a very great acquisitive interest in it because our Atomic Energy Commission is now using thorium as, I understand it, chiefly for experimental purposes and not for its production system. We would not want it to fall into anyone else's hands. We would like to purchase it, but if it is not possible for us to purchase it we would be satisfied with a straight embargo so that nobody got it." Acheson did not want to make the wheat sale contingent on an agreement on monazite. Referring to Indians, he added: "They are a very stubborn people and I think that sort of treatment would probably result in our having a worse chance."[65] But he felt that the United States needed some kind of a positive promise—of development or of saving lives. It could not be a quid pro quo officially, but in practice it would act as such, to protect the US arsenal.

The participants in the congressional hearing on India's wheat struggled to come to grips with what India's constant food and population challenges should mean for the United States. Should these natural crises evoke a sense of responsibility, or should they be exploited in the US interest? Senator J. William Fulbright in particular referred to Fairfield Osborn's book *Our Plundered Planet* (1948), one of the key intellectual works stimulating a postwar revival of worries about population pressures.[66] Fulbright asked: "Isn't this true every year? This is nothing new, that people die in India, is it?" He worried about the double-edged sword of scientific progress, fearing what kinds of responsibilities the United States would have to take on. Referring to Osborn's book, he said, "Isn't it true that the average span of life is about 25 years, and in this country it is somewhere in the neighborhood of 60? We could send some people in there to spray DDT and expect, assuming we fed them, that that would go to 35, and yet we undertake to both feed them and keep them alive. . . . And if you keep them alive from 25 to 35 they could really produce. . . . It is a very dangerous thing to do, and we become involved in a way we haven't ever been involved in any other Far Eastern area." He noted that although food aid had been given to China in the past, it was through private channels, not government. "We did not undertake it as a national policy to keep the Chinese alive." Senator Bourke Hickenlooper mused, "Maybe we are introducing rabbits into Australia, figuratively speaking." [67]

In the absence of colonialism, they wondered why the weight of responsibility should fall on the United States. "This isn't like the Marshall Plan," Senator Henry Cabot Lodge Jr. noted, "where you expect in five years to have everybody on their feet again." Hickenlooper stated the Malthusian situation in brutal terms: "The British had India for 150 or 200 years in one way or another and they had these recurring famines, and their solution was to let them die, apparently. . . . Are we now assuming whatever responsibility the British had there for seeing that people lived or died? Are we now assuming that, only assuming it on a far grander scale than the British or the Indians ever assumed it?"[68] Hickenlooper continued: "So long as the Methodist Board of Missions and the Ladies' Aid Society, which I used to attend with my mother as a kid, have been in existence," Hickenlooper stated, "we have seen pictures of starving Indians. They have starved for years over there." [69]

Some of the American politicians saw the need for a fair quid pro quo—food aid in return for access to strategic minerals—while others encouraged treading lightly in dealing with a former colonized people craving industrial development. Republican senator Alexander Wiley, referring to the wheat, complained: "If we give it to them we cannot get any of their [monazite] sand? I think we need a little more sand in our dealings with them." Conversely, Democratic senator Brien McMahon replied, "They think that is the source of future power, that thorium. Some day it is going to be the source of future commercial power. Maybe yes, maybe no. If they really believe it, and they do, you can hardly blame them, Senator Wiley, for wanting to keep such a valuable resource, because they have been for 150 years, as they see it, exploited and this is their chance to industrialize their country, do you see?" Wiley's retort was that "I would not rob them, but don't they think the lives of their people are worth something, too? They want us to keep them alive."[70]

Ultimately the president chose not to tie the wheat directly to strategic resources and instead characterized the aid as a humanitarian gesture. Truman emphasized "terrible natural disasters," against the advice of the senators who believed that structural problems in Indian society were to blame for the famine. He mentioned earthquakes, floods, droughts, and locust plagues as the culprits. Now the United States was stepping in to "save untold millions of our fellow human beings in India from great suffering." Moreover, he suggested that the aid was part of his Point Four plan, saying that the India Emergency Food Aid Act of 1951 provided for Indian students, professors, and technicians to come to the United States for study and training, and for Americans to provide technical assistance to India. "This kind of help to stricken humanity is a tradition of the American people—whether to the sufferers of the great Russian famine and the victims of the Japanese earthquake in the early twenties or to the starving in Rumania in the late forties."[71]

Although US officials avoided explicit quid pro quo agreements regarding food aid, they were routinely confronted with an expectation that they should help other nations develop non-military applications of atomic energy. They had seen such requests from nationalist China, Brazil, Argentina, and other countries holding minerals critical for the atomic bomb. The top secret agreement eventually negotiated in 1951 between the United States, the United Kingdom, and Belgium, for example, revealed the extent to which scientific expertise and equipment had become assets in negotiation. The Americans and British agreed to assist in "the prompt development of a well-trained corps of Belgian scientists and engineers in the field of atomic energy," granting access to declassified material and facilities, assisting students to find placements for advanced study, and furnishing declassified equipment and materials, even for programs that involved reactors.[72]

Before the early 1950s, US officials typically resisted such agreements unless they were confined to agriculture and medicine. Yet they were tempting: here was a quid pro quo that did not make the Americans look as though they were extorting vulnerable countries but instead as though they were being generous and willing to assist. Both the AEC and State

Department found themselves bending on the issue of physics research, as officials perceived pathways toward favorable terms on strategic minerals. Brazil, in addition to its sources of monazite, also was exploring for uranium, making it even more important to the United States. In late 1951, the president of Brazil's Academy of Sciences, Álvaro Alberto a Mota e Silva, visited Washington, DC, and discussed acquiring cyclotrons for Brazil. These machines were used to produce isotopes, and indeed the cyclotron at the University of California had been the site of American scientists' first production of plutonium. The presence of cyclotrons in Japan at war's end had led occupation authorities to publicly dismantle them and blow them up with dynamite. Brazil wanted the US government to approve a sale from General Electric. In fact, GE did not want to produce the cyclotron, citing the cost and difficulty of obtaining materials for it, and told the AEC that it would not do so unless formally asked to by the US government. [73] The American ambassador in Brazil, Herschel Johnson, wanted GE to make the cyclotron for Brazil—and even saw it as a crucial moment in which Brazil would decide whether to look to the United States or Europe on matters of atomic energy. Because of the need to get uranium and monazite from Brazil, Ambassador Johnson wrote that "our willingness to help the Brazilians here will have a considerable influence on our whole program of cooperation in the atomic energy field, and conversely if we are not willing to assist it will have an unfortunate effect." Besides, refusing the order would not stop Brazil from acquiring a cyclotron, as it would simply shop elsewhere, such as the Netherlands-based company Philips, and then create enormous uncertainty about the future of Brazil's precious fuel resources.[74]

American diplomats were swiftly realizing that US control over atomic energy developments, despite secrecy, was rapidly diminishing. The British program was developing; and the direction of the French atomic energy program was increasingly unclear, though an experimental reactor was well under way by 1951. Joliot-Curie's involvement in communist causes had led to his dismissal as director of the Commissariat à l'Énergie Atomique in April 1950. While that left open questions about the kind of atomic energy program desired by the French government, there was little question that it posed a serious threat to the joint control of strategic minerals by the United States and the United Kingdom. The Americans seemed wholly unprepared for it. France's "appetite for atomic energy materials" already was posing difficulties, especially because French businesses seemed willing to construct facilities in India to process monazite, making India quite happy. And any minerals in the French colonial holdings in Africa would go to France first, of course. [75]

The American weapons arsenal never turned toward thorium and had no reason to do so given the difficulty in securing it from two unpredictable former colonial countries, Brazil and India. And its strategic mineral challenge would soon diminish: one of the richest sources of uranium was actually in the United States, in the region known as the Colorado Plateau—linking the states of Colorado, Utah, Arizona, and New Mexico. Uranium was known to exist there but its extent was unknown. In 1948 the Atomic Energy Commission sparked a uranium mining boom by offering cash bonuses for new discoveries, top dollar for tonnage, and guaranteed purchases. It even issued a how-to guide, *Prospecting for Uranium*, to encourage private businesses to scour the land for the yellowy substance.[76]

Much of this uranium existed on and near land occupied by the Diné people, known widely as Navajo Indians, and the federal government exploited their labor. Using underground shafts and open-pit techniques, mining companies began to extract uranium from the Carrizo Mountains in 1948, drawing in the Diné as low-wage laborers. For the next decade or so, uranium mining would be big business in the region, with several major centers of operation within the Navajo Nation reservation, but not without price for the miners. Studies conducted half a century later on the Diné miners revealed that exposure to radioactivity in the mines had led to increased rates of lung cancer, pneumoconiosis and other respiratory diseases, and tuberculosis.[77] Although exposure to radiation was strictly monitored in laboratories or during Bomb tests, in which the workers were predominantly white, the same standards did not apply to the mines.[78]

Although the reservation was within US borders, the federal government's treatment of the Diné was similar to the colonial relationships it abetted in its other quests for strategic resources. The people who suffered the direct consequences were non-white people with little or no understanding of dangers to their health—in this case they were US citizens. Although individual workers were paid, they were not tracked or monitored in any way, and the government's sense of responsibility toward them was minimal. The highest priority was to extract the uranium. Scientists were at that time studying the reasons that radon and its isotope progeny caused increased rates of lung cancer, but the Diné workers—many of whom did not speak English—were not notified of the risk or protected from it. Instead, they were studied. One white scientist, in charge of a medical fieldwork study in 1950, later recalled how surprised he was that the miners were simply being studied as subjects rather than treated:

> When I reported for duty in 1950, I asked about the objective of the study. I was told that it was to determine whether the deaths of miners in Joachimstal,

Czechoslovakia, and Schneeberg, Germany, in the 15th and 16th centuries were caused by radiation or other causes, such as silicosis. In the face of this long-term objective of the studies, acute problems among the Navajo in Utah were being ignored. Typhoid was endemic in the area, and 6% of the miners from Monument Valley had open, cavitary tuberculosis. When I reported this to the medical director of the Indian Service on my return to Washington, he said he would do what he could; but he wasn't very optimistic that he could do anything.[79]

Cases of lung cancer among the Diné would be widespread by the 1960s.[80]

The callous treatment of the Diné, as with colonial peoples elsewhere, was barely perceived at government levels where officials made the military arsenal their highest priority. The United States turned a blind eye to colonialism when trying to secure uranium, relying on Africans and indigenous peoples to extract it and pay the biological consequences. Further, when dealing with those parts of world it still considered "backward" (even if now independent of colonial rule), the United States was primarily interested in offering only the waste by-products of its arsenal, in the form of radioisotopes. The government-mandated shaping of what "peaceful" atomic energy looked like—radioisotopes rather than electricity—would soon change. The discovery of such large deposits of uranium within the United States offered a reprieve from the pressures of the global "scramble" for uranium, though the US government continued to act as the "dog in the manger" to thwart the Soviet Union from securing access to uranium sites elsewhere in the world. More important, the notion that atomic energy might itself hold the key to future development—addressing not only food and health but also energy—was becoming an unexpectedly powerful asset in negotiations, one on which Americans would increasingly rely. Mastery of strategic minerals would also be crucial in the thinking of the next president, Dwight Eisenhower, though in time the notion of "peaceful atomic energy" would broaden considerably and become a major propaganda initiative. As Truman had done, Eisenhower would leverage the suffering of the world, particularly the vulnerability of poor countries to nature's whims, and offer atomic technologies as potential solutions.

CHAPTER 2

A Thousand Years into One

When the elected leaders of the United States, Britain, and France met in Bermuda in December 1953, one carried a speech draft, another a painting box, and the other a nasty case of the flu. It was supposed to be a summit meeting of Dwight Eisenhower, Winston Churchill, and Joseph Laniel—and their chief diplomats—to discuss their alliance, the Soviet Union, the colonial wars, and atomic bombs. Eisenhower liked to golf, but Churchill had given the sport up in favor of painting, and the two tried to make time to paint together. Laniel was not given to painting, but it did not matter because he spent much of the summit sick in his room. Eisenhower asked the two men for guidance on a speech about atomic energy he was about to give at the United Nations. It would be dubbed his "Atoms for Peace" speech, a term that also would long define American efforts to promote civilian uses of atomic energy. It made the United States seem serious about both disarmament and about sharing technology for the social uplift of the world, and it provided the idea that would lead to the creation of the International Atomic Energy Agency in 1957.

Ironically, this peaceful proposal was designed to mitigate the political damage from what the United States really intended—to integrate nuclear weapons more fully into American and allied military plans and to embark on an extraordinary series of atmospheric nuclear weapons tests. Declassified meeting minutes show that the Bermuda discussions provided a great deal to think about: Eisenhower believed that atomic bombs needed to be considered conventional weapons, and he planned to use them in Korea if hostilities were to reignite; Churchill tried to reestablish atomic sharing between the two countries and informed the president that the

British atomic arsenal was well under way; the French made a plea for greater military assistance in holding on to Indochina against communist forces there. To his allies, Eisenhower described the speech as one that offered something positive to a world clamoring for disarmament. But Eisenhower had no intention of disarming. If he could offer peaceful atomic energy, it might convince the world that the United States was willing to take actions toward peace even if it did not do so in the area of disarmament. He suggested that the rest of the world might be distracted from disarmament and instead direct its attention toward promoting peaceful applications of atomic energy. The speech promised to supply uranium to a global agency, while also challenging the Soviet Union (and the UK) to do the same. Such a plan would siphon off precious supplies from the Soviet arsenal if they agreed. If they did not, it would be a propaganda win for the West.

The president was hazy on the details. He mentioned that atomic reactors had medical and agricultural applications and that perhaps reactors could be used to "run tractors." The truth is Eisenhower had no clear concept of what peaceful atomic energy entailed. The specifics were less important to him than the act of making the proposal, and vagueness would be key to making it credible. Like many atomic promises in the decades to come, Eisenhower was basing the proposal on an imagined future—no one could demand evidence, but it would need to appear realistic. "We would have to word this carefully so as not to raise hopes that if you gave a man a ball of plutonium he might be able to plow his field for the next hundred years," Eisenhower cautioned, "but we had here an area where we could do something that would bring a large number of people to our side."[1] It was aimed in large part at those countries perceived as backward—the newly independent and unpredictable states of the Third World, and those countries still recovering from war.

Later dubbed a "Madison Avenue gimmick," as if hatched by advertising agencies, Eisenhower's "Atoms for Peace" speech is often seen as the founding story of atomic energy's peaceful side. In fact, it was not such a dramatic break from the past. Atomic energy was already being promoted, officially or otherwise, as a boon to the downtrodden of the world. The Democrats had begun to use the atom in this way, first with radioisotopes and then with other intriguing ideas, such as irradiating seeds in the hope of generating wondrous mutations. In fact the Democrats hatched the germ of the idea of "Atoms for Peace," calling for a global atomic Marshall Plan, shortly after President Truman announced in 1949 his decision to pursue development of the hydrogen bomb—another case of offering a peaceful vision while in reality intensifying weapons efforts. Truman had done it even earlier, too, making an audacious plan for peace in 1946 just weeks before launching the first postwar atomic tests at Bikini, in the Marshall Islands. In all these cases, the idea of the peaceful atom was deployed rhetorically, with no genuine plans for implementation, to mitigate the political consequences of a significant escalation in weapons development. Eisenhower's pledge delivered not a new program but American political consensus about how the atom should be discussed as a matter of state, focusing on how atomic technologies—most of them not yet achieved—would serve the betterment of the world's downtrodden peoples. Doing so explicitly gave the US government a political stake in the success of civilian applications of atomic energy, because they were conceived as strategies for protecting and even expanding the weapons program.

* * *

The basic foreign policy articulated by the US Department of State at the close of 1945 was that scientific information ought to be shared "for industrial and humanitarian purposes," as long it did not encourage military programs.[2] Diplomatic conversations around atomic energy in 1946 even revolved around questions of international control of atomic energy. American diplomats helped create the United Nations Atomic Energy Commission, and for a short time it appeared a real possibility that atomic bombs, peaceful technologies, and even supplies of uranium and thorium might be under its control. The Truman administration sent the wealthy financier Bernard Baruch to address that United Nations body on June 14, 1946, to propose a specific plan for such control. Baruch proposed that the manufacture of bombs cease, that existing ones be destroyed, and that a new international body be created to manage all activities, inspect facilities, and foster beneficial uses of atomic energy, while bringing under its dominion all of the world's supplies of uranium and thorium.[3]

At the time, the Baruch proposal astonished the world. Here was the only nation armed with atomic bombs making the most radical gesture of peace imaginable. Not only did the United States offer to give up bombs, but also it seemed willing to set aside its own sovereignty in favor of some form of world government. Critics at the time (and since) have pointed out that the plan was never likely to succeed, and the Truman administration knew the Soviets would never accept its intrusive mechanisms of inspection and enforcement. But simply making the proposal was enough to capture headlines and compel the world to consider that arguably the most ambitious peace initiative in history had come from the United States. The speech was filled with many memorable images. Baruch began it thus: "We are here to make a choice between the quick and the dead. That is our business." He referred to the "black portents of the new atomic age." He framed the atomic age in spiritual terms, saying that atomic fear had to be supplanted by hope. "There is famine throughout the world today," he said. "It starves men's bodies. But there is a greater famine—the hunger of men's spirit. That starvation can be cured by the conquest of fear, and the substitution of hope, from which springs faith—faith in each other; faith that we want to work together toward salvation; and determination that those who threaten the peace and safety shall be punished."[4]

Baruch was offering a new world order, and the proposal dominated headlines at a time when the Americans were eager to counteract what really was in store that summer, the first atomic bomb explosions since the wartime destruction of Nagasaki. Two weeks after announcing Baruch's peace plan, the United States began Operation Crossroads, as if to punctuate Baruch's framing of humanity's choice between the quick and the dead. Admiral William H. P. Blandy, who commanded the task force overseeing the tests of atomic bombs in June 1946, said, "I named the project 'Operation Crossroads' because it was apparent that warfare—perhaps civilization itself—had been brought to a turning point in history by this revolutionary weapon."[5] He and others touted the tests as being "for the good of mankind," to take place on a little-known coral atoll in the Pacific called Bikini. The Navy brought film crews, invited international observers, and provided enormous publicity. Most famously, French designer Louis Réard was inspired by the atomic blasts and adopted the name "bikini" for his two-piece swimsuit.

The first to be offered the rationale of "the good of mankind" were the Bikinians themselves. The Americans were new faces to them. Bikini was one of the twenty-nine coral atolls making up America's new territorial possession, the Marshall Islands, wrested from Japan during the Gilbert and Marshall Islands naval campaign in 1943 and 1944. The bloodiest battles occurred when American troops invaded Majuro, Kwajalein, and Eniwetok, where bombardments and fierce ground fighting resulted in some 14,000 Japanese and Americans killed or wounded. With the end of the war, American existing territories in the Pacific—Hawaii and the Philippines being the most prominent—were enhanced by ousting the Japanese from the Marshalls, the Marianas, and the Carolines. Previously, the island of Guam—won from Spain in 1898—had acted as the country's strategic outpost in the South Pacific. Now the United States was the unchallenged master of the Pacific, and it dominated an extraordinarily large region, with hundreds of islands stretching many thousands of miles. It seemed to have islands, and peoples, to spare. The US Navy evacuated Bikini's inhabitants, telling them—incorrectly, as the Marshallese learned over the next half-century—that their relocation was only temporary and that they soon would return to their homes.

Once the Bikinians had been removed, American and British scientists tried to imagine the Bikini atoll as a controlled experiment to understand modern war and the transformative possibilities of the atom. In reality the first tests in the summer of 1946 were not controlled, and both defied expectations. The first of them (codenamed Able) had been off-target, and most scientific problem solving was oriented toward salvaging some useful results from a poorly executed experiment. It was also a problem politically. Baruch's peace plan was predicated on the atom bomb being perceived as an unprecedented factor in the history of war and civilization, and Operation Crossroads intended to demonstrate that. But the blast itself, by many accounts, was a dud. From many miles away, it did not measure up to the expectations and hype of the vaunted "atomic age." It just looked like a giant plume of smoke in the middle of the ocean. Invited observers expected something more spectacular. Brazilian military officer Orlando Rangel, when asked by reporters for a reaction, said he felt "so so" after seeing the explosion. Russian scientist Simon Alexandrov was seen shrugging his shoulders. Mexican explosion expert and military officer Juan Loyo González noted that apparently even atomic bombs have their limitations.[6]

That perception changed dramatically with the next blast, Baker. It was more spectacular visually because it was detonated underwater. The uplift of water, described by one officer as "Niagara Falls in reverse," inspired awe, and Crossroads planners breathed a sigh of relief that the operation had been redeemed by something that appeared to be worthy of the world's expectations.[7] Although many ships stayed afloat after Able, the underwater blast spelled the end for tough ships from the Second World War. The *Saratoga* had survived torpedo bombers and kamikaze attacks, but she was no match for Baker. Writing to colleagues back home, English mathematician William Penney provided some detail about it: detonated ninety feet underwater, it created a torrent of contaminated water that not only knocked into the ships but also assaulted them from above. Some fifteen hundred feet from the blast, it created waves forty feet high. The water spout going up from the blast reached a height of more than a mile. When that water came crashing back down, it saturated the vessels with radioactivity.[8]

The Baker explosion had created an environmental disaster area unlike anything in the world. Radioactivity was everywhere and it paralyzed military and scientific work. Writing to his colleague Sir James Chadwick, Penney said that daily dose limits set by the navy "confounded everything badly and practically nobody has been on any of the actual ships for more than 2 or 3 minutes. Quite a few are sinking steadily simply from their normal leakage."[9] The ships stayed "hot" for quite some time, and they accumulated radioactivity in unexpected ways, creating new sources of exposure over time. Stafford Warren, who headed the radiological safety team, wrote that the second Bikini bomb "demonstrated an entirely new danger of atomic warfare." In *Life* magazine a year later, he wrote that an hour after the explosion, his team of radiological monitors tried to enter the Bikini lagoon and "recorded a solid wall of contamination." Only radio-controlled boats could be used to collect water samples, and it was more than a month before some of the ships could be boarded for longer than an hour at a time. Warren wrote that the contamination had "penetrated every crevice of the target ships." [10]

In keeping with Baruch's proposal and Blandy's rhetoric about the "good of mankind," Operation Crossroads blended studies of weapons effects with some potential peacetime applications. Nineteen of the target ships at Operation Crossroads carried items intended for radiation exposure study, including canned fruits and vegetables and a variety of clothing and fuel. But there were also seeds for commodity crops, such as wheat, barley, corn, and cotton. Shortly after the conclusion of the tests in the summer of 1946, these seeds were taken up by scientists at agricultural experiment stations, many of them connected to American land-grant universities. Perhaps, they imagined, the bomb might induce life as well as death.

The juxtaposition of death against life had been a recurring theme about radioactivity since its discovery a half century earlier. Radium enthusiasts at the dawn of the twentieth century had imagined it held the secret to health and long life, yet the radium tonics sold to the wealthy made them sick or killed them. English scientist John Butler Burke claimed in 1904 to have produced some kind of life artificially by stimulating sterile beef bouillon with radium. He would go on to claim that "all matter is alive." And yet the high-profile case of the radium watch dial painters in the 1920s—the so-called radium girls—revealed a heartbreaking and gruesome link between occupational exposure to radium and cancer.[11] Now it was the bomb that threatened the world. Baruch was proposing that atomic energy be controlled by an international body and then bent toward uses to help humankind rather than harm it.

The possibility of using radioactivity to transform nature itself and overcome its apparent limitations had inspired scientists from numerous disciplines. The interpretation of radioactivity by chemists Ernest Rutherford and Frederick Soddy in the first years of the twentieth century had made it seem like the modern equivalent of alchemy. Their so-called transformation theory revealed that elements could indeed change—like the age-old dream of changing lead into gold. Soddy's 1911 textbook, *The Chemistry of the Radio-Elements*, showed how uranium could become thorium, and radium would become lead.[12] Such malleability in nature inspired scientists to imagine reordering nature according to human needs. For example, Russian geochemist Vladimir Vernadsky saw anthropogenic (human-caused) changes to the earth as salvation, and he believed atomic energy was the leading candidate for the role of Messiah. If humans played by nature's rules, Vernadsky believed, population pressures would lead to wars and famines, just as Thomas Malthus stated in his 1798 *Essay on the Principle of Population*. Vernadsky rejected the specter of Malthusian population catastrophe, writing to Soviet leader Joseph Stalin in 1931 that "the study of cosmic rays and nuclei of atoms will lead us to the discovery of new, powerful sources of energy. . . . We are facing the future sovereignty of radioactive energy, more powerful than electricity."[13]

Some of the most provocative notions about a future transformed by radiation came from genetics. Even before the postwar heyday of comic book heroes there were scientists imagining biological improvement from mutation. American scientist Hermann J. Muller in the 1920s showed that radiation had discernible effects on heredity, as X-rays readily induced mutations in fruit flies. A flurry of research in the 1930s suggested that genetic characters could be altered. In theory, inducing new—and possibly beneficial—mutations put the power of design back into the hands of scientists. Muller's 1927 work, published prominently in *Science*, became the foundational text for modern mutation plant breeding.[14] After a meeting of the American Association for the Advancement of Science—at which Muller received an award of $1,000 for having presented the most notable paper—one writer reflected: "It is agreed on all sides at the gatherings of scientific men that the past year has been one of revolution in the study of heredity among living things, comparable with 1859, when Darwin published the *Origin of Species*, and 1900, the year of the rediscovery of Mendel's law."[15]

Using radiation from X-rays (requiring electricity as a source) or radioactive substances had not yet lived up to the hype generated in 1927. In the decade before World War II, induced mutations in flies and plants had not produced viable new species.[16] One of the most prolific irradiators of seeds was American geneticist Lewis Stadler, who cultivated corn, barley, and other crops—all prior to the atomic bomb. Stadler's extensive work on X-rays led him to conclude that most genetic changes were deleterious and that useful variations were rare. He also used radium to induce mutations and found that there was no obvious difference between an extremely expensive radium source and the widely available X-ray machine.¹⁷ As a way of producing radiation to induce mutations, radioactivity seemed to be a red herring. Not only were radioactive sources expensive, Stadler said, but the number of harmful mutations made the whole endeavor inefficient.¹⁸

Operation Crossroads reinvigorated the idea that radioactivity from the atom might empower human beings over nature. Just as the comic book hero Atoman (who made his first appearance in February 1946) acquired super strength, superhuman speed, and the ability to fly because of atomic radiation, plants appeared to be acquiring new traits in real life. Scientists remained intrigued by mutation, and Muller won a Nobel Prize in 1946 for his earlier work. Prior to Muller's banquet speech accepting the award, the president of the Royal Academy of Sciences, Sigurd Curman, marveled that Muller had found a way "to intervene in the strange manifestations of what was formerly called 'the blind play of Nature.'"¹⁹ Muller's prewar enthusiasm for generating beneficial mutations continued to resonate in scientific work, especially among his former students and colleagues at the University of Texas. There, geneticist J. T. Patterson continued an intensive research program on radiation and mutation on fruit flies after Muller's departure in 1932, influencing a generation of young geneticists. Among these was Texas A&M researcher Meta Suche Brown, who—like most geneticists in the 1930s—had focused on fruit flies to study chromosomes but turned to *Gossypium* (cotton), the staple commodity of the American South.²⁰ When she studied the Bikini cotton seed plants that were harvested in the summer of 1947, she noticed that some of them were strange looking. Talking to fellow geneticists at an annual scholarly meeting, Brown said that the chromosomes—the part of the cell that carried genetic information—had been altered or destroyed.²¹

Meta Brown's plants were new creations of the atomic age. Her Texas studies showed that the radiation altered cotton plants, producing squat, compact plants compared to the taller and less dense plants that grew from unexposed seeds. Very few of the seeds produced such striking differences, but because of the laws of inheritance the new traits were likely to appear more obviously in subsequent generations, she believed. All of the plants seemed to have had chromosome alterations from the intense radiation.²² Thus they raised serious questions about the stock of varieties available for breeding and about the pace of evolutionary change. At the time, cotton specialists debated whether the New World and Old World cottons had evolved to their current state from a point of divergence a very long time ago, from ancient human migration, or from an even more distant past, from continental drift.²³ The Bikini bombs made a provocative intervention into that timescale. With one enormous dose of radiation, a new mutation had defied the slow pace of evolutionary change.

Such intriguing results fell short of providing a clear path for the development of peaceful atomic energy, because the radiation was not unique to atomic energy. Though several scientists claimed to have altered growth patterns from subjecting crop plants to either X-rays or radioactive elements, they were unable to demonstrate statistically significant differences. Despite the press attention garnered for growing Bikini seeds, geneticist Luther Smith pointed out that "exposure to atomic-bomb-induced radiations resulted in effects in every way comparable to exposure to X-rays," whether it was germination, mottling on leaves, chimeras, or mutation frequencies.[24] In fact, the US Department of Agriculture launched a study in several states, using some sixteen different crops, to test claims by companies selling radioactive fertilizer. They found no significant difference between X-rays and sources from atomic energy.[25]

It seemed as if mutation plant breeding, as a peaceful application of atomic energy, was a dead end. Ironically, what saved it was the vast scale of the bomb program. The reactors used to create fuel for the bomb produced radioactive isotopes (radioisotopes) at a lower cost than anyone anticipated. The most notable site of research was the new national laboratory created in Brookhaven, New York, in 1947. It was owned by the Atomic Energy Commission but operated by a non-profit corporation called Associated Universities, sponsored by several elite northeastern universities. Two of Brookhaven's first employees were Arnold Sparrow, a specialist in plant cells and genetics who had an infatuation with exposing flowers to X-rays, and W. Ralph Singleton, a geneticist intrigued with the idea of inducing mutations with radioactive cobalt.[26] They made an ideal scientific pair, and together they decided that one did not need to wait for atomic tests to create a research program devoted to the effects of radioactivity on plants. They could do it themselves, using the radioisotopes from production reactors. Within a decade, the president of Associated Universities, Lloyd Berkner, would be so effusive about inducing mutations with radioisotopes that he said, "It is as though, for evolutionary purposes, we had collapsed a thousand years into one."[27]

In a reverse of the 1930s situation, the primary advantage of using a radioactive source for radiation, as opposed to X-rays, was the cost. Plant researchers could obtain enough radioisotopes to irradiate plants at high dose rates continuously during their entire life cycle. Using a cheap radioactive source also allowed a very different kind of study: instead of analyzing the results of an acute dose of radiation, such as that provided by an atomic bomb, one could trace continuous exposure over time. It was even possible to calibrate that exposure much more carefully and reliably. Sparrow and Singleton chose cobalt, a brittle silvery-gray metal whose radioactive isotope (cobalt-60) emitted high-energy gamma rays. As cobalt-60 has a half-life of 5.3 years, a researcher could use a single sample of it for studies spanning several growing seasons. Using a technique that soon would be copied by scientists all over the world, Sparrow and Singleton placed the source in the middle of a field, with plants arranged in concentric circles around it. The scientists began the radiocobalt-exposed growing season in 1949, and the first of the so-called gamma gardens was born.[28]

The gamma gardens were especially promising because they suggested a degree of control over agricultural production and hinted at a cornucopian future. Food plants such as potatoes, tomatoes, corn, broccoli, and strawberries each responded differently, as did the gladiolas, tobacco, and spiderwort flowers. Some exhibited signs of sterility, stunted growth, or other abnormalities, while others seemed relatively unaffected. The *Gladiolus*, for example, seemed tolerant of radiation even at doses of 2,000 roentgens (R) per day, whereas the spiderwort (*Tradescantia paludosa*) showed severe effects at merely 30 R per day. For Sparrow, who would spend his whole career at Brookhaven, these studies opened up a world of possibilities for scientific research. Exploring individual plants' "radiosensitivity" could alone fill many volumes of scientific journals, as could the inheritance of new mutations from gamma exposure.[29]

Some Democrats in government cast these agricultural techniques as non-military uses for the greater good. Just as the Baruch proposal was timed in parallel with the blasts at Bikini, so too did peaceful atomic techniques see a revival along with the US's decision to build a new super weapon larger than the atomic bomb. In August 1949, within months of Truman's announcement to share scientific knowledge and technologies under the Point Four programs, the Soviet Union tested its own atomic bomb. The president swiftly pressed forward with the development of hydrogen bombs which, powered by fusion rather than only fission, could have a thousand times the explosive power of the bomb that destroyed Hiroshima. The president's Democratic allies immediately attempted to mitigate the announcement by making proposals about peaceful uses, specifically to offer to remake the natural environment in those countries with large numbers of people living on the edge of survival. Referring to Truman's decision, Senator Brien McMahon noted in the *Bulletin of the Atomic Scientists* that "[h]e had no choice, and his decision under present circumstances is right." McMahon lamented: "We are plunged into a truly terrible arms race! What are we going to do about it?"[30] In a February 2, 1950, speech to the Senate, McMahon called for a "moral crusade for peace" that would have atomic energy as its focal point. Accompanying a printed version of the speech in the *Bulletin of the Atomic Scientists* was a cartoon showing two visions of American intentions, one well-meaning and peaceful and the other evil and malcontent. It was called "Dr. Jekyll and Mr. Hydrogen." McMahon proposed something radical to help erase the image of Mr. Hydrogen. Noting that the government spent about $15 billion annually on weapons, he suggested taking $10 billion of that and using it for peaceful purposes. Instead of building weapons with that money, the United States could hand some of it over to Point Four programs, to use science for good—even developing atomic energy everywhere. "Such a global Marshall Plan," he observed, "might combine with the marvelous power of peacetime atomic energy to generate universal material progress and a universal cooperative spirit."[31]

At the time, McMahon had his eyes on a presidential run in 1952, and his political allies tried to draw attention to the speech, one calling it "extraordinarily brilliant, moving, of the highest statesmanship in Christian ethics," and another saying it was a "great public document."[32] More accurate was economist James P. Warburg, who also liked the speech but guessed "that its echoes will die away within a few weeks or months, if the flame of hope which it kindled is allowed to flicker and die out."[33]

The plan went nowhere, and the speech is a forgotten document of the Cold War, but it is worth asking: what would McMahon have done with this $10 billion annually? Knowledge of what peaceful applications were feasible was not much clearer in 1950 than it had been in 1946, when Baruch made his proposal and when bombs exploded over Bikini "for the good of mankind." So McMahon drew on the unspecific idea that atomic energy was going to remake the natural world. "It is almost impossible to overestimate what all-out concentration upon atomic energy for peace might accomplish in terms of remaking and improving the physical environment of mankind." He did not say what remaking meant—he may have imagined grand engineering projects using atomic detonations or perhaps new kinds of crops with mutants. He did say that the frightful alternative was also to be seen in the natural world: each American leader "should glance at the sun and reflect that what he sees there, millions of miles away, threatens to be recreated on this earth, in our own cities, in Washington, New York, Los Angeles, and Chicago." [34]

While McMahon called for transforming the physical environment, Soviet leaders claimed to be doing it already. They too tried to balance their weapons program with publicity about constructive uses of the atom. After Truman announced the Soviet test in 1949, Soviet foreign minister Andrei Vishinsky attended a political committee of the United Nations and pointed out how the USSR planned to remake nature with the bomb. Rather than merely stockpiling bombs, Soviet scientists and engineers would be moving mountains and diverting water to desert regions in order to make the landscape more productive. "We are razing mountains; we are irrigating deserts; we are cutting through the jungle and the Tundra; we are spreading life, happiness, prosperity and welfare in places where the human footstep had not been seen for thousands of years."[35] Such statements from the USSR stretched even the most generous bounds of credibility, since it seemed that the Soviets had only exploded one atomic bomb thus far.

The outlandish claims emanating from the Soviet Union outraged some but inspired others—notably Brien McMahon. He complained that Vishinsky no doubt had "deceived multitudes," and he called for American agencies to step up their own propaganda efforts. The Soviets, he believed, were winning the war of opinion. Communist organizations dominated peace organizations, and the Soviets were having better luck framing their atomic activities not as weapons but as transformers of nature. McMahon called for major broadcasts by the United States with similarly audacious claims and wanted to print millions of leaflets for worldwide circulation, providing details of an American atomic peace proposal.

In McMahon's view, the United States needed better advertising—he wanted the federal government to step up its propaganda efforts to paint the atom as the savior it could be, not the world destroyer it was. Like other governments, the US government at the time manipulated the media and sponsored broadcasts to portray the nation favorably. One of these was Voice of America, broadcast outside the United States. McMahon derisively called it the "Whisper of America," given its low annual budget of $29 million. "We spend over $30,000,000 a year to advertise cosmetics," he complained, "and $29,000,000 to sell the precious commodity of freedom!" Nevertheless, the world continued to see the United States as a warmonger. "They see that we devote billions to guns, tanks, planes, and atomic weapons—and day and night the Communist propaganda machine hammers into them the theme that American armaments are designed for conquest." [36]

The American intelligence community took such calls to action seriously. The newly created Central Intelligence Agency, for example, identified newspapers and other kinds of media as crucial venues of pro-American propaganda. It tried to counter communist-linked peace efforts such as the Partisans for Peace and the 1949 Cultural and Scientific Conference for World Peace, held in New York City. These organizations had the Nobel Laureate (and nuclear physicist) Frederic Joliot-Curie and the world-famous artist

Pablo Picasso among their ranks—Picasso had even designed the memorable peace dove for the movement. The CIA wanted similar groups that were populated by well-known intellectuals and artists who were pro-West. One of these was the Congress for Cultural Freedom, a collaborative project between academic scholars and the CIA's Psychological Strategy Board. It sponsored publications and events favoring liberal democracy rather than communism, though the CIA role was known only to a few.[37] One of its reliable outlets was the *Bulletin of the Atomic Scientists*, which published on a range of issues tying science to policies. Some contributors (including its editor, Eugene Rabinowitch) were connected to the Congress for Cultural Freedom, and it would become a forum for laying out peaceful visions of the atom.[38]

Among those speaking at the first meeting of the pro-West "Congress" were public intellectuals such as Bertrand Russell, John Dewey, and Benedetto Croce. Speaking on atomic energy were the nuclear physicist Hans Thirring, geneticist Hermann Muller, and David Lilienthal, who had stepped down as US Atomic Energy Chairman earlier that year. Muller was still basking in his public notoriety for winning a Nobel Prize in 1946, but he also made an intriguing government ally. He had been attracted to communism in the 1930s and moved to the USSR, only to depart in disillusionment with Stalinism.[39] He and other speakers warned about the dangers of communism and endorsed Western-style liberal democracy. Some also made promises of a peaceful nuclear future. Lilienthal had opposed the development of the hydrogen bomb and had seen himself as the chief of a commission for the betterment of the world, not just an arms agency. He was echoing a theme of 1949 book *This I Do Believe: An American Credo*. Its theme was one of faith—in democracy, in individual freedom, and in a future in which the atomic bomb was reshaped into a more positive force.

In other speeches, Lilienthal cast democracy as a kind of religion, with the atom entwined within it. Addressing the American Association of School Administrators, he said that humans now lived in the "Age of Radiation." For educators, it was the fourth "R." Reading, Riting, Rithmetic, and Radiation. "We shall need knowledge and we shall need courage, but more than anything else we shall need faith. We shall need faith in the institutions of freedom. With faith in each other, with faith in our institutions, with faith that the Creator of us all did not endow men with the ability to unlock the secrets that lie within the atom in order that they should destroy this beautiful earth and all that is on it—with that kind of faith, I want to share with you my deep and abiding belief that we shall make these atomic discoveries serve the betterment of humanity and the glory of God."[40] For Lilienthal, the peaceful atom had become a symbol of faith and commitment.

Politicians in advance of the 1952 presidential election highlighted the need to turn around the warlike image of the United States by cleaning up the atom's image—especially since the president had decided to push forward with developing a fusion weapon. The most creative ideas for doing so came from the Democrats, allied as they were to the tenets of Point Four, which explicitly tied US scientific innovation and technical know-how to foreign aid programs in the developing world. McMahon himself was the leading Democrat with expertise in atomic affairs. He had sponsored the Atomic Energy Act in Congress, had argued for civilian control of it, and had chaired Congress's Joint Committee on Atomic Energy. His aspirations ran high—his name was on the nomination ballot for the presidency at the Democratic National Convention in 1952. But he withdrew before the convention due to illness, and an aggressive cancer killed him just two days afterward when he was only forty-eight. One of his last messages was relayed in an essay in the *Bulletin of Atomic Scientists*, published in the same issue as his obituary. It was called "Survival—the Real Issue of Our Times," and it had originally been sent by wire from a hospital bed in Washington to be delivered at the Democratic State Convention in Connecticut.

In that essay, McMahon leaned on a familiar theme: the two roads ahead, one of peace and plenty, the other of destruction. He recalled the Baruch plan of 1946, that moment when "we went before the United Nations and offered to share with the world all that is good in atomic energy."[41] He also reiterated his belief that atomic energy could be used to conquer poverty. The United States, he felt sure, was still willing to spend billions of dollars annually on "enlarged Point Four programs" designed to develop atomic energy for peace. If the United Nations could be given control of all atomic armaments, and if the Soviet Union would promise to contribute a similar proportion of its arms budget to the cause of peace, the United States was ready to move forward and focus on the constructive uses of atomic energy—to "bring the suffering and the hungry bread and medicine and clothing and shelter." While some, especially Republicans, had pilloried the idea as yet another Democrat-inspired global "giveaway" program like the Marshall Plan, McMahon argued that it represented a mere fraction of what was spent already on arms. McMahon hoped that instead of simply thinking in terms of disarmament and banishing weapons, what he termed a negative goal, Americans would focus on "the positive goal of substituting for weapons a better life everywhere." He wanted to "wage peace," tackling two problems at once, "disarming this earth and developing this earth."

The vision of a global Marshall Plan for atomic energy development was not to be. The winner of the general election was Republican Dwight Eisenhower, president of Columbia University and military hero—wartime

Supreme Allied Commander in Europe, then Army Chief of Staff, and then NATO Supreme Commander. To the historian, the title of Eisenhower's presidential memoirs—*Waging Peace*—might suggest that he agreed with McMahon. But there were stark differences. Though a moderate Republican, he viewed state-sponsored development programs with disdain, preferring to see them taken up by private enterprise. His approach to government spending was to cut back where possible. Moreover, Eisenhower was determined to treat the atom as a usable weapon, and he thought seriously about using atomic bombs to end the Korean War.[42] Yet there were also similarities to McMahon's vision. The most important was that Eisenhower would come to believe that escalation of weapons production would need to be countered by pro-US propaganda and that peaceful applications of atomic energy should play a role. It would be Eisenhower's name, rather than McMahon's, that would become inextricably linked to the peaceful atom.

Initially, Eisenhower's thoughts on atomic energy focused principally on their military value. In early 1953, just two months into his presidency, faced with a national deficit and an unclear future of American troops in Korea, he told his National Security Council that atomic bombs might be the answer to the United States' fiscal and strategic challenges. After all, if the Americans increased their conventional forces, the Soviets would strengthen the communist conventional forces. Pretty soon the United States would again be at the state of general mobilization, as it had been during World War II. Atomic weapons, on the other hand, might prove decisive in ending the conflict in Korea without putting severe strains on the US economy or requiring Americans to go fight abroad.[43] The president considered using atomic bombs in Korea, weighing their military value against the possible negative opinion of allies. Even after the armistice in July 1953, Eisenhower's advisors had to consider what it would mean to be attacked again by the communist Chinese. Now-declassified documents make clear that, had China renewed the fighting, American military plans called for atomic bombings of both North Korea and China.[44]

One crucial change had occurred by 1953 that altered how government advisors in the United States thought about peaceful atoms. Uranium turned out to be more abundant than expected. The extraordinary investments in prospecting begun in the late 1940s had begun to pay off. Not only were there domestic sources in the Colorado Plateau, but another foreign source in neighboring Canada, at Elliot Lake, made the future prospect of uranium supplies appear bright. This was not true of the Soviet Union, which failed to find such promising new sources during the same period. While the United States Atomic Energy Commission even began experimenting with novel military uses for uranium, especially ships and planes powered by reactors, the Soviet Union still worried about its reliance on foreign sources to supply its arsenal.[45]

Shortly after taking office, Eisenhower received a note from AEC chairman Gordon Dean outlining a plan for attaining economically competitive nuclear power plants. Doing so would require extensive liberalization of laws, such as allowing entities besides the AEC to own and operate nuclear power reactors and permitting the sale and transfer of fissionable material. In addition, it would mean a substantial incentive program by the federal government to minimize risk to the private sector. Dean's main justification for providing this was that American prestige was tightly wrapped up in nuclear technology. Letting another country take leadership in the field of electricity generation "would be a major setback to the position of this country in the world."[46] Later drafts of the policy massaged this anxiety into a more positive message, saying, "We believe that the United States should continue in its present position of leadership among those nations striving to promote the peacetime applications of atomic energy."[47] Rather than engage in a massive new subsidy, the AEC suggested cannibalizing existing military projects. The most notable of these were nuclear-propelled aircraft and large ships and submarines.[48]

As one official, R. Gordon Arneson, observed, supporting a commercial reactor program "would give tangible evidence to refute the oft-repeated Soviet charges that the United States is interested only in the destructive aspects of atomic energy, while the Soviet Union has been developing it for peaceful purposes." Arneson, who had worked on atomic energy during the Truman administration and called himself "Mr. Atom" in his memoirs, helped the State Department to see the potential diplomatic dividends in nuclear power. One was negative: "If some other country, particularly the Soviet Union, developed useful atomic power first, it would be a major psychological, cold war setback to the United States." But the other was positive. Loosening restrictions and allowing other countries access might prove a useful way to tether them to the United States. "It might also be possible to use such a card to bind our allies closer to us and even influence certain countries presently neutral to be more positively cooperative."[49] Arneson, previously concerned primarily with securing strategic minerals, came to see commercial power as a high-stakes propaganda issue as well.

Originating from Dean and Arneson, carryovers from the Truman administration, the proposal was treated with skepticism by Eisenhower's advisors. None felt that commercial nuclear reactors were worth government investment if the goal were simply to generate electricity. Developing nuclear power was fraught with uncertainties, especially economically.

They were not interested in "give-away programs," having criticized them during the Truman years. Monsanto representatives advised the president that a subsidy would be needed to move forward with power plants.[50] The president's own special advisor for atomic energy, Lewis Strauss, was at that time no booster for commercial atomic energy. He supported reactor development for the navy, as a way to fuel surface ships and submarines over long distances, but such applications did not require strict calculations of costs and benefits. More important, he was developing a personal dislike for Arneson, whose moniker "Mr. Atom" served as a direct challenge to his own role in the White House. But even Strauss saw some value in the proposal as a way to win friends around the world as America waged the Cold War against the Soviet Union.[51]

The dire need for a major "peaceful" propaganda initiative came in the second half of 1953, because Eisenhower expected widespread opposition to a new series of bomb tests in the Marshall Islands to begin in 1954. The United States had tested a fusion device in 1952, in the waning months of the Truman administration. In the summer of 1953, prospects for peace seemed momentarily bright with an armistice ending the fighting in Korea. But the respite was short. On August 12, 1953, just weeks after the armistice, the Soviet Union tested a thermonuclear device of its own, far ahead of American intelligence analysts' projections. If American political leaders were unified on anything, it was in their desire to maintain the technological edge over the Soviet Union. For President Eisenhower, that would mean an ambitious program of nuclear weapons testing. This would require an equally ambitious counter-propaganda initiative, like what Truman had accomplished when pairing the Bikini tests with the Baruch peace proposal in the summer of 1946.

The strongest backing for strengthening thermonuclear weapons capabilities came from Congress, specifically the chairman of the Joint Committee on Atomic Energy, Sterling Cole. He urged that the thermonuclear weapons program "be characterized by even greater vigor, imagination, and boldness," and he recommended that the AEC's activities should focus on hydrogen bombs even more than already was the case. Yet at the same time, Cole urged the president not to lose hope in the idea of international arms control or to abandon the idea of sharing "the benefits of peacetime atomic energy with decent people everywhere." He was no Brien McMahon—he did not envision an atomic Marshall Plan for all peoples. Instead, he backed the domestic power reactor program and was in favor of helping allies to build them too.[52] The president told Cole that he was trying to find a way to strengthen the United States' military preparation, keep ahead in terms of science and technology, while offering a credible vision for peace. He mentioned he had been working on a "talk," to be delivered in the fall, that would address his views on the subject.[53]

The germ of that idea would eventually become one of the most notable proposals of the Cold War, Eisenhower's "Atoms for Peace" speech at the United Nations General Assembly in December 1953, leading to the institutional apparatus for promoting atomic energy throughout the world. But in the summer of 1953, it was just that, a germ of an idea. The speech itself can be interpreted as a creative distraction from the administration's lack of progress on disarmament. The president and his National Security Council already had agreed that serious disarmament was likely to occur only as an agreement between a couple or a few nations and would need to settle major issues such as the fate of Korea, Germany, and Austria. On the question of disarmament discussions at the United Nations, Eisenhower had decided to "conduct a holding operation," doing nothing of substance. That left a gaping hole in American policies that would be filled primarily with propaganda.[54] By September, the administration had nothing new to say and was floundering, trying to concoct something interesting to put forth at the UN meeting. At one point Vice President Richard Nixon asked whether it was possible to simply "dress up" the old position of the United States so that it looked like a "new story."[55] In an earlier speech, Eisenhower had toyed with the idea of a "new kind of war," taking the savings from disarmament and declaring total war against the "brute forces of poverty and need," devoting considerable sums to world aid and reconstruction. But he abandoned it, believing it to be too similar to Point Four and the global Marshall Plan ideas favored by Democrats.[56]

In talking with his special assistant Robert Cutler, the president was drawn to an idea that might have great propaganda value but also would pose a material challenge to the Soviet Union. "Suppose the United States and the Soviets were each to turn over to the United Nations, for peaceful use, X kilograms of fissionable material. The amount X could be fixed at a figure which we could handle from our stockpile, but which it would be difficult for the Soviets to match."[57] The idea emerged from a worldview centered on concern for strategic minerals. Both the Truman and Eisenhower administrations had been obsessed with securing them and denying them to the enemy. And the USSR was clearly making progress in weapons development. What if the president were to challenge the Soviets to siphon off some of the fuel from their stockpile?

The idea at first met with tepid enthusiasm, since it seemed unwise (to AEC Chairman Strauss, for example) to set fissionable materials aside and thus diminish what was available for weapons use. With the advent of thermonuclear weapons, Strauss reasoned that trying to hamper the Soviet

Union in this way might be fruitless, since fissionable materials would only be needed as a primer. The only positive outcome in the proposal would be its propaganda value. Would the propaganda gains be substantial enough?[58]

What eventually became the "Atoms for Peace" proposal was the result of discussions within the administration about balancing frankness concerning the hydrogen bomb with "some kind of equally significant hopeful alternative," as presidential advisor and speech writer C. D. Jackson put it.[59] He told the president that it had to be "a packaged concept" fulfilling three requirements outlined by Secretary of State John Foster Dulles. First, it had to be "new and fresh" and potentially acceptable to the Soviets. Second, if the Soviets did accept, the Western position must not be hampered. And third, if the Soviets rejected it, it would need to leave the United States occupying the moral high ground—placing blame for the arms race—and possibly war—firmly on the Soviet Union. Jackson told the president that they already had done a great deal of drafting of speeches about disarmament and the threat of thermonuclear weapons. "What is missing," he wrote, "is the 'package.'" With dramatic flair, Jackson added, "This can not only be the most important pronouncement ever made by any President of the United States, it could also save mankind. It therefore rates the concentrated attention of the Government's top brains."[60]

In the days before delivering the speech, Eisenhower tried to shore up other commitments, meeting in Bermuda with the prime ministers of France and the UK. To Churchill, privately, Eisenhower laid bare his view that should the communists break the armistice in Korea, the United States would respond by attacking military targets with atomic bombs.[61] He urged the French to recommit to holding their colony in Indochina. During this meeting, just days before the invited speech before the United Nations, the president had not even decided for certain that he would make his nuclear sharing proposal—or so he claimed to his allies—and he presented the basic ideas to the French and British for some feedback.[62]

To his close allies, Eisenhower framed the proposal a bit differently than he did publicly. The world, he said, was in a rather "hysterical condition" about the bomb, and his plan was to work through the United Nations to emphasize constructive work rather than destructive power. He had publicly stated that if the Korean dispute reignited, the United States would strike military targets in reprisal—and it was crucial to appear also as struggling for peace. Donating fissionable material could be interpreted as a kind of disarmament since it diverted the stockpile that otherwise would have been used for bombs. The United States would make a much larger donation than the Soviets (or the British) would, but even that small amount would compel a reduction in the Soviet stockpile and slow their progress on weapons.

The president framed the proposal to his allies as a means to recruit countries into the Western side of the Cold War. Thus far, he said, the world seemed to think the struggle was between the USSR and China on one side and the United States, the United Kingdom, and France on the other. Other nations needed to be drawn in, he said, and to be shown they had a stake in the outcome of the Cold War. Perhaps with the atom, the West could make a hopeful promise to the desperate countries of the world. "Men needed power everywhere," he said. "If we could give hope, it would give these nations a stronger feeling of participation in the struggle of East and West, and such a feeling of participation would be on our side, and hope might be engendered from a fairly insignificant start."[63] The speech would need to give the entire world a stake.

The British and French gave the president the support he needed to confidently make the address at the UN. Laniel approved of it entirely, eager to offer support at a time when France craved American military assistance holding on to its colony in Indochina. Churchill was skeptical at first, sensing a finer line between the commercial nuclear world and the military one. Why encourage other countries to develop any kind of atomic infrastructure? Eisenhower assured him that there were "technical means of rendering it safe." While it was true that there were methods to convert reactors to military use, the president was unconcerned about it. His stance on what later would be called the danger of nuclear weapons proliferation could be boiled down to this: whatever other countries might have would be insignificant compared to what already existed in the USSR.[64]

Promoting atomic energy in other countries was a gamble, but Eisenhower was willing to take the risk. One reason he was not particularly concerned with weapons proliferation was that he did not personally consider atomic bombs to be worthy of a special category. If some smaller country had a few bombs, he believed the US arsenal would possess an adequate deterrent. His approach to national defense was to rely on them more than non-nuclear armaments—they were cheaper and more destructive—and he counted on the arsenal to be a real and usable one. In Bermuda, while discussing the British nuclear weapons program, he expressed his belief that atomic bombs were being regarded as a "proper part of conventional armament," which was well and good. Churchill agreed with him—all the while complaining that US legislation since 1946 had made it hard to get information about these new bombs, should British planes ever be required to drop American bombs.[65]

Eisenhower left Bermuda on December 8 and arrived in New York in time to address the United Nations, delivering what would become the defining speech of the global nuclear order for decades to come. Buttressed by the support of his most important allies, he was able to speak eloquently and candidly about the dangers facing the world, while making what seemed like a constructive plan for peace.

The speech itself had been through several revisions, with the president's advisors and speech writers searching for the right pitch to the rest of the world. As Eisenhower commented to his allies in Bermuda, their chief aim was to encourage other countries to see their own stake in the Cold War struggle and to choose the Western side. In the speech, this was framed as shared danger and shared hope, with the president referring to the "tensions of today's world" rather than between the United States and Soviet Union. In an early draft, the speech boldly challenged the complacency of other nations and invoked a sense of belonging to one planet: "No area of the world, no matter how remote, could consider itself completely immune to some of the results were atomic warfare to occur on our planet." [66] That sentence was cut prior to delivery and replaced with one noting that "this subject is global, not merely national in character." In his address to the United Nations, Eisenhower did say that the two "atomic colossi" faced each other, but "across a trembling world." The language was evocative—the United States' purpose was to find a way "out of this dark chamber of horrors," helping "the minds of men, the hopes of men, the souls of men everywhere" to find peace, happiness, and well-being. Eisenhower spoke of salvation "in a world divided." He deliberately used words that were far-reaching and inclusive, drawing in all peoples, speaking of the "human race" and "every other nation." He offered the word "mankind" seven times and hammered home the word "world" two dozen times.[67]

The president was setting the United States on a path that would have ramifications for the world's nuclear programs, military and peaceful alike, for the next half-century and beyond. What gave his speech appeal was that it leveraged the aspirations of other nations hoping for technological solutions to poverty, disease, and economic stagnation. The speech institutionalized US government endorsement not only of commercial atomic technologies in general but also of the idea that they had a special role to play in the social uplift of the world. It went beyond a willingness to share and also embraced a responsibility to promote civilian applications of atomic energy in other countries. Eisenhower's speech committed the country to creating what became the International Atomic Energy Agency in 1957 and to sharing technologies that might conceivably make good on the promise to bring "salvation" to the world. The president mentioned agriculture and medicine, and he also said that "a special purpose would be to provide abundant electrical energy in the power-starved areas of the world."

Despite their ambitious scope, Eisenhower's words looked toward future possibility, not present reality. The United States in 1953 and 1954 still relied heavily on byproducts of the weapons arsenal, namely, radioisotope production, as its main "peaceful" technology to be exported abroad. No country had yet built a commercial nuclear reactor, and few anticipated that anyone outside North America or Europe would be in a position to attempt it for many years to come (the Soviet Union would surprise the world in mid-1954 with a small 5-megawatt reactor connected to an electricity network).[68] The American plan certainly lacked details. The conservative French newspaper *Le Figaro* guardedly observed, "The plan presented by the president is conceived in very general terms." Another French newspaper, the communist *L'Humanité*, expressed more candid skepticism, noting that genuine disarmament was not part of the plan, and that "behind these grand words it is rather easy, we can see, to recognize a new version of the famous Baruch plan," an insincere propaganda ploy.[69]

Despite the rhetoric about "power-starved areas" in the speech, the United States had no intention to export reactors for electricity generation in the near future and would not know how to handle other countries' demands for them, especially those countries outside Europe and North America. Most of the civilian applications were in the realm of general research, medical therapies using radioactive material, or those intriguing agricultural possibilities such as gamma gardens and mutation plant breeding. Even when thinking about motive power, the president himself had imagined that most of the poor countries would want to "run tractors" to plow their fields. It was a remarkable moment in which a US president tied foreign policy to an imagined set of technologies that relied on a cornucopian fiction. In lieu of making a genuine proposal about disarmament, he was gambling that other nations would assent that the abundance provided by atomic energy was a legitimate vision of the future. Whether these were real or not mattered little, but officials would begin looking in earnest for success stories in atomic energy to match the American promise.

PART II
Atomic Propaganda

CHAPTER 3

Forgetting the Bad Dreams of the Past

John Jay Hopkins's visit to Japan in 1955, as an informal emissary of "Atoms for Peace," must have seemed surreal to everyone involved. Hopkins was the head of an old American shipbuilding firm based out of Groton, Connecticut. Electric Boat Company had struggled in the 1920s and 1930s with its reputation as a "merchant of death," having sold warships to all sides in major wars. During the Second World War, it had stuck to the Allied war effort, producing several hundred patrol torpedo boats that became decisive in the island-hopping campaigns in the Pacific between American and Japanese forces. The Japanese had called them "devil boats," harassing Japanese ships and helping American marines to take control of the vast Japanese Pacific empire. The company had also produced dozens of submarines that killed Japanese sailors. One of these, the USS *Barb*, was alone credited with sinking seventeen Japanese vessels, including the aircraft carrier *Un'yō*. The *Barb* even had pioneered the use of submarine-launched rockets, bombarding civilians in towns on Japan's home islands in 1945.[1]

Just ten years after Japan's defeat, and only three years after the departure of US occupation forces, Hopkins was in Japan being treated not as a foe but as a hero. He had made some changes to his company, including its name. It was now called General Dynamics, with Electric Boat one of its subsidiaries, mostly hidden from view. He had hired a graphic designer to help him to rebrand, creating a series of posters with the words "Atoms for Peace" next to "General Dynamics" in several different languages. He made speeches suggesting that American technology was going to provide power and food to the world and that his company stood ready to participate in a kind of global Marshall Plan that harnessed the atom. Perhaps surprisingly, the first country to take him seriously—and to capitalize on President Eisenhower's "Atoms for Peace" speech—was Japan, the only country to have been attacked with atomic bombs. Hopkins was surprised to be invited there by rich newspaper magnate Matsutarō Shōriki, and after his arrival his astonishment only escalated. He was treated as a celebrity and dignitary, more like a head of state than the head of an infamous defense contracting company. His visit was heralded in local newspapers as the dawn of the new era in the nation's history. There were lectures and presentations about science, and there was entertainment galore, "on a scale lavish even by Japanese standards," one CIA document put it. The event was pure pageantry, with women in geisha costumes, and a thousand of Shōriki's employees chanting "Banzai!" in his honor.[2]

Although the promise of the peaceful atom has been imagined as a successful vision in the 1950s, only to be complicated by nuclear weapons proliferation and environmental concerns in subsequent decades, in reality "Atoms for Peace" opened a Pandora's Box right from the start. The speech itself was part of a concerted American propaganda campaign, and in some ways it worked like magic, providing the United States with a positive agenda at a time when genuine disarmament simply was not happening. It was launched cynically as a propaganda strategy, without a genuine peaceful program in place, and was nurtured with considerable publicity—including working with cartoon filmmaker Walt Disney to turn the atom into a "friend." The United States government eagerly sought success stories that showed the atom as a pathway to abundance and health, but it would struggle in the years to come to offer genuine solutions to developing countries.

The Americans were not the only ones capable of embracing a cornucopian vision of the atom. Eisenhower's initiative provided rhetorical tools to others who pursued political or even personal goals in their own countries. The first major efforts to take "Atoms for Peace" seriously were in East Asia, particularly post-occupation Japan and also South Korea, freshly emerging from the Korean War. In both cases the United States would be confronted with its own empty promises, because these countries explicitly asked for American help to build nuclear reactors to power their economic resurgence. Instead, US officials stalled for time and wavered, unsure how—or if—they should genuinely encourage a peaceful nuclear industry outside the United States and Europe. Japan's was a particularly striking case, because of the sharp shift in attitudes about peaceful atomic energy—moving from deep skepticism in the late 1940s, to outrage at American weapons testing in mid-1954, to a rapid about-face that favored peaceful atomic energy, mid-decade. The apparent reversal surprised everyone, and soon American officials took credit for it as a propaganda win. Yet it also revealed troubling uncertainties about peaceful nuclear technologies, as US government officials realized they were unable to control the pace and direction of Japan's nuclear ambitions.

***

Because the US president's atomic proposal of late 1953 was conceptualized within a psychological warfare framework, the administration worked closely with newspapers to shape public discussion—starting within the United States. The president counted on political allies in the press, such as William Laurence of the *New York Times*. Laurence was long accustomed to helping "sell the bomb," as one scholar put it, having been paid by both the newspaper and the US government to report in precisely the way government officials wanted, adding his own insights and vivid writing style. His eye-witness account of the bombing of Nagasaki and subsequent essays on the meaning of atomic energy had won him the 1946 Pulitzer Prize for reporting. After the war, "Atomic Bill" Laurence played a crucial role in framing public attitudes about atomic bombings and about the Bikini bombs, and he was tapped to do the same for "Atoms for Peace." News articles bearing Laurence's byline, while not exactly as "official" as press releases, were reflections of what US officials hoped to convey to the public, in the guise of detached reporting.[3]

Together with the newspaper's longtime science editor, Waldemar Kaempffert, Laurence launched a publicity campaign on the pages of the *New York Times* focusing on the wonder of the atom, the importance of private enterprise, and the peace-loving attitudes of the president. Just after the new year, Laurence penned "Atomic Power Being Tamed to Turn Industry's Wheels," looking back at 1953 as the year marking a transition from military to peaceful atomic energy, as if that had been the intent all along. He expected the coming decade to bring "epoch-making progress" to detect and treat diseases and to put the atom to use "in a thousand and one fields of endeavor, as widely divergent as are archaeology and agriculture." He predicted that all the heretofore-unheralded applications might turn out as "tails wagging the atomic dog."[4]

Laurence's predictions included the so-called breeder reactor, which would be able to use by-products of fission as fuel, allowing humans "to multiply nature's niggardly store of atomic fuels by a factor of 140, or about 14,000 per cent." That was twenty-three times what was produced by all conventional fuels combined, he enthused. The article led with an image of the naval submarine USS *Nautilus* at the center—labeled "power"—surrounded by other images representing oil research, new metals, chemicals and medicine, and plants and foods. The latter was one of Brookhaven's gamma gardens.[5]

Laurence made the world seem wide open to fantastic possibility, and he hewed closely to the administration's line that peaceful uses of atomic energy were themselves a form of arms control. He spoke of the "transition" from military to peaceful uses as if playing a zero-sum game with the world's supply of uranium. The more it was used for peace, the less it would be used for war. He also reported on the first "atomic battery" made by RCA, using strontium-90. It was initially employed by the company's chairman of the board David Sarnoff to send a message via telegraph: "Atoms for peace. Man is still the greatest miracle and the greatest problem on this earth." Laurence heralded it as an important new source of electricity, and he believed strontium-90 would be widely available, cheap, and destined to "find thousands of potential uses in the developments of atomic energy for the peaceful pursuits of mankind the world over."[6]

Major publishing houses helped promote the government initiative as well. Random House's series on science, "All About Books" included a volume on atomic energy, eventually published in 1955. Written by Rutgers University professor Ira M. Freeman, *All about the Atom* contained all of the optimism found in the president's program, especially for the poorest countries of the world. "The United States and other countries could lend nuclear materials and engineering help to the undeveloped regions of Asia and Africa," he wrote. "This would make the neglected parts of the world flourish. In just a few years, they could make more progress than in many centuries before."[7]

Although Eisenhower did not use the term "Atoms for Peace" in his original speech, newspapers picked it up immediately. It was an old term—already employed from time to time, such as when discussing nuclear-powered electricity.[8] Going forward it would be linked unmistakably to this particular speech and plan by Eisenhower. Other phrases would soon be added, notably "plowshare." It was a reference to the prophet Isaiah, whose memorable words from the Bible referred to soldiers beating their swords into plowshares, turning weapons of war into farm implements.

One corporate ally who immediately latched onto the president's speech was John Jay Hopkins, chairman of the board of General Dynamics. One of the company's biggest government contracts was the USS *Nautilus*, a submarine built for war, powered by an atomic reactor, and named after the submersible craft in Jules Verne's *Twenty Thousand Leagues under the Sea*. The work on the ship was begun during the Truman administration, but the *Nautilus*'s launch occurred on January 21, 1954, less than two months after Eisenhower's historic speech. Hopkins spun the launch of the *Nautilus* less as a victory for the US Navy and more as a step forward for humanity. One company-produced brochure about the launch noted, "The 'Nautilus' will be listed in the annals of man as the first demonstration of his ability to curb the destructive force of the atom and to turn it in positive directions." Gwilym Price, the president of Westinghouse (which manufactured the reactor itself), observed that the *Nautilus* was "a testimonial to the ability and determination of free men to act in the defense of human rights and dignity."[9] The navy had a new class of submarine that could stay submerged for extended periods without the need for refueling, but those at the christening ceremony described it as a boon to humanity and a part of the new peaceful direction of the atom.

Hopkins saw the opportunity of using "Atoms for Peace" to consolidate the rebranding of General Dynamics as a purveyor of technologies beyond the conventional wartime domains of Electric Boat. He dreamed of atomic ships and airplanes and eventually would create a subsidiary—General Atomics—to sell research reactors to countries around the world. He had his sights set on August 1955, when the Eisenhower administration planned to sponsor a major international conference on the peaceful atom in Geneva, Switzerland. There would be opportunities for contractors to put up exhibits, and among these contractors were American household names like General Electric, Westinghouse, and Union Carbide. Hopkins was determined to seize the opportunity to mark his newly named company as modern, progressive, and futuristic. His primary publicity instrument was the Swiss-born graphic designer Erik Nitsche, whose style fit this vision. Nitsche's work for General Dynamics would mark him as one of the most influential modernist graphic designers. His drawings were suggestive of a scientific mindset, with an aesthetic sensibility that blended imagination with clarity and orderliness. Simple yet elegant, with precise shapes and lines but abstract in concept, his artistic renderings were the perfect fit for the relatively unknown future of atomic energy. As one writer later wrote, "Nitsche's brand of artful futurism was copied by many others at the time and might be seen today as representative of the so-called 'Atomic Style' that emerged in the mid- to late-1950s." He made six posters for Hopkins for the 1955 conference, each featuring the firm's name along with the phrase "Atoms for Peace" in one language or another. The French one featured the word "hydrodynamics" along with a visual of the *Nautilus*, positioned not as a war vessel but as a harbinger of peace. The German one, on "aerodynamics," showed the atomic-powered airplane then under development. There was a Japanese one too, on "nucleodynamics," and it was highly abstract—a series of colored squares (some have described it as a rendering of isotopes), with an inset photograph of two physicians.[10]

There was no better friend to the atom, however, than cartoonist and film producer Walt Disney, who agreed to promote the peaceful atom with a new film to be aired on television. Disney producers later explained to the FBI that it took about a year and a half to prepare for it and to film it. "This type of film is usually not profitable for the company; however, Mr. Disney likes to do films of this type occasionally as a public service."[11] Disney was already a household name for inventing Mickey Mouse in 1928 and making the 1937 blockbuster *Snow White and the Seven Dwarfs*. In early 1954, when "Atoms for Peace" needed some publicity, Disney was coming off the success of *Peter Pan* (1953) and was in the process of planning an ambitious theme park, to be built in Anaheim, California. He also had partnered with the American Broadcasting Company to produce a series of television programs for children. All of this put him in an important position to influence young families' attitudes about all manner of things, including atomic energy. The FBI's 1954 assessment of Disney was that he was reliable, cooperative, and "extremely prominent in the motion picture industry," and that year he became an approved FBI contact for the bureau's "Special Agent in Charge" in Los Angeles.[12]

Disney's production, *Our Friend the Atom*, borrowed ideas already established by General Dynamics. On screen, Disney himself provides some introductory remarks while standing in front of several of the Nitsche posters. He makes a reference to Jules Verne's 1870 *Twenty Thousand Leagues under the Sea*. "Fiction often has a way of becoming fact," he says, holding up the Verne book. Then he moves over to two scale models of submarines, one styled after the one in the story and another a replica of the "real" *Nautilus*—the USS *Nautilus*, the first ship to be powered by a nuclear reactor. He does not mention that it is a war vessel. "It's the first example of the useful power of the atom that will drive the machines of our atomic age," Disney states, adding, "The atom is our future." He then goes on to describe the many atomic projects that the Disney studio is planning in addition to the television program, including a book and ambitious exhibits as part of the Tomorrowland portion of the amusement park in southern California.

For Disney, this "public service" was a collaboration that would draw potential visitors to his new theme park. For his program on the atom, he drew from the same network of scientists he was already using to make a similar television program on space exploration. As narrator he chose Heinz Haber, whose gentle demeanor, foreign accent, and silvery hair lent the discussion some scientific gravitas. He was not a nuclear physicist, though. In the previous decade, Haber had been working as a rocket scientist in Nazi Germany and was likely introduced to Disney producers by fellow rocket specialist Werner von Braun. Both von Braun and Haber had been captured toward the end of the war by Americans under Operation Paperclip and went to work for the US Army. Together with another colleague, Willy Ley, the two had written a series of essays on space exploration in *Collier's* magazine. These had captured the attention of executives at Disney, who saw space as the perfect subject for Tomorrowland. Producing educational television programs about space exploration seemed like a great advertising opportunity for the new theme park. Kimball reached out to von Braun and soon both he and Haber became technical consultants for Disney. The first of the space programs aired on ABC on March 9, 1955.[13] Von Braun focused on space, while Haber became the face of Disney's atom.

The Disney version channeled US policy perfectly, with the book and television program both titled *Our Friend the Atom*. In the 1957 program, Haber eases into the discussion by saying that, yes, it was a science story, but that "it was almost like a fairytale. By a strange coincidence, our story turned out to be like the old fable from the Arabian Nights, "The Fisherman and the Genie." Rather than discuss technical details, Haber begins by telling the story of a fisherman attempting to convince a magical creature, living in an ancient-looking container pulled from the sea, to do his bidding. Cartoons, orchestral music, and voice actors play out the story, before Haber reappears on screen to say that "we are like the fisherman. For centuries, we have been casting our net in the sea of the great unknown in search of knowledge. And finally," he says, holding up a rock, "we found a vessel. And like the one in the fable, it contains a genie. A genie hidden in the atoms of this metal, uranium." The cartoon genie then shows that it is radioactive by holding a Geiger counter next to it and drives the theme home: the genie is liberated, it first threatens to kill, and then it is "finally harnessed to grant us three wishes."

The publicity campaign for the television program and book was enormous. It involved syndicated news stories, magazine features, brochures, and even a school donation program calling on businesses to buy prints of the film to distribute in schools. The brochure for the donation program stated that "at the threshold of the atomic age we find our nation critically short of trained scientists and engineers so necessary if we are to reap the many benefits the friendly atom can bestow upon us." Of course, all of the cross-promotion was tied to Tomorrowland at Disneyland.[14]

The television program proposed the atom not merely as a "friend," to be juxtaposed with the warlike atomic bomb, but also as a solution to a serious problem confronting the world—the limitations of nature. Haber notes that "the coal and oil resources of our planet are dwindling" and calls upon the genie to provide power. He also notes that humans continue to suffer from hunger and disease and says that our second wish for the genie should be "food and health." Finally the last wish is peace—to let the genie be a friend forever.[15]

The president's allies in the corporate world hoped to harness this publicity and create markets for American companies. One such ally was Walker Cisler, who had been part of Eisenhower's wartime staff in 1944 and had had the duty of rehabilitating electrical power, along with gas and water, after the D-Day landings. In subsequent years he rose high in the ranks of Detroit Edison. In 1948, he leveraged his wartime role to become one of the principal designers of European electric power infrastructure under the Marshall Plan.[16] As president of Detroit Edison, he teamed up with Dow Chemical to conduct a 1951 study on the feasibility of commercial nuclear power for the Atomic Energy Commission. After Eisenhower became president, Cisler headed up the first association of businesses—called Atomic Industrial Forum, Inc.—formed in 1953 to promote the nuclear industry in the United States. He was eager to see atomic energy enter the private sector and was very supportive when the University of Michigan started fundraising for an atom-themed research project to honor its alumni killed in World War II. The unique Michigan Memorial-Phoenix Project drew on the imagery of the mythical creature rising from the ashes, and it represented a vision of the future marked by alliances between major corporations and university research laboratories—rather than domination by the AEC.[17] With such partnerships in view, Cisler and others lobbied to amend the Atomic Energy Act of 1946 to allow nuclear development to take place outside the direct management of the Atomic Energy Commission. As it happened, Cisler's view fit Eisenhower's (and that of most Republicans at the time) very well, and Congress amended the act in 1954 to allow more opportunity for private industry.[18]

Despite such enthusiasm from the private sector, the United States was neither ready nor even planning to build reactors for electricity generation anywhere beyond US borders. The prevailing view among American electricity companies in 1954 and 1955 was that the future of atomic energy in the United States would lie in breeder reactors. These would recycle the irradiated fuel in a fission reaction, thereby increasing the fuel efficiency of a reactor. One of the by-products of the fission of uranium was the element plutonium, which itself could be used in fission: the reactor would breed its own fuel. Cisler believed breeders would mitigate US dependence on foreign sources of uranium, and they would be economically competitive with other forms of energy, without constant subsidies from government.[19] This view had the backing of the nuclear physicists who directed major national laboratories such as Walter Zinn (Argonne National Laboratory, in Illinois) and Alvin Weinberg (Oak Ridge National Laboratory, in Tennessee). Although they both supported and (in the case of Zinn) helped to design pressurized water reactors for the navy, they believed the future of US commercial atomic energy would be in breeder reactors.[20]

Cisler and others founded a new organization called the Fund for Peaceful Atomic Development (FPAD), financed largely by the Ford Foundation and other charitable donors, to align "Atoms for Peace" with the opportunities abroad perceived by US industries. While ostensibly speaking for private industry and financed by private foundations, the FPAD aligned itself closely with the agenda of the Department of State.[21] In addition, it may have been linked indirectly to US intelligence. The Ford Foundation was one of many philanthropic foundations used by the CIA for monitoring and influencing activities abroad while concealing the source of funding.[22] Cisler would in 1955 be tapped by Eisenhower's special advisor on disarmament, Harold Stassen, to lead a task force on inspections of industrial power in other countries with the aim of identifying production or diversion of strategic resources such as uranium. He had a close working relationship with CIA director Allen Dulles throughout the 1950s.[23]

FPAD provided a means by which the US government monitored the atomic energy capabilities of countries around the world. A French correspondent reported that most activities in his country were oriented toward shoring up access to fuel resources and starting up a reactor-heavy nuclear program at home. The French had discovered a "vast mineral zone" of uranium and thorium in southern Madagascar. "Our scientists estimate that this may be one of the largest thorium deposits known to date, and one which is in no way smaller than those of India and Brazil."[24] The Fund also received letters from the Mexican Light and Power Company and from the Universidad Nacional Autónoma de México to coordinate information about developing nuclear energy there. Others were interested in radioisotopes and research reactors. In just the first year of its existence, the Fund reported to Congress that it was in contact with colleagues from Cuba, India, Turkey, Pakistan, and Egypt.[25] Under the auspices of the Atomic Industrial Forum, Cisler sent an information request to foreign embassies to canvass atomic activities, political interest, and overall aims of potential atomic energy programs. It had received nearly forty responses by April 1954.[26]

Although the United States was promoting a range of atomic applications—in agriculture, medicine, and research, for example—it was clear to Cisler's organization in 1954 that most countries were far less interested in these than in electricity generation. It was the one application that seemed directly tied to economic development. A correspondent from India, for example, noted that "easily available and abundant power is the key to all industrialization," and that atomic energy may be competitive compared to hydroelectricity. While India was perceived by many as a source of raw materials, such as monazite and beryl, the objective of the nation's atomic energy program clearly was electricity.[27]

Eisenhower had captured the world's imagination, but even by the mid-1950s other nations were competing with the United States as a source of atomic development. France was cooperating with both India and Brazil to develop their own atomic-related industries, including uranium extraction in Brazil and a monazite processing facility in India. The nation most "ahead" in peaceful applications, including sharing them with the world, arguably was the United Kingdom. As British delegate Pierson Dixon crowed to the United Nations in November 1954, "I believe that the United Kingdom is at present the greatest exporter of radioactive isotopes in the world."[28] Even prior to Eisenhower's speech, Prime Minister Winston Churchill had told Parliament that industrial power from the atom was destined to play a major role in the world economy and that "the exploitation of nuclear energy may come to be regarded as the most important step taken by man in the mastery of nature since the discovery of fire." By then the British had begun construction on an atomic-powered electricity plant, Calder Hall, to be part of their plutonium production facility at Windscale. This would be a gas-cooled, graphite-moderated reactor, using natural uranium rather than enriched uranium, and it was to have a power capacity of some 50 megawatts, about ten times that of the modest Soviet reactor unveiled in 1954. In addition, just a few months after Eisenhower's speech, the United Kingdom announced plans to build a breeder reactor on the northern coast of Scotland, at Dounreay. Neither plant would turn a profit, but they were intended to demonstrate future directions of British nuclear energy to be in place by the 1970s.[29]

In the United States, the pressure to be perceived as the leader was strong. Faith in breeder reactors required patience, which was in short supply in 1954 and 1955. Aside from the progress being made by the United Kingdom and France, the Soviet Union built a demonstration reactor in Obninsk in June 1954 and claimed it as the world's first nuclear power plant. It produced only a small amount of electricity (capacity of 5 megawatts), but it was a "first," thus it represented a challenge to US leadership in the field. Behind the scenes, Soviet scientists resented the diversion of resources to the small reactor because they too favored breeder reactor research. But peaceful atomic energy was becoming a significant vehicle for propaganda, and Soviet officials were as determined as the Americans to utilize it. In fact, after the death of Joseph Stalin in 1953, new political leaders relied on such "firsts" to bolster their credibility. Communist Party secretary Nikita Khrushchev embraced international competition in peaceful atomic energy, and soon he would send representatives to international meetings to tout the achievements of Soviet science and technology.[30]

In tense hearings before Congress's Joint Committee on Atomic Energy in 1955, Cisler defended the sluggish pace of the US atomic energy industry. Representative Carl T. Durham pressed Cisler, saying "It is getting to where this thing is still research, research, research. I believe in it, but after a while I want some results." He was not just worried about the Soviet Union. He also sensed that the British were getting into the reactor business earlier than the Americans. "If we have to mess around here for another period of years, somebody else might beat us to it." Senator John O. Pastore asked Cisler whether the government could be doing more to nudge businesses along. "I have always felt that we are in a contest or a race with other countries of the world in achieving this objective of producing electric power by use of atomic energy," he said. But Cisler still held firm, doubting the wisdom of a faster pace. "If we were to go into a crash program," he asked, "what would be the justification from an economic standpoint?" The United States had sufficient power already and in fact produced more than 40 percent of the total electrical power worldwide.[31]

President Eisenhower too was motivated to stay ahead and already had ordered the construction of a commercial atomic power plant for demonstration purposes to be located in Shippingport, Pennsylvania. It was not a breeder but instead was cannibalized from the naval program that produced the *Nautilus*. It used a pressurized water reactor (PWR), whose defining feature was its compact size, making it seem suitable for use aboard ships. Construction on the commercial reactor began in September 1954, and when it was completed in 1957, the Americans heralded it as the world's first.[32] It was really the third, but the truth of such "firsts" boiled down to certain details. The Americans said theirs was the first such reactor devoted exclusively to peaceful uses, thereby allowing them to sidestep the knowledge that both the USSR (Obninsk in 1954) and UK (Calder Hall in 1956) already had developed reactors for electricity generation. Even so, it was not completely true in the US case. It was the navy's reactor, refashioned as a civilian one.

The US decision to build the Shippingport reactor was political but it had far-reaching implications. The future US nuclear industry would be based on pressurized water reactors (PWRs) and boiling water reactors (BWRs), both of which used ordinary (or "light") water as a coolant and enriched uranium as fuel. Weinberg and Zinn, the national lab directors, had supported the navy's preference for PWRs for use in submarines but were disappointed to see the ideal concept for a commercial reactor—the breeder—cast aside. Weinberg later argued that most other major design possibilities, using alternative coolants, such as gas, heavy water, hydrocarbons, or sodium, had advantages in civilian use over those using plain water. But the American companies making reactors for the navy's new class of submarines, such as Westinghouse (*Nautilus*) and General Electric (*Seawolf*), were getting a lot of experience with water-cooled reactors, and speed was the priority. In the years to come, despite continued interest in breeders, American-made reactors would be water-cooled and fueled by enriched uranium. "The national laboratories, although they gave support to the main line," Weinberg lamented years later, "found themselves rather bypassed in their preoccupation with breeders."[33] After the navy design was chosen, there was no turning back.

Some American corporations saw near-term export opportunities abroad for civilian reactors but not for electricity generation. One of these was General Dynamics, which created a subsidiary in 1955 called General Atomics to build and sell research reactors. Over the next few years it designed a reactor that could not suffer a meltdown, making it relatively safe and marketable.[34] The company targeted customers within the United States but also abroad. Known by the acronym TRIGA (Training, Research, Isotopes, General Atomics), these reactors used enriched uranium as fuel, requiring the buyer to strike an ongoing fuel deal with a country (ideally the United States) that had invested in facilities to separate uranium isotopes. TRIGA reactors could serve to placate the desires of those countries wanting a modern reactor without requiring the extensive infrastructure of an electricity grid.

Research reactors would become an important means of trying to fulfill the promise of "Atoms for Peace" in developing countries. One of the first tests of Eisenhower's initiative occurred in Korea, where war between the communist North and the UN-supported South had been ongoing for three years, ending less than five months before the president's speech. The signing of the Korean Armistice Agreement in July 1953 did not establish permanent peace. Americans and Koreans seeking to strengthen South Korea knew that much of Korea's industrial strength lay in the North, and they turned to US foreign aid to build up the South's infrastructure. As scholars of Korea note, they sought to create a showcase "developmental state" in South Korea, working with UN specialized agencies and state agencies such as the US International Cooperation Administration.[35] Given the rhetoric of "Atoms for Peace," the South Koreans might have expected a big push for putting reactors in their country. But most of the peaceful applications advocated by Eisenhower were in the realm of agriculture and medicine, not necessarily electricity.

To South Koreans, electricity was the most prized application of all. In the years between World War II and the Korean War, the South suffered from its lack of access to the North's thriving chemical industry and hydroelectricity grid constructed during the years of Japanese rule. The South's predominantly agricultural society relied on the North as a source of chemical fertilizers and electricity, which was cut off in 1948. This move bolstered the North's claims of independence and political legitimacy, as it could provide for Koreans in ways the South could not. North Korea lorded this superiority over the South in material ways and in symbolic ones, using the unmistakable images of a river dam and electricity power line on its national emblem.[36]

Atomic energy appeared to offer autonomy for the South, overcoming the constraints of nature while also ensuring independence from North Korea. As historian John Dimoia has noted, "Atoms for Peace" came at the same moment that South Korea was attempting to implement a long-term development plan. Internal plans, along with plans developed in concert with American and other UN allies, all pointed to electricity generation as the crucial foundation. Not only would it provide needed infrastructure but it would also be a symbolic move to achieve a level of technological self-sufficiency. Were nuclear reactors part of the answer? The South Korean government sent Japanese-educated Korean scientists such as chemist Chul-Jae Park to train in nuclear techniques at US national laboratories and other training programs in the United Kingdom, France, and Germany. Chul-Jae Park returned to Korea motivated by the desire to develop a plan for nuclear power in Korea.[37]

Park, along with officials within the Ministry of Education, had hopes of large-scale development aid packages from the United States. High-profile Americans seemed to be making such promises. Walker Cisler came to Seoul in 1956 and delivered a series of lectures about the benefits of atomic energy, though he focused on the Fermi breeder reactor then under development by his company, Detroit Edison. South Korean President Syngman Rhee was intrigued.[38]

At any suggestion of electricity, the United States deflected Korean overtures of cooperation. The Americans pushed for a research reactor with strong ties to universities and routinely tried to slow the Koreans' enthusiasm for jumping into electricity generation full throttle. Much of the technical collaboration took place under the auspices of the Michigan Memorial Phoenix Project, part of the University of Michigan. Its faculty already had decided to build an on-campus reactor, and the Phoenix Project aligned itself with US foreign policy goals to promote similar approaches elsewhere. They were not prepared for the South Korean government's wish to embark on a crash atomic energy program to address its serious natural shortfalls. The reactor ultimately purchased in the short term by South Korea was a TRIGA Mark II, one of the research reactors developed by General Atomics, which was not designed to generate electricity. The Koreans followed the Americans' lead while still holding out hope for a future of electricity generation. As DiMoia notes, the banner at its 1959 groundbreaking ceremony for the TRIGA reactor displayed the words "Peace, Research, Power," underscoring the importance of electricity.[39]

In South Korea, the Americans dictated both the pace and the model of development by insisting first on a university research reactor, to be followed many years or decades later by electricity production. This was a matter of unspoken US policy, and as early as 1954 intelligence analysts anticipated criticism and resentment, stating how important it was to properly present atomic research as capacity-building—start with research, train scientists and technicians, then proceed ultimately to their application—"the development of power reactors could be expected to follow in due course."[40]

Meanwhile politicians in Japan focused on self-sufficiency—given the loss of resource-rich Manchuria and Korea during World War II and the rules against deep-sea fishing during US occupation. Energy demands, especially for coal and oil, had been a major motivator for Japanese expansion in the 1930s. In the postwar years the nation wondered whether nuclear power could address those concerns peacefully. It might have seemed unlikely that Japan would turn toward atomic energy. Defeated, under military occupation, and the victim of two atomic bombings, Japan had every reason to be resistant to it.

By early 1954, the track record of the United States toward Japanese atomic energy research was not good. A few months after the war, occupation authorities had ordered the destruction of two cyclotrons operated by physicist Yoshio Nishina's laboratory at the Institute of Physical and Chemical Research in Tokyo. Nishina interpreted this as a sign of American concern that the Japanese would try to build an atomic bomb, and he complained that the cyclotrons could have aided research in agriculture, forestry, animal husbandry, fisheries, and medicine.[41] It seemed ironic that now the US president was proclaiming to want the Japanese to do precisely these things, despite occupation authorities having made it harder rather than easier to do so. Numerous scientists remained enthusiastic about non-military uses of the atom, but aside from the use of radioisotopes, very little atomic research was reported when Cisler's group queried the Japanese in 1954. Plans were modest: the Science Council of Japan hoped to build a laboratory for nuclear physics, to be associated with Tokyo University, where a new cyclotron had been built after the American occupiers departed in 1952. Other universities planned to build cyclotrons of their own, to conduct particle acceleration research and also to produce radioisotopes on a small scale.[42]

The first serious "atomic" event to occur in Japan after the war threatened, rather than encouraged, Japanese self-sufficiency. By 1952 Japanese industries were recovering, especially in textiles, because American occupation authorities lifted trade restrictions to allow Japan to help supply troops fighting in Korea. Yet Japan was still trying to find sufficient sources of food. The government issued sweeping reforms, seizing land from absentee landowners and forcing locals to sell uncultivated land. Japan's rice fields, under heavy fertilizer use, began to produce impressively—and supplemented by wheat, oats, and sweet potatoes, Japan's food production began to recover too. But it was not enough to provide even minimal calories for the Japanese, which in 1952 amounted to 1,978 calories per capita per day, compared to the 1936–40 average of 2,280. That is why the deep-sea fishing industry was so important to the Japanese people and their politics. Despite the limits the American occupation authorities had placed on the area in which the Japanese could fish, Japan had nearly regained its prewar fishing catch by 1951, and the peace treaty that went into effect in 1952 abolished that limit altogether.[43] So by early 1954, Japan had just entered a period of expansion in Japanese deep-sea fishing, designed to make the country self-sufficient in food, at just the moment when the United States began an ambitious series of hydrogen bomb tests in the Pacific Ocean.

One of these tests, codenamed Bravo, occurred in March 1954 and was part of the "Castle" series of blasts at the Pacific Proving Ground in the Marshall Islands. The "Atoms for Peace" initiative had been created in part to blunt the expected negative publicity from this new class of weapon utilizing nuclear fusion, with fission bombs as triggers. The Bravo shot alone was an estimated 15 megatons in size, a thousand times the size of the bomb that destroyed Hiroshima. By all accounts, it exceeded the expectations of scientists. But what made it controversial was its fallout—the debris from the blast that shot up into the sky and, carried by atmospheric currents, fell out in many parts of the South Pacific, including the Marshall Islands. In addition, contaminated ash fell onto a Japanese fishing boat called the *Daigo Fukuryū Maru* (usually translated into English as *Lucky Dragon*). When the boat returned home, some of the crew were hospitalized and one died; the fish were sold before it was widely realized they were contaminated.[44]

The international scandal over the *Daigo Fukuryū Maru* incident renewed antagonisms between the United States and Japan while also undermining the message of "Atoms for Peace." In other Asian countries, the incident became a symbol of American warmongering. In a public statement, Indian prime minister Jawaharlal Nehru pointed out the obvious, that disarmament clearly was not happening. Moreover, it seemed that "the open ocean appears no longer open, except in that those who sail on it for fishing or other legitimate purposes take greater and unknown risks caused by these explosions." He observed that the burdens of atomic energy fell heavily on Asia: "her peoples appear to be always nearer these occurrences and experiments and their fearsome consequences, actual and potential."[45] In summarizing Japanese reactions, the Central Intelligence Agency noted a "wave of anti-American feeling" as "sensational reports about the harmful radioaction [sic] continue to fill the Japanese press."[46] In Japanese media, the United States—until quite recently an occupying power—came across in much the same way as a colonial power, wielding its unchallenged technological and military power over the entire Pacific.

Despite the furor over the *Daigo Fukuryū Maru*, the Japanese government made its first budget allocation for atomic energy that same month. It did so against the outspoken views of many Japanese scientists, though the Science Council of Japan issued a declaration that atomic energy should be supported only if three principles were followed: non-secrecy, democracy, and independence. When physicist Sin-itirō Tomonaga and others convinced the government not to proceed without major investment in basic science, they considered it a success. But when they tried to make plans for a nuclear research institute in Tanashi, outside Tokyo, they discovered that there was widespread opposition to it there, mainly because of fears that it would eventually become a site for military work.[47]

It was an inauspicious beginning for civilian atomic energy in Japan, marked not by hope and cooperation but by distrust and resentment. Yet atomic energy continued to have advocates who saw it as a pathway to national self-sufficiency. The young conservative politician Yasuhiro Nakasone had openly criticized the long American occupation and urged other Japanese to think of atomic energy as key to the country's postwar resurgence. He had been behind the government's budget allocation for atomic energy research. Though in Japan there would continue to be strong opposition to nuclear weapons in the 1950s, resistance to civilian atomic energy diminished considerably. This was in part due to successful American propaganda and the efforts by Japanese politicians such as

Nakasone.⁴⁸ It was also aided by favorable coverage of the peaceful atom in the television and newspaper outlets of media mogul Matsutarō Shōriki. His role is greatly understated in most English-language accounts of the spread of atomic energy programs, and yet it is a fascinating early example of how easily the American promises could be bent in unpredictable and uncontrollable directions.⁴⁹

Shōriki used his newspaper and television outlets to sell the peaceful atom to the Japanese people at a time when the *Daigo Fukuryū Maru* incident seemed to doom atomic energy in the country. "The bloodshot eyes of the Japanese," he later boasted, "sparkling with hatred of atomic energy, changed overnight to serene eyes adoring the goddess of peace!" Shōriki described atomic energy in terms of natural limitations, impending crisis, and the need to quicken the pace of development. "In a nation suffering from population pressure, loss of territory, and paucity of natural resources, and in need of speedy improvements in industrial technology, agriculture, and medicine, and in promotion and expansion of new industries, the time has come for the whole nation to forge ahead without any hesitation whatsoever." ⁵⁰

Shōriki seemed to be an ideal partner for a 1950s American government that fought communism tooth and nail. His early career was spent in the police force, where in the 1920s he rose to chief of staff of Tokyo's metropolitan police. A staunch anti-communist, he had been charged with rooting out communism among labor groups, and he instituted the practice of raiding educational institutions. He left the force in shame when a young socialist came close to assassinating Crown Prince Hirohito. When he bought the newspaper *Yomiuri Shimbun*, he turned it into a voice for the establishment, unfriendly to communism but very friendly to right-wing politics and celebratory of Japanese imperial conquests. After the war he resisted American demands for "democratization" of the press and refused to give up autocratic control of his paper's overall tone and editorial decisions. That resistance ended only when occupation authorities arrested him for having used his newspaper to cooperate with Japanese militarists during the war. At the time, the Americans suspected that he had hoped to use the newspaper to climb to further political influence, including obtaining Cabinet rank.⁵¹ When others took over the paper, American authorities noted approvingly, "those who had propagandized the nation into war and conquest were not qualified to serve as heralds of peace or spokesmen for democracy."⁵²

After the occupation government released him from Sugamo prison in August 1947, Shōriki quickly rebuilt his influence. He did so first with baseball, one of his passions (he was the owner of the Tokyo Giants), and he was appointed baseball commissioner—only to resign under intense pressure from the Americans. To Courtney Whitney, a high-level official in the US occupation government, Shōriki's regaining of his prewar influence was a symptom of backsliding in American reform efforts.[53] Shōriki was not easily repressed, and soon he found ways to align his interests with the United States in ways that the Americans were unable to resist.

Before long the Americans saw value in Shōriki as a good propagandist. While in prison, he developed an idea to take control of television in the same way that he had dominated the newspaper industry. Shōriki's plan, according to CIA analysts, was to use the threat of exposing corruption by several government officials to persuade them to support him. In other words, he would rise again through blackmail. One of his associates, Hidetoshi Shibata, worked for the planned government-sponsored television network and thought that the Americans might help Shōriki achieve his goal of taking control of it—providing technical assistance, money, and political influence—in return for cooperating in American propaganda. This proved to be correct, but it ended up with Shōriki gaining control of a different network altogether, a private one called Nippon TV.[54]

The relationship with the Americans began when US senator Karl Mundt gave a speech in June 1950 suggesting that the United States should promote Voice of America television programs in Japan to consolidate the country's orientation toward the democratic free world. Shōriki seized the opportunity to gain an American ally, and he sent Shibata to meet in Mundt's office with some Americans who had gotten into the field of television broadcasting: New York attorney Henry Holthusen, and the engineers William S. Halstead and Walter Duschinsky.[55] Those three Americans went to Japan in 1951 to help Shōriki set up a new nationwide television network, headquartered in Tokyo and with relay stations throughout the home islands. These Americans went on to form the Unitel corporation, with Halstead as president. Holthusen worked as a consultant to the US Senate Foreign Relations Committee and led efforts to find appropriate outlets for Voice of America. He was doing the same in other countries, including Brazil, Greece, and Turkey, with an eye toward a worldwide network of pro-American television programming, using broadcasting standards that mimicked American ones. Though US administrators in Japan initially balked at the idea of a television network not controlled by the state, Holthusen stressed the role Nippon TV could play in American psychological warfare around the world, working with corporate partners rather than governments.[56] Shōriki was off the purge list in 1951 and was running Japan's first commercial television network by early 1953.[57]

American intelligence agents characterized Shōriki as a man of ambition and influence who was willing to act as a mouthpiece for American ideas in exchange for US support for his personal ambitions. Shōriki knew he was working with Americans but willfully remained aloof on the details. As one CIA official estimated Shōriki's motivation, "Subject is anti-communistic, a highly successful businessman and promoter of sports, i.e. baseball, racing, etc., Subject is interested in maintaining his position as such." He seemed to be a shrewd opportunist with ambitions that matched American goals for Japan. What Shōriki wanted was money to build the television network and political help obtaining the necessary licenses.[58]

Even before working with him on atomic energy, the CIA wished to use Shōriki in 1953 as an unwitting collaborator or "cutout" for funding Project KMCASHIER, the plan to develop an international microwave communication network among Japan, South Korea, Taiwan, and the Philippines.[59] The plan relied on Unitel to create a global relay network, linking major cities of every non-communist nation, to allow close to real-time dissemination of information. It would enable global reach to the televisions of the world.[60] In 1954, Shōriki, Halstead, and others were actively collaborating to serve corporate interests, US government propaganda, and Shōriki's own reputation in Japan. Nippon TV was growing, and Unitel was expanding, as was the regional impact of Voice of America.

Shōriki's interest in "Atoms for Peace" was sparked by a late 1954 speech, reported in the *New York Times*, by General Dynamics president John Jay Hopkins. The speech identified atomic reactors as a way of raising living standards in underdeveloped areas, while creating "vast new world markets for our products." It would be like an "Atomic Marshall Plan," Hopkins said. He set forth an ambitious construction scheme in which private enterprise and national governments would cooperate over a whole century. Although Hopkins spoke of electric power, he saw it as a long process of development that could take decades or more. It would start with research reactors; then move to small-scale portable power reactors; then larger-scale stationary reactors; and ultimately to breeder reactors. "The real wealth of Asia," Hopkins observed, "is locked under deserts, in mountains, and mainly in the billion people who hunger for food, for equality, and for all that is implied in the term 'American standard of living.'"[61]

Shōriki paid little attention to the pace of development laid out by Hopkins and instead focused on the idea of building an electricity-generating reactor in Japan. Through his associate Shibata, who met regularly with a CIA agent, Shōriki communicated to the Americans that he wanted to do everything he could to promote Eisenhower's peaceful atomic energy agenda in Japan. Meanwhile Shibata had Halstead make contact with Hopkins to invite him to Japan. Both Halstead and Shibata already were acquainted with General Dynamics vice president Vernon Welsh, who helped convince Hopkins to go to Japan. To the CIA, Shibata urged that someone in the US government should contact Hopkins and endorse his trip, and then send a top-level atomic physicist with him to Japan. He also suggested that Eisenhower should personally mention the Hopkins trip, to allow Shōriki to make the most of the publicity in newspapers and on television.[62]

By finding an influential figure with personal ambitions, the Americans seemed to have a particularly important ally who would be pro-American and who would adopt similar rhetoric—namely, that atomic energy could free Japan of its natural limitations. Some CIA agents speculated that Shōriki might become an extraordinary asset. His political ambitions ran high. In early 1955 he was seeking a place in the Japanese Diet and, if successful, he and his trusted colleague Shibata would become CIA assets within the Japanese government. A CIA report noted one of its reliable sources, a Japanese journalist, saying, "He may become president of the Japan Democratic Party in the near future. . . . He may become Prime Minister if he succeeds in unifying the conservative parties."[63]

Despite such enthusiasm among intelligence agents, Shōriki had a different vision for Japan than did Hopkins, Cisler, or any of the other Americans. He would not be satisfied with research reactors. He wanted electric power. Running for election to the Diet as a conservative, he wished to show the importance of atomic energy for the Japanese private sector. That is why inviting Hopkins, rather than a government official, was so important. A connection with him could be shaped in the press as a promising business relationship with an important US corporation while avoiding the charge that it was direct collaboration with the US government—or worse, seeking a handout from the Americans. Since the Japanese election was slated for late February 1955, Shōriki urged Hopkins to arrive in early February at the latest. Meanwhile Shibata wrote to his American contact at the company, Vernon Welsh, that such a visit would effectively silence what he called communist-influenced propaganda against the atom in Japan. Although Hopkins did not visit before the election, Shōriki was elected to the Diet as a non-partisan candidate in late February 1955, having campaigned heavily on a platform stressing the connection between atomic energy and Japan's self-sufficiency.[64]

Shōriki tied his political fortunes to a vision in which nuclear power would make up for Japan's natural resource shortfalls and supplant them with abundance. Rhetorically he followed "Atoms for Peace" precisely but in practice went far beyond genuine US intentions, imagining the near-term development of electrical power stations. He used the considerable power at his disposal—his newspaper and his television network—to promote atomic energy in Japan. He gave up his presidency of the newspaper when he joined the Diet, but he did not give up ownership control. He convinced Prime Minister Ichirō Hatoyama and other Japanese politicians to endorse the visit by Hopkins.[65] His political campaign rhetoric made atomic energy into a marker of national power and prestige while also portraying it as a liberator from the constraints of nature. He stood as the candidate who could help Japan defy the world's expectations and restore its global standing. It had happened before, he proclaimed: skeptics had said Japan was not ready for a television industry, and Shōriki had proved them wrong. Now he would do the same with atomic energy.

Hopkins came to Japan in May 1955 with an entourage that included his General Dynamics colleague Vernon Welsh and scientists Ernest Lawrence and Lawrence Hafstad. Also present was Philip Reed from the General Electric Corporation. Reed's presence was not widely advertised, but he likely had a dual corporate and government role, having held advisory roles to several US government bodies, including the US Information Agency, and often acted as an informal advisor and envoy to President Eisenhower. Hopkins was received by the newly formed Organizing Committee of Japan Atoms for Peace Council. This official-sounding group had been formed just prior to the visit, and its Japanese translation was the "Atoms-for-Peace Friendly Talking Society." Shōriki, naturally, was the leader. Other members of that committee included key leaders in the industrial and manufacturing sector.

Hopkins gave an address about civilian atomic energy on May 13, 1955, in Hibiya Hall, the largest auditorium in Tokyo. He was treated as if he were an important celebrity or dignitary rather than a corporate executive. The American scientists did their part, giving speeches to counteract the negative views of atomic energy among Japanese scientists. "These men were knowledgeable and expert to the point where they repeatedly reduced their Japanese opponents to nothing," one CIA officer exulted. "They succeeded in the Japan press in revealing to the Japanese people for the first time that many of the so-called Japanese atomic scientists were hardly distinguishable from charlatans or at best somewhat misguided."[66]

Even on the Science Council of Japan, which had previously seemed like such an implacable foe of atomic energy, the so-called Hopkins Mission won some converts. This was the "most profound and lasting effect" that the CIA rejoiced in, because it helped to label even scientific objections as politically motivated. "The Japan Science Council appeared to shake itself out of its political trauma and finally agree with the American scientists that a great deal could indeed be done on a scientific basis for Japan's welfare."[67]

Among intelligence analysts, the consensus view was that Shōriki's television and newspaper propaganda had significantly reversed public perceptions. One CIA case officer noted: "When the arrival of Mr. Hopkins and his party began to materialize [Shōriki] committed his empire to a full blast favorable treatment of the atom, not neglecting to feature himself as the Prometheus who was bringing this fire to Japan. This was interesting because it was the first time since the war that major Japanese media had done anything but look askance at the atom."[68]

The apparent readiness of Japan to accept, indeed embrace, a nuclear future, startled virtually everyone in the US government. Shōriki was not just a newspaper mogul but an influential member of the Diet with dreams of becoming prime minister, and he had made the visit of the president of General Dynamics into a dazzling spectacle. As one CIA analyst wrote, the Hopkins Mission had a "press play unparalleled in recent Japanese history." The General Dynamics leader "departed amidst a welter of Geisha girls and Banzais by thousands of *Yomiuri* employees, somewhat confused about just what it was the Friendly Talking Society expected of him."[69]

What Shōriki wanted was a reactor for electricity generation in Japan as soon as possible. He asked if the United States was willing to provide "on a long-term lend-lease basis—as the first sign of encouragement and assistance—an atomic power reactor." The request came inside a gushing follow-up letter to Hopkins signed by nineteen members of the Organizing Committee. The letter reported that the "sudden surge of ardor" after his visit had completely reversed public opinion about atomic energy, giving the Hatoyama Cabinet the confidence to accept enriched uranium, a possibility previously disallowed. The Hatoyama government also had started to negotiate a bilateral agreement on nuclear sharing with the Americans. Other measures were picking up as well—an official committee on peaceful atomic applications had been created in the Diet, and new legislation had been set aside for purchasing reactors. "It is our earnest hope that Japan, by becoming a participant in a broad scale atomic energy program, will help to free the one billion people of Asia from poverty and disease, and help to build a world filled with friendship and love." The letter spoke of the solemn duty to continue on this course, "even with a serious cold war going on," and "affirm anew our indomitable determination to achieve our goal, no matter what the cost."[70]

The letter, sent to Hopkins but then circulated within the US government, spoke of "turning misfortune into fortune," "our common destiny," and using atomic energy as a "symbol of the joining together of our two countries" that would permit everyone "to forget the bad dreams of the past." The letter laid on the hyperbole, closing by saying how grateful the nearly 90 million Japanese people were to Hopkins personally "for the effort you have expended in opening a new page in our history."[71]

The peaceful atom was finally getting more attention in Japan than weapons testing. CIA director Allen Dulles received a heartening cable from agents in Japan: "Hopkins trip and his public statements have made extremely good impression, and for first time have forcefully directed public attention to US program in field peaceful uses of atom. All media playing up heavily; even recent underwater atomic explosion California crowded off front page."[72] The underwater test referred to Operation Wigwam (May 14, 1955), an underwater blast some 500 miles southwest of the California coast. Given the uproar after the 1954 Bravo shot, the Americans expected criticism but found little on the pages of Shōriki's *Yomiuri*.

By the end of 1955, the State Department had helped to provide Japan with an atomic energy library, was facilitating the training of Japanese students in nuclear science and engineering, and had reached a bilateral deal on reactor assistance and material transfer. The United States Information Service launched in Tokyo a year-long exhibit on reactors, instruments, and medical and industrial applications of atomic energy, and sent the exhibit to travel all over Japan. Even in Hiroshima, US officials created an exhibit on the great benefits of atomic energy. Despite expecting strong opposition from *hibakusha* (atomic bomb survivors) and from the Council against Atomic and Hydrogen Bombs, the Americans—and Shōriki—persuaded local officials in the city to openly support the educational goals of the exhibit. American planes dropped 100,000 leaflets in the surrounding area, encouraging Japanese to visit, and American films celebrating atomic energy were screened throughout Hiroshima. Television broadcasts on Shōriki's Nippon TV and many special symposia were devoted to turning public opinion toward supporting peaceful applications of atomic energy. Numerous *hibakusha* and prominent peace activists visited the exhibit and publicly praised it. One even donated a television set to a young boy who was the exhibit's millionth visitor.[73]

It was in these exhibitions that Shōriki proved his worth, offering official sponsorship from his newspaper *Yomiuri Shimbun*. Shibata pointed out to his American contact that the Japanese public was unlikely to accept an event that was clearly sponsored by the US Information Agency. One CIA memo noted that "his basic plan is to use Japanese artists, make up men and printers who would rework CIA furnished material to (1) play down or conceal the original source of this material, (2) fit current attitude [to the] Japanese public and general Japanese psychology. Emphasis would be placed on Russian refusal participate all-out [in] Atoms-for-Peace plans."[74]

Shōriki wrote directly to Eisenhower to highlight what he was doing for the US cause: "We have done our utmost to publish the true facts of atomic energy through the media of newspapers and television, in order to calm the storms of violent controversy and combat the activities of leftists and rightists."[75] In his message, Shōriki reinforced his own role in the success of the "Atoms for Peace" exhibition, which helped ameliorate the bitter memories of the Japanese. "As I watch the number of people enlightened by this Exhibition grow day by day, I feel a deep satisfaction which is a full reward for the part I have played therein." The Japanese, he said, "have not failed to see through the flames in which they were baptized into the atomic age, into the dawn of peace, prosperity, and civilization rising beyond."[76] He may have overstated the turnaround in Japanese public opinion, which remained divided on whether atomic energy—and especially the United States—could be trusted. Yet public opinion surveys in subsequent years indicated that the combined efforts of American propaganda and Japanese media were having a strong effect.[77]

Less than two years into the era of "Atoms for Peace," the United States was confronted with a situation in which a local figure hoped to use nuclear energy in ways that served personal and national ambitions. Shōriki was using American rhetoric, but was he pursuing goals that Americans truly wanted? He seemed to suggest that Japan was willing to set aside the past and to leap forward with the United States toward an atomic-powered future. But the question of what to offer Japan was freighted with memories of the recent Pacific war. Even if Shōriki failed to achieve his goal of becoming prime minister, the CIA's connection with him might be helping not to simply resuscitate Japan from the war but to restore Japan to Great Power status. "This is not said lightly," one analyst concluded, "for when one considers the final potential of what the man is doing, the mind begins to boggle. For one thing, the microwave [television broadcasting] scheme, if carried to its logical conclusion, will put into Japanese hands a tremendous propaganda organ capable in some degree of influencing all of Free Asia. The nuclear energy proposals, if carried to their logical conclusion, will put Japan in possession of an atomic bomb. These are certainly instruments which will put Japan, if only in her potential as a troublemaker, in the first rank of world powers." In their discussions with the Americans, of course, the Japanese never mentioned the atomic bomb. Yet it would be astonishing if "these clever gentry have not considered the implications of this useful byproduct of the peaceful uses of the atom."[78]

When Japan's Atomic Energy Commission was created in January 1956, Shōriki became its first chairman. Cables to the director of Central Intelligence, summarizing views of sources, grew more alarmed. "If Shōriki becomes premier, he is determined to streamline Japanese govt structure and cut number of govt officials," one stated. "He would also stress amendment of disarmament clause in constitution."[79]

The Americans were in no hurry to provide reactors, which would prove deeply frustrating to Shōriki, who felt that he had done everything in his power to amplify Eisenhower's message in Japan and to establish a friendly political climate for atomic energy in Japan. Yet Hopkins did not respond to his letter, interpreting it as a "thank you" note rather than a request for a business arrangement. Only after CIA intervention did he finally phone Tokyo.[80] The results were disappointing. General Dynamics was interested in developing export markets for research reactors (the so-called TRIGA reactors). Shōriki, however, wanted electricity generation. Then, in the final week of the six-week Tokyo exhibit, Shōriki learned that the US State Department had decided to build a regional "Asian Nuclear Center" in the Philippines, not Japan. He was furious. Twice he phoned Vernon Welsh at General Dynamics, hoping he would intervene somehow, but to no avail.[81] Shōriki had staked his political future on atomic energy, and he was making no progress on getting a power reactor from Hopkins. The US government added insult to injury by looking to a different country in the region for its nuclear center. What more could Shōriki have done to welcome peaceful atomic energy?

Despite the fanfare of the "Hopkins mission," it was a different visitor who told the Japanese precisely what they wished to hear. Sir Christopher Hinton came to Japan in late April 1956 to persuade Shōriki and others that Japan's best bet for atomic energy lay with British reactors, not American ones. Hinton later kept a copy of one of his three lectures in Japan, with the title "A Talk to People in the Inner Circle of Atomic Energy in Japan." In it, he outlined the history of atomic development in Britain, including its initial military objectives from 1946, setting up a research establishment at Harwell, and building factories for fabricating fuel in the reactors. He pointed to their new facility at Calder Hall, an experimental power reactor attached to a military facility, as the prototype of the future.[82] Unlike the American reactors (cooled by water and relying on enriched uranium), it was cooled by gas and used natural uranium. Hinton compared the Calder Hall reactor to the slow speed reciprocating engine of the steam age—it was well established and well tried, capable of being a "safe, reliable and reasonably economical source of power." It would be superseded in the future but it would hold its own for some time. "I think that reactors of this type will still be sold in 30 or even 40 years time and that they will be in use in 50 years time."[83]

Hinton framed his discussion in terms of resource shortfalls, especially the serious coal shortages predicted for the future. He drew parallels between Japan and Britain: both produced present fuel requirements internally, but demands were rising more rapidly than production of coal; and both made up for it with oil imports, putting pressure on the economy—which "will impose an impossible strain in the future unless an alternative form of power can be developed."[84] Nuclear power would provide a solution to these natural resource constraints. In drawing parallels between the two island nations, Hinton emphasized the nuclear kinship between the United Kingdom and Japan, a kinship not shared by the Americans. The United States had massive diffusion plants for enriching uranium, operated by the relatively cheap electricity in the United States. "In the UK we are short of power and we are reluctant to erect large diffusion plants which would, in the first instance, only aggravate our troubles." Hinton presumed the Japanese had similar problems. Adopting American designs would mean a commitment to building facilities or relying on the Americans for fuel, neither of which was ideal for a country wishing to achieve self-sufficiency.[85]

Hinton knew exactly what to say. He encouraged Shōriki to think big and to buck American advice to move forward slowly. If the Japanese were serious about nuclear power, they should not simply start a research program. They needed an industrial reactor as soon as possible. Research was like military reconnaissance, he said—useless if not consolidated by the main body of the army. "I imagine that you feel that, with a pressing need for nuclear energy, you are making a late start," Hinton said. "We, in England had something of that feeling when, well behind the United States, we laid the foundations of our industry in 1946. We found however, that careful planning and wise concentration of effort enabled us to make satisfactory progress and that we were right in regarding our late start as a challenge rather than a handicap."

Whereas Hopkins had remained noncommittal, the British were eagerly knocking on the door to sell Calder Hall–type reactors. Hinton made clear that Britain saw itself as competing for Japan's business against the United States. Japan soon sent a team to the United Kingdom to further explore options with the Calder Hall reactor. In the discussion with Hinton, Shōriki praised Britain's program, which was successful despite unfavorable circumstances. He then called to mind the fact that Japan's economy was worse off than Hungary's or Argentina's, a situation that would continue due to its lack of energy resources. "Japan can never become one of the world's leading powers so long as she persists in a negative program for power generation, that is, a program which will merely try to cover the shortage of electric power."[86]

After Hinton departed in May 1956, Shōriki had options—and the United States learned this the hard way when it resumed nuclear weapons testing that month. Operation Redwing brought the Americans back to Bikini and Enewetak in May 1956 with a series of seventeen tests to try out a new generation of thermonuclear weapons, new fission triggers, and tactical fission weapons. On May 21, the Cherokee test deployed the first thermonuclear weapon delivered by air—demonstrating that fusion weapons could be integrated with fission weapons into the strategic bombing fleet. Although no official details were available, the *New York Times* estimated the yield of the blast to be in the range of 10 megatons, with a fireball some three miles in diameter. In Japan, the Kyodo News Service reported changes in air pressure similar to the Bravo test of 1954 and warned that the fallout from the test would get to Japan in a week or so.[87]

The Americans had no reason to suspect that Shōriki's press would be unfriendly, but they had not considered the impact of the Hinton visit. An editorial in the *Yomiuri Shimbun* condemned the United States, which "seems to be very proud of its hydrogen bomb test" despite blinding two people, and it criticized the Americans for casually referring to it as a human error. "Do they not think," the editorial asked, "that the very testing of nuclear weapons constitutes an intolerable 'human error' from the standpoint of humanity?" It then went on to criticize the United States' interpretation of its security pact with Japan, which the Americans believed gave them control of Okinawa for the next couple of centuries. Okinawa would soon become the Cyprus of Asia, the newspaper complained, and it made sarcastic remarks of how grateful Japan was to American kindness in extending its protection. "This 'kindness' is what is making the United States more and more unpopular in all parts of the world."[88]

All of the CIA handlers of Shōriki were appalled at the editorial. Knowing Shōriki's close monitoring of the newspaper, and his subordinates' fawning desire to please him, it seemed impossible to imagine that he was not behind it. The chief of the CIA's Far East Division wrote to the CIA chief in charge of Japan that a clear message needed to be sent to Shōriki that the United States was "not interested in a 'mutuality of interests' relationship that is chameleon in nature, depending on whether at the moment there is something [Shōriki] desires from us; and that one more such harangue and [Shōriki] may expect no further friendship from [the CIA]."[89]

Shōriki was not getting what he needed from the Americans. He had already done the legwork in Japan, convincing the Kansai Electric Power Company to ask for a 10-megawatt demonstration reactor from the United

States, and was just waiting for government approvals. But Shōriki's frenetic pace could not be matched by the Americans. When Brookhaven scientist Marvin Fox visited Japan to discuss the country's participation in Asia-wide atomic cooperation through the Asian Nuclear Center, Fox was interested in talking about gamma gardens and medical techniques, not nuclear power. He told Shōriki that Japan was unlikely to receive a US reactor in fewer than five years, and even that seemed optimistic. "This reservation apparently came as a considerable shock to [Shōriki]," the CIA's chief in Japan noted, "and prompted his overtures for the procurement of a reactor from the British."[90]

Matsui Sashichiro, a Japanese diplomat and one of the boosters of the American program, conveyed his distress to an American colleague in July 1956 that Hinton's "sales talk" had the ideal effect. "Shōriki is basically a man of action and is impatient with efforts to take a more cautious study approach to any problem. On the other hand, Dr. Fox, who urged a cautious approach publicly, made a rather poor impression on Shōriki and convinced him that the U.S. was not anxious to push early development of atomic power." As soon as Fox had gone, Shōriki wanted to sign a contract with the British. "Hinton's talk about the economic feasibility and lack of security safeguards in the British reactors completely convinced Shōriki."[91] Evidently he was not alone. Japanese interest in nuclear power was now aroused, but few wished to have the pace dictated by the United States with talk of caution. Japan was no South Korea and would not be put off so easily. The American attitude seemed not only arrogant but hypocritical—after all, the United States did not seem overly cautious when building weapons.[92] Spurned by the Americans and forced to wait, Japan was ready to do the spurning.

While the Americans peddled research reactors, the Japanese wanted electricity. They did ultimately buy research reactors from American firms but also pressed forward without delay with reactors destined for the electricity grid. Shōriki and others formed the Japan Atomic Power Company (JAPCO) in 1957 and struck a deal with the British. Construction on an electricity-producing atomic power station would begin in 1960, in Tokai-Mura, operated by JAPCO. It was a gas-cooled reactor, using natural uranium, based on the designs at Calder Hall—the British design, not the American one.[93]

In the meantime, Japan became the first non-Western power to fully embrace a future of atomic energy, not only in agricultural and medical uses but also in reactors for electricity production. It gave the appearance of having overcome the "bad dreams" of Hiroshima and Nagasaki and the more recent sting of the *Daigo Fukuryū Maru* incident. US State Department officials saw the change in political winds as a propaganda coup, but the reality was more complicated. The rhetoric of American politicians certainly established the talking points—the ability to overcome resource shortfalls and establish self-sufficiency were chief among them. But the "Atoms for Peace" initiative was not the agent of change in Japan. The American initiative became the vehicle of choice by an already powerful media mogul with political ambitions, one who already had found ways to leverage American propaganda goals to serve his own interests when he created Nippon TV. This initiative also played into the hands of Shōriki and other conservative politicians as they tethered their perception of Japan's future to a broad vision of civilian atomic energy.[94] When the Americans were not willing to practice what they preached, the Japanese were able to collaborate with others—the British, who deployed the same rhetoric even more expertly than the Americans did, emphasizing the similar paths and challenges of the British and Japanese island empires.

The turnaround startled virtually everyone, especially the Americans, who suddenly had to imagine a resurgent Japan committed to a major nuclear program just a little more than a decade after the end of the Pacific War. Had the United States been wrong to tie so many developmental visions—self-sufficiency, food production, medicine, and power—to the atom? The United States had put extraordinary effort into propaganda at home and abroad, selling a future of plenty. In practice, however, most officials still imagined South America, Asia, and Africa as "backward" areas more suited to agricultural or medical applications, not capable or ready for electricity generation. Japan challenged that and showed how little control the United States really had. Other countries would soon do the same, forcing the US government to decide how to react when other governments—even in newly independent nations—made ambitious plans for a future powered by atomic energy.

CHAPTER 4

Colored and White Atoms

The unfolding situation in Japan and Korea made clear that American officials and businesses, when pressed, were not prepared to provide reactors for electrical power in the so-called undeveloped or "backward" areas of the world. They preferred to emphasize medical or agricultural uses—including mutation plant breeding, food irradiation, fertilizer studies—or research reactors. While many of these held attractions, the prospect of proceeding without electricity as an aspiration was fraught with meaning. Electric-powered industry was a signifier of development, certainly, but just as important it was a symbol of independence and self-sufficiency. Some of the countries that took atomic energy seriously were newly independent after years of colonial rule, such as India; others had recently been occupied, such as Japan; some were clamoring for independence still, including African states such as Ghana. All of these looked for an economic path forward that would ensure political and economic stability in the long term.

Were there colonial and racial dimensions of "Atoms for Peace"? When proposed in 1953, empires were alive if not well—Europeans and Americans asserted control, formally and informally, over peoples all over the world and tried to manage their natural resources. In Southeast Asia, for example, Britain had deployed troops to hold on to Malaya, while France battled to keep its colony in Indochina. Indeed when Eisenhower first broached his plan to Joseph Laniel at Bermuda, the French leader was more interested in soliciting American military assistance fighting Ho Chi Minh's forces. The Americans had granted independence to the Philippines in 1946, after half a century of rule, but still kept dozens of military bases there and enforced trade laws highly advantageous to

American businesses. The United States itself was deeply divided racially, with Jim Crow laws enforcing separation of "colored" and "white" in many parts of the country. That included Tennessee, the site of the Oak Ridge National Laboratory, home not only to "isotope alley" but also to state codes outlawing interracial marriage and requiring racial segregation in public transportation and in washrooms.

Eisenhower had offered up a vision of the peaceful atom that suited the outlook of an American president in 1953—one in which there were industrial centers in Europe and North America, and most of the rest of the world was either colonized or, if independent, disdained as "backward." He believed that certain applications of atomic energy might be relevant to such backward areas, namely, those in agriculture and medicine. After all, these were people with age-old problems of disease, overpopulation, and food insecurity. It must have seemed a reasonable premise, but it raised a couple of sticky problems. One was the presumption that the first countries to develop nuclear power for electricity ought to be the predominantly white nations of the United States and Europe, with the nonwhite nations to follow after many years had passed. Another was that the so-called backward countries ought to be content with applications oriented not toward industry but toward agriculture and medicine. Such perspectives hinted that there were two kinds of atomic energy: one suited to the traditional, predominantly white, colonial powers, and the other suited to the impoverished, brown-skinned, formerly occupied or colonized peoples of the world.

American presidents over the next decade would be eager to disavow this impression, starting with Eisenhower and continuing with American politicians through the mid-1960s. Atomic energy was supposed to be a liberator, not a means of reinforcing the historical divisions of the world. As with its overall foreign policy, the United States framed its atomic energy offerings as part of the global struggle between the "free world" and the communists, a division that masked the firm US military alignment with colonial powers such as Britain, France, Belgium, and the Netherlands. The United States continued that framing even as nations such as India and Ghana tried to forge a different path that associated atomic energy with the struggle for national or even racial liberation. The specter haunting Eisenhower and his successors was the emergence of a bloc of countries whose concerns were primarily racial and anti-colonial. Given the reality of racial segregation at home and the government's close alliance with colonial powers of Europe, including military assistance for maintaining political control over colonies, such a framing would put the United States on the side of the old colonial masters.[1] American politicians utilized the promise of atomic energy to dim such perceptions amid numerous racially charged challenges in the 1950s and '60s.

***

"Atoms for Peace" appeared as a winning propaganda tool because even some of the most vigorous critics of American policies abroad were remarkably uncritical of the peaceful atom. For example, renowned Mexican artist Diego Rivera usually was critical of the United States, as when he skewered its foreign policy in a 1954 "mobile mural" depicting the nation as the architect of the 1954 coup in Guatemala, showing dead bodies and a giant bomb with Eisenhower's face on it.[2] Yet on atomic energy, Rivera was a booster. One of his patrons was Nabor Carrillo Flores, a Mexican atomic physicist who had been invited to witness the 1946 Bikini tests and who in 1953 became the rector of the Universidad Nacional Autónoma de México, where he encouraged the creation of a peaceful nuclear research community. Rivera's 1953 mural *The History of Medicine in Mexico* depicted a patient receiving radiation therapy, a procedure Rivera himself would undergo in the Soviet Union beginning in 1955. Similarly, Chilean (and communist) poet Pablo Neruda's vision of rearranging nature for the good of all was reminiscent of American "Atoms for Peace" propaganda. As part of his 1954 *Odas Elementales*, Neruda penned an "Ode to the Atom," which implored the atom to abandon the criminals ("los bandidos") and to collaborate instead with life, agriculture, machines, and electricity, to enrich the world.[3]

In 1955 there was little beyond medicine and radioisotopes to offer as a "peaceful" technology. Already Japan was clamoring for nuclear reactors for electricity, and the US government was not genuinely willing to provide them. Rather than say no to reactors completely, Eisenhower's government offered up the idea of the research reactor, like those being planned by General Dynamics. It would aid scientific research, it had all the appearance of modernity, but it could not be used as a significant source of either electricity generation or bomb fuel. The National Security Council document calling for these reactors had stated that they would be useful for psychological advantage in international cooperation.[4] In June 1955, Eisenhower made nuclear reactors the theme of his commencement speech at Pennsylvania State University, congratulating it on the first research reactor of its kind at a university. In the speech, he offered such research reactors, with the United States contributing half the cost, to "the people of free nations."[5]

While publicly downplaying the importance of commercial power in the short term, the United States worked feverishly to finish its own demonstration reactor in Shippingport, Pennsylvania. After visiting the United Kingdom in late spring 1955, AEC Chairman Lewis Strauss worried that the British might get ahead of the United States in commercial power. To prevent that, Strauss planned to do a quick repurposing of a reactor at West Milton, New York, which had been the prototype of a nuclear submarine. That way they could begin producing electricity in a matter of weeks and declare a "first." If anyone raised eyebrows about it being a conversion from a now-unneeded military reactor—not a true purpose-built civilian plant—Strauss would play up the propaganda of turning a military project into a peaceful one.[6]

In the meantime, the US government planned an international conference that would dazzle the world. Held in Geneva in August 1955, it featured much fanfare and press coverage and an extensive exposition hall to highlight various national programs. It would include the latest examples of mutation plant breeding and medical applications. The Americans tried to highlight a development path for other nations that led to research reactors. Secretary of State John Foster Dulles pointed out that even that would be too ambitious for some, because "the level of scientific competence of most countries appears to be too low to make profitable use of such a complex scientific tool as a research reactor." Even with American training courses for foreign students, progress would be slow; only after some time would there be "sufficient skilled cadres of scientists and engineers" abroad to justify reactors.[7] But the Americans presented the research reactor as a worthy goal for any nation and planned to build a working reactor just for the occasion of the conference, at a projected cost of some $300,000 to $400,000.[8]

American diplomats worried that their showcase event would be tainted by accusations of racism and colonialism from nonaligned and nonwhite nations—particularly India, whose leaders were critical of US nuclear weapons testing. The Indians seemed to want to be involved in international atomic energy affairs, not simply as a recipient of American largesse but as a full participant—even a leader. Several notable scientists in India had promoted nuclear physics since the late 1930s and claimed to have proposed electricity production from uranium fission prior to the bombings of Hiroshima and Nagasaki. India saw electricity generation from nuclear reactions as a goal, ultimately to be based on the thorium in its vast monazite sands. The leading scientist in this effort by the early 1950s was Homi Bhabha, who had convinced the wealthy Tata Foundation to partner with the Indian government to support a nuclear program. The Indian government proposed that Bhabha serve as the Geneva meeting's president.[9] AEC chairman Lewis Strauss tried to convince American diplomats to block the appointment, suspecting that the Indians would hijack "Atoms for Peace" and use the Geneva conference as a platform to criticize nuclear weapons testing, to remind the world of the horrors of Hiroshima and Nagasaki, or to make a case for neutralism. However, the British and the Soviets agreed that an Indian president made political sense, and many in the US State Department thought it was fruitless to object. Instead they worked behind the scenes, acquiescing in Bhabha's appointment in return for assurance that MIT chemist Walter Whitman would be installed as secretary-general to act as the real gatekeeper: reviewing papers, making chairperson appointments, and overseeing other logistical details that could shape the proceedings. Let India have the position of prestige, they reasoned, and put a loyal American into the position to make decisions.[10]

The timing of the conference made Eisenhower nervous, because it was going to be preceded by another international conference with a very different tone: the meeting of African and Asian countries, scheduled to take place in April 1955 in Bandung, Indonesia. On its agenda were issues of colonialism, white supremacist regimes, and the perils of nuclear weapons. The Americans were not invited. Eisenhower brainstormed potential distractions and pressed his National Security Council to be imaginative about civilian atomic energy, given that many of the projects "were being done for psychological and political advantages to the United States." He suggested pulling a nuclear propulsion unit from a naval submarine and putting it onto a merchant vessel to send around the world as a "traveling showcase." Such a plan was already under way, and AEC chairman Lewis Strauss said so. The president was delighted and asked that the press be notified, but Strauss reluctantly added that if they implemented it only "as a stunt," it would take three months. To do it properly would take two years.[11] Unfortunately, that would be too late to make an impression on the Africans and Asians in Bandung.

The Americans had reason to be worried about the Bandung conference. It brought together representatives from more than two dozen governments in Asia, Africa, and the Middle East to discuss issues common to them all. From the Americans' perspective, it threatened to become a vehicle for neutralism and accusations of racism. The United States relied heavily on its allies in these regions to make speeches clearly orienting the world toward East-West rather than North-South conflicts. Numerous delegates (Pakistan, Thailand, Iraq, and Turkey, for example) made anti-communist remarks. But the Bandung conference also gave voice to simmering resentments about US actions toward the non-white peoples of the world. China's premier Zhou Enlai reminded his listeners that the first victims of nuclear weapons were Asians. Others pointed out that the United

States claimed to support sovereignty and independence, yet relied heavily on colonial Europeans as military allies in the struggle against the Soviet Union. Numerous participants questioned American commitment to racial equality, given that only in 1954 had the US Supreme Court declared public school segregation unconstitutional and that "Jim Crow" discriminatory laws continued to be enforced nationwide. Even in atomic energy matters, the United States had made tempting promises under "Atoms for Peace," yet due to its uranium needs, it still maintained strong ties to the historically brutal colonial regime of the Belgian Congo and the white supremacist government of South Africa.[12]

In a final communiqué, the twenty-nine nations of the Bandung conference outlined hopes for a future of economic development, denounced colonialism as evil, and challenged the United States to make good on its promise to share knowledge about atomic energy. They urged the creation of a "Special Fund" under the United Nations, to be provided for the purpose of economic development. The Bandung nations welcomed the offer by "the Powers principally concerned" to share information about atomic energy for peaceful purposes. They urged the establishment of the promised International Atomic Energy Agency and observed that it should include adequate representation from Asian and African nations in the agency's executive branch. They encouraged all Asian and African governments to take full advantage of training and opportunities to gain experience in other facilities.[13]

Despite many criticisms of the United States at Bandung, American leaders breathed a sigh of relief when the final communiqué simply asked them to make good on the promises Eisenhower already had made. The diplomatic power of the peaceful atom was working. The timing was perfect, given that the Geneva meeting on peaceful uses of atomic energy was scheduled to take place a few months later. Still, Eisenhower took no risks and made sure there was positive press about disarmament. In July 1955, also at Geneva, at a political summit with the leaders of the USSR, Great Britain, and France, the president made a speech welcoming aerial reconnaissance of military facilities. What became known as the "Open Skies" proposal was another distraction—it did not suggest genuine disarmament but seemed to move in that direction, and no one expected the Soviets to accept the proposal (they did not).[14] It was perfectly timed to maximize positive feeling during the meeting on peaceful applications of atomic energy, which turned out to be a showcase of American ambitions. Strauss would later boast that the success of the conference itself was largely due to the new climate of opinion resulting from Eisenhower's remarkable proposal.[15] The president was becoming skilled at "waging peace."

The August 1955 Conference on the Peaceful Uses of Atomic Energy was gigantic, and Strauss guessed it was the largest scientific gathering the world had ever seen, with 1,110 papers presented over a period of fourteen days, and with nearly eighty countries represented. The American exhibit was the most extensive and included a functioning research reactor. The Soviets also had a display, as did the French, Germans, Belgians, Canadians, and Scandinavian countries. Strauss thought the conference "had provided the United States a handsome dividend in the shape of a victory for our fundamental national policy," effectively countering enemy propaganda that the United States was a warmonger. Everyone in attendance was "perfectly astonished," he stated, to see how thoroughly the reverse was true, and they would carry that impression back to their home countries.[16]

Soviet participation in the conference served as a potent reminder that the USSR expected to compete for propaganda victories in peaceful nuclear technology. The preparations in Moscow were intense: the Soviet Academy of Sciences even staged a kind of dress rehearsal for scientists a few weeks before the conference. At Geneva, Soviet scientists delivered 102 papers, including reports on the recently commissioned Obninsk reactor. Moreover, Party Secretary Nikita Khrushchev later led some of the delegates on a visit to the United Kingdom's Atomic Energy Research Establishment in Harwell, England. There he gave a speech about peaceful atomic energy and made it crystal clear that the Soviet Union was making it a top priority.[17]

The United States followed up the Geneva conference with a plan to collaborate directly with Asians, to speak to the aspirations of the earlier Bandung meeting. The State Department sent John Hollister, director of the newly created International Cooperation Administration, to meet with Asian delegates in October 1955. This time it was a gathering of the so-called Colombo Plan, a regional economic development body made up initially of former British colonies but soon extended throughout the region. Hollister announced that the United States would finance the creation of an Asian Nuclear Center to make the peaceful atom a reality in that part of the world.

In a press release about the proposed center, the United States estimated that the government would commit some $20 million to the project, an extraordinary sum that dwarfed any previous contributions for nuclear activities in Asia. It was all part of the American plan of "putting atomic energy to work for the economic and social progress of Asia," the press release noted, saying that the center would exist in the spirit of President Eisenhower's "Atoms for Peace" program. Speaking on behalf of the International Cooperation Administration, US official William F. Russell called it an enormously ambitious nuclear project that would serve "the needs of all humanity."

The idea of the Asian Nuclear Center was hatched by political operators, not scientists, and with little specificity. First, it was unclear what kind of work would occur at the center. Second, and more important, Hollister had not said where the center would be located—and it sparked an immediate competition for hosting it. One possibility was Pakistan, already negotiating with the Americans for a research reactor, and on the verge of creating its own Atomic Energy Commission. Another was Ceylon, whose capital Colombo already enjoyed a symbolic position as a center of Asian cooperation. Another was Japan, where Matsutarō Shōriki was doing his best to set the political stage for atomic energy. Like many others, Shōriki viewed hosting the center as a prize to be won. Of course another possibility was India, with its strong community of physicists and Homi Bhabha's demonstrated leadership during the Geneva conference.

Despite the appearance of high-stakes competition, the United States already had decided where to locate the center. The choice was obvious only to Americans: the Philippines. It was a country relatively free of any troubling Bandung-like notions, it was amenable to promoting a positive cornucopian message, and it was easy to control. The country had become independent of the United States in 1946, with many strings attached—such as the retention of US military bases and guarantees of access to Philippine natural resources. The United States maintained close watch and control over the country, its most reliable foothold in Asia. For example, before the Bandung conference, General Carlos P. Romulo of the Philippines had circulated and discussed his opening statement with Secretary of State Dulles, and he dutifully returned afterward to report on his efforts to oppose the neutralists.[18] The Philippines was an ally that could be trusted to toe the US line. It was also so far "behind" anyone else that its activities were likely to stay in the realm of agriculture, medicine, and other kinds of developmental research. The US agreed in July 1955, a month before the Geneva meeting, to supply the Philippines with a research reactor. The Philippine ambassador to the UN, Felixberto M. Serrano, chaired the country's delegation to the Geneva meeting on peaceful atomic energy. In a radio broadcast in the Philippines, Serrano echoed the American view that the world was effectively turning swords into plowshares, and he described the American peaceful atomic energy initiative as "an act of peace and of faith in a world of mounting tensions." He hoped that "the little group of Filipino scientists who are with me today" would help to extend the uses of atomic energy.[19]

Given how "backward" the Philippines was perceived to be, the choice of Manila seemed to suggest that Americans expected Asian atomic energy to be confined to research on agriculture and medicine, not electric-powered industry. It was a choice that spurned both Japan and India, whose aspirations and scientific communities were substantial. To justify its decision, the United States claimed that there were already appropriate educational institutions with English-speaking scientists in Manila. It was a claim that baffled the Indians, whose educational institutions were English-speaking and whose scientists were renowned—including a Nobel Prize winning physicist, C. V. Raman. The Philippines, by contrast, was not known for scientific work at all.[20] A British diplomat in Manila described the educational institutions there as having "shockingly low" standards, noting that when foreign students were asked to compare the University of the Philippines with universities in Ceylon or Pakistan, they were only able to smile.[21]

The Americans used their most reliable form of diplomacy, the power of the purse, to mollify offended sensibilities. For example, the Ceylonese had hoped to have the center in their country, but they did not make a fuss when the United States chose the Philippines. They accepted that the latter had a special place under American protection. "Indeed Ceylon would find it hard to understand any other view," one British diplomat surmised. "An Eastern people expects rewards to go first to friends." It did not hurt that the US International Cooperation Administration sent a mission to Ceylon at the same time with $5 million to give away in the coming year, a gesture of continued friendship.[22]

Dubbed "Project Colombo" by American scientists, the plan for the Asian Nuclear Center had been given no forethought by scientists, American or Asian. Most of the Colombo Plan countries assumed that a working group, consisting of leading regional scientists such as Homi Bhabha, would meet to discuss the best plan of action. Instead of inviting Bhabha or even soliciting his advice, however, the United States sent a team of American scientists from the Brookhaven National Laboratory, led by reactor expert Marvin Fox, to visit each country. Instead of a joint undertaking, the Americans were providing the "blueprint."[23] Fox tried to explain that the idea of the center had been hatched by bureaucrats in Washington, and the details had been very hazy. Brookhaven then received a quarter million dollars for the project, employing scientists from several government agencies as well as diplomats, political scientists, and businessmen. Brookhaven scientists were supposed to figure out what to do, based on consultations with Asians. Yet there was little to consult about, given that none would have suggested that putting the center in the Philippines was a good idea.[24] Fox was almost apologetic when discussing the program with British diplomats in India. He asked them whether they thought the scheme could succeed, given that the only two countries with robust nuclear programs in the region—India and Japan—felt snubbed. The British could do little more than shrug their shoulders and say the way the Americans had done it was not really regional scientific cooperation. It was more of a donor-recipient approach. The Americans seemed to think that Asians should be grateful for whatever they received rather than expecting to be consulted.[25]

Such American behavior may have seemed undiplomatic but it was not atypical of long-standing American attempts to wed scientific and technical expertise with foreign policy goals. Despite the link with the Colombo Plan, it went against the usual British approach, which focused on coordination rather than direct aid. The Americans, by contrast, tended to think of science and technology as something to be given, with programs focused on assistance rather than coordination. One British official complained, "It would be the greatest pity to allow the system of technical cooperation under the Colombo Plan to become messed up with United States methods."[26] Such methods simply meant spending more money and presuming to make all the important decisions. The center in Manila was projected to cost $20 million. With that price tag, it is no wonder that the Americans intended to remain in control.[27]

The American scientists seemed overwhelmed by the notion of introducing atomic energy to Asians. The Brookhaven team faced intense culture shock that left them wondering how any kind of atomic energy program could be possible. The poverty, the lack of infrastructure, and the wide cultural rift between the United States and Asian countries left some of them stunned. Upon arriving in Ceylon, one of them suggested that they should all just go home again, since explaining atomic power to such a backward people would be hopeless.[28] British diplomats in many of the countries found the Brookhaven team to be hopelessly naïve and typically American, in that they imagined the only way to proceed was to get good American instructors to tell everyone what to do. Commenting on the attitudes of the Brookhaven team leader Marvin Fox, one said that the American's "remarks almost suggested that he was doubtful whether the countries of the region were far enough advanced to be able even to discuss the matter usefully," but that with competent teachers the center held great promise for the whole area.[29]

Instead of promoting regional cooperation, the Asian Nuclear Center became a regional joke and encouraged independent nuclear programs in Asia using bilateral relationships with Westerners. Aspiring nuclear communities in Pakistan, India, and Japan scoffed at the notion of looking to Manila to gain anything useful—especially since the Americans seemed to think its main purpose would be in rudimentary training. No one took seriously the idea of sending the most promising experts to Manila, especially if that meant learning only what the Americans thought they ought to know. They could as easily send scientists directly to US universities and laboratories, or better yet to Canada, the United Kingdom, or elsewhere in Europe. In Pakistan, where in 1956 the government negotiated the legislation to establish the country's Atomic Energy Commission, the nuclear community was at a crossroads. Physicist Nazir Ahmed, who would shortly become the commission's first chairman, was blunt about the consequences of the Americans' unilateral decision, telling British diplomats that Pakistan would rather send scientists to train in the United Kingdom than send them to Manila. It seemed clear to Nazir Ahmed that India, snubbed by the Americans, would not open its own reactor training facilities to scientists in the region and would foster their bilateral relations with the Canadians instead. Pakistan was still interested in working with the Americans, but not through Manila.[30]

The British recommended that the majority of the new center's board of trustees should be Asians, but this seemed impossible to accomplish. The Americans were willing to staff the center with some Filipinos, but handing over control would be another matter. Robert Schaetzel, an American State Department official, confided to colleagues at the British embassy in Washington that high-level American officials such as Hollister or Strauss were unlikely to relinquish control of the center to ethnic Asians. Strauss was skeptical of the whole project and hoped only second-rate American scientists would be posted there. Not only might it be a colossally expensive flop but it might also draw good scientists away from the United States and post them fruitlessly in Manila.[31] According to British diplomats in Burma, the Brookhaven team were also taken aback when they "realized just how 'un-Asian' the Philippines appear to other countries in the area."[32]

Hostility in the worst case, apathy in the best—that was how many non-Americans viewed the attempt to create an Asian Nuclear Center. Even some British diplomats, who were willing to go along with a great deal, balked at giving active support to something that was offered on a "take it or leave it basis" by the United States.[33] Despite trying to be supportive publicly, behind the scenes the British diplomats from London to Washington, and in every Asian country concerned, universally thought the American plan did more harm than good. It was embarrassing in its lack of forethought and alienated the countries with genuine nuclear aspirations.[34] As a British diplomat in Burma put it—if Asians had to turn to the West, they ought to send trainees to the United States or the United Kingdom "and not to a half-way house in the Philippines."[35]

Given the experiences of the Asian Nuclear Center, it is no wonder that skepticism about the new global nuclear body, the International Atomic Energy Agency, ran high. This new organization had been at the center of Eisenhower's "Atoms for Peace" proposal, and the United States was committed to creating it. But the lack of consultation with Asians and Africans continued. The first draft of its organizing structure, developed by a team led by American Morehead Patterson, was a collaborative effort among predominantly white and/or colonial powers in the Anglophone (United States, Britain, Canada, Australia, South Africa) and Francophone (France, Belgium) countries—as well as Portugal. The Americans were keen to include strategic suppliers of uranium—South Africa, Belgium (Congo), and Portugal. That negotiated document was then sent to the USSR in 1955 for comment. These consultations did not include any of the countries that purportedly would gain from the benefits to the developing world.[36]

While the Americans were consulting only with the white world, Indians were asserting leadership in a growing group of countries from Africa and Asia, while not inviting Americans or Europeans for consultation. After presiding over the Geneva meeting, Homi Bhabha reoriented the Indian nuclear program by abandoning its focus on making particle accelerators for research and instead emphasized the construction of reactors. A year after the meeting, India's first research reactor went into operation.[37] In that summer of 1956, some of the Colombo Plan members met in Bombay to discuss their cooperation in atomic energy. Included were Indians, Burmese, Ceylonese, Indonesians, and Egyptians. Neither the Americans nor the British were invited. American diplomats guessed that the Indians were trying to drum up opposition to the Americans because of the Asian Nuclear Center debacle. State Department official Robert Schaetzel voiced these concerns to a British colleague and got an exasperated lecture on diplomacy in return; the British diplomat stated that the Americans might "try to give them the feeling of being genuinely consulted."[38]

It is true that India was gearing up to oppose the United States, establishing a distinct alternative voice in creating the International Atomic Energy Agency. When the Colombo Plan delegates came to Bombay that summer of 1956, resentment about the Americans' unilateral behavior was expressed through criticism of proposals for an IAEA governing board. Once again, Indian delegates noted, the Americans were designing the IAEA in such a way as to give Americans disproportionately large representation, by insisting on priority for countries with "atomic know-how" and those giving technical assistance. British observers noted that at the meeting, Indians such as Homi Bhabha did most of the talking, while others listened—so much that it seemed as if "the object of the meeting had been to prepare the ground for the emergence of a group which would follow India's leadership in atomic affairs."[39]

As India maneuvered, the Americans tried to maneuver back. The conflict set the tone of the IAEA's eventual creation. Morehead Patterson, the official US representative, dreaded the prospect of India securing a permanent seat on the IAEA's governing board, which would have executive control over the agency, would be much narrower in scope than its wider membership, and would hold the real power. Some of its members would be elected by the member states, and some would be permanent.[40] Henry Cabot Lodge, the US representative at the United Nations, regaled Patterson with tales of how difficult Indian representatives were at the UN, and they hoped to avoid having India on that board. But both men agreed that "it would be politically desirable and almost necessary to include a colored and underdeveloped country among the permanent members" of the board. But which country? Was there a less independent-minded "colored" country than India? In conversation with each other, Lodge and Patterson tried to make a case for the Philippines or Pakistan, both of them compliant allies, or possibly Japan. But it was hard to get around India as the obvious choice.[41]

American diplomats feared the consequences of "colored" influence in the IAEA, especially if it might mean introducing issues of racism and colonialism. After the Bandung meeting, it seemed clear that changing the discourse from East-West to North-South was a high priority for India. Was there a way to blunt India's efforts to bring such worldviews into the new IAEA? Lodge suggested that locating the organization away from the United Nations headquarters would be essential to keep Indian delegates (and others) from acting in lockstep with their national counterparts. And it should be made clear that IAEA representatives had to be scientists, not politicians. He and Patterson mused about the possibility of expanding the "colored" permanent membership to offset India's influence while expanding into Latin America. To them, the question was which of the colored nations could be trusted not to bring up racism? Lodge believed that Brazil could be counted on to support American positions.[42]

In the negotiations that followed, India's goals ended up conforming with American ones in an unexpected way. India achieved permanent representation, but other countries such as Brazil gained permanent representation too, reducing India's ability to fully represent the "colored" world. The formula, proposed by India and described as "complex but ingenious" by the IAEA's official historian, divided the world into zones: North

America; Latin America; Western Europe; Eastern Europe; Africa and the Middle East; South Asia; Southeast Asia and the Pacific; and the Far East. It assigned "quasi-permanent" status to five countries deemed the most technologically advanced in atomic technology (including the production of source materials). These countries went unnamed, but in practice they were the United States, the Soviet Union, the United Kingdom, France, and Canada. The formula then assigned the same quasi-permanent status to the most advanced countries from each of the different regions, if these regions did not yet have a permanent member. That brought in Brazil for Latin America and Japan for the Far East, both of which the United States believed would be easier to handle than India, which represented South Asia. Then there were added complexities that brought in several other countries (such as Belgium, Czechoslovakia, and the Scandinavian countries) on a rotating basis because of their roles producing source materials or providing technical assistance.[43]

Although it might be considered a victory for the aspirations of the Bandung conference to have permanent seats on the board of governors of the IAEA held by countries from African-Asian countries, there were glaring reasons for skepticism. Because of its role in mining and milling uranium, the permanent member from Africa and the Middle East ended up as the Union of South Africa, the world's bastion of white supremacy and the government whose policies were most antithetical to the Bandung principles. Indeed the final communiqué at Bandung had explicitly condemned South Africa for its apartheid policies formalized in the late 1940s and early 1950s. Also, the representative for Southeast Asia and the Pacific was Australia, making it the fourth permanent member from the British Commonwealth whose government was virtually all white. Those in executive control of the agency were still the weapons-makers and their uranium suppliers. Syndicated columnist Holmes Alexander later scoffed that some American diplomats came close to giving leadership of the agency "to one of the loincloth nations," but that "thus far common sense has prevailed."[44]

In the new structure of the IAEA, racially segregated South Africa appeared to represent all Africans in atomic energy matters. The only other contender was Belgium, with its colonial hold on Congo. Because both regions were crucial for supplying uranium to the United States and Britain, and both had strong allegiance to the non-communist West, these white-dominated and racially segregated regimes enjoyed ironclad US support during the Eisenhower years. Not only were atomic energy matters all white, but Africa itself also seemed inescapably colonial—a site of uranium extraction, with minimal peaceful applications that seemed tailor-made for colonized peoples. Rather than focus on industries, the continent's countries focused on agriculture and, to some extent, on health. Both South Africa and the Belgian Congo were "advanced" principally in terms of supplying uranium; their leadership roles on the board of governors seemed a tacit acknowledgment that Africa would continue to be perceived as a source of strategic materials rather than a place for industrial development through atomic energy.

In Africa itself, colonial officials tried to use atomic energy to smooth over racial tensions. The Belgians had ambitious plans to bring peaceful atoms to Congo, in concert with the construction of a new university outside Leopoldville, called Lovanium University. The university itself, founded in 1954, offered an idealistic vision: it was supposed to mitigate the tensions of colonialism through education. According to one promotional film for the university, it was to be an interracial university to make the "complete citizen" in a country where two civilizations found themselves, creating the "necessary climate for a fertile and friendly collaboration between blacks and whites." The film shows men and women of both races together eating, researching in the library, and playing games such as chess, table football, table tennis, and pocket billiards.[45] The university also hosted, by US-Belgian agreement, a TRIGA Mark I research reactor, which went into operation in June 1959.[46] Lovanium would attempt to decouple racism from colonialism, and the ultra-modern atomic reactor seemed a symbol of interracial scientific collaboration.

Outside Congo, white commentators struggled to understand what ostensibly primitive people might do with atomic energy. Only when framed as development did it appeared comprehensible. American reporter Clyde Farnsworth would call the TRIGA reactor work "a new witchcraft," providing not nuclear power but rather radioisotopes to help Africans understand water sources, pests, parasites, food preservation, and the treatment of disease.[47] The imagery of witchcraft suggested a vision of Africans that tied them to tribal, pre-modern concerns. Africans would not need industrial-scale electricity but instead would need to address either their basic needs in food and health or an economy based on agriculture and extraction of raw materials.

In the late 1950s, the presence of sub-Saharan Africa in atomic energy affairs consisted almost entirely of black workers in uranium mines, and entirely white representatives—either due to European colonial rule or to apartheid rule in the Union of South Africa. At the second international conference on peaceful uses of atomic energy, in 1958, there were merely hints that changes might be under way. Although representatives from several states from northern Africa (Morocco, Tunisia, and Egypt's United Arab Republic) attended, the only ones from sub-Saharan Africa were from the Union of South Africa and Ghana. Ghana, in West Africa, had been the British colony of Gold Coast until declaring independence in 1957 and joining the British Commonwealth. Its prime minister, Kwame Nkrumah, had become the figurehead of anti-colonial independence in Gold Coast and elsewhere in Africa too. His government asserted a role in atomic energy, sending representatives to the 1958 conference. Nkrumah took very seriously the importance of assigning black Africans to important posts, but doing so on atomic energy was difficult to accomplish in 1958. Although the delegation included black Africans (such as Richard Quarshie, an embassy official), it was only the white, British physicist Alan H. Ward who had a scientific reputation outside Ghana.

The rise of Ghana as a major regional voice was a complication for the United States, as was the prospect of many newly independent states in Africa. Such developments, if not handled properly, promised a future bloc of neutral countries at the United Nations and in atomic energy affairs. Kwame Nkrumah espoused African unity and neutralism, and he was openly friendly to socialist ideas. He took stances similar to those of Egyptian leader Gamal Nasser, who favored pan-Arabism, and the Eisenhower administration treated him with caution. Nkrumah was the only black African leader to contend with in atomic energy affairs.[48]

That seemed about to change, as many nations in Africa were becoming independent of their colonial rulers. A few political developments allowed this to happen with remarkable rapidity. Both the Somali Republic and Nigeria gained independence from Britain 1960, encouraged by British prime minister Harold Macmillan's so-called Wind of Change speech on February 3, 1960, which acknowledged the inevitability of independence for those wanting it. Also that year, Ghana shed its status as a Commonwealth nation, declaring itself a republic, with Nkrumah abandoning the title of prime minister and adopting that of president. African American intellectual and Nobel Laureate Ralph J. Bunche, then under-secretary of the United Nations, predicted early in the year that 1960 would be the "Year of Africa," noting that despite the diversity of languages and traditions there was remarkable unity among Africans "in their aspirations for independence, human rights and dignity."[49] The cascade of declarations of independence that year seemed to prove him correct. Fighting in Algeria prompted in 1958 an enormous political crisis in France, resulting not only in the fall of the Fourth Republic but also a major restructuring of the empire as a voluntary federation. Thirteen sub-Saharan colonial states declared independence from France in 1960.

Among those declaring greater independence amid these "winds of change" was South Africa, but it offered a starkly different vision of the future. South Africans would strengthen discriminatory laws in the late 1950s and 1960s. In 1960, white voters by referendum ended their status as subjects of the British monarchy, choosing to abandon their Commonwealth status and instead to become a republic in 1961. The prime minister during that transition, Hendrik Verwoerd, was a staunch believer in separation of the races. Verwoerd stated that "the republic is the only sure and stable friend that the Western nations have in Africa. We are here to stay, and we are here to aid all others in whatever they may need and can get from us." In remarks made before a television camera, while sitting in an orderly, comfortable office, he calmly described South Africa as representative of stability and order. Discussing race relations, he noted, "We seek gradual development of each of our groups in a certain direction. Here the solution is sought by openly retaining the white man's guiding hand, which elsewhere is the hidden guarantee of industrial development and even good administration."[50] Verwoerd extended apartheid to other domains, such as refusing to allow black ambassadors into the country. Describing South Africa as a friend to the West, he was quick to draw links between "communistically conditioned people" and anti-apartheid agitators.[51]

After independence Verwoerd moved to solidify his country's position as Africa's leading nuclear nation. The IAEA would be an important vehicle for South Africa's conduct of international affairs, especially given the sudden presence of newly independent African states in other bodies such as the United Nations. South Africa created an Atomic Energy Board and began research on peaceful applications, adopting the full range of ideas coming from the United States and elsewhere. Although it claimed no immediate plans to adopt nuclear power, it oriented research toward it. To do otherwise might have undermined the notion of the white man's role in industrial development. In addition, toward the end of 1961, South Africa's first year as a republic, Atomic Energy Board director Abraham J. A. Roux made the peculiar statement that South Africa had the knowledge and industrial potential to produce atomic bombs, adding that he hoped South Africa would never have to make them.[52]

Two other developments in 1960 complicated Africa's relationship to nuclear matters, both of them related to bloody racial struggles. One of these was the independence of Congo from Belgium, established in June 1960 with independence leader Patrice Lumumba as the new prime minister. Just a couple of months prior to independence, the Belgians had the uranium mine at Shinkolobwe closed down and sealed with concrete. Taking Congo out of Belgium's hands put the fate of its remaining uranium and other valuable minerals into question—a fact immediately recognized by American leaders, leading the United States down a complex path of clandestine behavior in Congo. The other development was France's first test of an atomic bomb in February 1960. Not only had another colonial power joined the nuclear weapons club, but it had also used its North African territory Algeria as the test site, in the midst of a protracted war between French forces and the National Liberation Front there. Both events would be rallying points for those hoping to establish pan-African solidarity. After the French nuclear test, for example, Ghanaian foreign minister Ebenezer Ako Adjei called for a summit of black Africans, with an eye toward some kind of union of African states.[53]

When Nkrumah came into power, he stated that Ghana's independence was meaningless without the liberation of all of Africa. Time and again he stated that Africa's principal goal should be for Africa to be controlled entirely by Africans. That would mean the end of colonial relationships: no more French in Algeria, no more Belgians in Congo, no more Portuguese in Angola. It would also mean the abolition of laws intended to reinforce white minority rule, as in South Africa. Nkrumah, the leader of a relatively rich African state, saw himself at the forefront of the pan-African movement, and his public speeches dwelled as much on the future of Africa as on Ghana itself. He saw the divisions of territory and political infighting among Africans as playing into the hands of Europeans who sought, even in the post-colonial era, to disempower the peoples of the whole continent. When France detonated a nuclear bomb in Algeria, Nkrumah stated that France had "defied the conscience of mankind and has this morning exploded a nuclear device on African soil." He echoed the sentiments of the Arab League, which called on all Afro-Asian countries to unite in opposition to the French test on African soil. Nkrumah used the event to illustrate the meaning of foreign domination, artificial territorial divisions, and European practices of "divide and rule." He paired France's "nuclear imperialism" with the apartheid policies of South Africa as one of "two threatening swords of Damocles hanging over our continent."[54]

Algeria was at the time the site of violence and torture as the French government attempted to hold on to the country, treating it not as a colony but as an "integral" part of metropolitan France. Algeria would gain independence in 1962. To many observers of the Algerian war, including writer and political theorist Frantz Fanon, even the waves of independence were unlikely to alter long-standing patterns of exploitation. Fanon warned of a new kind of informal colonialism he and others called neocolonialism. "Independence does not bring a change of direction," Fanon wrote in his widely read *Les Damnés de la Terre* (*The Wretched of the Earth*). "The same old groundnut harvest, cocoa harvest, and olive harvest. . . . No industry is established in the country." In Fanon's view, non-white peoples had been, and would continue to be, treated as part of the landscape to be exploited and harvested. He recounted a conversation with an official who told him, "Nature must be tamed, not talked into reason."[55]

Nkrumah adamantly opposed claims by Europeans to see any part of Africa as an extension of European territory. That France had chosen Algeria as the site of its nuclear tests struck him as a classic colonial decision, forcing colonized people in Algeria—and even in other parts of Africa—to bear the human cost of the test. "Let us remember," he said, "that the poisonous fall-out did not, and never will respect the arbitrary and artificial divisions forged by colonialism across our beloved continent." He used the nuclear tests to showcase how insincere Europeans were. Africans "must firmly and resolutely refuse any concessions to nuclear powers for the establishment of nuclear bases on our continent," he said in an address to Ghanaian women. "Military bases should not be made a condition for the granting of independence. The acceptance of such a condition makes independence fake and unreal." He said in July 1960 that colonial powers were granting independence insincerely. "Chaos ensues and this enables the ex-colonial master to re-enter the territory on the pretext of maintaining law and order. Their idea is to grant independence with one hand and to take it back with the other. This chicanery of granting fake independence must stop. We demand real independence. We demand that when the colonial powers quit, they quit for good, baggage and all, and leave us to sink or swim according to our own efforts."[56]

In 1960, the United States and its allies faced the possibility that the sealed Shinkolobwe uranium mines in Congo would fall under the jurisdiction of an independent black African state—one that might turn to the Soviet Union. After Congo became independent in 1960 under the leadership of Patrice Lumumba, a crisis ensued centered upon the attempt by the Katanga region to break away and create a separate state. Katanga was important not only to Belgium but also to the United States, and its new government was widely perceived as loyal to the mining industries and their consumers. The Belgians formally recognized the different government in Katanga—led by Moïse Tshombé, an outspokenly anti-communist African who seemed willing to submit himself to the demands of the mining company and who sought to continue strong links with Belgium. From Ghana, Nkrumah saw this as textbook neocolonialism: "There is a real danger," he stated, "that the colonial powers will grant a nominal type of political independence to individual small units so as to ensure that the same old colonial type of economical organization continues long after independence has been achieved."[57]

Though not publicly, US intelligence analysts viewed Katanga in the same vein. It was easily the richest province of Congo, accounting for about half of the nation's entire income. "Since its mineral properties still remain in Belgian hands, and since Tshombé relies heavily on Belgian technical and military advice, his regime has drawn sharp criticism from Africans and Asians generally as a colonial puppet." The Americans had to concede the point: "While Tshombé is today general master in much of Katanga," explained a special National Intelligence Estimate in early 1961, "he would almost certainly be unable to survive without Belgian help."[58]

The Eisenhower administration viewed the changes in Africa with caution, often viewing independent African states as unreliable and untrustworthy. The crisis in Congo was one of the last events that Eisenhower had to contend with before leaving office, and he disliked Lumumba and his socialist tendencies. [59] He also disliked the influence of left-leaning, purportedly neutralist countries such as Egypt (formally known as the United Arab Republic) and Ghana. At a January 12, 1961, meeting of the National Security Council, in the last days of his presidency, Eisenhower lamented that the United Nations was getting out of US control and "felt the UN had made a major error in admitting to membership any nation claiming independence. Ultimately, the UN [headquarters] may have to leave US territory."[60] It was a fatalistic view of African independence that looked with trepidation on a future of chaos as the colored people of the world gathered strength in the United Nations. A few days later, Lumumba and two of his associates were killed by the Katanga government, and scholars have been looking for evidence of US involvement ever since.[61]

Alignment with Belgium and South Africa due to uranium mining presented a public relations challenge to the US government in the 1960s during the era of decolonization abroad and civil rights activism at home. Eisenhower's successor, John F. Kennedy, wanted to be seen supporting black Africans, but a future of collaboration with the South African government seemed inevitable. Shortly after his inauguration, Kennedy convened the National Security Council to discuss military needs moving forward, and one part of that discussion centered on uranium. Most of the planned foreign uranium purchases would come from Canada and the Union of South Africa.[62] Because Kennedy believed the United States needed to be seen backing the right horse, namely, the so-called Afro-Asian countries, his administration developed a policy that strengthened the UN and tried to avoid alienating African countries. "Africa is much more emotional and unsophisticated than Europe and Asia," one US policy document put it, "and the game must be played there in a different way."[63] In 1962, during a meeting between President Kennedy and Prime Minister Macmillan,

Undersecretary of State George Ball observed that he believed Union Minière in Congo still harbored "hopes for a white enclave in Katanga" and that both the United States and Britain needed to make clear this was simply not possible.[64]

There was no ignoring the South African government's intention to remain such a white enclave, and South Africa—increasingly criticized at the United Nations—relied heavily on the new IAEA to wield influence in world affairs. It shielded itself, and the Americans and Europeans shielded it, by describing the agency as scientific and technical, supposedly devoid of politics. The agency's scientific advisory committee was designed to draw leading scientists from member states without actually representing those states. Such scientists were supposed to be free to have candid discussions about technical issues. It was a tricky position to put them in because the IAEA also allowed these scientific advisors to be "assisted" by political advisors. As South African IAEA governor Donald B. Sole noted in 1959, "It was to be feared that the presence of political advisers might cast doubt on the impartiality of any recommendations the Committees made to the Director General and to the Board." The scientific body was supposed to have "no political character" and to "be free of all outside influence."[65] As historian Gabrielle Hecht has pointed out, South Africa was committed to "presenting a depoliticized, technical vision of nuclearity" that would ensure its presence in the IAEA in spite of the mounting opposition to its racially segregated regime.[66]

When exploring ways to extend peaceful atomic energy in Africa, the IAEA made its most extensive links with South Africa. Even in the field of agriculture, IAEA officials went to South Africa first, hoping its scientists would apply for grants and take up positions in the agency. The head of IAEA's agricultural work at that time was the American soil chemist Nathaniel Coleman, on leave from North Carolina State University. Charged with creating a global network of atomic-related agricultural work, Coleman turned to South Africa. Writing to South African scientist Pieter Marais, Coleman stated in late 1960, "We have no agricultural research contract with any country on the continent of Africa, and in case you or some of your colleagues would be interested in submitting proposals to the Agency, we would be glad to consider them."[67]

The South Africans leaped at the opportunity to take a leadership role in the field, despite having made almost no commitment thus far. Its Atomic Energy Board agreed to send South Africans to training courses offered by the IAEA and to expand radioisotope research at major agricultural centers throughout the country. At the time, the only agricultural laboratory in South Africa equipped to do radioisotope research was the

W. P. Fruit Research Station in Stellenbosch, but Pieter Marais wrote that South Africa would soon have such centers throughout the country. One of his staff was about to travel to the United States to gain experience at the US Department of Agriculture, where scientist Maurice Fried was using radioisotopes to study soil nutrients.[68] In fact Fried was about to become Coleman's replacement at the IAEA.[69] South Africa, meanwhile, kept pace with whatever expectations the IAEA seemed to have. In the summer of 1961 it reported its capacity to conduct agricultural research "on an extensive scale" and announced ambitious hiring plans to conduct research using several different radioisotopes on both plant mutation and entomological studies.[70]

South Africa gave every indication of ramping up its nuclear expertise beyond simply providing uranium. It began to build what it called a research reactor near Pretoria. Unlike the TRIGA research reactors, such as the 50-kilowatt one built in Congo, it was designed also for "materials testing" and would have a capacity of 20 megawatts. As a point of comparison, the Soviet Union had claimed that its 1954 reactor of 5 megawatts was the first electricity-generating reactor, and the first generation of British and American electricity reactors were in the range of 50–60 megawatts. The United States agreed to supply the South African reactor with enriched uranium as fuel. In 1962 the University of Capetown and the University of Stellenbosch agreed to combine resources to create the Southern Universities Nuclear Institute, with a costly 5.5 volt Van de Graaf accelerator as its focal point. The same year, both Potchefstroom University and the University of Witwatersrand opened Cockcroft-Walton accelerator facilities for research and training of nuclear physicists.[71] All this indicated that South Africa was determined to maintain its position on the governing board of the IAEA by being unrivaled as the most advanced nuclear nation in Africa.

Ghana, on the other hand, was trying to represent black Africans. Maurice Fried at the IAEA also reached out to colleagues working in Ghana, including Alan H. Ward, a British-born agricultural scientist. In late 1961 Ward reported what seemed like promising radioisotope work using phosphorus-32 to study the micro-structure of soil and using other isotopes to study dwarfism in animals. The press reports in Ghana were encouraging and framed as pan-Africanism: "Ghana's programme in the field of agricultural research should be extended, with the help of international funds, to benefit the entire development of African agriculture."[72]

Both Ghana and South Africa embraced the promises of the peaceful atom as paths to asserting or maintaining political roles on the continent of Africa. The economic or scientific arguments for these projects were less compelling than the political ones. While Maurice Fried was charged with building up "atomic" agriculture at the IAEA, many of his former colleagues at the USDA scoffed at it. Regarding the notion of irradiating grain to kill pests, USDA scientist M. E. Jefferson wrote in 1961 that the point was likely "prestige building" rather than genuine economic development. Non-atomic methods were more effective, "and these I think merit greater consideration than they will ever receive because they are not directly or indirectly tied to the glamorous atom."[73] Similarly, British biologist Scott Russell chided Fried in 1964 for overstating "the glamour of [radioactive] tracers."[74]

The stakes were high for Ghana, seeking to lead a pan-African movement, and for South Africa, wishing to shore up its diplomatic standing in the face of outcry about its blatantly racist laws. The United Nations passed a resolution in 1962 condemning the South African regime's policies, including the imprisonment and execution of "political prisoners under arbitrary laws prescribing the death sentence."[75] The UN Security Council in 1963 even passed a resolution calling for a voluntary arms embargo on the country. [76] But South Africa found refuge in the IAEA, where it still represented Africa, and where political discussions were supposed to be avoided.

Although many in the nuclear sector in the United States supported the status quo with South Africa, deals between the two countries were politically fraught. Oak Ridge National Laboratory scientist Paul Aebersold visited South Africa in 1963 and was impressed by the range of work at several universities. South Africa imported an Allis-Chalmers experimental reactor in 1964 under the terms of an existing bilateral agreement with the United States. American suppliers had already gained a license to provide the reactor with fuel. After the Kennedy assassination, when President Lyndon Johnson faced the prospect of running for a true election, his advisors worried that these nuclear contracts might undermine his image as a supporter of civil rights. "These events will be publicized in South Africa, which will unquestionably kick up a nice propaganda storm elsewhere about US nuclear cooperation with South Africa." The Johnson administration ensured that there was no fuel shipment or other cause for publicity until December 1964, knowing that by then his presidential election would be resolved.[77]

The embrace of civilian atomic energy by South Africa would prove extremely complicated for Johnson, who had committed to addressing racial problems in the United States with changes to the laws—guaranteeing civil rights and voting rights on equal footing with whites—that were precisely the opposite of South Africa's political direction. Johnson spoke of creating a "Great Society" in the United States, with new laws and programs to eliminate poverty and racial injustice. Cozying up to South Africa contradicted that agenda. South Africa was embracing the atom, not just as a supplier of uranium but with a program of its own. It was being empowered by the United States to do so.[78] Dozens of white South African specialists had trained abroad, many of them at American institutions and laboratories. As the reactor at Pelindaba (near Pretoria) began, Americans went to South Africa as consultants. An American firm, Allis-Chalmers, was the major construction contractor. Key atomic scientists visited it for the opening ceremonies, such as Oak Ridge director Alvin Weinberg.[79]

On the twentieth anniversary of the bombing of Hiroshima, the president of the United States signed into law the Voting Rights Act. The same day, the *New York Times* reported that the government of South Africa had started a nuclear reactor, acquired from the United States. "Prime Minister Hendrik F. Verwoerd led his country into the nuclear age today," the newspaper observed, "and told the black African states of the north that they would be welcome to come along." In what was perceived by some as a double entendre, Verwoerd noted that South Africa's reactor was intended to be for the advancement of "the rest of Africa when it is prepared to take what we have to offer." South Africa had no formal relations with its neighbors, refusing to allow black diplomats to establish themselves in Pretoria. Yet Verwoerd saw civilian atomic energy in the same way that Eisenhower had, as a means of ameliorating tension despite lacking progress on the most important issues. He imagined that nuclear reactors in South Africa might eventually be used by other countries as well. As the *New York Times* reported it, "the offer was part of an effort the Government has been making to show that it does not want to live in eternal hostility with the rest of Africa. If the black states will learn to live with its policies of racial separation, the Government seems to be saying, then they will be handsomely rewarded."[80]

In Ghana, Kwame Nkrumah's government embraced the peaceful atom as well, but hardly seemed a politically reliable partner to the United States. The University of Ghana gained a well-known physicist in 1961 on its faculty: the Englishman Alan Nunn May, whose claim to fame thus far had been serving as a spy for the Soviet Union during the wartime Manhattan Project. He had been released from a British prison in 1952 and finally had found employment in a university.[81] One American editorialist described him as "a fascinating study in reptility." It seemed bewildering that Nunn May should find a place to continue his career in Ghana. One commentator put it thus: "And now, the man who freely admitted his part in handing over our atomic secrets to the Soviets, goes back to work for them again in Ghana, for a decidedly leftist dictator named Nkrumah, and I am willing to bet that America's recent donation of millions to the Ghana government will find its way into the communal fund which will help finance the atomic reactor the Russians have thoughtfully provided for Nunn May to play with."[82]

Although Alan Nunn May was perhaps the strangest of them, Ghana attracted numerous prominent figures who were critics of Western governments. Among the visitors were W. E. B. Du Bois, Bayard Rustin, Malcolm X, Yuri Kochiyama, and Paul Robeson. Most of these drew parallels between Africa's anti-colonial struggles and African American struggles for rights. When Rustin, an influential civil rights activist, visited, he combined these concerns with nuclear disarmament and peace and tried to cultivate a sense that they were all connected issues. From Ghana he organized a protest demonstration in which he and others drove into the Sahara desert several times and were apprehended by French authorities.[83] The most prominent of Ghana's visitors during that era was Du Bois, whose 1903 *The Souls of Black Folk* had declared that the problem of the twentieth century would be that of the "color line—the relation of the darker to the lighter races of men in Asia and Africa, in America and the islands of the sea."[84] Having inspired a generation of American civil rights activists, his outlook had become increasingly Marxist. While abroad, he made speeches that the FBI used to justify barring his reentry into the United States.[85]

The FBI worried about the common themes between civil rights advocates in the United States and the anti-colonial rhetoric of pan-Africanism. On a May 1964 visit to Ghana, Malcolm X gave several speeches, including one at the University of Ghana titled "Will Africa Ignite America's Racial Powder Keg?" An FBI report pointed out that one of his themes was that the United States was the "master of imperialism." He drew parallels between the overt racism of South Africa and the hypocrisy of the United States. "If America is not interested in human rights in America," he was quoted, "how can she be interested in human rights in Africa?" One interviewer, referring to Malcolm X's personal meetings with various leaders in Africa, including Nkrumah, asked how much influence revolutionary Africa had on the thinking of black people in the United States. "All the influence in the world," he responded. "You can't separate the militancy that's displayed on the African continent from the militancy that's displayed right here among American blacks."[86]

Ghana under Nkrumah's leadership became a pan-African cultural mecca that openly opposed colonialism and apartheid, and attempted to build a nuclear science community. But Nkrumah also courted American money, believing his country needed to industrialize. Thus far, Ghana's relevance to the global economy had been in its abundant supplies of cocoa and bauxite ore, the source of aluminum. The latter, a light but strong metal, was crucial for military production and a range of manufactured goods. Nkrumah attracted an American firm, Kaiser Aluminum, to help build a dam on the Volta River and an aluminum smelter. In return, he promised access to the bauxite mines and to the hydroelectricity produced from the dam. Like leaders of other developing countries, Nkrumah saw industrial development, powered by electricity, as the key to moving his nation beyond resource extraction. As he explained to Ghana's National Assembly on February 21, 1961, "The industrialization of Europe, of America, of Canada, or Russia and of other countries, emerged as a result of the invention of sources of power of hitherto undreamt of size. . . . Electricity is the basis for industrialization."[87]

In addition to seeing the benefits of the Volta dam project, Nkrumah looked to other miracles of science as tools for rapid advancement. "Ghana must force the pace of our growth in science and make Ghanaians science-minded," he stated. "We must produce Ghanaian scientists and technologists to help in the rapid development of Ghana." He installed himself as chancellor of the Kwame Nkrumah University of Science and Technology. At its inauguration ceremony, he repeated his theme of forced, rapid development. "In a sense," he said, "we must move swiftly from the stone age to the age of the atom. What has taken other peoples and nations centuries to achieve, we have to carry out in a decade or generation." Science would be essential to the life and progress of the nation. "The ivory tower concept of the university is dead," he said, "and may it rest in peace!" Science would be harnessed to introduce new kinds of crops, to mechanize agriculture, to control diseases and plants and animals, and to make infertile lands yield abundant harvests. "The future scientists of Africa must make our deserts bloom," he said. "Where one blade of grass grew before, they must make two blades grow."[88]

Atomic energy had an important place in Nkrumah's vision of the future. Fossil fuels, he said, were of limited use because they would reinforce African dependence on outsiders. "The most important other sources of power in the world are from atomic reactors, and Ghanaians will soon share in the work and responsibilities of using modern reactors."[89] Solar energy too was a possibility. These had great appeal because they appeared to break the bonds of dependence. Soon Ghana would have a dam of its own to produce hydroelectricity, and if nuclear reactors and solar power could be generated within Africa—without the need to import fossil fuels such as oil and coal—these technologies could be part of the story of African liberation. From power generation to communication technology and transportation infrastructure, Nkrumah believed, Africans had to stop relying on Europe and instead look within the continent.

Ghana swiftly gained a voice in the IAEA, and its representatives carried the torch of pan-Africanism. Nkrumah created an Atomic Energy Commission and appointed at its head Robert P. Baffour, the vice-chancellor of the university. When Baffour served as president of the IAEA General Conference in September 1962, he asked that "assistance continue to be given to member States in the introduction of nuclear power and that closer co-operation be established . . . on matters relating to power and particularly to the economics of power."[90] Like South Africa, Ghana followed the IAEA recommendations closely, creating a "Health Physics and Radioisotope Unit" at the University of Ghana. Then in 1962 it asked the IAEA for a technical advisor on the agricultural uses of radioisotopes. The advisor was to assist Ghanaian institutions, such as the West African Cocoa Research Institute and the Central Agricultural Station at Kwadazo, in studies of soil fertility and plant physiology.[91] At Kwadazo, Ghana began construction of a radioisotope laboratory to study the movement of phosphorus in the soil and to examine organic matter with the aid of carbon-14.[92]

Ghana and South Africa represented two different visions for Africa, both of them utilizing the promise of atomic energy, but ultimately the United States backed the racially segregated government of South Africa. This was partly due to the uranium in South Africa, and partly due to Nkrumah's emphasis on colonialism and racism, but also because of the apparent influence of the Soviet Union in Ghana. Nkrumah planned to get its first research reactor from the USSR, and several promising Ghanaian students went to Moscow to study. By 1965, physicist Alan Ward—who hoped to cultivate ties with the West, found himself marginalized and replaced in the project by Alan Nunn May, the former Soviet spy.[93] Even the IAEA's primary technical advisor on atomic agriculture turned out to be a Soviet scientist, Vladimir Alexseevich Golikov. The thirty-three-year-old had been head of a laboratory on radioactive isotopes within the Institute of Vegetable Economy in the USSR's Ministry of Agriculture.[94] Details of his selection are murky, and in at least one respect Golikov was a disastrous selection because, although the job posting specifically mentioned an English language requirement, Golikov spent a good deal of time in Accra taking language lessons. As one of his new colleagues wrote, "I'm extremely worried—surely IAEA must check up on this sort of thing? It's impossible even to introduce Mr. Golikov to the agriculturalists here he's to work with."[95] Over a couple of years Golikov's English improved and he advised on building up laboratories for radioisotope research in agriculture and encouraged Ghanaians to go abroad to study. He urged speed: "It is necessary to take into consideration that in the nearest future the Republic of Ghana will have its own atomic reactor." There had to be Ghanaians who were in a position to use it.[96]

Golikov was not the only Soviet specialist in Ghana at the time; dozens of Soviet specialists arrived in the early 1960s to advise on building a research reactor, and they began promising a reactor for electricity generation. The Englishman Harold Miller, a different IAEA specialist (in medical physics, such as radiation therapy and occupational exposure) wrote that there was a bizarre separation between his work and that of the reactor. He was working with universities, but the reactor seemed to be under the purview of a new nuclear research institute, and the reactor site was being developed by Soviet specialists. "There is considerable secrecy and a security barrier about this project and I am not in touch with the developments at all," Miller stated. Surely, given the limited Ghanaian resources and the presumably peaceful nature of the project, more collaboration would make sense. He wanted, for example, to make use of the dosimetry and exposure experts he presumed were working at the reactor site, but he found his overtures unwelcome. "It would be a valuable thing if the security barrier on this subject could be removed," he wrote to IAEA colleagues in Vienna, wondering if his attitude was even appropriate. "Or am I quite out of touch with the situation here?"[97]

The Soviet role in Ghana's reactor project was disturbing to Americans who already distrusted Nkrumah's pan-African politics and his penchant for associating the United States with the ideas of colonialism and imperialism. President Johnson's advisors agonized about how to respond to Nkrumah's increasingly sharp anti-American rhetoric. They did not want to pull the plug on the Volta dam project being financed by Kaiser Aluminum, knowing that it might result in a repeat of Egypt's efforts on the ambitious dam at Aswan, in which the Soviets would simply intervene and finish it, scoring a propaganda victory in Africa. Further, abandoning the dam would be giving up the United States' primary instrument of influence in the country.[98]

The Americans kept watch on Nkrumah primarily through the dam project. The chairman of Kaiser Aluminum, Edgar Kaiser Sr., had a close working relationship not only with Nkrumah but also with both Johnson and his CIA director, John McCone. Declassified documents reveal Kaiser as a crucial informal emissary during a period of intense distrust. Nkrumah tried to calm the Americans' nerves about Soviet influence by writing to Johnson directly, repeating his policy of non-alignment. Yet in the same letter, he did not hold back his concern with the CIA's activities in Ghana.

"There appear to be two conflicting establishments representing the United States in our part of the world," he wrote. "There is the United States Embassy as a diplomatic institution doing formal diplomatic business with us; there is also the C.I.A. organization which functions presumably within or outside this recognized body. This latter organization, that is, the C.I.A., seems to devote all its attention to fomenting ill-will, misunderstanding and even clandestine and subversive activities among our people, to the impairment of the good relations which exist between our two Governments." McCone, formerly the face of atomic energy as AEC chairman, had become the face of the much-feared CIA. In that letter, Nkrumah wrote about his commitment to a planned economy as a socialist ideal, but he also pointed out the important role of foreign investment in such an economy. "Ghana welcomes foreign investors in a spirit of partnership; they can earn their profits here, provided they leave us an agreed portion for promoting the welfare and happiness of the majority of our people, as against the greedy ambitions of the few."[99]

Nkrumah's reassurances did not matter, and the United States, Britain, and France all had already committed to removing him from power. On May 27, 1965, National Security Advisor McGeorge Bundy was told by his staffer Robert Komer that a pro-Western coup was likely imminent. "The plotters are keeping us briefed, and State [Department] thinks we're more on the inside than the British. While we're not directly involved (I'm told), we and other Western countries (including France) have been helping to set up the situation by ignoring Nkrumah's pleas for economic aid. . . . All in all, looks good."[100]

In October 1965 Nkrumah published a book called *Neo-Colonialism—the Last Stage of Imperialism*. "The essence of neo-colonialism," he wrote, "is that the State which is subject to it is, in theory, independent and has all the outward trappings of international sovereignty. In reality its economic system and thus its political policy is directed from outside." He took aim not only at the CIA but also the Peace Corps and the US Information Agency, all of which conspired with bribes, direct financing, and arms supplies to manipulate and undermine the newly independent African states. The book continued Nkrumah's plea for African unity against the divide-and-conquer tactics of the United States and European powers, and its publication in October 1965 was timed to coincide with the annual meeting of the Organization of African Unity, held in Ghana's capital, Accra.[101] Relations between the United States and Ghana deteriorated rapidly, with American diplomats expressing dismay at the unprecedented, "deeply disturbing and offensive" critiques coming from a supposedly friendly country.[102]

On February 24, 1966, while Nkrumah was visiting North Vietnam and China, the long-awaited coup d'état took place in Ghana. General Joseph Arthur Ankrah, chairman of the National Liberation Council, quickly consolidated power. The US ambassador sent a telegram to Washington a week after the coup: "General Akhrah requested I inform President Johnson that Ghana will never look east again."[103] White House insider Robert Komer described the new regime to the president as "pathetically pro-Western."[104] Another advisor noted that Ankrah even supported the American war in Vietnam. "The General's only problem with our policy on Vietnam is that it is too soft to suit him—he may well ask you why we are not using nuclear weapons." [105]

In Ghana, both socialism and pan-Africanism had been dealt a severe blow. So too had the prospect of an ambitious peaceful nuclear program by an independent African nation not ruled by whites. The United States helped to crush it. After Nkrumah's ouster, the reactor was put on hold—the Soviet Union recalled its advisors, and they took their designs with them. There would be no reactor for electricity, and indeed there would be no reactor of any kind for decades. Atomic energy continued in Ghana at a lethargic pace, and with traditional, agricultural goals in mind, such as acquiring a source of radioactive cobalt in 1972 to study cocoa crops.[106] Despite its overtly racially segregated society and white minority rule, South Africa's diplomatic position as representative of Africa in atomic energy affairs would go unchallenged for many years to come—until 1976, when its human rights abuses and suspicions about its nuclear weapons program convinced other IAEA members to find a new representative of Africa—not Ghana, but Egypt, with its Soviet-supplied research reactor.[107]

In 1946, American intellectual W. E. B. Du Bois had predicted that if colored people ever developed the bomb, "it will be the people with massed cities, with sky-scrapers and factories, with piled material wealth, which will suffer all the more easily before desperate men in forest and on steppe, with nothing to lose but their chains."[108] Denied reentry into the United States, Du Bois had stayed in Ghana at Nkrumah's invitation to write his magisterial *Encyclopedia Africana*. He died there in 1963, at the age of ninety-five; a day later, hundreds of thousands of civil rights activists in the United States honored him with a moment of silence during the historic "March on Washington."[109] What Du Bois never witnessed, however, was a particular achievement of people of color—joining the so-called nuclear club. The year after his death, it was not Africans but Asians who broke the white monopoly on the bomb. China exploded a device on October 17, 1964, and immediately called for disarmament. President Johnson played down its significance, saying that it was a shame that a country with so much poverty should divert its resources in such a way. Behind the scenes, however, the US government anticipated a new era in nuclear politics, one that would continue to be marked by racial overtones. As one US intelligence analysis put it prior to the bomb's detonation, the Chinese sought leadership of the non-white world, and this was "to be done by exacerbating racial animosities, adopting the stance of the spiritual leader of all oppressed peoples and proving by example that China is the only militant and reliable source of aid to revolutionaries seeking to overthrow the existing order by force."[110]

Was the Chinese test perceived as a victory for colored people? Nkrumah's reaction was lukewarm. He stated that he understood China's point of view in pursuing the bomb, but he regretted the test itself.[111] Civil rights activist Malcolm X lauded the Chinese bomb. "I, for one, was very happy to hear that the great people of China were able to display their scientific advancement, their advanced knowledge of science, to the point where a country which is as backward as this country keeps saying China is, and so behind everybody, and so poor, could come up with an atomic bomb. Why, I had to marvel at that. It made me realize that poor people can do it as well as rich people."[112] He lauded the bomb for crossing the so-called color line in a way few had anticipated. "All these little advances were made by oppressed people in other parts of the world during 1964," Malcolm X stated. "These were tangible gains, and the reason that they were able to make these gains—they realized that power was the magic word—power against power." He ridiculed President Johnson's Great Society as a sham, filled with gimmicks that would reinforce the status quo. It was a "doublecross" to be juxtaposed against the greater progress made by oppressed peoples in other countries. "Power recognizes only power," he said, "and all of them who realize this have made gains." He pointed out that the March on Washington and the Civil Rights Bill were like release valves, never designed to solve the problem. The Civil Rights Bill "was designed to lessen the explosion, because everyone in his right mind knows there should have been an explosion." He wondered what else the Western countries would do to placate the ambitions of colored people without actually giving up or sharing their power. "What will they give us in 1965?"[113]

CHAPTER 5
Turf Wars and Green Revolutions

"The champion needlepointer of Steuben County" is how the *New York Times* referred to W. Sterling "Stubby" Cole, the first director-general of the International Atomic Energy Agency. He had won first prize in the open needlepoint class at the Steuben County Fair, and witty reporters used Cole's hobby as a metaphor, opining that he was "about to attempt to stitch together the most intricate, demanding design of the atomic age: an international organization to direct the power of the atom to peaceful purposes." The *New York Times* pointed out that it was Cole who was "a principal architect" of the 1954 Atomic Energy Act and that he was the one to suggest the ideas that became "Atoms for Peace" to President Eisenhower in the first place.[1]

Cole was an odd choice to lead the international agency. He spoke no foreign languages, had no diplomatic experience, and had no background working in a large international organization. He first became a congressman in 1934 at the age of twenty-nine, after a short career practicing law, and he had been in Congress ever since. Even before he went to Vienna to head the agency, colleagues described him as "inclined to introversion and moments of pensive moodiness. Occasionally his temper flashes and his face flushes." Colleagues recalled that he was also the kind of man who always remembered your birthday.[2] His most important characteristic, however, was that he would reliably guide the IAEA according to US goals. President Eisenhower had ensured that a loyal, anti-communist Republican politician was steering it. He could be counted on to avoid letting African and Asian states bring in the politics of colonialism and to maintain the president's vision of the atom—with its promise of a future of abundance, breaking through the constraints of nature in even the poorest countries of the world. When Cole departed the IAEA, that tradition continued. His successor, Sigvard Eklund (a Swede), would carry on the notion that the IAEA was a non-political technical agency with a mission to contribute to humanity's overall well-being through atomic energy.

Behind the fiction of the IAEA's non-political status was a tremendous amount of political maneuvering. The agency embarked on numerous programs in the developing world, backed by substantial financial commitments from the United States and other governments with robust weapons programs. It became a vehicle for implementing positive rhetoric about peaceful nuclear technology on a global scale. The agency's apparent status as a non-political technical agency obscured its role in propaganda, while its wide membership provided an illusion of global norms and consensus. The agency provided an authoritative international voice for a cornucopian vision of the atom that exaggerated the problem-solving aspects of atomic energy and constantly tried to identify success stories in health, agriculture, and other domains. The agency provided a positive counter-narrative when other international bodies, such as the United Nations General Assembly or the UN Specialized Agencies, seemed vulnerable to infiltration by critics of nuclear weapons tests.

In the early 1960s, the IAEA engaged in a turf war against two of these agencies, the World Health Organization and the Food and Agricultural Organization (FAO). These amounted to more than bureaucratic spats. The IAEA attempted to edge out the World Health Organization as an authoritative voice on the environmental and public health dimensions of atomic energy. Similarly, IAEA officials tried to outmaneuver critics in the Food and Agriculture Organization who questioned the legitimacy of agency projects related to food and grain irradiation, insect control, and mutation plant breeding. These obscure research projects had a powerful public relations body that propped them up, far beyond the scientific consensus of the time, as legitimate and feasible solutions for food crises, for population growth, and even for mitigating the use of chemical pesticides. Many specialists in these other bodies did not see the IAEA as providing legitimate solutions. No matter what problem arose, its solution was always "atomic energy." Both of these existing agencies clashed bitterly with the IAEA, not just because the IAEA was infringing on their turf within the United Nations family of agencies, but also because IAEA's approach seemed lopsided—always playing up the benefits of atomic energy while playing down the dangers, quashing dissent, and ignoring alternative solutions.

***

The International Atomic Energy Agency never became the "bank of fissionable material" that Eisenhower proposed in 1953. Even though the United States declared it would make available some 5000 kg of uranium-235, the Soviet Union pledged up to 50 kg, the United Kingdom offered 20 kg, and several other countries offered materials, these donations were never made. The major powers agreed to back the agency, with Britain seeing a pathway to regaining its nuclear collaboration with the United States, and with the Soviet Union seeing opportunities for continuing influence worldwide.[3] "With some minute exceptions," IAEA official historian David Fischer later wrote, "none of this material was physically transferred to Vienna, the IAEA never felt the need to acquire facilities for storing nuclear material, and no guards were recruited." Instead, the IAEA played the role of broker between governments, occasionally providing a "legal fiction" when a government did not wish to reveal which other country was providing materials and technology.[4]

In the absence of any bank of uranium, it was unclear what this well-funded new agency was supposed to do or how its members should cooperate. "During the first few years," Fischer later wrote, "hardly any matter could be discussed without provoking lengthy, ideologically tinged arguments." The discussions in the board of governors meetings were so acrimonious that, on the suggestion of several Western delegations, including the United States, its meetings were held in private and the records kept under a veil of secrecy. Both the Soviet Union and India, whose participation had helped to provoke the move toward secret meetings, opposed this move, but they did so in vain. Even though the agency was not a military body, and despite the fact that its mission was to promote peaceful applications of atomic energy, the meeting minutes of the board of governors were classified.[5]

Despite the Cold War tension between the superpowers, the two were allied in their commitment to the atom's bountiful promise. Here too the Soviets competed to achieve technological "firsts," ahead of the Americans. They had already beaten the Americans to building a reactor for electricity generation in 1954, and Soviet premier Nikita Khrushchev boasted in 1958 that his country was the first to approve the irradiation of potatoes. By the early 1960s, scientific journals in the USSR routinely reported work on the benefits of irradiation in preserving fruits, vegetables, meat, and fish, or in killing the insects that infested grain. In almost every Soviet republic, health officials promoted food irradiation from cheap sources of gamma radiation, such as cobalt-60. They also sponsored the manufacture of portable grain irradiators using

Cesium-137, to be used by farmers. The Soviet government, like the US government, became deeply involved in the IAEA and endorsed the idea that such efforts were benefits of the atomic age.[6]

Some of the acrimonious disputes about the IAEA arose not between geopolitical rivals but between the IAEA and other international bodies. The World Health Organization (WHO) began to carve out its own role in atomic energy as early as March 1955, when its deputy director-general Pierre Dorolle organized a conference of experts on the public health aspects of radiation protection. He did so on the advice of a group of consultants who wanted to ensure that standards on nuclear sites be differentiated from standards to the general public.[7] In practice, WHO established early that its domain—that of public health—would necessitate its involvement in atomic energy issues. Specifically, WHO put itself in the position of evaluating the broad environmental effects. Its domain "includes the problem of air, soil and water pollution, the problem of wastes from the public health point of view and, as a consequence, the problems related to the location of nuclear facilities."[8]

The entry of WHO into atomic energy affairs highlighted an early clash of two environmental narratives about atomic energy. One of these saw radiation and radioactive debris as a contaminant and a source of pollution. It acknowledged the worldwide controversy about US, Soviet, and British atmospheric nuclear weapons testing and widespread concerns about their long-term effects on human health and genetics. The agency's emphasis on public health implications contrasted sharply with the narrative that portrayed atomic energy as a solution to natural resource challenges, and it did not sit well with atomic energy enthusiasts. Perhaps André Cipriani, the Canadian scientist working for Atomic Energy of Canada Ltd. at Chalk River, put it best when he wrote to WHO officials that it seemed extremely important that the atomic energy and public health communities not develop confrontational attitudes toward each other: "The two should work hand in hand rather than have public health regarded as a stone around the neck of atomic power."[9]

Collaboration between atomic energy scientists and public health scientists were marked by mutual distrust from the start, with some highlighting cases of pollution or contamination and others emphasizing the need to avoid hampering development of nuclear technology. Maurice Tubiana, a prominent French professor of medical physics at the University of Villejuif, criticized Cipriani and others for playing down health problems. "Long-term contamination by radio-active elements is a cumulative process which cannot be reversed," he wrote. "An imprudent act in our generation could endanger not only our own, but also future generations which would probably have no means of decontaminating the air and the soil. With such a risk of compromising the future of the human race, therefore, too much rather than too little prudence should be advocated."[10] Tubiana pointed to the wider public health threat. "Any rash act by a country or laboratory means a risk not only for the country or laboratory concerned, but also for the neighboring populations, and if radio-active waste is discharged into the sea, for a large part of the inhabitants of the globe." He advocated setting up an international protection organization with enough regulatory teeth to ensure that all countries abided by its rules.[11]

With creation of the IAEA in 1957, the cornucopian narrative of atomic energy had an institutional home within the family of UN-related international agencies. It immediately set out to counteract the influence of the World Health Organization. Its board of governors created a committee to advise Director-General Cole about how to make up for lost time and assert its pro-atomic voice on matters of public health. When WHO submitted its list of proposed programs to its own executive board in January 1958, IAEA officials noted that there would soon be various meetings about radioactive waste disposal, radiochemical analysis, and radiation protection standards.[12] Should such meetings have been IAEA's territory? Cole thought so. But Marcolino Candau, the director-general of the World Health Organization, believed the answer was no. These were not subjects related to promoting atomic technologies but to protecting people from their effects.[13]

The agencies' officials became deeply partisan and distrustful of one another. In preparing for the 1958 UN meeting on peaceful uses of atomic energy, Marcolino Candau wrote to Sterling Cole that—though the IAEA had not requested it—he would be happy to provide any public health data needed, and he "would also request you kindly to clear with us any statement you might wish to include in your document regarding international health activities in the atomic field."[14] Cole bristled at the suggestion that he had to get approval from a rival agency. "With regard to your request that we 'clear' with you any statement we make related to international health activities in the atomic field, did you have in mind that we should submit our statement to you for comment and editing, or simply for comment? It seems to me it would be advantageous at this stage to clear up what is meant by the expression 'to clear' with you our statement."[15]

The letters between the heads of the two agencies were polite but they were clearly guarding their perceived territory. Several WHO officials worried that nuclear states were attempting to use the IAEA to play down health impacts of their weapons programs. Pierre Dorolle pointed out that the IAEA was supposed to focus on peaceful applications but actually was putting itself in a position to downplay the effects of US, Soviet, and British nuclear tests. It was trying to weigh in on questions of worldwide sampling, monitoring, and radiation effects. The new agency was primed to become a public relations arm for the nuclear weapons states.[16] Another like-minded official, R. Lowry Dobson, WHO's chief medical officer for radiation and isotopes, saw himself protecting an international venue for probing the effects of radiation from fallout. Dobson had co-authored with Sweden scientist Bo Lindell the WHO study on radiation effects and subsequently published it in 1961 as *Ionizing Radiation and Health*. The two observed pointedly that WHO "has clear responsibilities in the broad field of radiation health including radiation protection." They noted that Swedish studies of nuclear tests revealed that radioactive material might stay aloft in the stratosphere for a shorter period than previously believed, before returning to the earth as fallout. They also pointed out possible induction of leukemia by radiation and the lack of known threshold levels for inducing genetic effects.[17]

Dobson was incensed at how the IAEA tried to establish itself as the authoritative voice on atomic energy's environmental impacts, given that it showed no genuine commitment to impartiality. In 1959, for example, the IAEA announced—without consulting other agencies—that it was convening a panel of experts on the best methods of collecting and measuring traces of radioactivity in the biosphere. "Such systematic measurement could be used as the basis for controls to forestall any dangers to health and property," a press release announced. The goal of the meeting was to draft recommendations for member governments.[18] Dobson fumed, "The motivation we of course understand, as we know something of human behaviour; but we can hardly overlook this action."[19] So WHO countered by doing the same thing, planning a 1962 conference on the public health aspects of ionizing radiation, without consulting the IAEA. When challenged by the IAEA about it, Dobson wrote back emphasizing the extent to which the subject was about health, not peaceful applications of atomic energy. In one paragraph alone he used the phrase "public health" nine times.[20]

By the early 1960s, the IAEA was shoring up its credibility as a scientific agency with an authoritative voice on all nuclear matters, including the potential health dangers from weapons programs. From the perspective of the United States, having Cole in charge of the agency ensured that its worldview would prevail, but it also made the American manipulation of the agency too obvious to other members. At the fifth annual conference of the IAEA, in September and October of 1961, Soviet representative Vasily Emelyanov complained that the IAEA should not be treated as a corporation in which the United States held the majority share.[21] IAEA historian David Fischer later wrote that the Soviets and others had a "concern that the IAEA would be run as an instrument of US policy."[22] When Cole's term as director-general ended in 1961, US officials felt that having an American in charge had become a liability, opening the agency up to criticism of projecting American views onto the world. The United States under President John F. Kennedy put its political support behind the Swedish scientist Sigvard Eklund, significantly bolstering the agency's credibility as a scientific and technical agency.

Under Eklund, the agency continued to assert itself on issues related to public health, environmental contamination, and food and agriculture. Eklund felt that the agency's statutes gave it a special role in making recommendations to governments. He believed that other bodies, such as the World Health Organization, should defer to it. Eklund's strategy was to leverage his impressive budget, largely supplied by the United States, to buy the agency's way into these issues. A draft briefing for the IAEA director-general, to be used in a February 1963 discussion with the WHO director-general Marcolino Candau, reveals that the IAEA believed its statute set it up as a regulatory agency. "There is no reason why IAEA should not serve as the watchdog in health and safety matters," the briefing note stated.[23] It particularly hoped to wrest radiation protection and radiation medicine from WHO's realm of responsibility. IAEA argued that it devoted far more resources to it and employed more specialists on its staff than the WHO. "Practically speaking, it could be argued the most efficient solution would be for WHO, which has many other more pressing interests, to leave these two fields to us."[24]

The IAEA outmaneuvered the WHO because of its extraordinary budget, supplied primarily by the nuclear weapons states. Although WHO officials continued to believe the public health effects of fallout, waste disposal, and other nuclear matters were their responsibility, they could not compete with the array of programs launched by the IAEA. To back up their credibility, the IAEA launched an extraordinary number of events and projects around the world, particularly in the so-called developing countries. Some of these were centered on training, as with the Mobile Radioisotope Laboratory that traveled around Mexico in 1960. One widely used photograph showed the training laboratory—itself housed in a large bus—parked outside the University of Guanajuato in February 1960, as rural Mexicans and their donkeys walked by. The photo was staged (and perhaps juxtaposing two different photographs) to highlight the IAEA's role in bringing modern techniques to unlikely places in the developing world.[25] From a modest support of nine student fellowships in 1958, by

1963 the IAEA had supported 130 fellowships, several training courses, exchange professorships, laboratories, research contracts, conferences, and original research at the new Seibersdorf Laboratory near its headquarters in Austria.[26]

Many of the IAEA's projects were aimed at enhancing agricultural production and combating major diseases, which put the nuclear agency at odds with the Food and Agriculture Organization. The IAEA coordinated mutation research on rice and wheat, on the sterilization of disease-vector insects, and on food and grain irradiation. In a 1963 summary of activities related to food irradiation, IAEA scientist Maurice Fried (an American) emphasized that they were particularly important for "technologically less developed countries, where it is difficult to maintain satisfactory sanitary conditions." Such countries' economic potential could be expanded if animal products could be preserved for longer periods. He pointed to Thailand as an example of a country with a variety of animal products that might find markets in Europe and the United States if only its heavy contamination by salmonella could be overcome. Similarly, in Mali, Uganda, and East Pakistan (later Bangladesh), irradiation to kill insects could prevent dried fish from being eaten during transport, which Fried said currently accounted for more than half of the fish being lost during transport to market.[27]

Few of the IAEA's techniques enjoyed widespread endorsement. One example was the sterile male insect technique for disease eradication. In theory, if irradiation could be used to render male flies sterile, millions of such flies could be released in certain areas and out-compete the non-irradiated male flies for female mates. The offspring would not be viable, and thus the main vector of disease could be eliminated. The technique had been pioneered by American entomologist Edward Knipling and had even been used successfully to eliminate screwworm in an island environment (Curaçao, off Venezuela). It was touted as a kind of biological control of insects that might replace the use of dangerous chemical insecticides. But skepticism ran high. A. W. Lindquist, part of the US Department of Agriculture, wrote to a colleague at the IAEA in 1959, "Unfortunately several people have the idea that atomic radiation is some new, magic tool that can be used in almost all types of situations to control insects," he wrote. "This is not true and we hope that capable scientists will understand that the sterile male technique has numerous limitations." He imagined that it would be useful only in small areas that were "completely isolated or sufficiently isolated so that reinfestation will not occur."[28]

Similarly, although some scientists were inspired by the new creations of the atomic age—mutants spawned by exposure to radiation—mutation plant breeding was never perceived as the most promising way to find new varieties of crops. There were some true believers at Brookhaven National Laboratory such as Arnold Sparrow and Ralph Singleton, who continued to be optimistic about the future of radiation-induced mutations. As historian Helen Anne Curry has noted, the "political demand for work such as theirs was significant, and this demand kept the Brookhaven research program afloat in the mid-1950s in spite of criticisms that arose."[29] That criticism continued into the 1960s. Perry R. Stout, a professor of soil science at the University of California, was one of several who told IAEA in the early 1960s to focus on fertilizer studies, not plant breeding.[30] "Except in very favorable cases," British radiobiologist R. Scott Russell similarly stated, "the labour involved in selecting the valuable mutations from the much larger number of useless ones is a formidable task."[31] Cambridge plant breeder G. D. H. Bell wrote to colleagues at the IAEA, "Personally I feel that the application of any method for the artificial induction of mutations is more in the nature of being an interesting scientific experiment rather than directly useful in the economic sense of the term, i.e. the production of improved varieties." Bell put greater confidence in traditional methods, namely, selecting the best of the existing varieties and/or hybridizing them. Bell tried to be positive about the IAEA's work but wrote adamantly that there was no good evidence to suggest that mutation plant breeding made economic sense.[32] Even Brookhaven National Laboratory scientists were dismissive of the usefulness of gamma gardens for economically important agricultural research, with one remarking, "I have grave doubts."[33]

Despite such widespread skepticism, IAEA officials developed strategies to support scientists who were willing to take a chance on the atom. They were inspired by the machinations of Japanese scientist Kiyoshi Kawara, who was creating a government-sponsored National Gamma Field. The US Atomic Energy Commission in 1957 had offered to provide Japan, free of cost, with a 200-curie cobalt source to make a gamma field, or gamma garden. The US offer lent such fields a sense of importance and helped Kawara and others to get even more money from the Japanese government. Kawara benefited so much from Japan's atomic energy ambitions that he was able to decline the American offer and secure another source. He announced that the Japanese were in the process of exposing just about every conceivable plant to gamma radiation and that there already were promising new mutations in roses, carnations, and other flowers.[34]

Scientists at the IAEA saw in Kawara's experience an intriguing path forward. What if the IAEA could offer research contracts to mutation plant breeders around the world, simply to show national governments that the prestigious international agency supported the work? The "contracts" themselves would have the appearance of financial support but would not even have to come up with real money. Such was the strategy pursued by Icelandic botanist Björn Sigurbjörnsson when he took a post at the IAEA. He created an "International Mutation Group" that included anyone working on methods to produce and use induced mutations in plant breeding. The IAEA organized annual conferences, printed an information circular, and offered what appeared to be grants.[35] Upon closer inspection these were "cost-free" contracts, involving no expenditure on the part of the IAEA. They were designed to give the appearance of support from the IAEA, to open a pathway to funding from national governments that had openly committed to financially supporting some IAEA programs. Sigurbjörnsson was offering the indirect benefits of IAEA endorsement without actually paying anything.

In a letter to an American colleague, Sigurbjörnsson was explicit about the strategy behind the "cost-free" contracts, referring to the German breeder Horst Gaul. "This thing started as a way to help Horst get money to continue his research after the AEC called it quits," he wrote. "The idea was that the Agency could give him moral support by awarding him a 'cost-free' contract and by dropping the right hint in the right places." Sigurbjörnsson then decided to think of it as a lifeline for researchers who had been marginalized at home.[36]

As its hollow grant system propped up mutation plant breeding, IAEA administrators craved high-profile success stories from the developing world. They tried to collaborate with the International Rice Research Institute (IRRI), an organization in the Philippines financed by the Ford and Rockefeller Foundations. Takeshi Kawai and Mankombu S. Swaminathan, mutation breeders in Japan and India who were both members of Sigurbjörnsson's group, visited IRRI and tried to drum up enthusiasm for the IAEA's work. But at the time they visited in 1966, IRRI scientists scoffed at the atom. As Kawai told Sigurbjörnsson, IRRI scientists already had "a huge gene source in their excellent collection of rice varieties, and triple crops in a year enable them to breed new 'spectacular' varieties in three or four years." They saw little reason to divert energy and resources to mutation breeding.[37] For IRRI, it was an exciting time for breeding rice—figuring out how to make hybrids efficiently, break dormancy in grains, and imagine what an ideal high-yielding plant might look like. They already had identified a hybrid that resembled the ideal—a high-yielding variety called "IR8," soon to become a huge success story in Asia.[38]

IAEA officials began in the 1960s to make audacious claims about the quality of radiation-induced varieties of grain. One of these was in durum (or "hard") wheat, typically used for pasta, couscous, and the bulgur in

Middle East dishes such as tabbouleh. The Italian standard was an old variety called Cappelli, but it did not respond well to the chemical fertilizers increasingly used by farmers. When scientists at an Italian nuclear research center in Casaccia treated Cappelli seeds with neutron bombardment, they produced a couple of promising mutant varieties, Castelfusano and Castelporziano. Sigurbjörnsson wrote, "Their grain quality remains nearly the same as that of Cappelli for one of the mutants; the other has a quality that is lower but still acceptable."[39] This was hardly a rave review but it counted as a success for Sigurbjörnsson. The IAEA, along with the Food and Agriculture Organization, sponsored a project to plant these durum wheat varieties in several countries in the Middle East.

The durum wheat trials yielded mixed results in these countries for unexpected reasons. Even though the IAEA saw them as successful, they did not always match the interests or practices of local people. In Egypt, for example, plant breeders were looking for ways to improve bread wheat, not durum wheat. In Iran, where wheat and barley were the most important crops, farmers disliked the new varieties' heavy reliance on expensive fertilizer—not a problem in Italy, but definitely a problem in Iran. In other places, such as Israel and Turkey, the durum wheat mutants were faring well compared to local varieties. Sigurbjörnsson encouraged scientists in these countries to apply to the IAEA for aid. If any of these varieties could be shown as viable, it would be a great boon to the IAEA and bolster the credibility of the science.[40]

Sigurbjörnsson's boosterism met with some resistance among his colleagues, especially those at FAO. Botanist Ronald Silow, for example, noted that the IAEA's official report on the durum wheat trials incorrectly stated that the mutants tested in nine countries in North Africa and the Middle East had out-yielded all local and other common varieties. Silow wrote to Sigurbjörnsson, "That statement is patently contrary to the scientific evidence available . . . from those trials and should be deleted. From that statement member governments are being led to the false conclusion that radiation-induced mutation has already provided varieties of wheat better than any other varieties available to farmers in that wide region."[41]

Silow's critique was just one early salvo of an intense feud between the IAEA and the FAO—one that had some bizarre twists and turns. To prevent a turf war, the two agencies set up the FAO/IAEA Joint Division for Atomic Energy in Agriculture in 1964, which Silow joined. But the agencies made an odd personnel swap, intended to indicate compromise and diminish inter-agency rivalry: IAEA made its top agricultural scientist, Maurice Fried, an FAO employee, and FAO likewise moved Silow to the IAEA. Fried became the director of the joint division, with Silow his deputy. This gave the appearance of FAO leadership, when in fact Fried was in charge. The whole division stayed at IAEA headquarters in Vienna. When Silow and his FAO colleagues arrived in Vienna, Fried welcomed them with a party, with Austrian wine and Viennese songs. Björn Sigurbjörnsson exulted, "Our colleagues interpreted this as a celebration of our victory over them. Maybe this was not so far from the truth: we had stayed in Vienna and our beloved chief, Mac Fried, continued as our boss."[42] The FAO/IAEA joint division would continue for decades to give the appearance of a cooperative operation but would be dominated by atomic energy enthusiasts working in Vienna for the IAEA.

As they had with the World Health Organization, IAEA officials tried to deflect any FAO skepticism of atomic energy and instead stuck to its narrative that it was a technology of abundance. Having moved to the IAEA headquarters in Vienna, Silow came to see the agency as little more than a promotional agency. In early 1966 he sent a report to the IAEA's director-general and to Fried, his boss in the joint division, and copied it to his former colleagues at FAO. He claimed that FAO and its member governments were "being seriously misled," and that the IAEA had misspent $1.5 million between 1962 and 1966, about half a million of it from the already cash-strapped coffers of developing countries.[43] He felt that such poor countries had asked FAO not to encourage them to adopt techniques until they had been proven feasible by the industrialized countries. Yet the joint division had done the opposite, using the developing world as an experimental zone. Silow alleged that atomic energy advocates promoted the atom as "modern" and "advanced" in the developing world, masking how marginal these techniques really were.[44]

The IAEA leadership tried to silence Silow's dissent. After reading the memo, Director-General Sigvard Eklund reassigned him to different duties, telling him to focus on writing a history of nuclear techniques in food and agriculture.[45] Isolated within IAEA, Silow reached out to FAO for help, writing to Director-General Binay Ranjan Sen. In a twenty-six-page handwritten letter, he complained that his IAEA colleagues had begun to make personal comments disparaging his role in the development of FAO's work and to question his competence to comment on scientific matters.[46] Instead of helping Silow, Sen delegated the lengthy letters (which Silow had marked as confidential) to subordinates to read. And so Silow's personal appeals, because they were in letters mixed with his policy objections, reached an audience of mid-level functionaries at FAO, including his enemies Fried and Sigurbjörnsson.

In March 1967 Silow wrote to both agencies' directors-general with a forty-nine-page memorandum reiterating that techniques should not be encouraged in the developing countries until they had been proven to be successful in industrialized countries. He pointed out that because of stark policy differences, IAEA attitudes toward him had become "vindictive" and "hostile." The execution of his responsibilities on behalf of FAO, he stated, "has led to the virtual termination of normal professional life for me for the past two-and-a-half years since being transferred to the IAEA staff." He was not allowed to travel to relevant conferences, was excluded from policy discussions, and was an object of ridicule. "I have been almost completely isolated from my professional contacts, both inside and outside the United Nations family, and from my agricultural profession of a previous 35 years standing."[47]

As Silow became increasingly marginalized, his allegations grew in number. He claimed that the agency caved to commercial and government demands, for example, referring to Isochem, an American company that salvaged isotopes from radioactive waste. In 1967, Isochem openly worried that production was beginning to outstrip demand and that new markets for isotopes in the Western world were hard to come by. Such isotope production had turned into a "white elephant" doomed to failure. Thus they increasingly looked to foreign markets, especially in the developing world. For Silow, such "sales pressures" translated into "programmatic pressures" in international agencies, which tried to convince developing countries to buy radioisotopes.[48] Further, he observed that the only major buyer in the United States for irradiated food was the Department of Defense and that the USDA hesitated to approve irradiated foods despite over $20 million in research in the United States.[49] Yet, because of IAEA advice, the Tanzanian government recently agreed to cooperate with an American firm to build its own $4 million irradiation plant to produce sterilized beef for domestic consumption, with isotopes provided by Atomic Energy of Canada. This facility was intended to start production in 1969, even before the first American one. Silow objected: "There should be at least three years commercial production and consumer experience with such a radically new process, in a country like the United States with almost unlimited resources for technical and economic evaluation of the process, before thought is given to transferring such an extremely complex technology to countries in the very early stages of their technical and economic development."[50]

Silow and others perceived scientists using the IAEA not only as a safe haven for their marginalized ideas, but also as a vehicle for rehabilitating their research projects. As an example, he pointed to Henry Seligman, who had come from the United Kingdom's Wantage Radiation Laboratory. After the British government reduced the agricultural program at Wantage to about a third of its previous size and eliminated several projects, Seligman moved to the IAEA as a deputy director-general and started up the IAEA's Seibersdorf Laboratory. Silow noted that "the grain irradiation project . . . was immediately reconstituted in virtually identical form here on the international level."[51] Silow's assessment would be repeated decades later by IAEA's official historian, David Fischer. In a footnote he observed that Seligman and another physicist, Italian Carlo Salvetti, had been "dissatisfied with the direction their establishments were taking and sought scientific refuge in the IAEA."[52]

In April 1967, Silow tried to take a public stand with his ideas and wanted to present a paper to the IAEA General Conference.[53] Silow's strategy in the paper was to outline the objections to food irradiation made by experts within the United States, particularly by the President's Science Advisory Committee (PSAC). It had issued a report in 1967 titled "The World Food Problem," in which it suggested that there was some uncertainty about whether irradiation imparted toxicity to food. The PSAC had stated that "these and other problems indicate that radiation is not likely to have a significant application for food preservation in the foreseeable future."[54] He mentioned experiments showing toxic effects in organisms raised on irradiated food. Symptoms included reduction in cell growth and cell division rates, increased rates of mutation, and also chromosome breakage. These effects had been observed in fruit flies, rats, mice, and cultures of human tissue. Silow saw this as evidence that food irradiation had not been approved in the wealthy, industrialized countries, and therefore promoting it in poor countries was "clearly entirely premature and unwise."[55]

As they had with the WHO, the scientists at the IAEA tried to counter any narrative that might cast radiation as a contaminant, preferring one that portrayed it as improving the food supply. Ironically, the IAEA had to choose between civilian and military experts in this case, and opted for the military ones. The PSAC was a civilian body—the highest such advisory body in the United States, reporting directly to the president. When commenting internally on Silow's proposed paper, those in the IAEA/FAO joint division in Vienna belittled the person who had prepared the PSAC statements, calling him a mere employee of Campbell Soup Company. This was a reference to Stuart G. Younkin, the soup company's vice-president for Agricultural Research, who chaired a seven-author panel of the PSAC report's chapter that mentioned food irradiation. The other authors of that chapter included W. Richard Graham Jr., director of research at Quaker Oats Company; Harvard professor of agriculture and business Henry B. Arthur; and four administrators from the US Department of Agriculture. But IAEA experts dismissed their concerns and preferred the more optimistic statements of the US Army, which declared food irradiation to be wholesome. They also cited fellow atomic energy booster Glenn T. Seaborg, the Nobel Prize-winning chemist—and chairman of the US Atomic Energy Commission—who had written in a letter to the PSAC that massive feeding experiments (of animals) had shown no evidence of harm. Members of Congress's Joint Committee on Atomic Energy also challenged the PSAC. All of the typical boosters of atomic energy lined up to oppose the report, and the IAEA simply followed suit. In the words of Silow's critics within the IAEA, the PSAC report had been "published without consulting the American authorities in the field of food irradiation."[56] Such "authorities" were not disinterested parties; the army and the nuclear weapons establishment all had interests in showing that this particular application of atomic energy was wholesome, harmless, and beneficial to the world.[57]

In an internal critique, IAEA staffers devoted some twenty-five pages to refuting Silow's criticisms, saying that past research was justification for optimism rather than pessimism. They pointed to research successes in the United States and reported commercial successes in the USSR, which already had approved irradiated food for consumption and was called "one of the most advanced countries in the industrial application of food irradiation." Besides, the IAEA authors pointed out, "technical assistance is requested by Governments and . . . the IAEA is the servant of the Member States and not in a position to dictate what assistance is best for them." If member states wanted atomic energy, they would get it.[58]

In the end, Silow's document was suppressed by both the IAEA and FAO and never saw the light of day. IAEA director-general Eklund wrote simply to FAO director-general Sen, "It is clear that statements in the papers will not stand critical examination and I do not consider it appropriate to give any of the documents broader distribution, for instance as a document for our General Conference."[59] Eklund had tried to sideline Silow before; but doing so over a document that simply repeated the arguments of the US President's Science Advisory Committee was an even more decisive step to silence dissent.

Fortunately for his enemies in the IAEA, the mandatory retirement age forced Silow out in March 1968. His place as deputy director was assumed by an IAEA insider, the decidedly pro-atomic Björn Sigurbjörnsson. According to prior arrangement, Silow returned to FAO, where the retirement age was slightly higher. But by then, FAO no longer offered friendly faces. In 1968 it appointed a new director, Addeke Hendrik Boerma of the Netherlands, whose outlook complemented the technophile leanings of atomic energy advocates.[60] Maurice Fried had cultivated allies at FAO, including its assistant director-general for agriculture, Otto E. Fischnich. Like Fried, both

Boerma and Fischnich saw Silow not as attempting to help the UN but rather as personally invested in destroying the joint division's program.[61]

By the spring of 1968, the IAEA was trying to put its agricultural work into media headlines, to assert a role in the so-called Green Revolution. That was a term used by William Gaud, head of the US Agency for International Development, to describe radical changes in agricultural practices made possible by "modern agriculture"—meaning, to him, intensive use of chemical fertilizers, pesticides, irrigation, and improved seeds. The *New York Times* reported record crops across Asia, particularly India, and gave credit to the new kinds of wheat and rice. It predicted an "agricultural revolution that may prove as important to mankind as the Industrial Revolution of the early nineteenth century."[62] Some were skeptical. The Green Revolution also would mean heavy reliance on government subsidies, expensive chemicals, and infrastructural investment, while "monoculture" (relying on one particular crop) could ultimately lead to less rather than more food security. Still, giddy predictions of ending world hunger, fending off population pressures, and solving the problems of the developing world through high technology ensued.[63]

IAEA officials tried to tie atomic energy to the Green Revolution, again by looking for success stories in mutation plant breeding. One of the most promising projects was led by Mankombu Swaminathan of India. He had leveraged the prestige of the IAEA, along with its "joint" division with FAO, to rise in influence within India and gain both financial and political support for mutation plant breeding there. The timing was ideal: after the death of longtime Prime Minister Jawaharlal Nehru in 1964, the new (but brief) regime under Lal Bahadur Shastri wanted a more aggressive program to address his country's food needs. The path he took was in crop intensification, using technology to maximize yields. Shastri's minister of food and agriculture, Chidambaram Subramaniam, wrote to FAO's director-general, his countryman Binay Ranjan Sen, that India was "deeply interested in exploiting atomic energy to the fullest possible extent for the betterment of human welfare" and wanted FAO's help to increase production on existing land through a program of what Subramaniam called "scientific cropping." Atomic energy seemed so promising, particularly in plant breeding and radioactive tracer studies, that his ministry decided to include in its Fourth Five Year Plan a major expansion of such research. Hoping for FAO assistance in gaining funds, Subramaniam reminded Sen that India was "in a stage of transition from a traditional to a progressive agriculture," and that it needed at least one national institution capable of using these modern research tools.[64] That institution was the Indian Agricultural Research Institute, which Swaminathan had directed since 1961. At a time of population pressure, famine threats, and war—India was at war with Pakistan in 1965—food security through a dynamic and aggressive line of genetic research became a central part of India's vision of future national security.[65]

The Indian government had every reason to be optimistic, given the results emerging from Swaminathan's institute. Scientists under Swaminathan's direction took some of the most promising new "Sonora-64" wheat varieties developed at the International Maize and Wheat Improvement Center in Mexico and irradiated them with gamma rays. One result was an amber-colored variety that looked closer to what Indians typically consumed. Swaminathan rechristened it "Sharbati Sonora" wheat. It appeared to be high in protein and lysine, an essential amino acid found in higher levels in animal proteins rather than plants. In 1967 Swaminathan claimed that these levels were nearly comparable to the lysine found in milk protein. Because such protein was crucial for child brain development, he wrote, Sharbati Sonora wheat offered a cheap and practical way of "diminishing the threat of intellectual dwarfism."[66]

At last, the IAEA seemed to be making good on the atom's abundant promise. By highlighting Sharbati Sonora's protein content, the IAEA could say its work had helped to alter the limits that nature had imposed on a region, Asia, under immense population pressure. Nonetheless, some skeptics argued that protein content was too often treated as an unqualified measure of health. One researcher, R. O. Whyte, noted, "I am concerned that the present stress on the protein content of cereals as the answer to Asia's problems is not giving due account to the equally important role of vitamins, minerals and fats, nor to the question of the relative merits of plant and animal protein in the Asian diet." Whyte also pointed out that India's stress on raising lysine content might disrupt the balance of other essential amino acids in the grain.[67] The IAEA's reply to this critique was to say that vitamins, minerals, and fats could be added as dietary supplements. IAEA scientist Robert A. Luse, a chemist trained at the University of California, believed the best path was to alter the foods that the population already consumed, as Swaminathan had done.[68] Luse argued that there were millions of people on the edge of starvation who had little access or money to pay for animal protein. Research on increasing protein in grain—whether by finding mutations, hybridizing existing ones, or inducing new ones with radiation—seemed to be the path toward helping the poorest people of the world.[69]

It was an extraordinary claim to make: atomic energy had provided the crucial nutrient to address Asia's perennial problems with famine. Sharbati Sonora gave atomic energy a place in the narrative of the Green Revolution.

The announcement seemed to convince even diehard skeptics. In 1969 Maurice Fried at the IAEA/FAO joint division received a contrite letter from Robert Rabson of the US Atomic Energy Commission, where experts heretofore had felt mutation plant breeding was little more than a gimmick. He said that he had been surprised that their American contractors were interested in finding ways to stimulate yield with radiation. "So you see we are getting drawn into the question just a little further with time."[70]

But was Sharbati Sonora really the miracle grain it seemed to be? Unsurprisingly, Silow—working at FAO—was deeply skeptical. First, he pointed out, the role of atomic energy had been to change the color of the grain. The evidence of increased protein content, or that any such increase was due to radiation, seemed dubious. But Silow's successor, Björn Sigurbjörnssen, trumpeted it as a huge win for mutation plant breeding. The irradiation undertaken in India had changed the seed color of the Mexican wheat variety Sonora-64 in a matter of three and a half years. "It is very difficult to match this by using any other technique of breeding," he said. "I see no reason why developing countries should be deprived of a proven method of efficient plant improvement." He believed that a shift toward plant protein improvement programs in the developing world was fully justified.[71]

Those protein claims would become a point of considerable controversy in the ensuing years. Scientists at Purdue University, Edwin Mertz and Oliver Nelson, had been working on improving the lysine content of maize for a number of years, and they had been successful—though other aspects of the maize made it nonviable for farmers.[72] Their attempts to replicate Swaminathan's findings proved futile. They saw insignificant differences in lysine between the Sonora-64 wheat and the new Sharbati Sonora. Other scientists at the University of Nebraska went so far as to say that Sharbati Sonora wheat had less lysine than its parent, Sonora-64. In the space of a year Swaminathan went from comparing his new wheat favorably to milk protein to saying that it had only slightly higher amounts of protein. Those saying there were no differences included geneticists in Mexico at CIMMYT, the International Maize and Wheat Improvement Center, which had produced the Sonora-64 variety initially. Yet Swaminathan continued to publish, and he won accolades for his work allegedly increasing protein in wheat. In 1972, an Indian scientist working for him, Vinod Shah, committed suicide and left the accusation in a note to Swaminathan that "a lot of unscientific data are collected and passed on to you to fit your line of thinking."[73]

Silow became convinced that Swaminathan was a fraud as soon as the Indian scientist began to tone down his claims about the extent of the protein increases. Moreover, he believed the IAEA was covering for Swaminathan so that it could hold on to atomic energy's tenuous link to the Green Revolution.[74] At FAO, he continued to oppose funds for irradiation programs, and he complained the joint division was propping up institutes in places like Iran, where previously enthusiastic backers such as the Central Treaty Organization (CENTO) had become disillusioned and withdrawn their support. He chastised his FAO colleagues, saying that they were just going along with the IAEA. "The world history of food irradiation is one long story of excessive claims of its economic value and repeated financial failure and bankruptcy, without a single commercial success, coupled now with lack of confidence on the part of the public health authorities in the data, purporting to demonstrate the safety of irradiated foods, that have been given to them by the promoters of food irradiation."[75]

Silow made few friends and many enemies by sticking to this critique. He resorted to accusations of corruption and deception among colleagues within the joint division. He accused one (without naming him) of falsifying his degree and lying about his affiliation to a university, and accused Fried and Sigurbjörnssen of covering it up. He also accused them of making public claims that could not be justified by scientific data. They had wanted to believe Swaminathan's claim about increased protein content, he alleged, and had not bothered to verify it. In the meantime, other geneticists had shown that the Indian claim was grossly exaggerated.[76]

FAO and IAEA leadership silenced Silow in several ways. Fried wrote a long condemnation of him, attaching a handwritten note to a subordinate with the observation "This is much stronger than the form of my usual answer but it is all true and somehow a stop has got to be made."[77] Fried said that technically FAO had not explicitly stated that Swaminathan had indeed increased the protein content. Fried even tape-recorded a meeting during which Silow said these claims had been made, and (he said) he had evidence that the subject had come up only once and the claims had been duly qualified as still unsubstantiated. Thus, Fried wrote to Silow's supervisor at FAO, Silow's basic accusation was false and he "stands exposed as having deliberately lied to you." Fried's descriptions were resentful, referring to Silow's "crusade against the joint division," calling him a "self-appointed policeman." Fried resented "being asked time and again to answer fabricated and false, malicious and slanderous accusations by Dr. Silow against myself, my staff, and the Joint Division's activities." Fried wanted the FAO to take some disciplinary action against Silow: "I would now kindly request that a stop be put to this nonsense."[78] One official suggested suspending him with pay for a few months, "to keep him out of the building and worrying delegates."[79]

Despite Fried's desire to have Silow punished, FAO leaders decided to wait until Silow's mandatory retirement age and in the meantime concealed from him any activities that might provide him with further ammunition. One example of this occurred when another individual began to criticize atomic energy in agriculture. Oddvar Aresvik had been a professor of agriculture economics at the Norwegian University of Agriculture, had worked under the Ford Foundation in Pakistan and Lebanon, and was writing a book about his experiences. Upon finishing a draft, he sent a copy to his own country's FAO national committee for comments. From there it reached the attention of the FAO's director-general, Addeke Boerma. The manuscript was highly critical of grain irradiation and the fundamental critique was identical to Silow's.[80] Aresvik felt that the joint division's encouragement of such research led cost-cutting politicians in developing countries to make dubious choices in priority. It led to greater support for radiation research, and because the best scientists followed the money, huge stores of existing genetic material went without study. National pride encouraged politicians to focus on such cutting-edge research, because "they have got the impression that to be considered developed they have to have atomic reactors and institutes for irradiation genetics." Aresvik wrote, "I have no objection to rich countries, which are experimenting with moon rockets and similar projects, sacrificing large amounts on radiation genetics." International agencies should know better, he stated, and not encourage developing nations to build expensive "white elephants."[81]

FAO leaders tried to determine the best response to Aresvik, while hiding the entire discussion from Silow, their "exasperating" employee. Fried nitpicked, saying that the joint division supported new buildings, not whole institutions. He also cast doubt on Aresvik's assertion about disproportional government funding of irradiation. He did not believe irradiation researchers were paid more, for example. Further, he stated that it was unfair to insist that only rich countries should work on such research, calling it the "spoon-feeding of crop varieties."[82]

Someone, accidentally or surreptitiously, took Fried's comments about Aresvik's draft and delivered a copy to Silow. He saw the copy on his desk, reviewed its contents, then left his office for a time. When he returned, he found his secretary in an argument with his supervisor's secretary, who had come to retrieve the document without Silow's permission. The ranking secretary had the document in her hands and left. Outraged, Silow railed against the "increasing trend toward secrecy in scientific matters" at FAO, which he said was surely a sign that something was wrong with the program.[83] Aresvik himself seems to have been humbled by Fried's hostile critique and likely never learned of the matter. His subsequent books on agriculture in developing countries were not especially critical of atomic energy.[84]

The controversy came and went. After his mandatory retirement in 1972, Silow tried to attend an FAO meeting on agriculture and was barred from doing so.[85] In a desperate move in 1973 he contacted a BBC correspondent with a story about "fraudulent conspiracy" at FAO to continue research on false science.[86] He also worked with a journalist at the *New Scientist* to tell the story, which came into the news after Vinod Shah committed suicide and the Indian government launched an investigation into Swaminathan's work.[87] Yet Swaminathan's reputation remained intact, and he went on to great fame and influence. He would become director of the International Rice Research Institute—the same organization that first had dismissed the importance of radiation-induced mutation breeding. He later went into politics in India and a 2009 retrospective interview in *Science* dubbed him a "guru of the Green Revolution."[88]

It is clear that by the early 1970s, the IAEA was a community looking for success stories and its leaders were willing to take actions that suppressed negative information about atomic energy. In *Personal Reflections*, a companion volume to Fischer's history, Björn Sigurbjörnsson relates the controversy without mentioning Silow's name, describing how the IAEA fought for its program's survival in the late 1960s. He notes how, before major conferences attended by Silow, IAEA staffers would prepare, as if for battle:

> We all stayed in the same hotel. Mac Fried held strategy meetings and we, in effect, divided the delegations between us and made contacts.... This was certainly not very ethical but in the face of hundreds of memo pages which had been distributed to delegates by our adversary, our choice was either to fight or give up—which would have certainly meant the end of the Joint Division.[89]

Sigurbjörnsson suggests that the joint division's coherence and unity probably was due in part to the constant need to defend itself against this unnamed "adversary."

By the early 1970s the IAEA was accustomed to blending the Malthusian rhetoric about population pressures and food supplies with the developmental ethos of FAO and other agencies. Its leaders carefully curated this positive image. The Green Revolution was an ideal vehicle for promoting a technological solution to global crises, if only the atom could be linked to it. In his Nobel Peace Prize lecture in 1970, plant breeder Norman Borlaug (whose team had produced Sonora-64) implored governments and scientists to invest heavily in agricultural research to address the population crisis, including mutation plant breeding, rather than in nuclear arms for the destruction of humanity.[90] IAEA scientists pointed to "successes," such as Sharbati Sonora, as well as the durum wheat trials in the Mediterranean region, and a high-yielding Japanese rice called Reimei.[91] Because numerous crop varieties around the world had been altered by radiation treatment, the IAEA attempted to claim these as successes. Most of these accomplished the same feat as the Italian durum wheats—increasing the stiffness of a stem, or making it shorter, so that vast increases in fertilizer inputs could be maintained without making plants fall under their own weight. Other traits included early maturity or disease resistance. These were rarely improvements in nutritional quality. Most of the success stories were subjective, as in the aesthetics of ornamental flowers. And most of those were from X-ray treatments, not from gamma sources requiring radioactive materials. The IAEA claimed radiation was responsible for saving peppermint from extinction—because American researchers had used it to produce disease-resistant varieties.[92] Björn Sigurbjörnsson wrote in 1971 that the work of the IAEA was "quickening the pulse of nature." Radiation promised to speed up the rate of spontaneous mutation to give researchers a larger number of plants to work with.[93]

Making such claims was part of the agency's practice of protecting the image of the peaceful atom as a technological agent of positive change in the world. The agency's conflict with other bodies can be read as a contest of narratives, with the IAEA strongly promoting one showing the manifold ways that atomic energy was ready to resolve the world's problems of disease, famine, and overpopulation. Prior to the 1963 ban on atmospheric nuclear tests, the IAEA's principal foe seemed to be the World Health Organization, whose scientists did not shy away from speaking about the dangers of radioactive fallout. In the mid-1960s, the IAEA courted trouble from the Food and Agriculture Organization but successfully outmaneuvered opponents there to position the atom as a key part of the Green Revolution. By the late 1960s and early 1970s, however, the international situation was changing in ways that would provide a permanent raison d'être for the agency, while giving nuclear weapons states another incentive to support its work. Americans, Soviets, British, and others sought a treaty to limit the spread of nuclear weapons and imagined the IAEA in a policing and monitoring role. They needed the IAEA more than ever, heightening the urgency to bolster its civilian dimensions. That would mean continued reliance on rhetoric that emphasized natural resource constraints, famine, and disease, along with water and energy insecurity. As the IAEA was drawn more into nuclear security issues, its need for positive rhetoric only intensified.

Figure 1. President Dwight Eisenhower addressing the General Assembly of the United Nations on December 8, 1953, suggesting the creation of an international atomic energy agency. Courtesy of the United Nations.

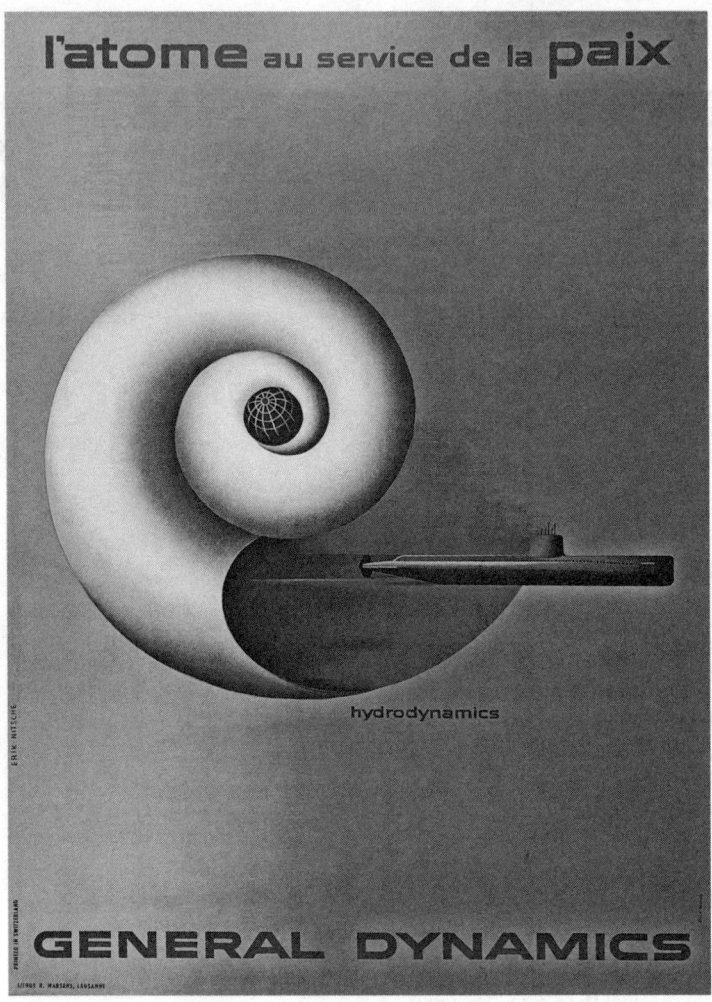

Figure 2. One of several posters designed by Erik Nitsche for General Dynamics on the "Atoms for Peace" theme. The French one depicts "hydrodynamics" and features an image of the USS *Nautilus*. Courtesy of General Dynamics.

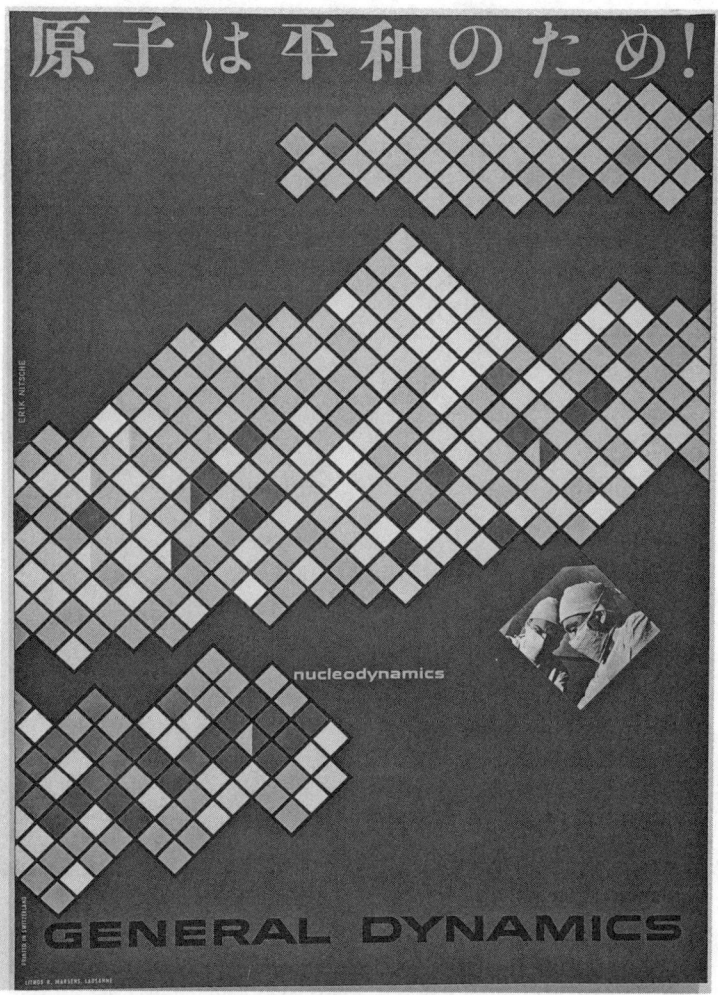

Figure 3. Another poster designed by Erik Nitsche for General Dynamics on the "Atoms for Peace" theme. The Japanese one depicts "nucleodynamics" and features physicians with surgical masks. Courtesy of General Dynamics.

Figure 4. The opening ceremonies of the 1955 International Conference on the Peaceful Uses of Atomic Energy, in Geneva, Switzerland. UN Secretary-General Dag Hammarskjöld (*center*) and others look at a model of an experimental boiling water reactor, part of the United States display. American scientist Walter G. Whitman (*far left*) was the conference's secretary general. To his *right* is Ahmed S. Bokhari, Pakistan's permanent representative to the United Nations. Courtesy of the United Nations.

Figure 5. Indian physicist Homi J. Bhabha (*right*) served as president during the 1955 International Conference on the Peaceful Uses of Atomic Energy, in Geneva, Switzerland. Pictured here at the closing session with UN Under-Secretaries Ralph Bunche (*center*) and Ilya S. Tchernychev. Courtesy of the United Nations.

Figure 6. Ghana's President Kwame Nkrumah (*left*) visiting the United Nations Headquarters in New York in 1961, talking with UN Under-Secretary Ralph Bunche. Courtesy of the United Nations.

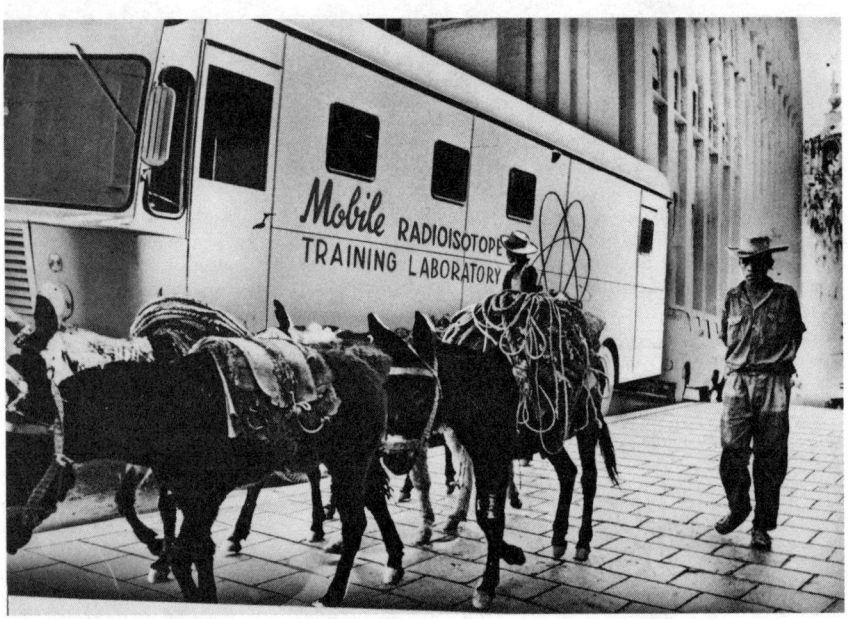

Figure 7. This widely used IAEA photograph depicts a mobile radioisotope laboratory outside the University of Guanajuato, Mexico, in 1960. Courtesy of the United Nations.

Figure 8. "Gamma gardens" or "gamma fields" were used to induce mutations or to study the effects of radiation on plants at various distances throughout a growing season. The photo depicts the radiation tower at the National Institute of Radiation Breeding in Japan in 1967. Photo credit: Goldberger. Courtesy of the International Atomic Energy Agency.

Figure 9. Durum wheat varieties produced from radiation exposure were grown experimentally in twelve countries of North Africa and the Middle East in the 1960s. This undated photograph depicts one such site in Syria, and the scientist on the *left* is identified as Italian plant geneticist G. T. Scarascia. Courtesy of the International Atomic Energy Agency.

Figure 10. Botanist Ronald Silow in 1964. Silow was the first deputy director of the FAO/IAEA Joint Division for Atomic Energy in Agriculture. He criticized the agencies' work on agricultural techniques in developing countries and accused them of covering up scientific results. John Innes Archives, courtesy of the John Innes Foundation.

Figure 11. Japanese mutation plant breeder Takeshi Kawai standing with the Rei Mei rice he produced in the 1960s. Courtesy of the International Atomic Energy Agency.

Figure 12. Maurice Fried (*center*) in 1961 at a conference in Mexico City co-sponsored by the World Health Organization and International Atomic Energy Agency. Also pictured are Ribeiro Pieroni (*right*) of Brazil and A. A. Kudriavtsev (*left*) of the USSR. Kudriavtsev delivered a lecture on the use of radioisotopes in animal husbandry and veterinary medicine. Photo credit: W. Joseph. Courtesy of the International Atomic Energy Agency.

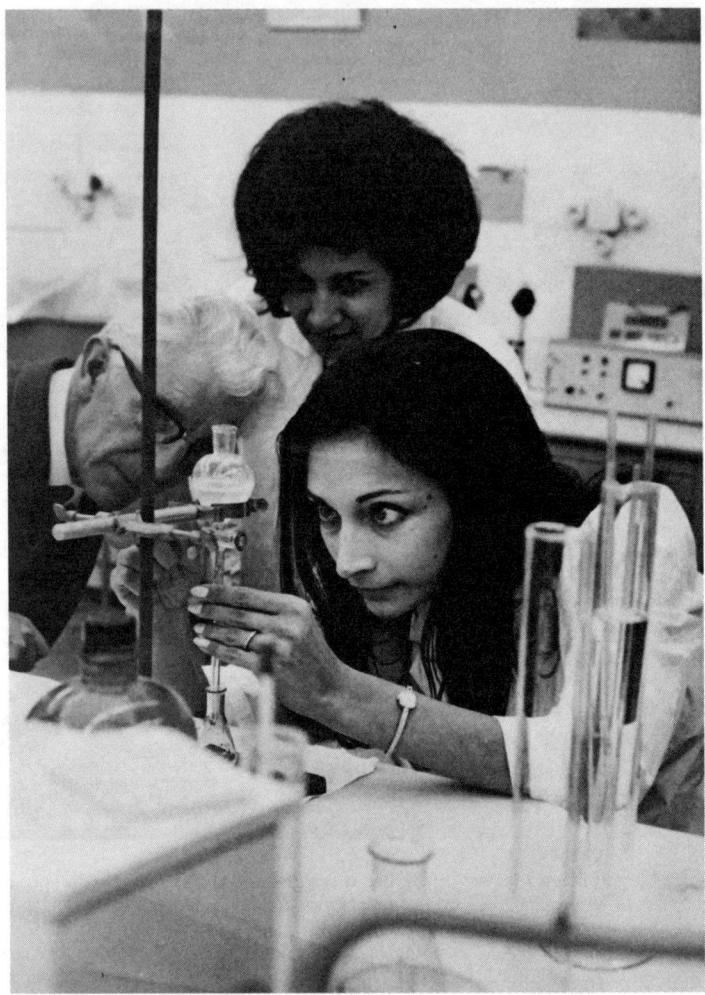

Figure 13. The research reactor at Tehran University went into operation in 1967, and the IAEA assisted it by sending experts for training purposes. Pictured here in 1970 is Thomas Hayes (United Kingdom), an IAEA expert in radioisotope production, working with Iranian scientists Zhila Khalkhali (*top*) and Zohreh Abedin-Zadeh. Photo credit: Muldoon Jr. Courtesy of the United Nations.

Figure 14. President Lyndon Johnson (*right*) visiting exhibits at the Water for Peace symposium in Washington, DC, May 1967. With him (*from right to left*) are Secretary of the Interior Stewart Udall, Philippine diplomat Carlos P. Romulo, and Greek architect and city planner Constantos A. Doxiadias. Courtesy of the Lyndon B. Johnson Presidential Library, National Archives and Records Administration.

Figure 15. American architect Edward Durell Stone designed the Pakistan Institute of Nuclear Science and Technology to blend modernity with touches of Mughal history. On a visit to Pakistan in 1961, Stone (*left*) discussed the concept with Pakistan's president Muhammad Ayub Khan (*next to Stone*). Next to President Khan in the photo is Ishrat Hussain Usmani, chair of the Pakistan Atomic Energy Commission. Courtesy of Edward Durell Stone Papers, University of Arkansas Libraries.

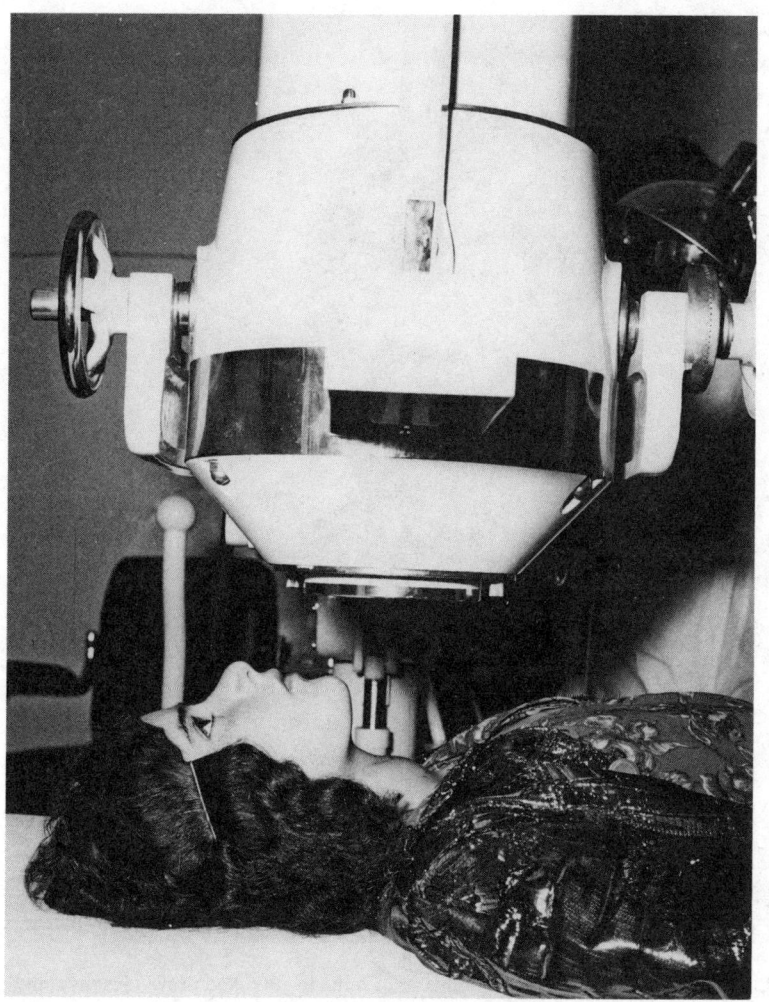

Figure 16. The IAEA used this photo, from Tehran's Razi Hospital in 1967, to show medical applications of atomic energy in the developing world. Pictured is an Iranian patient who has received radioiodine treatment for an enlarged thyroid gland. She is positioned under a gamma camera to determine the distribution pattern of the iodine. Photo credit: P. J. Gillespie. Courtesy of the International Atomic Energy Agency.

Figure 17. Indira Gandhi became prime minister of India in 1966 and proved just as committed to nuclear programs as her predecessors had been, despite US efforts to persuade her to join the non-proliferation treaty. The photo is from a visit to UN Headquarters in New York in 1968. Under Gandhi's leadership India detonated its first atomic device in 1974, calling it a Peaceful Nuclear Explosion (PNE). Courtesy of the United Nations.

Figure 18. President Gerald Ford and Secretary of State Henry Kissinger, meeting in the Oval Office with Iranian economic minister Hushang Ansari in 1975. Courtesy of the Gerald R. Ford Presidential Library, National Archives and Records Administration.

Figure 19. Israel's peacetime air attack on Iraq's nuclear facility in 1981 forced several countries, including the United States, to reconsider their commitments to civilian nuclear programs around the world. Here the UN Security Council debates actions to take against Israel. Pictured speaking is Zehdi Labib Terzi, representing the Palestinian Liberation Organization. Next to him is Oleg A. Troyanovsky of the USSR. Courtesy of the United Nations.

Figure 20. Hans Blix (left) led the International Atomic Energy Agency from 1981 to 1997, as the agency became increasingly associated with weapons inspections and nonproliferation. He is pictured here with Chief Inspector David Kay of the IAEA after an assessment of Iraq's nuclear capabilities in 1991. Courtesy of the United Nations.

PART III
Atomic Prohibition

CHAPTER 6

Water, Blood, and the Nuclear Club

What the People's Republic of China accomplished in 1964 had a profound impact on nuclear affairs, deeply upsetting the prevailing nuclear order and putting peaceful atomic energy firmly onto a new path that paired it with proliferation concerns. China's was the colored bomb and the people's bomb. It was the first atomic bomb to cross W. E. B. Du Bois's "color line," and it did not fit comfortably in any existing political category. China was an enemy of the United States, having a communist government that had fought against the US-supported Chinese nationalists. Yet it also was estranged from the Soviet Union, for reasons that included the USSR's decision not to share nuclear weapons. Moreover, it had a bitter history of colonialism, with British-controlled Hong Kong a constant reminder. Further, its war with imperial Japan had ended nearly two decades earlier, but the countries could not be considered friends—China had suffered some of the highest losses of life in World War II. And it was not a keen ally of neutralists, having waged a border war with India as recently as 1962. It operated outside the domain of international bodies, such as the United Nations, because many countries (including the United States) still recognized the exiled government in Taiwan as the only legitimate "China." If commentators of the 1960s spoke like those of the 1990s, they would have called China a "rogue" nuclear state. What would a country like China do with the bomb?[1]

China's bomb set into a motion a series of events that resulted in the late 1960s in the signing of a non-proliferation treaty—an agreement that, by century's end, would bind together nearly 200 participating governments. In their zeal to attract other countries into agreements about non-proliferation and safeguards, nuclear states—led by the United States—recommitted to the promises of plenty from the peaceful atom. They already had dreamed of new plant mutations, new ways of preserving food, new medical applications, and uses of radioisotopes for research. They made even bolder promises to make radical transformations to the earth, to reconfigure entire socioeconomic systems, and to make deserts bloom. For more than a decade, Americans had urged caution in building reactors for electricity. But now the United States and several European states threw such caution to the wind. They instead imagined that collaboration in extensive nuclear programs was a means of exercising influence, much like efforts to sell conventional arms.

Two of the most politically volatile regions on earth, the Indian subcontinent and the Middle East, would see bloody conflict in the 1960s and beyond at the same time that politicians promoted nuclear programs there under the banner of the peaceful atom. Both India and Israel were widely perceived as the next countries that might go nuclear. Could they be convinced to forgo weapons programs? If so, was there a way to leverage "peaceful" atomic energy to make it happen, perhaps by making promises of a cornucopian future? Not only did nuclear programs grow, but so too did nuclear collaboration. The United States made ambitious plans to build nuclear reactors in Israel that could produce electricity for water desalination plants. Other countries, notably Canada, helped India with its project, even as India made plans to detonate nuclear explosives. Doing so made governments' promotion of civilian nuclear energy an even higher-stakes game. If non-nuclear nations agreed to forgo weapons development in exchange for access to the atom's civilian applications, those applications needed to be perceived as valuable, even if based on a mirage.

***

Although the United States had, since 1945, nominally opposed the proliferation of nuclear weapons, it had made no serious attempt to enact that view after the 1946 Baruch Plan to eliminate atomic weapons had fizzled. Between President Dwight Eisenhower's 1953 suggestion to create an international atomic energy agency and the IAEA's official birth in 1957, scientists and diplomats focused on how to encourage the proliferation of civilian nuclear technology without actually contributing to bomb projects. Since the 1950s, countries all over the world, having no particular knowledge or infrastructure to build atomic bombs, steadily amassed the expertise, training, material, and technology to enter the nuclear world.

Some of the crucial discussions about transferring technology occurred through IAEA safeguard negotiations. "Safeguard" was a term that described not safety in nuclear technology but rather the legal and logistical procedures for ensuring that nuclear materials and equipment were not diverted to bomb projects. In the 1950s, thinking through such safeguards was new, with many unanswered questions. Should agreements be bilateral, at the discretion of two states? Should norms be created, perhaps at the IAEA? How could any country be enticed to adhere to these norms? Who would enforce them? Although in 1953 scientists had in mind a range of less disquieting applications in developing countries—radioisotopes in fertilizer research or mutation plant breeding, for example—it was clear after the creation of the IAEA that many countries would want to develop nuclear power and hoped to use the new international availability of technology and material as a way of accomplishing it. Because this would entail the creation of large reactors, many equipment acquisitions would be indistinguishable from those of bomb projects.

Initially such safeguards were imposed by governments and built into bilateral trade deals between importers and exporters. The United States, for example, insisted that its nuclear deals with its recent enemy, Japan, include sufficient safeguard procedures. In the late 1950s, the United States, Japan, and others hoped that the task of overseeing these safeguards would fall on the IAEA. By 1961 the agency had established the principles of a safeguard system covering research facilities and smaller (100 megawatt or less) reactors. Trying to extend the safeguards to larger reactor systems, the IAEA reopened discussion in 1963 to hash out an agreement about safeguards for larger reactors. In September 1963 the Americans and Japanese took their own bilateral agreement and signed over the responsibilities for administering the safeguards to the IAEA. Japan also planned to have the IAEA administer safeguards for its bilateral deals with Australia, South Africa, and the United Kingdom.

The IAEA was attractive because of convenience, but it also served as a means for Americans (and others) to monitor the development of nuclear programs, as a complement to other kinds of intelligence gathering. In 1964, the US Central Intelligence Agency had few eyes "on the ground" and relied heavily on aerial reconnaissance. The 1964 Chinese test was a case in point. American analysts had guessed that the test would occur no earlier than 1965, based on U-2 aircraft and satellite photography of the test site at Lop Nor and the production of fissionable material by the reactor at Pao Tou. That estimate was revised on October 15 to be "at any time," because the test site itself seemed complete—with a 340-foot shot tower surrounded by a double fence, arrays for instruments around it at various distances, other smaller towers, and bunkers. Looking again at the reactor site, CIA analysts judged that they had been wrong about when the Chinese had begun to produce fuel for the bomb.[2] The next day, October 16, 1964, the bomb detonated.

Only after this test did the US government take significant steps toward what became the Treaty on the Non-proliferation of Nuclear Weapons (NPT) several years later. Despite Nationalist China's immediate panic ("We are the target!" Chiang Kai-Shek told American officials in Taipei),[3] most key American advisors thought in terms of deterrence. Should Japan or India be encouraged to build a bomb of their own? Just days after the event, US secretary of defense Robert McNamara reminded members of Congress that there were several countries that could similarly develop a bomb, and that the cost of doing so was on the order of $120 million, well within the reach of governments.[4] Military advisors in the Joint Chiefs of Staff began advising the secretary of defense that nuclear sharing among Asian allies might become necessary with increasing pressures from China.[5] After perceiving India as the key "colored" adversary in the nuclear realm because of its focus on colonial history and race in the 1950s, the Americans now were considering the prospect of encouraging India to arm, as a counter to China. Secretary of State Dean Rusk, for example, posed the question baldly to his colleagues: should it always be the United States that would have to deter China? Would it not be preferable for India or Japan to act as a deterrent? That Rusk and others were entertaining this option was to remain highly classified, at the urging of Secretary of Defense McNamara.[6] In meetings between President Lyndon Johnson and Soviet Foreign Minister Andrei Gromyko, it seemed clear that the Soviets wondered if the Chinese situation would lead to the Americans allowing West Germany to become nuclear-armed, thus developing its own independent nuclear deterrent. Suddenly, the Soviets were very interested in working with the Americans to maintain a global status quo in nuclear weapons.[7]

Needing a strategy, two weeks after the Chinese bomb test, President Johnson announced the creation of a special panel—the Task Force on Nuclear Proliferation, chaired by former deputy secretary of defense Roswell Gilpatric. Its members framed their choice as having to pick one of two worlds. What McNamara called "Model A" was for the United States to push for a world with no additional nuclear weapons states. "Model B" would have the United States accept a limited number of further nuclear powers. Several of the task force participants began with Model B—accepting that it was in the US interest to have a few more nuclear powers—but by the end they came around to a new conviction that American policy should follow Model A. Cornell University president James A. Perkins argued that to ensure that Model A happened, even in advance of an international agreement—and possibly even without one, "we should beef up the IAEA to make it the inspectorial system around the world."[8] Although the IAEA was not designed to be a policing agency, or a "watchdog," the task force increasingly saw it that way. The "Atoms for Peace" agency would need to be transformed into a tool for keeping nuclear weapons out of the hands of all states except the United States, the Soviet Union, the United Kingdom, France—and now China.

These advisors recognized a paradox in their recommendation. Promoting peaceful atoms and promising an abundant future would be crucial to getting countries to agree to forgo weapons. And yet promoting atomic energy made bomb projects more likely. Seeing what happened in China—and the resultant belief that developing a bomb had enhanced China's position in world affairs—made the committee members look anew at pathways to nuclear weapons in the rest of the world. They recognized explicitly that the promotion of peaceful nuclear power was part of the problem. "The world is fast approaching a point of no return in the prospects of controlling the spread of nuclear weapons," the committee stated. "Nuclear power programs are placing within the hands of many nations much of the knowledge, equipment and materials for making nuclear weapons." They recommended helping only friendly countries with nuclear power.[9]

Only after this committee made its recommendations did the United States government commit itself to non-proliferation. Other nuclear powers followed suit. The report itself was made available—leaked, some stated—to the British, to ensure support from the United States' most important ally. Britain needed little convincing, as Prime Minister Harold Wilson had stated forcefully in 1964 that there should be no new fingers on the nuclear trigger, a remark aimed as much at the Federal Republic of Germany as any. The French and Germans would prove reluctant allies in the goal of non-proliferation in the years to come. But treaty negotiations with the USSR moved swiftly, and the two superpower rivals—along with the United Kingdom—would be among the first signers in 1968.[10]

The IAEA figured at the center of US non-proliferation strategy, but could the agency truly put the world under surveillance? At IAEA meetings, delegates routinely doubted the effectiveness of establishing some kind of technological barrier in formal agreements. The parties in a nuclear deal would find ways to get around the rules, as Oscar Quihillalt, the head of Argentina's National Atomic Energy Commission, observed. Deception was easy to accomplish, he noted. He argued that there needed to be a sense of moral obligation, not simply a legal one, for countries to adhere to the safeguards system. The development of new techniques over time made it a simple matter, he stated, to deceive inspectors.[11]

Quihillalt knew how toothless safeguards could be. In 1964 he was questioned by American diplomats about Argentina's secret sale of eighty tons of uranium oxide to Israel. This was eight times more than the maximum sale permitted under the auspices of the IAEA. Had the IAEA arranged the deal, there would have been specific safeguard agreements that included inspection. Argentina had signed a sales contract with Israel in early 1963, with nothing more specific than an assurance by the government of Israel that the material would not be used for military purposes. The Americans had "expressed its serious concern" because they believed the Argentines supported a common position not to sell uranium without some kinds of safeguards. But Quihillalt's attitude was that his country was not part of a common agreement, formal or otherwise, and there had been nothing to stop Argentina from making the sale. After all, major uranium suppliers like South Africa did this all the time, he noted. Why should any country put itself at a commercial disadvantage?[12]

The prospect of a non-proliferation treaty raised anew the question of neocolonialism. Not only did it explicitly separate the world into haves and have-nots, but it also threatened to interfere with developing countries' access to nuclear reactors. As Indian atomic energy chief Homi Bhabha put it to the IAEA board of governors in 1965, such agreements should be "implemented in a spirit of reason and common sense."[13] He complained that safeguards unfairly hindered the development of nuclear power for electricity while doing little to prevent military applications. From a technological point of view, Bhabha noted, it was easier to use atomic energy for military purposes than economic ones.[14] Similarly, Hassan M. Tohamy of the United Arab Republic (Egypt) argued that rules about safeguards might lead to "the unnecessary domination of foreign powers in the scientific and economic fields."[15]

Bhabha's concerns about neocolonialism were real enough, but India itself was at a crossroads in its nuclear program for reasons right across its borders. China's atomic bomb sent ripples of discord through the Indian political scene, given that the two countries had been at war over a border dispute in 1962—and India had lost. India's primary nuclear goal under Prime Minister Jawaharlal Nehru had been industrialization. With the detonation of the Chinese bomb in 1964, political debates shifted dramatically to the question of whether India should develop its own bomb. Nehru died of a heart attack in 1964, prior to the Chinese bomb test. His successor, Lal Bahadur Shastri, reiterated India's commitment to a peaceful program, but the question still lingered. At least one major survey of Indians suggested that some 70 percent supported moving toward a nuclear weapons program. After all, border disputes would continue, if not with China then with Pakistan. Would India always be subject to nuclear blackmail? Shastri gave a speech in late 1964 indicating that India might have to change its position in the coming years, and he also mentioned that India's peaceful program would include explosives for civilian earthmoving projects.[16]

The mention of explosives made clear that India was leaving its options open, and thus it seemed unpredictable. Colleagues of Bhabha outside India understood from him that he was confident in his country's ability to build a bomb in short order, especially since India had stepped up construction of facilities producing plutonium. Shastri continued to support the nuclear program over the next year, even as India engaged in war with Pakistan.[17] The final peace treaty ending that war was signed at Tashkent, in the USSR, by Shastri and his Pakistani counterpart Muhammad Ayub Khan, on January 10, 1966. Shastri was dead before morning, apparently of a heart attack overnight. Bhabha was killed in a commercial airline crash over the Alps just two weeks later, on January 24. Both men's deaths have sparked numerous conspiracy theories about other countries' possible attempts to quash an Indian bomb.[18]

India's claim of developing a "peaceful nuclear explosive" (PNE) would spark ridicule and consternation outside India in subsequent years, but it is worth remembering that the idea was taken directly from the United States. Americans called their atomic earthmoving plans "plowshare" projects, after a passage in the Bible about beating swords into plowshares. The first of these was a plan to build a harbor in Alaska with a series of nuclear detonations, but it was canceled by the Kennedy administration. Throughout the 1960s, the US Atomic Energy Commission held on to the idea that its atomic detonations could be used to transform landscapes, liberating humans from the constraints of nature by rerouting rivers, building giant harbors, and embarking on other earthmoving projects.[19]

The United States had already shown how the promise of PNEs could be useful in wielding geopolitical power, as it did in relation to the Panama Canal. After violent clashes between anti-American protesters and US troops in 1964, the government of Panama broke diplomatic relations with the United States and insisted that a new treaty be signed to replace that of 1903. The Johnson administration floated the idea of building an entirely new canal in a different location—possibly outside Panama—using atomic blasts. With PNEs, the United States had the appearance of being able to construct a new canal in far less time than with conventional earthmoving. Critics of the idea called it a bluff, and Johnson tried to lend the project credibility by launching major scientific feasibility studies of specific sites in Panama, Colombia, and Nicaragua. A new canal even had the appearance of being less imperialistic because a deeper, larger canal without a complicated system of locks would not require a permanent colony of foreign staff and troops. The Americans did not advertise PNEs as geopolitical leverage, of course, but instead characterized them as serious development projects and even advocated providing "PNE services" to other countries. In the case of the canal, the peaceful atom was part of a public conversation that Johnson hoped would weaken Panama's negotiating position.[20]

Americans were highly selective about their worries over the connection between peaceful atomic energy and weapons programs. India was a proliferation possibility, true, but it also condemned the American war in Vietnam and seemed on too-friendly terms with the Soviet Union. President Johnson hoped India would explicitly disavow nuclear weapons and commit to signing on to a non-proliferation treaty. He considered withholding food aid to accomplish it, and he tried to signal his power over India by intervening to delay the delivery of parts for some American-made reactors being built at India's Tarapur site. That tactic continued into 1966, after the installation of the new prime minister of India—Nehru's daughter Indira Gandhi. The American tactics backfired and only strengthened Gandhi's resolve to avoid dependence on any foreign power, particularly the United States. She would prove just as committed to the nation's nuclear program as Shastri had been, perhaps more so.[21]

In contrast to its attitudes toward India, the Johnson administration bent over backward to accommodate the ambitions of Israel, even though it too posed a proliferation threat. Israel's weapons program has long been a subject of controversy, as historians continue to debate the timing of it, the role of other nations as collaborators, and the complicity of the United States. What was widely known in the 1960s was simple: Israel had been supplied with uranium fuel by Argentina and was being furnished with a large reactor by France. The French and Israeli governments had collaborated closely on nuclear technology in the late 1950s. Both nations had been humiliated during the Suez crisis of 1956. They invaded the canal zone when seized by Gamal Nasser's pan-Arab government, only to bow to international pressure and withdraw. Kept secret at the time, France recommitted to Israel's security in the late 1950s, trading not only in high-quality conventional arms but also making an effort to help Israel build an atomic bomb. Israel began the construction of a French-made reactor in 1958, at a town in the Negev desert called Dimona. By the early 1960s the reactor was complete—and producing plutonium for a weapons arsenal.[22]

Although the extent of US knowledge remains a contentious issue, the United States made several efforts to maintain a controlling hand over

Israel's weapons program.[23] Israel allowed Americans to make some on-site inspections. Reports of visits by US Atomic Energy Commission scientists to the Dimona reactor, in 1961 and 1963, provided no clear evidence of a military dimension. Secretary of State Dean Rusk advised diplomatic posts in the area that it was a research reactor with a 24-megawatt capacity. When it was fully operational, it would produce some plutonium, he said, but "our experts found no evidence Israelis [were] preparing nuclear weapons."[24] Yet (in the 1980s) a key Israeli informant, Dimona technician Mordechai Vanunu, claimed that the reprocessing facility was buried deep underground and that access points were bricked up and plastered over before each scheduled visit.[25]

In the early 1960s, American inspectors and intelligence analysts recognized the possibility that Israel might try to build a bomb and use the premise of civilian atomic energy to do it. The French justified their sale of the reactor on the grounds that it was peaceful. The Canadians had done the same when they agreed to help India build reactors in the mid-1950s. CIA analysts in 1963 guessed that Israel probably had sufficient "access to nuclear technology in the international scientific community" to acquire a bomb design. Israel's "special relationship with the French" struck them as a distinct possibility for a pathway to a bomb.[26] Within the US government, officials saw that peaceful uses of atomic energy had the net effect of establishing a capacity to create a realistic weapons program while giving every outward appearance of a non-military program. American diplomats even acknowledged to Egypt's Gamal Nasser that Israel's reactor facilities may have been laying a foundation for moving into weapons.[27]

Israeli politicians had just as little interest in disavowing an atomic bomb program as Indian ones. They too were surrounded by hostile neighbors. Golda Meir, at that time Israel's foreign minister, was unambiguous about what she thought Egypt's intentions were under its leader Gamal Nasser. On a September 1963 New York visit to participate in the UN General Assembly, she met with Secretary of State Dean Rusk and painted a bleak picture of a man spreading socialism and Soviet influence under the banner of pan-Arabism. The Egyptians were embroiled in a costly commitment to the republican side in the civil war in Yemen, and Meir felt that Egyptian soldiers were getting much-needed training. She noted that Nasser's forces had begun to use chemical weapons, including mustard gas, against supporters of the royalist regime there. Although the Americans doubted it, saying that Nasser was likely using concentrated tear gas, Meir held firm.[28] She turned out to be right. Nasser's troops, on several occasions from June 1963 forward, made the war in Yemen the center stage of the most extensive use of chemical weapons since the First World War. Meir believed in

1963 that Nasser was trying to develop not just chemical weapons but also radiological weapons (using radioactive debris) and even nuclear ones.[29] Israel's own facility at Dimona moved in the same direction—its reactor went into operation in late 1963, meaning that the Israelis would soon be able to produce plutonium for bomb construction or radiological warfare if they had the desire to do so.

The United States under Lyndon Johnson attempted to leverage the abundant potential of the atom as a way of drawing the Americans and Israelis closer together in collaboration. At a 1964 dinner in New York for Israel's Weizmann Institute of Science, he spoke eloquently about the American role in helping generate water in parched lands. "Water can banish hunger and can reclaim the desert and change the course of history." That very day, he said, the Cuban government had shut off water to the US naval base at Guantanamo, but the Americans had stockpiled enough to manage the crisis. Likewise, water security would be crucial to a vulnerable nation such as Israel. "Water should never be a cause of war," he said. "It should always be a force for peace." The president announced that the United States and Israel already were beginning a cooperative scheme to use nuclear energy to generate electricity for massive desalination (or desalting) facilities, to turn salt water into fresh water and thus improve Israel's water security.[30] Later that year he repeated the promise during a toast at a White House dinner with Israeli leader Levi Eshkol. "Mr. Prime Minister, you told me only this morning that water was blood for Israel," Johnson said. "So we shall make a joint attack on Israel's water shortage through the highly promising technique of desalting. Indeed, let us hope that this technique will bring benefit to all of the peoples of the parched Middle East."[31]

It was reminiscent of "Atoms for Peace," but Johnson put his own stamp on the program. He took some flak initially from Israel's neighbors, who saw it as favoritism. One Lebanese newspaper dubbed him "Johnson the Jew."[32] But Johnson was undeterred. It became "Water for Peace," but atomic energy was still at the heart of it. Linking environmental crisis to armed conflict, Johnson touted technological solutions as a route to lasting peace. It was a perfect storm of various goals. It gave the United States something to offer that others could not. It might end up as the "carrot" to persuade countries to permit inspections of their facilities. It also fit into the president's broader goals of social uplift in his Great Society political platform. At least rhetorically, it offered a means to bend nature toward human needs on a large scale. Further, it promised an impressive example of a peaceful application of atomic technology at a time when one of the most promising ones, peaceful nuclear explosions (PNEs), had been dealt a blow by the 1963 Limited Test Ban Treaty, which forbade above-ground explosions.

Enthusiasm for dual-use nuclear plants for electricity and desalting initially came from a small number of people, mostly centered in the Oak Ridge National Laboratory in Tennessee. Its director, Alvin Weinberg, had come to the conclusion that desalting might become a major selling point for nuclear power, to make it even more attractive to governments. A colleague later described Weinberg as a "prophet for the nuclear age" who saw nuclear energy as a "way to extricate mankind from the Malthusian curse."[33] He persuaded the previous administration's science advisor, Jerome Wiesner, to form an interagency task group to do a feasibility study. It began work in January 1963 and was headed by oceanographer Roger Revelle, serving as science advisor to the secretary of the interior. Even before that could be completed, Johnson announced the US commitment to it.

Nuclear desalination appeared at an opportune moment in the history of environmental concerns and nuclear issues. The Department of Interior then was headed by former Arizona congressman Stewart Udall, whose concerns about environmental challenges ran deep. Having been inspired by Rachel Carson's 1962 *Silent Spring*, he wrote his own conservation manifesto in 1963, *The Quiet Crisis*. It echoed Carson's misgivings about pesticide use and argued for a shift away from strict economic conservation in favor of quality of life issues such as clean air and water.[34] Udall was instrumental in gathering support for key legislative acts during the Johnson years, including the Wilderness Act and the Endangered Species Act, and he helped to put environmental concerns into Johnson's "Great Society" agenda. Like many others of his time, he had complete faith in nuclear technology to resolve a host of human ills, and he specifically marked it as an alternative to unrestrained resource extraction. Later in life, Udall would regret his unremitting enthusiasm for nuclear power, especially because of the radiation exposures to people living in his native Southwest. But in the early 1960s he was one of its most reliable boosters. One of Udall's chief aides, Sharon Francis, later called his discussion in *The Quiet Crisis* "a hymn to nuclear power."[35]

Udall made the ideal ally for Atomic Energy Commission chairman Glenn Seaborg, who was no environmentalist but was looking for a "win" in the arena of peaceful uses of atomic energy. The AEC was increasingly perceived on the wrong side of environmental issues. It polluted the air, with radioactive fallout from nuclear tests; it contaminated rivers and streams, with effluent releases from nuclear facilities; and it dumped radioactive waste into the oceans. Rachel Carson, for example, criticized the AEC's ocean dumping in an updated edition of her book *The Sea around*

Us. Outrage at dumping radioactive waste off of coastal cities and in the Gulf of Mexico had plagued the AEC so much that by 1963 it decided to phase out ocean dumping.[36] Worse was that its technological approach to addressing resource limitations had been dealt a severe blow by diplomats. The Limited Test Ban Treaty in 1963 banned above-ground nuclear tests, undermining the AEC's Project Plowshare—its ambitious effort to use nuclear detonations for big construction projects.[37] Despite that setback, Udall's belief in nuclear power as a solution to the "quiet crisis" created an opportunity to renew the atom's place as an ally in addressing environmental concerns. Seaborg and Udall together argued forcefully in favor of nuclear-powered desalination. Their enthusiasm infected President Johnson, who saw it as a potential foreign policy lever that worked well with his "Great Society" agenda, already oriented toward poverty and civil rights within the United States.

Johnson was so enthusiastic about putting reactors in the desert that he began to promise more than scientists and engineers could deliver. Donald Hornig, chief scientific advisor and head of the President's Science Advisory Committee (PSAC), tried to tone down the promises but without success. Hornig knew Weinberg well and was familiar the AEC's enthusiasm for finding viable and creative applications of atomic energy, and he knew that Interior Secretary Udall had high hopes for nuclear power. But he also knew that the technology was still just science fiction. The United States itself had never built such large-scale facilities to take salt out of water, even at home. There was no existing program ready to export to Israel. The largest desalination plants the Americans had built thus far could produce a little more than a million gallons of water per day. That may seem like a lot, but the feasibility study that led to such sanguine views about nuclear desalting required facilities capable of producing 500 million gallons per day.

In hindsight it is perhaps tempting to think of Johnson as foolish in over-promising. But his predecessor had embraced the challenge of putting a man on the moon "before this decade is out," despite immense technical obstacles. Indeed, Kennedy also had made a virtually identical (but far less remembered) challenge to build dual-use nuclear and desalting facilities.[38] A similar approach to miracle technologies in arid lands seemed appropriate to Johnson, and the potential foreign policy dividends seemed to justify the expense. To Hornig, Johnson did not exactly offer a blank check, but it was not far from that. The existing annual budget at the Department of Interior's Office of Saline Water was about $10 million, which appalled the president. He told Hornig that $50 million or $100 million were not out of the question and that the project was, according to Hornig's note for the record, "just as important as space." Johnson had already made the speeches, built up expectations, and would need to create a bold and imaginative program to match it.[39]

In theory, the project had the potential to remove a potential cause for war in the Middle East, namely, access to freshwater sources around Israel. The most significant source was the Jordan River, which flowed through Lake Tiberias (also known as the Sea of Galilee). These were sources of water for Israel, Syria, and Jordan. In the 1950s, the United States tried to broker a deal between the Arab states and Israel about how much freshwater each could take from these sources, but no formal agreement had been reached.[40] Israel began to improve its infrastructure in the early 1960s, in order to take more freshwater from Lake Tiberias. Although the Israeli government did not state that it intended to draw substantially more water than before, its new National Water Conduit would have the capability to divert far more on an annual basis, cutting deeply into the informal allocations to other states. By late 1963, American policy analysts were advising the secretary of state that conflict over the Jordan Waters, long foreseen as the issue most likely to precipitate an Arab-Israeli war, was only going to intensify and "the strains will be great at best."[41] The source of the river water was in Syrian territory, at Mount Hermon, and the governments of Jordan and Syria in 1964 started their own infrastructure redesign, which included the possibility of redirecting the water before Israel would have a chance to use it.[42]

In July 1965, Americans and Israelis convened in Philadelphia at the offices of the Catalytic Construction company to consider practical details of a technological fix to the Jordan River problem. The Americans were drawn from government agencies, and among the Israelis were nuclear scientist Shimon Yiftah, director of Israel's Atomic Energy Commission; Chaim Cats, chief of Israel's electric power company; and Zvi Zur, general manager of Mekorot, the national water company. In efforts to reassure observers of Israel's peaceful intentions, Yiftah had publicly insisted for years that Israel's nuclear reactor site at Dimona would be completed without a facility for separating plutonium.[43] Zur until recently had been chief of staff of Israel's military forces and was uniquely positioned to appreciate the nexus between conventional arms, water security, and nuclear reactors.[44] The construction of nuclear reactors connected to a visible economic (rather than military) purpose no doubt appealed to officials hoping to proceed with a robust nuclear program that kept its weapon option open. It is now known that Israel had a clandestine project to build a chemical separation plant for plutonium production, so any new reactors would be a potential contributor to bomb fuel.[45]

Although there was a legitimate concern over water security, all of those involved were much more interested in seeing a successful implementation of nuclear technology than finding the best means of desalting water. The Israelis consistently rebuffed suggestions that desalination might move forward using non-nuclear fuels. During a discussion about the promising future of using light water reactors to power desalination at 100 million gallons of water per day, Zur, Yiftah, and the other Israelis present argued that any other kind of fuel besides nuclear should henceforth be eliminated from consideration. The Americans, equally glad to see the project proceed as a nuclear one, agreed. Phase II of the project originally was to include "comparison of the economics of the favored alternative nuclear plant with those of a fossil-fueled dual-purpose plant of comparable capacity." After the July 1965 meeting with the Israelis, however, this part of the plan was deleted. The goal would be to produce water, certainly, but it would be a nuclear project.[46]

The Israelis wanted to move quickly beyond feasibility studies—much faster than the Americans imagined. They insisted that even preliminary reports be written in sufficient detail to meet World Bank and Export-Import Bank requirements for securing loans. They did not quibble about designs or worry about making the facilities economically self-sufficient; the only major qualms they had about the engineering plans had to do with sabotage and wartime vulnerability. For example, they favored one particular design based on vapor suppression primarily because of its smaller physical size, which if made of concrete would give the greatest protection from an external bomb blast.[47] They worried that the economics of scale—which the Americans focused on—would mean building enormous targets for enemies to bomb.

Despite plenty of reasons for skepticism, the plan to put reactors in Israel under the banner of water security became a major initiative of the Johnson administration. Myer Feldman, a high-profile attorney who advised presidents Kennedy and Johnson on numerous matters involving Israel, advised incorporating desalination into the president's Great Society program and framing it as something to offer other countries too, such as Egypt and Mexico.[48] Shortly after that, in an effort to bring some concerted thought to the issue, an inter-agency committee of the State Department, Atomic Energy Commission, and others began meeting regularly to lay out practical plans. To emphasize the peaceful aspects of atomic energy, the United States instigated an exchange of technical reports with the Soviet Union and offered to host the first international symposium on desalination in Washington, DC, in October 1965. There, one could lay out the extent of the actual water crisis at hand and show how nuclear technology might solve it.

Desalination had momentum, but whether it could become reality remained unclear. "It seems that desalting has a mystique of its own," presidential advisor Charles Johnson mused, noting the mounting pressure to announce a "a foreign aid 'spectacular'" to bring nuclear-powered desalination to reality in arid lands.[49] Desalination plants would have to be heavily subsidized wherever they were built. Science advisor Don Hornig believed the project might become a "white elephant"—huge, unwieldy, and unprofitable. Worse, the presence of the reactors—and perceptions of favoritism toward Israel—might inflame Arab-Israeli tensions rather than contribute to peace.[50]

Carried along by the enthusiasm of Chairman Glenn Seaborg of the AEC and Interior Secretary Stewart Udall, Johnson announced a major initiative at the 1965 symposium. It was an opportunity he could not miss, with over 2,500 registrants from sixty-five nations and six international organizations. He invited the official delegates to the East Room of the White House on October 7, 1965, and unveiled his plan for a new effort to find solutions to man's water problems. That is when it took on the name "Water for Peace." He promised to ask Congress to approve construction of prototype plants. He also announced the creation of a special international fund to help and offered several commitments to international ventures, including sending scientists abroad and increasing funding resources for scientific research. "Let future generations remember us," he stated to his White House guests, "as those who freed man forever from his most ancient and dreaded enemies—drought and famine."[51]

Desalting with nuclear power would have necessitated a "crash" program like the one under way to put a man on the moon. Some of the most ambitious ideas were based on massive terrestrial transformations. Coastal deserts accounted for about 20,000 miles of the earth, and since they offered easy ocean transportation, they seemed to have enormous potential—if only the saltwater could be turned fresh. Hot deserts on the shores of the Red Sea, the Persian Gulf, the Gulf of California, and great stretches of Australia, along with moderate and cool deserts in the Mediterranean Sahara and the west coast of South America, might all yield bountiful harvests and become homes for millions of people—with a little faith and imagination. Caught up in the enthusiasm, American geographer Peveril Meigs went so far as to suggest setting aside some of the desert as national parks or wildlife preserves because doing so would be cheaper while the lands were waterless.[52]

Nuclear boosters reveled in the president's rhetoric, because it positioned atomic energy as the ultimate technological fix to a huge social challenge. Indeed the term "technological fix" is typically associated with Alvin Weinberg, director of the Oak Ridge National Laboratory, who in 1966 challenged readers of the *Bulletin of the Atomic Scientists* to consider whether complex social problems could be circumvented by reducing them to technological ones.[53] Social change was difficult to accomplish, he admitted. "One must persuade many people from having fewer babies, or to drive more carefully, or to refrain from disliking Negroes." Similarly, equitable water use was too difficult to solve by asking individuals or nations to behave responsibly. Rather than ask people to change their behaviors, he recommended using technology to make problems go away. Weinberg specifically identified nuclear desalination as a leading example. "I have little doubt that within the next ten to twenty years we shall see huge dual-purpose desalting plants springing up on many parched sea coasts of the world." It took a visionary engineer to solve such problems, he wrote, or at least to buy some time, that "precious commodity that converts violent social revolution into acceptable social evolution."[54]

With such a broad commitment, Israel saw the United States as a key partner in developing its nuclear program, either by providing reactors or helping to finance them. In late 1965, Israeli nuclear engineer Joseph Adar visited Oak Ridge to discuss reactor designs. What really concerned him was whether an American reactor could sustain a bombing attack. The experts at Oak Ridge could not reassure him on that score. Although the Americans had several creative ideas for siting the plant away from population centers, such as building an artificial island offshore, or even a "deep water caisson containing the entire plant and a floating station," these simply carried the project further into the realm of science fiction. Adar reminded the Americans that it was not a hypothetical problem. Given the hostility of Israel's neighbors, nuclear reactors might very well be bombed. The Arabs might think there were nuclear weapons or fuel being produced by them.[55]

Arab states were not the only ones concerned about an Israeli bomb. The Americans were too, but they were torn on whether to tether Water for Peace to any non-proliferation agreement. Myer Feldman saw the program as part and parcel of the Great Society, not as a carrot for agreeing to site inspections. Similarly, former presidential science advisor Jerome Wiesner wrote to the president that pulling unlimited amounts of fresh water from the sea had "the aura of a scientific miracle and in your hands, could bring about a political miracle." He was convinced that the earlier announcement of a US-Israel project had played an enormous role in relieving the crisis over the Jordan waters. Yet he also saw some benefit in using it as leverage: why not promise nuclear desalination for both Egypt and Israel in return for a promise not to undertake nuclear weapons development?[56] Others were skeptical, including presidential advisor Robert Komer, who derided the "glorious scheme" to use nuclear desalination as "sweeteners" for arms reduction. He called it "a long shot." Israel would never accept IAEA inspectors, he stated. "The Israelis already allow us to secretly police Dimona, anyway." Besides, it seemed unwise to single out Israel. The idea of supplying Gamal Nasser with a reactor in Egypt in return for not developing a weapon, when he had no existing nuclear capability, struck Komer as illogical.[57]

A formal tie between Water for Peace and nuclear safeguards would have stalled the program—and in 1966, when Johnson was repeatedly promising to make deserts bloom, this seemed unacceptable to him. In mid-1965, the president had asked Israeli prime minister Levi Eshkol to agree to IAEA safeguards, but Eshkol did not reply. It seemed unlikely that Israel would give up its nuclear option. A number of advisors, including Hornig and Special Assistant to the President Walt Rostow, pointed out that offering reactors to Israel, and possibly Egypt, put the United States in a tricky position. "If they could get away with it, we would have enhanced the potential of each to build nuclear weapons without establishing compensating controls," Rostow wrote the president. "From the viewpoint of preventing nuclear proliferation, it might be better to have no new nuclear reactors in the Middle East and to look more closely at desalting with non-nuclear fuels, especially if nuclear desalting shows no clear-cut economic advantage."[58] Although some, like Wiesner and Secretary of State Rusk, thought there might be merit in using desalting as a "carrot" for disarmament in the region, nothing of the kind was being attempted seriously. Some of Johnson's advisors characterized the debate as the "desalters" versus the "disarmers." Enthusiastic "desalters" were the AEC and the Department of Interior, where Seaborg and Udall both championed nuclear power's potential to resolve issues ranging from energy use to food production and water security. Others, notably the State Department, wished to avoid moving forward without explicitly linking them with a major US objective like getting the Israelis to agree to foreswear nuclear weapons and agree to IAEA inspectors.[59]

In practice, President Johnson made no progress on proliferation and he continued to negotiate conventional weapons agreements along with "Water for Peace," touting it as a crucial piece of Israel's water security vis-à-vis its hostile neighbors. He wrote personal notes, in vain, inviting the Israeli prime minister to accept IAEA safeguards. He then spoke of the era of peace that desalination would bring while he was also agreeing to sell American warplanes, the A-4 Skyhawk, produced by Douglas Aircraft. Discussions with the Israeli ambassador in mid-1966 moved back and forth between Israel's desire for nuclear desalting and its need for napalm bombs, anti-tank cluster bombs, and Sidewinder missiles. Surrounded by hostile neighbors possessing Soviet-supplied MiG fighter jets, Israel lobbied the United States for the best military equipment it could get, including the Hawk surface-to-air missile system. The United States was trying to build up nuclear infrastructure in what was shaping up to be a war zone.[60]

Border clashes in 1967 reinforced this perception, and that year the United States lost its illusions about whether Israel intended to maintain its option to build a nuclear weapon. Although visits to the Dimona site had not uncovered evidence of a weapons program, other indicators told a different tale. One was an intelligence report that Israel had acquired a chemical separation plant, thus giving it the ability to salvage plutonium from spent fuel of any nuclear reactor. Another more troubling red flag was that the Israelis were unwilling to explain to the Americans what had happened to the 80 to 100 tons of unsafeguarded uranium they had bought from Argentina a few years earlier.[61]

Amid such uncertainties in 1967, "Water for Peace" continued its forward momentum, with advocates on all sides pinning expectations on its nuclear component. The president appointed a special envoy, Ellsworth Bunker, ambassador to the Organization of American States.[62] The State Department coached him to strike a deal with Israel that made the acceptance of IAEA safeguards on all reactors, including Dimona, the price for getting nuclear reactors for desalination.[63] Others, notably the AEC and Department of Interior, were simply eager to see Israel choose American designs and commit to large facilities, addressing water conservation and the peaceful atom. They knew the economics made no sense—but neither did the economics of the space program or any of the Great Society programs, for that matter. To those who foresaw "white elephants" emerging from nuclear-powered desalination, Rostow retorted with a note of optimism. "I keep remembering," he observed to the president, "that we would not have built the transcontinental railway on a conventional cost/benefit basis."[64]

Optimism about Water for Peace reached its height in May 1967 during yet another international conference. Johnson spoke of his desire to "share the fruits of this technology" among all the countries of the world. One presenter, R. Philip Hammond, boldly estimated that food could be grown with water costing a mere 3 cents per day per person. In addition to reshaping nature, all of society would have to be rethought. People in developing countries, powered by nuclear reactors, could produce food in "agro-industrial complexes" rather than farms, with agriculture converted into a factory operation, making it more efficient and economical. Weinberg was intrigued and immediately set his staff to work evaluating this proposal. It fit his vision of the technological fix. "The idea of producing food in underdeveloped countries in 'food factories' rather than on farms seems very appealing to me," he wrote to Rockefeller Foundation official J. George Harrar. "For if agriculture can be converted into an industrial operation in which a few experts make the primary decisions, and the workers carry out carefully specified tasks, one in principle avoids the problem of convincing countless peasants to change their individual farming methods."[65]

Amid such optimism about technological solutions, war broke out between Israel and its neighbors. As the conference wrapped up, Jordan and Egypt were signing a defense pact, and both countries began shoring up military forces. On June 5, Israel, aware of these preparations, launched a surprise attack on Egyptian air bases in the Sinai Peninsula, and the conflict soon widened to include Jordan and Syria. In a matter of days, Israeli ground forces changed the map of the region dramatically, occupying the Sinai Peninsula and the Gaza Strip (previously held by Egypt), the West Bank, including eastern Jerusalem (previously held by Jordan), and the Golan Heights (previously held by Syria). That conflict, known as the Six Day War, not only reinforced the potential for outbreaks of extreme violence in the area but also set the stage for even deeper grievances between Israelis and their neighbors, and between the Israeli government and the Palestinians living in occupied territories.

The links between the Six Day War and water security could not be ignored. The director-general of Mekorot, Israel's national water company, had been Zvi Zur, former chief of staff of the Israel Defense Force. Zur had been a crucial figure in negotiations with the Americans about nuclear desalination. With President Johnson's Water for Peace conference approaching in May 1967, Zur left Mokorot at the request of Israel's new minister of defense, Moshe Dayan, to become an advisor on such issues as natural resources, scientific development, and the production of arms.[66] Within weeks, Israel was at war. Crucial areas targeted for occupation by Israel were sources of potable water. Once occupied, the territories would prove difficult to give up. To the south of Lake Tiberias, Jordan's forces retreated to the eastern bank of the Jordan river, leaving the entire region known as the West Bank to Israel. In addition to extending Israel's border to the river, this retreat gave Israel the West Bank's extensive freshwater aquifer. East of Lake Tiberias and along the river to the north was the Golan Heights, previously part of Syria, which stretched into the foothills of

Mount Hermon and the river's source. Occupying the West Bank and Golan Heights thus secured more of the river, brought Israeli territory closer to its source, and put all of Lake Tiberias farther behind Israel's borders.

In the aftermath of the Six Day War, the future of nuclear reactors in Israel seemed uncertain. Given widespread suspicions about an Israeli bomb program, the war heightened the urgency of ongoing negotiations regarding a global non-proliferation agreement, and this opened for signatures just a year later in the summer of 1968. The text of the treaty was liberal in its discussion of peaceful applications, stating in no uncertain terms that each state had "the inalienable right" to do research and production on atomic energy for peaceful purposes. It even required existing nuclear states to contribute to such development, "with due consideration for the needs of the developing areas of the world."[67] Israel, however, refused to sign. It would remain outside the non-proliferation regime throughout the twentieth century and beyond. Other non-signers in the early years of the treaty included France and Argentina (both of which were helping Israel's program with equipment, training, or fuel), South Africa, and India and Pakistan.

Perhaps surprisingly, the Six Day War did not lay to rest discussions about ramping up Israel's nuclear program under the banner of "Water for Peace." AEC chairman Glenn Seaborg was undeterred by the violence on every side of Israel. He felt that Israel might be willing to put its entire nuclear program under safeguards in return for reactors. He wrote to the secretary of state, "It seems to me that the recent events may well intensify the problem of water allocation in the area rather than ease it."[68]

A couple of weeks after the Six Day War, former president Dwight Eisenhower met with Johnson and emphasized his view that the water problem in the Middle East had to be solved before any of the other outstanding issues could be addressed. Eisenhower had his own nuclear cheerleader, former AEC chairman Lewis Strauss, who was feeding him ideas just as ambitious as those yet offered under Water for Peace. Strauss had diplomatic leverage in mind too and wanted to set up a corporation owning the reactors, with the United States owning 51 percent of the stock. One potential investor, Edmond de Rothschild, proposed building nuclear desalting facilities for Israel and Jordan, and another in the Gaza Strip, with the ostensible aim of assisting the livelihoods of hundreds of thousands of refugees looking for land and water.[69] The new project promised an unprecedented amount of political control over any country setting up the reactors.

Johnson's project had been ambitious enough and far beyond what had been technically feasible. Eisenhower was suggesting facilities ten times as big, to be put into the most contested areas of the recent Arab-Israeli conflict. The ideas put forth by Strauss and Eisenhower were similar to those of R. Philip Hammond and Alvin Weinberg. They embraced the idea of creating agricultural factories, with intensive, highly managed farming. Trying to predict the future, they believed that such intensive management would optimize water use, dramatically reducing the amount needed. For example, instead of the US average of 4,000 gallons of water per day to feed one person, "one could get by on 200 gallons/day."[70]

As a former "Atoms for Peace" booster, Lewis Strauss had no trouble imagining a nuclear technological fix to the region's fundamental problems, namely, water and displaced people. "By a simple, bold, and imaginative step," he proclaimed confidently in a memorandum to Eisenhower, "it is in our power to solve both problems." Three new, gigantic facilities could produce cheap electricity to attract industry and fresh water, "opening to settlement many hundred square miles which heretofore have never supported human life," mooting the controversy over the Jordan River waters. Strauss envisioned massive construction projects that would employ thousands of refugees building plants, laying pipelines, constructing an electricity grid, and digging irrigation ditches and reservoirs. When finished, those workers "could be settled in irrigated areas under conditions far superior to any life that they have ever experienced." All of this would be achieved, Strauss observed, for "substantially less than one year's expenditure on the moon program." He urged Eisenhower to take the plan to President Johnson so that he could "electrify the world by such a proposal," much as Eisenhower's famous atomic energy speech had done. Strauss predicted that it would be hailed by millions and that it "might well be the beginning of a new life in the lands of the oldest civilizations."[71]

In the wake of war in the Middle East, American nuclear boosters were locked in a battle over whose vision was more inspired, more ambitious, and more dramatic. *New York Times* columnist C. L. Sulzberger wrote about Strauss's plan in three installments in July 1967, calling it at various turns bold, imaginative, and visionary, always implying that the idea was brand new, sponsored by Eisenhower, "our Number One elder statesman," and handed over for consideration to the administration. He wrote, "The general's face lights up when he discusses the project he now advocates."[72] Sulzberger made no mention of Water for Peace but did say that the Eisenhower proposal dwarfed previous ideas. Readers of the *New York Times* might have gotten the impression that nuclear desalination was not part of the Great Society, but a new Republican technological fix. Subsequent coverage called it a "Republican peacemaking initiative for the Middle East" and noted that President Johnson gave it only "lukewarm endorsement." That apparent sluggishness led Republican Senator Howard Baker Jr. to sponsor a resolution calling for the prompt design and construction of nuclear-powered desalting plants in the region not only for economic reasons but also as a pathway to peace. It passed unanimously in December 1967.[73]

On the surface, there appeared to be a relative degree of political unity on desalination in the Middle East. Eisenhower wrote to Johnson that his support was disinterested and non-partisan, and Johnson wrote back in a similar spirit, saying, "I know we have both long felt in our bones" that achieving cost-effective desalination for irrigation might become "a great constructive turning point in human history" and even a basis for lasting peace in the Middle East. But beyond such platitudes, Johnson and his advisors sensed that they had lost the initiative, and worse—they had done so while heading into an election year. The crisis in the Middle East, combined with nuclear-powered desalination, became a political opportunity for the Republicans trying to take shots at the Democrat in the White House. Interior Secretary Udall complained to Johnson, "At this point the Republicans have—through the Strauss-Eisenhower effort—'stolen our clothes' as far as the water issue in the Middle East is concerned." Strauss's plan seemed bold and imaginative, despite the fact that the Johnson administration planned to spend more on desalination in one year than Eisenhower had during his total eight years in office.[74]

With such political momentum, especially after the Baker resolution passed, the scientists and engineers at Oak Ridge thought their moment had come. The new Israeli ambassador to the United States (and future prime minister), Yitzhak Rabin, was amazed that so many scientists genuinely believed that the project might contribute to peace. Rabin had distinguished himself as chief of staff of the Israel Defense Forces during the Six Day War and earned himself one of the most prestigious ambassadorial posts. He was tasked with talking to Weinberg, a techno-fixer who had the gumption to tell him how to make peace. Years later, Weinberg recalled the encounter vividly. "I remember very clearly talking with Rabin about the whole idea, and Rabin shook his head and said how can you guys five thousand miles away from Israel in a little town in the hills of Tennessee cook up schemes for solving the problems in the Middle East? And I said, well is that any crazier than Herzl sitting in a café in Vienna?"[75] He was referring to nineteenth-century Austrian Zionist Theodor Herzl, the purported spiritual father of the state of Israel.

Alvin Weinberg was wrong to think political momentum was on his side. The president's own enthusiasm for nuclear desalination evaporated when Washington insiders began referring to it as the Eisenhower-Strauss Plan.

No one seemed to associate it with the Great Society at all. Because those plans were based on the enthusiasm of scientists such as Weinberg, the administration increasingly perceived them in political terms. As Rostow described Weinberg's ideas to the president: "We don't quarrel with its vision and hope, but it is naïve on two serious counts," namely, that nuclear desalting was not the most practical and economic way to bring water to the area, and that fresh water itself could not bring permanent peace to the Middle East. Rostow had turned a corner in his own thinking and was skeptical of nuclear boosters at the Atomic Energy Commission. The same man who had compared Water for Peace to building the transcontinental railway sputtered that the "AEC has a way of going wild with its ideas and getting nuclear desalting out of economic perspective."[76]

The lynchpin of the Water for Peace program had always been the president himself, and he became alienated from it. Arguments for the project's symbolic value no longer held sway—especially after he announced on March 31, 1968, that he would not run again for president amid the worsening situation in the Vietnam War. The idea of nuclear desalination did not go away, but it no longer had any urgency from the White House. The president appointed George D. Woods, former president of the World Bank, to take over the role Ellsworth Bunker had played in negotiating with Israel. With no clear marching orders from the president to turn it into a Great Society piece, Woods made short work of the problem, saying that an economically justifiable dual-purpose project was almost certainly impossible. Although he thought the Israeli project should continue on a small scale, he dismissed the notion that desalting projects were good business opportunities. He proposed a much smaller venture with Israel—40 million gallons of water per day rather than 100–150—and wanted to move forward without necessarily coupling desalination with nuclear reactors.[77]

For advocates of atomic energy, this recommendation to make nuclear reactors optional was the worst possible outcome. Given that so much of the impetus for the whole program came from atomic energy boosters, Chairman Seaborg of the AEC predicted that the whole program would fall apart without reactors. Proceeding without requiring them seemed to throw the proverbial baby out with the bathwater—after all, the beauty of the scheme was that it was a nuclear one, leveraging American technological know-how for prestige, and possibly using desalination to convince Israel to put its reactors under IAEA safeguards. The promise of nuclear energy was inextricably tied to American security goals and the president's political prestige. Providing potable water was never the primary goal. As Johnson left the presidency, he had lost all enthusiasm for the project.[78]

Having left the door open to decoupling the desalting project from the nuclear one, Johnson left the next president, Richard Nixon, with a weird project that had no significant government boosters. Seaborg was correct that what animated the whole project in the first place was its imaginative approach—taking a nuclear reactor and using it to make deserts bloom. Nixon himself had strongly supported the Strauss-Eisenhower idea during the election, but swiftly buried the project once in office. Key officials from various agencies met and, despite a great deal of study, could not figure out what the genuine payoff would be. Nixon's national security advisor, Henry Kissinger, suggested that they might simply do nothing, unless suddenly the Israelis seemed to want it badly enough to make it a high priority.[79] Nixon had no Great Society to create, and Kissinger could not see what advantage such programs offered to American interests.

And yet changes were under way, as the United States had clearly broken free of its earlier taboo against encouraging nuclear reactors for electricity generation in other countries. By the early 1970s it was actively encouraging them, with some political advisors hoping it would convince other countries to sign the non-proliferation agreement. Both India and Israel had robust electricity goals while keeping their bomb options open. American politicians tried in vain to leverage civilian atomic energy to rein in these bomb programs. With Israel, the Americans waded deeply into muddy waters that blended peaceful atomic energy, nuclear weapons, conventional arms deals, and actual bloody conflict. That precedent would be repeated in ensuing years, in other countries. Nuclear technology was proffered as the solution to the environmental crisis, and even as a means of preventing war. Though enthusiasm for "Water for Peace" disappeared with Lyndon Johnson's presidency, the cornucopian rhetoric surrounding nuclear reactors would prove diplomatically useful for decades to come.

CHAPTER 7
Nuclear Mosques and Monuments

The summer of 1974 was a season of angry Canadians, and Indian foreign secretary Kewal Singh felt its full force on a diplomatic visit to Ottawa in July. Newspapers abused him and Canadian officials berated him for what they saw as a betrayal of trust and a threat to world peace. From one Commonwealth nation to another, the conversations had the air of a sibling rivalry. For years, Canada and others had provided food aid and technical assistance to India, and Canada in particular had helped with nuclear reactors for electricity generation. In the past half-decade, the IAEA had upheld India as the symbol of atomic energy in the developing world, with its mutation plant breeding program. But India had done the unthinkable—and to some, unforgivable—by detonating an atomic explosive. Singh and other Indian officials insisted it was a peaceful one, like the ones promoted by the US Atomic Energy Commission. It was dubbed the Smiling Buddha, but the Canadians were not amused. For Singh, it was an exhausting visit to Canada, during which he had been treated to hostile criticism, threats to halt assistance, and embittered lectures about his nation's world responsibilities.[1]

When the visit ended, Singh and his diplomatic entourage went on to Washington for some frank discussions at the US State Department. There he met with Henry Kissinger, who was having a bad summer, as President Richard Nixon was embroiled in controversy about illegal conduct in the Watergate scandal. Over the previous week, the US House of Representatives had adopted three articles of impeachment against Nixon, creating an aura of intense stress and tumult in Washington (Kissinger, ever the diplomat, simply referred to it as an "unsettled situation" to Singh;

the president resigned a week later). If this were not enough to make diplomatic conversations a challenge, Kissinger was suffering from a painful in-grown toenail, only recently cut by a doctor. When Singh met with Kissinger on August 2, the secretary of state sat with his foot up on the table. Singh, who had been treated as an uppity stepchild by the Canadians in Ottawa, had to view Kissinger's foot as the two men discussed India's new place in the world.

"I don't believe in recriminations about past events," Kissinger stated to Singh, according to an official memorandum of conversation. "But I have wondered about the following. Intellectually, a peaceful nuclear explosion has a different meaning and significance for a developing country than it has for an advanced country." It is difficult to imagine a more candid statement of Kissinger's view of India's place, or a more explicit acknowledgment of the double standard in Kissinger's mind about nuclear technologies. Singh's noncommittal answer is recorded as simply "Yes?" Kissinger then softened his statement, saying he meant only that advanced countries could control explosions with precision, whereas developing countries could not.[2] He could not muster a stronger condemnation.

The test of the Smiling Buddha is typically seen as a fulcrum point in nuclear affairs, with the world growing more skeptical of the connections between economic uplift and nuclear programs in poor countries. A day after India's nuclear test, the *New York Times* ran an article called "India, Uninvited, Joins the Nuclear Club," quoting one US government official complaining, "I don't see how this is going to grow more rice."[3] North Americans and Europeans helped countries in central and South Asia to create robust nuclear programs. By the mid-1970s, the United States and its allies' abilities to direct the choice of technology was clearly on the wane. Though numerous countries had signed the 1968 Treaty on Non-Proliferation of Nuclear Weapons (NPT), Indian rejected it explicitly because of its perceived neocolonial character. Clearly, at least some countries saw the control of the entire fuel cycle, and all technologies, as markers of power, legitimacy, and sovereignty. Other countries aided by Westerners, such as Pakistan and Iran, held similar views, even when (in the case of Iran) embracing the treaty.[4]

Perhaps surprisingly, Smiling Buddha did not signal the end of cornucopian rhetoric surrounding nuclear development. Another event had occurred in 1973 that drew nuclear energy deep into very real struggles over the world's natural resources. The Yom Kippur War, a major clash between Israel and its neighbors Egypt and Syria, just six years after the Six Day War, led to a global economic standoff. The United States extended military aid to Israel, prompting retaliation by the region's members of the

Organization of Petroleum Exporting Countries (OPEC). First they raised oil prices, then announced steep cuts in production, limiting the availability of petroleum worldwide. Then the Arab members embargoed certain consumers, including the United States, Britain, Canada, Japan, and the Netherlands. For the time being, the United States found itself relatively poor in oil resources, while Europeans no longer held the colonial stranglehold they once enjoyed. To the contrary, they found themselves at the mercy of countries they still considered "backward."

How could the North Americans and Europeans reassert leverage over such purportedly backward peoples? What direct leverage they still had appeared to be in the very technologies that represented power, might, and independence—not the vague promises of technical assistance programs but direct aid in advanced equipment such as fighter planes, tanks, and missiles. As one US embassy official in Iran noted in 1973, "The latest supersonic jet fighters and most advanced military technology function as the mosques and monuments of past Persian dynasties. They are the marvels that are intended to dazzle Iran's neighbors with the power and prestige of the Pahlavi line."[5] Nuclear reactors, too, would prove to be prestige-building enterprises in India and Pakistan, and in some countries—notably Iran—they would be wielded as leverage in the energy crisis, to overturn the natural resources advantage held by OPEC.

***

In the 1950s and much of the 1960s, the Americans and British treated nuclear collaboration as a kind of colonial science, with specific outcomes oriented toward subsistence, especially in food and agriculture. They even worked through old colonial networks. As with the Asian Nuclear Center, the United States operated through the Colombo Plan countries (all former British colonies) but put the center in the Philippines, only recently granted independence by the United States. The British carved out a sphere of influence in central Asia, in an area of great strategic interest due to its wealth in petroleum. Unlike the American "Atoms for Peace" initiative, the British operated explicitly within a security framework, the Central Treaty Organization (CENTO), also known as the Baghdad Pact. Established in 1955 to bind nations along the USSR's southwestern flank, it put the United Kingdom into alliance with Iraq, Iran, Pakistan, and Turkey. It also became a site for collaboration in a regional nuclear center beginning in 1956. The UK Atomic Energy Research Establishment at Harwell sent scientists to staff the center, which took over a building initially designed for research on dates. Harwell's director, Sir John Cockcroft, wrote in *Nature* that the focus of the center would be on the use of radioisotopes in medicine, agriculture, water conservation, and petroleum extraction.[6]

As with the Americans and the Philippines, the British had chosen an ally—Iraq—they believed they could manipulate with ease. Shortly after the center opened, Britain was forced to recalibrate, however. It had occupied Iraq during World War II and its young King Faisal II was perceived as pliable. Indeed Faisal had even supported Britain's occupation of the Suez Canal in 1956, turning his back on Egypt's leader Gamal Nasser. It would prove a fateful decision, as Nasser was not just the ruler of Egypt but also the figurehead of a pan-Arab movement that argued for unity among Arab peoples against imperial powers. Nasser's ideas were in spirit very similar to, and served as an inspiration for, the pan-Africanism of Kwame Nkrumah. The Iraqi king's support of Britain, and even participation in the Baghdad Pact, provided justifications for the violent military coup that overthrew the monarchy in 1958. Faisal formally opened the nuclear center in March 1957, but just over a year later he was murdered in the coup.[7]

The British government rebooted the CENTO center in 1959 as the Institute of Nuclear Science, based in neighboring Iran, at Tehran University. Sir John Cockcroft again made a speech about the role of nuclear science aiding the development of the region. This time it was Mohammad Reza Pahlavi, Iran's shah, who presided over the opening ceremonies, with diplomats and dignitaries from the remaining CENTO countries in attendance.[8]

The institute in Tehran operated much like a colonial base. Indeed one scientist wrote that it was hard to shake the impression that it was an "outpost of Harwell."[9] Not only did its directors come from there, but all the staff from participating countries had to travel to England to take six-month training courses on the use of radioisotopes. Harwell's own director, Cockcroft, chaired the Tehran institute's advisory council.[10] The British organized symposia and visits by notable scientists and other celebrities, including one visit by mystery writer Agatha Christie. Although Cockcroft and others paid lip service to handing over the work to local scientists, in reality they hesitated, believing the Iranians were not yet ready to take the reins.[11]

The institute itself had no core scientific questions or major projects, and by 1961, it had become a hodge-podge of research whose "community" was based on British experts explaining how to use radioisotopes.[12] The British abandoned the pretense of collaboration and reoriented their efforts toward more familiar relationships, using the institute as a hub for British officials to provide advice on various national projects for economic development. In one proposed example, scientists from the institute would give advice to colleagues at Pakistan's Forest Products Laboratory on the use of isotopes to trace the penetration of preservative into wood. In another, they would advise on the use of isotopes to mark wasps, in an existing insect control project operated by the World Health Organization in Isfahan, Iran.[13]

Harwell scientists adopted a paternalistic attitude that confined most of the institute's work to traditional colonial projects focusing on natural resources, agriculture, and health. They realized that many in these countries dreamed of nuclear energy, but they viewed the possibility with scorn. One noted that "in practice the regional countries are barely capable of formulating for themselves a clear picture of their needs or even of their wants." While acknowledging that their own attitudes seemed a bit "high and mighty," the British managers of the institute believed that Pakistan, Iran, and Turkey "required fairly positive guidance in their own best interests."[14]

British observers wrote with some irony about racial dimensions of the Tehran center. Just as Asians had scoffed at the American plan to have them train with Filipinos, here too the Turks and Pakistanis had little interest in learning anything in an institute run by Iranians. After a discussion with Mehmet Batur, a major figure in Turkey's Atomic Energy Authority, one British scientist received the impression that "no Turk could be induced to go to Tehran except at bayonet-point." Educated Turks wanted to look West, not East.[15] British diplomat Angus Rae put it in terms of who were the "wogs" in the relationship, using an ethnic slur to describe non-white people. The Turks did not think of themselves as such. Rae observed that for Turks, "wogs begin at the Caucasus."[16]

Pakistani scientists and politicians also wanted more robust efforts for their budding nuclear program and wanted to move beyond radioisotopes in agriculture and medicine. They embraced collaboration with the United States in the 1950s under the rubric of "Atoms for Peace," acquiring their own research reactor and beginning a major training program, with a view toward a future of nuclear power.[17] Pakistan had several excellent scientists, including the Cambridge-trained theoretical physicist Abdus Salam, whose work on electroweak theory would later earn him the Nobel Prize in physics. Sensitive to the continued colonial attitudes even post-independence, Salam argued in favor of an international center for theoretical physics sponsored by the United Nations Educational, Scientific, and Cultural Organization (UNESCO), and away from the direct control of the United States and United Kingdom.[18] Another was physicist Munir Ahmad Khan, who had trained in the United States and joined the IAEA's Reactor Division, where he was in a position to influence IAEA reports and statements about the role of atomic energy in the developing world. Ishrat Hussain Usmani, who completed his PhD under Nobel Laureate Patrick Blackett at Imperial College, London, traveled to the United States to work for a few years at Oak Ridge National Laboratory, and then served with Cockcroft on the CENTO institute's scientific council. Usmani became chairman of the Pakistan Atomic Energy Commission in 1960 and started a manpower recruitment program, putting about fifty of the most promising university students through a nuclear training course in Pakistan before sending them abroad to get their PhDs or postdoctoral training.[19]

As with its neighbor and rival India, Pakistan was busy pairing nuclear science and technology with its self-image as a newly independent nation. Pakistan's reasons for doing so were complicated and should not simply be reduced to functionalist explanations about the desire to have atomic bombs—though ultimately both nations pursued that course. Nuclear technologies seemed spectacular, and they lent legitimacy to the governments who flaunted them. The words "atomic" and "nuclear" had great appeal not only because they seemed like the most modern technologies available, but also for their symbolic value as the technologies possessed only by the world's major nations, including the former colonial master, Britain. Moreover, as daunting as nuclear reactor development might appear, it was less so than resolving the massive and recurrent problems related to poverty and population.[20]

By the early 1960s, a kind of nuclear nationalism was under way in South Asia. Becoming an "atomic state" was freighted with meaning for the new nations and was an essential part of state-building for India and Pakistan after independence. Homi Bhabha, chairman of India's Atomic Energy Commission at its creation in 1954, envisioned a complex of laboratories, reactors, and facilities at a site in Trombay that would help India achieve its goals and also be a spectacle itself, the "Versailles of the scientific world." India even tried to emphasize a Gandhi-like artisanal aspect of its nuclear program by photographing poor workers at the site of CIRUS, its research reactor, highlighting how much of it was made from hand labor. Pakistan took a different tack, drawing on the grandeur of Islam's pre-colonial past, constructing a nuclear institute with architectural features hearkening back to the Mughal Empire. As historian Stuart W. Leslie has argued, these institutes "embodied the paradox of postcolonial science, necessarily borrowing from the West but determined to break the cycle of dependency, in defiance of Western expectations."[21]

In Pakistan, nuclear ambitions featured prominently in plans for the nation's new capital, to be built away from the urban centers of Lahore or Karachi. The government hired some of the world's leading architects to imagine Islamabad as a crossroads of the traditional and the modern. One of the city's first buildings was the Pakistan Institute of Nuclear Science and Technology (PINSTECH). For its headquarters, Usmani hired the American architect Edward Durell Stone, a proponent of modern architecture who designed the Kennedy Center for the Performing Arts and the National Geographic Museum in Washington, DC. He also had designed the US Embassy in New Delhi and provided it with a distinctly South Asian touch, inspired by the Taj Mahal. The PINSTECH headquarters had the same Mughal flair. "All of us were rather awed and overwhelmed by the grand artistic theme," one Pakistani scientist recalled, while saying of Usmani, "He would grow passionate in describing his vision for the country, how science and technology could do wonders, and the unlimited potential of nuclear energy."[22]

By the early 1960s, Usmani and others in Pakistan were able to tie their ambitions for reactor development to the rhetoric of economic development. Usmani's PhD mentor was Patrick Blackett, whose *Fear, War, and the Bomb* (1949) had highlighted the possibility of using nuclear power for good in countries in South Asia. Munir Khan—working for the IAEA—helped provide Usmani with the legitimacy Pakistan needed, an authoritative statement that building nuclear reactors was in Pakistan's best interests. The IAEA issued a report in 1962 on Pakistan's prospects, and it observed that Karachi's energy requirements should be met by nuclear power instead of the non-renewable natural gas nearby. Usmani used the report to argue that nuclear power plants would meet Pakistan's energy needs for decades to come while supporting industrial growth.[23] Construction of its Mughal-inspired institute began the following year, and Pakistan's first research reactor went into operation in 1965.

Pakistan did not have the petroleum reserves enjoyed by other regional powers to its west, but Usmani and others had high hopes for another natural resource: uranium. In the late 1960s, the IAEA encouraged numerous countries to engage in uranium prospecting in the name of economic development and sent seasoned British and American experts to help. One of these was British geologist James Cameron, who was tapped by the IAEA to do prospecting in countries ranging from Turkey to the Philippines, Uruguay, and Egypt.[24] In 1969 he went to Pakistan to scope out the Siwalik sandstones of the Dera Ghazi Khan district, where uranium recently had been detected. He then helped Pakistan write a request for aid from the UN Development Program. Whether the nation used the uranium domestically or sold it abroad, mining and prospecting, the request argued, would provide jobs, stimulate the mining industry as a whole, and provide "employment, training and benefits in backward areas."[25]

The IAEA was being used by Pakistan to justify the expansion of its nuclear program under the rubric of peaceful uses, but it also was being used by Western countries wishing to conduct informal surveillance. Over the next several years, the IAEA oversaw Pakistan's uranium prospecting, using experts from the West. It financed drilling operations, aerial radiometric surveys, and ground geochemical analyses, and it built new transportation infrastructure.[26] James Cameron was the author of Pakistan's financial proposal to the UN, and the project leader was Canadian geologist J. W. Hoadley. One of the major discoveries, of a paleostream channel in the Baghal Chur basin, was made by an American, G. W. Chase, who had worked on uranium exploration in Oklahoma during the war and worked for the US Atomic Energy Commission in the 1950s. Another participant, J. L. Bowman, was a longtime economic geologist working for American firms and the AEC. Both Chase and Bowman were doing the uranium mapping for Pakistan, under the auspices of the IAEA. Even if these men did not directly report to their own governments, everything about Pakistan's resource development would have been known at least to the United States and Britain, because the IAEA relied on the US Atomic Energy Commission and the British Institute of Geological Sciences to analyze all of the ores. [27]

Pakistan never intended to simply be a seller of uranium. The mining program provided a crucial justification for launching an ambitious nuclear program that would secretly also include a bomb project. At the time, Pakistan emphasized the role of nuclear power in economic development, specifically focusing on nuclear power's potential to overcome the nation's natural limitations. It was a country without much coal or petroleum, and with too little natural gas to meet demand. Hydroelectric dams were dismissed as too difficult and expensive. Nuclear power plants, on the other hand, seemed to have decisive economic advantages in parts of West Pakistan and all of East Pakistan. Embracing the mid-1960s rhetoric of "Water for Peace" emanating from the United States, Pakistan's request for aid stated that nuclear plants would generate large amounts of electricity and also desalinate water. It estimated that by 1985, nuclear reactors would account for 16 percent of electricity in West Pakistan, and 41 percent of electricity in East Pakistan. The program was already under way—it pointed to the Karachi Nuclear Power Project (KANUPP), under construction, and the planned Rooppur Nuclear Power Project, slated to begin construction in East Pakistan in 1973.[28]

The domestic uranium prospecting program, framed as development to a backward area, also helped to justify Pakistan's focus on reactors using natural uranium (rather than enriched uranium). Potentially, its nuclear fuel cycle could be self-contained, freeing the country from reliance on foreign purchases of enriched fuel or having to build an enrichment facility at home. The idea of using natural uranium was not unique to Pakistan; it was the same path pursued by India. And one of the leading manufacturers of nuclear reactors using natural uranium—Canada—spoke out strongly in their favor. India's early research reactor, CIRUS, was the result of collaboration with Canada, as was its planned first commercial reactor, Rajasthan-1 (which went into operation in 1973). The IAEA backed natural uranium reactors too—which should be no surprise, with Pakistani scientist Munir Ahmad Khan as director of the IAEA's reactor engineering division. In the 1960s, Khan privately had tried to make the case that Pakistan should build a bomb rather than stick to peaceful applications, but he had been rebuffed. Promoting natural uranium reactors kept that option open. Khan was also the scientific secretary at the Fourth International Conference on the Peaceful Uses of Atomic Energy, in September 1971 in Geneva, where reactors using natural uranium had many advocates—especially in countries without resources for expensive enrichment facilities.

Pakistan's fortunes were altered in dramatic fashion by war. First was a war with India in 1965 over Kashmir, ending in a UN-mandated ceasefire. Then, in 1971, Pakistan initiated a brutal crackdown on Bengali nationalism in East Pakistan, in what scholars often call the Bangladesh genocide. Refugees fearing rape and murder fled toward India, where Prime Minister Indira Gandhi had opened the country's eastern border to let them in. Jingoistic rhetoric between India and Pakistan continued throughout 1971, and Pakistan hit India with airstrikes in December. India countered by invading Pakistan on the ground and in the air, while attacking Pakistan's navy at sea. In a humiliatingly short two weeks, Indian forces soundly defeated the Pakistan military, taking more than 90,000 soldiers prisoner, and East Pakistan won its independence—henceforth becoming known as Bangladesh.[29]

Without its eastern province, Pakistan lost much of the justification for its peaceful nuclear efforts. More than half of the country's population had been there, and the east had been projected to rely heavily on nuclear power in the future, possibly even to include desalination plants. But it did not matter. After the spectacular defeat, Pakistani officials were determined to hold on to the nuclear program, using the unaltered rhetoric of peaceful atoms. Scholars of Pakistan's nuclear programs point out that the war's aftermath was the definitive decision point in Pakistan that reoriented its nuclear program toward weapons. After Zulfikar Ali Bhutto came to power in Pakistan, he fired Usmani and replaced him with Munir Ahmad Khan in early 1972, who began a bomb-building program in earnest.[30]

The IAEA's promises of economic independence and resource security proved useful in justifying an expanded nuclear program. Pakistan's first nuclear power plant, KANUPP, was completed with great fanfare in November 1972. Speaking at the inauguration of KANUPP, President Bhutto drew the link between nuclear technology and the uplift of the developing world. "The most menacing problem in the Subcontinent of South Asia is that of poverty and misery of its people," he said. "For our people atomic energy should become a symbol of hope rather than fear."[31] Sir Alan Cottrell, the UK's chief scientific advisor, attended the inauguration of the power plant, providing the well-wishes of the British government on the occasion. It was a symbolic gesture on the part of a former colonial power that helped to supply parts. The Canadians proudly pointed out that they also had assisted.[32] In the meantime, Pakistan in 1972 also solicited help in building a chemical reprocessing plant so that it could make plutonium from the spent nuclear fuel. Records in the UK National Archives suggest that British Foreign and Commonwealth Office specialists had little problem with this and encouraged the government-owned firm British Nuclear Fuels Limited (BNFL) to bid on the contract.[33]

Pakistan normalized its activities—uranium mining and building plants to enrich uranium and produce plutonium—by working closely with the IAEA and echoing the agency's rhetoric about taming nature with the atom. Khan's public relations director, Akhtar Mahmud Faruqui, wrote an essay in the *IAEA Bulletin* outlining the previous six years of work and pointed optimistically toward a future of nuclear power. To read Faruqui, one could imagine that Pakistan had embraced every promise made by the IAEA, with programs in agriculture—radioisotopes for food preservation, grain disinfestation, and mutation breeding had all been attempted at Pakistan's new research centers—and in medicine—using radioactive materials for diagnostics and therapy. They were eager to try more, including the dual-use desalination plants the United States was designing for Israel. The essay pointed to the grand design of the nuclear institute, which "stands as a symbol of the aspirations of the country's scientific community," recalling the role of architect Edward Durell Stone. "Blending utility with elegance, PINSTECH provides modern facilities in classical surroundings," demonstrating to all underdeveloped countries the immense potential of the atom, "to the ultimate advantage of the teeming millions of the Third World who will benefit from it."[34]

The IAEA predicted that the mines in Pakistan would provide jobs to "tribesmen" currently living at a subsistence level, and the new roads "would open up to vehicular traffic areas previously accessible only by camel trails and foot-paths."[35] In a 1975 study, the IAEA claimed to use new advanced computer models to make fresh assessments and recommendations about nuclear power. In fact, it simply rehashed the arguments made five years earlier: Pakistan was naturally poor in fossil fuels, financially too poor for hydroelectric power, and thus required salvation through nuclear power. The country should begin its nuclear program immediately, the report stated, and after 1982 its new electricity installations should be exclusively nuclear. "The crucial problem will be to find additional financing sources for an investment of this order of magnitude." Bangladesh too was suffering from natural pressures: severe floods of the Brahmaputra River and a high rate of population growth. Much as in the earlier study, this new one estimated that Bangladesh should have 40 percent of its electricity from nuclear power by 1995.[36]

Efforts by Pakistan to develop an indigenous source of uranium became complicated after India detonated a nuclear device in 1974. Like India, Pakistan was relying on equipment from Canada for the construction of a uranium fuel fabrication plant. It had signed an agreement with Atomic Energy of Canada in 1973 to have the new plant completed by 1975. Canada's response to the Indian nuclear test was to require that any country receiving its nuclear technology either sign the Treaty on the Nonproliferation of Nuclear Weapons (NPT) or accept full-scope safeguards under the IAEA on all facilities. In addition, it demanded that Canadian supplies not be used for nuclear explosions, whether "peaceful" or otherwise. Pakistan at the time was keeping its nuclear options open, and in addition to working with Canada, it had contracted with France to build a chemical reprocessing plant. Such a facility would allow spent uranium from KANUPP to be treated and plutonium extracted from it. Pakistan refused to comply with Canada's new requirements. Behind the scenes, having recently made the decision to pursue a bomb, Pakistan was not in a position to accept these new requirements. Canada cut off all nuclear cooperation with Pakistan in 1976—it stopped supplying fuel, heavy water, spare parts, and information, and it recalled its citizens from their positions at KANUPP.[37]

Pakistan's program continued and more than ever relied on the rhetoric of the IAEA to do so. The uranium mining went on, though IAEA experts complained that the whole project began to break down as soon as some of the equipment did. Drill rigs broke down, as did vehicles and machine parts. Nature also was uncooperative; rains in the monsoon season destroyed roads, requiring bulldozers that were not always on hand or in good repair. The Pakistanis were unprepared to do timely basic maintenance and were also unable to control theft. In the summer of 1977, a military coup led by Muhammad Zia ul-Haq toppled Bhutto, and mining operations came to a standstill. When, in September 1977, an army colonel took over leadership of the Pakistani side of the project, many of the machine parts immediately disappeared, leaving the drill rigs inoperable. Maintenance facilities were practically non-existent, and the operation went on "under extremely primitive conditions," wrote a disgusted IAEA expert.[38] The mining was going nowhere but the nuclear reactor and bomb programs were intact, and the promises of economic uplift continued to provide justification for them.

The effect of the Indian test on Pakistan's program was a microcosm of its effects all over the world. Suddenly the assumption that a nation should be self-sufficient in nuclear fuel was open to question. So was the possibility of building enrichment or reprocessing facilities in-country, or even relying on reactor designs using natural uranium. The rhetoric of uplifting the wretched of the earth that had maintained political traction for so long at the IAEA and at the UN Development Program, would be recast in language of distrust, as if self-sufficiency was code for a clandestine bomb program. While Pakistan was indeed hiding a weapons program, India's position was more brazen—it positioned its device as a challenge not only to the non-proliferation treaty specifically but also to the hypocrisy of the United States, the Soviet Union, and Europeans who attempted to manage and control access to the entirety of the civilian fuel cycle, keeping the Global South dependent on the Global North.

In May 1974, India was scheduled to begin a Five-Year Plan to achieve self-sufficiency from foreign aid. That had already been ridiculed outside India as wildly optimistic, especially given the upsurge in oil prices in the past year. India's vaunted Green Revolution was under threat too because of cost spikes in fertilizer, on which all of the new crops depended. India's prospects for self-sufficiency in food had virtually evaporated during a drought in 1973, and it had borrowed grain from the Soviet Union. US aid had dropped precipitously since the war with Pakistan in 1971. Even with excellent monsoon rains in the summer of 1973, the harvests in 1973–74 fell well below self-sufficiency. "Meanwhile the population rises relentlessly," one British aid memorandum observed, "and things are worsened by the high cost and disappearance of fertilizer." That memo, briefing British diplomats before meeting with their Indian counterparts, stated: "We want to see the Indian march towards development resumed and the current crisis overcome, and we are ready to play our part in this," and added that the United Kingdom and other countries should do more to mobilize food and non-traditional resources such as petroleum.[39]

The non-traditional resource in "development" that India announced later that month was its fission detonation, exploded at the Pokhran Test

Range on May 18, 1974. Embassies were notified by Foreign Secretary Kewal Singh that the bomb had been an implosion device, detonated some 100 meters underground. Although detonated by the Indian Army, at a secured military test site in Rajasthan, a desert region adjacent to neighboring Pakistan, India claimed that it was intended to keep India abreast of peaceful applications such as mining and earth moving and that it remained a committed opponent to the use of nuclear energy for military purposes.[40] In the jargon of nuclear affairs, Indira Gandhi's India had conducted a "PNE," a peaceful nuclear explosion.[41]

The explosion called into question the new Treaty on the Non-Proliferation of Nuclear Weapons (NPT) at a time when many states were still debating ratification. The Indians had not signed the treaty, so no law had been broken. But as the Indian newspaper *The Patriot* suggested, "what status should India now be given if she chooses to sign the treaty?" Was it a nuclear weapon state? Or still a non-nuclear weapon state? Perhaps there should be a third category? The director of the Institute for Defence Studies and Analysis in India, Krishnaswamy Subrahmanyam, wrote that "this explosion will remind the participants about the unviability of the structure of the Non-Proliferation Treaty."[42]

Most Western countries scoffed at the idea of classifying the detonation as merely a peaceful nuclear explosion. The initial reaction of the United States, by order of the State Department, was to be "low-key" yet firm in the notion that that the test amounted to weapons proliferation. And US aid appeared to have helped it along. "It appears probable that in developing their device," Deputy Secretary of State Kenneth Rush cabled other American diplomats, "the Indians used heavy water that we provided for the Canadian supplied Cirus research reactor."[43] The US response was also muted because of the Watergate scandal: just over a week prior to the India test, Congress had begun impeachment proceedings against the president, beginning a tumultuous period in Washington that absorbed the attention of the president and most of his closest advisors. By contrast, Canada took the detonation particularly hard, especially because it occurred less than two months in advance of the federal election in Canada. Newspapers portrayed the test as a betrayal of trust. Canada had been providing food aid as well as nuclear aid, including for agricultural uses, and India repaid that by using its nuclear reactors to produce fuel that could be turned into bombs.

Indian politicians and intellectuals urged the wider world not to interpret the move as a military one. Yet on its Himalayan border, India had been at war with China in 1962, before the latter had tested its own nuclear device in 1964. India had warred with Pakistan in 1965 and again in

1971. Still, when Ashok Kapor, a professor of political science at Canada's University of Waterloo, gave a presentation at Chatham House, the UK's Institute of International Affairs, he framed the detonation as a triumph for a developing country—and one that starkly revealed the most insulting flaw in the NPT. That document had divided the world into two camps, not leaving space for "nuclear-capable" states, which India had just become. It was up to the West, he said, to identify the real motive behind the treaty, which he regarded as giving a commercial advantage to the nuclear weapons states.[44]

After some India-Canada talks in Ottawa at the end of July 1974, candid discussions revealed that many of the Indian officials, including Foreign Secretary Kewal Singh, assumed the outrage was manufactured for the political campaign season and were surprised that the Canadians were genuinely affronted. One observer said that the talks were "rough going," especially for the Indians, who had not come prepared to have Canadians suddenly insist on strict safeguards for any further nuclear cooperation. The talks simply "stalemated." Although the bilateral talks were closed, the India Desk officer at Canada's Department of External Affairs, Rodney Irwin, was talkative with British diplomats afterward. "Although Irwin was at pains to stress to me that they were not using their aid as a form of blackmail, it is obvious that they would not object if the Indians interpreted it as such."[45]

Informal chatter among diplomats revealed a starkly changed environment in nuclear affairs. British diplomat J. J. Taylor said of the Canadians: "They are under no illusions that the stick with which they have to beat the Indians is not large and that the Indians may well decide that they can learn to live without the Canadians. . . . At the expense of stating the obvious, whatever the outcome of the present difference of opinion between the two countries things are never going to be the same again."[46] Another British diplomat reported a chat with Dwight Fulford, an official at Canada's Department of External Affairs, at a social event shortly after the talks. "He was scathing in his condemnation of the 'peaceful' nuclear explosion. He said that we could no doubt look forward to a 'peaceful' rocket launcher, a 'peaceful' re-entry vehicle and perhaps eventually a 'peaceful' nuclear war-head."[47]

India's designation of its test as a peaceful nuclear explosive should not have surprised anyone paying attention to the atomic energy program of its key diplomatic partner, the Soviet Union. The two countries signed the Treaty of Peace, Friendship and Cooperation in 1971, prior to the war with Pakistan, and they vowed to boost cooperation in numerous fields—including science and technology. Soviet programs for PNEs included mining, waste incineration, stimulating natural gas and oil fields, and large-scale earth-moving project to build dams, canals, and harbors. As historian Paul Josephson has noted, the Soviets saw geophysical engineering as a means of "correcting the mistakes of nature."[48] Unlike most countries in the West, the USSR did not openly condemn the Indian test as a nuclear weapon but instead followed India's characterization of it as a PNE.[49]

Because much of the cooperation with India took place under the auspices of the Colombo Plan, the postwar collaborative venture of British Commonwealth nations in the Asian region, British officials were embarrassed. They immediately suspended the processing of Indian applications for nuclear-related aid such as training programs.[50] One embassy official, J. A. Thomson, sent a newspaper clipping of an American political cartoon to colleagues at the Foreign and Commonwealth Office in late June 1974. Titled "All God's Chillun Got N-Power," it depicted eight figures holding up atomic bombs, led by Uncle Sam. Each represented a state possessing the bomb—and the last three in line were Israel, India, and Egypt. The Indian was emaciated and mostly naked, a stereotypical image of a primitive South Asian. "The attached cartoon makes powerfully and neatly the point that in the last few days the world has become more dangerous," Thomson wrote.[51]

Prime Minister Indira Gandhi was quick to point out the hypocrisy in others' outrage, asking whether it was "all right for the rich to use nuclear energy for destructive purposes but not right for a poor country to find out whether it can be used for construction?"[52] Indeed the Americans had touted explosives as part of the "peaceful atom," and in the 1960s US AEC chairman Glenn Seaborg held out hopes of offering nuclear explosions as a service to other countries. The market for such services had never materialized, and when India employed the same rhetoric, the only landscape that changed was the political one. PNEs seemed doomed. The test "made it easier for other potential nuclear powers to claim their 'right' to detonate underground 'peaceful' nuclear explosions," Under Secretary of State Kenneth Rush lamented on the day of the test.[53] American diplomat William J. Porter pointed out to European colleagues that the United States had offered PNEs to India time and again, under the condition that the PNEs not explode in the atmosphere. But India had refused such "services."[54] The Indians were instead offering PNE services to other countries, notably Brazil and Argentina. India had asked no one's permission, had consulted no one, and indeed seemed to think that it should have the same rights as the Europeans or superpowers to explode fission devices for civilian purposes. "There is no doubt that if the Indians continue their present line they will drive a coach and horses through the efforts which we and the other depositary powers of the Non-Proliferation Treaty have been making to achieve an effective international regime to limit and control the possession of nuclear explosive technology."[55] Soon the Indians could be exploding bombs in South America, under the name of PNEs, and under the guise of economic development.

Although Pakistan was secretly building a bomb as well, its officials took a sanctimonious approach that emphasized India's betrayal of the economic promise of the atom for developing countries. Munir Khan portrayed Pakistan as peace-loving, having signed the Limited Test Ban Treaty of 1963, and having voted in favor of the NPT in 1968 (though it had not become party to it). "We in the underdeveloped countries must acquire modern technology—technology for our economic and industrial development and not for mutual destruction," Munir Khan observed. "We must first address ourselves to the crying needs of our hungry, poor and illiterate masses and postpone the pursuit of illusionary prestige and power for later." He stated that "this shortsighted and selfish step by India has rendered a great disservice to all mankind and particularly to the developing countries of the world which desperately need nuclear power to meet their electric power requirements in the midst of the energy crisis." He lamented that the more advanced countries would make it harder to build nuclear programs going forward.[56]

Instead of reproach, Secretary of State Henry Kissinger tried to interest India in non-proliferation. "India clearly is militarily predominant now," he said to Kewal Singh, in an oblique reference to Pakistan. "But there is a curious thing about nuclear weapons. It is easy to equalize the situation if the other side develops nuclear weapons." He offered to treat India as a nuclear power and to bring it into the non-proliferation fold.[57]

While polite, the Indians consistently pointed out that their main concern was in the treatment of India, relegating it permanently to a different class of countries from the United States, the Soviet Union, and Europe. This was unacceptable to Indians, especially given the long history of colonialism. Behind the veil of non-proliferation politics were deeper questions about national sovereignty, dependence, and access to natural resources and technology. The idea of only some countries having control of PNEs, for example, they could not accept. Nor did they think it was fair that US congressmen were attempting to tie development loans to nuclear issues. The so-called Long Amendment (after Democratic Congressman Clarence Long), for example, authorized the United States to vote against loans from the International Development Agency to any country developing nuclear weapons unless it became a party to the Non-Proliferation Treaty. "We do not like discrimination," India's US ambassador, Triloki Nath "Tikki" Kaul, stated to Kissinger plainly. Kissinger tried to backtrack, stating that he and

President Nixon shared this view, and that he personally had opposed the Long Amendment. "I am opposed to such discrimination," Kissinger said. "I don't like what you did, but want no discrimination. It is not our policy to discriminate." [58]

Despite utter turmoil at the White House because of Watergate—the president resigned a week later—Kissinger himself provided continuity on these nuclear conversations, as he continued to serve under President Gerald Ford. He visited India in October 1974 and met with Prime Minister Indira Gandhi. Kissinger found her difficult to manipulate and detested her. President Nixon had called her an "old witch," and both he and Kissinger privately referred to her as a "bitch." She was never as pliable as the Americans hoped she would be and seemed friendly with the Soviets.[59] She also had the bomb. "Despite Mrs. Gandhi's almost pathological need to criticize the United States, she, too, desires to see relations between us improve on this new and more equal basis." As with Singh, Kissinger insisted that he was not interested in recriminations about the nuclear test. "With Mrs. Gandhi I said very frankly that their nuclear explosion was a bomb no matter how India described it" and that a future Indian government might treat it as such.[60] Kissinger soon began working with diplomats from other countries to tighten controls on the nuclear trade, initiating a long and contentious period of negotiations about where to draw the line between peaceful and dangerous nuclear programs. Gandhi, for her part, retained her opposition to the American-inspired non-proliferation treaty and insisted on her country's right to pursue peaceful nuclear technology, including explosions.[61]

Reactions to the Smiling Buddha test were further shaped by a seemingly unrelated development: the Yom Kippur War of 1973 that had ignited a global energy crisis by the summer of 1974. The war itself occurred between Israel and its neighbors, and many of the Arab states in coalition against Israel were major oil producers. When these members of the Organization of Petroleum Exporting Countries (OPEC) reduced petroleum production and embargoed some major consumers, they did so as a punitive move in response to supporting Israel in the Yom Kippur War. The ensuing crisis saw the price of oil skyrocket and the availability of oil in Europe and the United States plummet. It also fueled enthusiasm for developing nuclear power. The French and British already had felt similar pressure in 1956 during the Suez crisis, and both countries' enthusiasm for nuclear power intensified in the 1970s. Likewise, the Japanese began to focus more on nuclear power during the oil crisis, as did West Germany.[62]

Indian diplomats were eager to frame their nuclear tests in terms of energy shortfalls. Talking with Kissinger, Singh had pressed the connection between nuclear discrimination and India's grave human peril. "We are in the midst of an energy crisis," he said, explaining how oil, food, and fertilizer accounted for some 80 percent of imports. The high cost of gasoline had hit agriculture hard. "We are having enormous difficulties. We are overhauling our priorities." Singh said they were looking for oil deposits vigorously and even prospecting offshore with the help of American firms. "Please consider our requirements for food, fertilizer, and oil."[63]

At the IAEA, Director-General Sigvard Eklund was determined to prevent the Indian test from undermining the existing narrative connecting natural resource shortfalls to the adoption of nuclear technology. The big nuclear news of 1974 was still, to him, the petroleum crisis. "Since we last met the world has seen what can happen when supply problems arise with one of our principal energy sources," he observed in an official statement. "It has brought home to all of us how much modern life depends on the availability of energy, as well as the sensitivity of the world's economy to large changes in the cost of energy, and in particular the vulnerability of those countries that do not control large energy resources." He lamented that "in some countries there is, to put it mildly, a deep reluctance to accept nuclear power as a way out of the present difficulties."[64]

The oil crisis would feed atomic energy's narrative of energy salvation. US domestic crude oil production hit a peak of 9.6 million barrels a day in 1970 and did not reach that mark again in the next few years. "Many analysts doubt that it will be that high again," journalist Edward Cowan wrote in the *New York Times*. In the economic world of supply and demand, the United States no longer appeared able to meet increases in demand by drilling more oil. In 1975, the US Geological Survey acknowledged that it—and most American geologists—had overestimated domestic oil and natural gas resources. An exception was USGS scientist and former Shell petroleum geologist M. King Hubbert, who in 1956 had predicted a bell curve in US oil production that capped out in the early 1970s. In reality, by 1971, American oil wells were operating at full capacity, unable to increase production to meet demand.[65] By 1975, scientists wondered if Hubbert had been right.[66]

In 1974, Hubbert made another prediction: global oil production would peak in the mid-1990s. He believed that a crisis could be avoided if fossil fuel consumption could be replaced by a combination of solar and nuclear energy, with heavy reliance on breeder reactors. During the oil crisis, both the Nixon and Ford administrations signaled a desire to eliminate reliance on foreign oil sources. Hubbert warned, "If your hopes of independence are to supplant imports with domestic production . . . I say it can't be done." He worried that in desperation Americans would turn to hydraulic fracturing of shale (later known as "fracking"), which would be a short-term solution with a high environmental cost, due to leaching of alkaline materials into rivers.[67] Some even went so far as propose fracking with nuclear detonations—a creative use of the "peaceful nuclear explosion" that could unleash fossil fuels from deep within the earth.[68]

The fast breeder (fast because the neutrons were not slowed down by a moderator, as in a normal reactor) had all the appearances of a magical solution to the problem of depleting resources. The Atomic Energy Commission identified them to the president as a high priority item in 1962, and by 1967 it had narrowed its prediction to a particular technology that used liquid metal (sodium) as a coolant. That technology had a cumbersome acronym: LMFBR (Liquid Metal Fast Breeder Reactor). With the advice of the Atomic Energy Commission, President Richard Nixon in 1971 framed the LMFBR as a crucial part of the United States' energy strategy. He gave the program the highest priority on his energy agenda and committed to a demonstration of the technology by 1980. "Our best hope today for meeting the nation's growing demand for economical clean energy," Nixon declared, "lies with the fast breeder reactor." The Atomic Energy Commission predicted that by the year 2000, LMFBR technology would equal the present energy capacity of the United States.[69]

The breeder reactor itself had become a Janus-faced symbol of the future. On the one hand, it was part of a narrative of economic promise: breeders would supply a virtually endless supply of energy because the technology created more fuel than it consumed. On the other hand, it was a marker of complacency about the endlessly extractive capitalist economy and its blind faith in economic growth. The technological fix that made breeders so attractive were repugnant to others who saw them as enablers of destructive trends. When asked how he felt about the connection between the energy crisis and breeder reactors, Hubbert responded that he didn't think breeder development should stop: "I'm saying we're almost on a collision course. We don't know how to stop. We need power and we need the energy. It's moving along like a Greek drama."[70] Others were more critical of breeders. Gary Snyder's 1975 Pulitzer Prize–winning book of poetry, *Turtle Island*, was both a critique of society and an environmental manifesto. He captured his impressions of breeders with his poem "LMFBR," which described the breeder reactor as "Death himself/ (Liquid Metal Fast Breeder Reactor)/ stands grinning, beckoning/ Plutonium tooth-glow." It was not fear of the bomb that motivated Snyder but instead the notion that endless energy would enable the worst in humans: "Aluminum beer cans, plastic spoons/ plywood veneers, PVC pipe, vinyl seat covers; don't exactly burn, don't quite rot/ flood over us/ robes and garbs/ of the Kālī-yūga/ end of days."[71] Drawing on Hindu imagery about the coming age of the demon Kālī, Snyder cast the detritus of consumer society as the clothing of the end of the world.

While oil consumers hoped breeder reactors might end their dependence on Middle East oil, major oil producers were turning to nuclear power too. In the 1970s, the Shah of Iran decided to invest huge sums of petroleum dollars into building dozens of nuclear power plants across his country. In 1970, Iran ratified the Treaty on the Non-Proliferation of Nuclear Weapons (NPT), which affirmed its rights of access to nuclear fuel and technology as long as it foreswore building nuclear weapons. The shah relished the idea and opened negotiations with European and American firms to build an extensive network of reactors, to operate them safely, and to secure fuel. Despite sitting on top of enormous supplies of petroleum, Iran embarked on what seemed like an energy revolution in the mid-1970s. American nuclear power advocates even circulated an advertisement picturing the shah, stating "Guess Who's Building Nuclear Power Plants," arguing that if the shah felt nuclear solutions were safe and economical, others should too.[72]

Iran's engagement with nuclear technologies thus far had been largely symbolic. It housed the regional CENTO institute, though its regional partners took little interest. It also collaborated with the IAEA, and the shah's government embraced the American vision of atomic energy in a developing country: focusing on research reactors and attempting to apply atomic knowledge to agriculture and health domains. Its first such reactor was built by American Machine and Foundry in 1967. Such reactors were relatively easy to use and could be found in universities around the world. Iran also acquired a radioactive source, cobalt-60, in 1971. With this source, contained in a lead-lined box with a small door, scientists could study the impact of gamma radiation on any object, such as plants, animals, air, or water. Because the facility was cheap to construct and the cobalt could be acquired easily through the IAEA, it was one of the most common "nuclear" tools found in developing countries.[73]

The IAEA used Iran to publicize the crossroads between traditional non-scientific cultures and the modern era of atomic energy. Publicity photographs, for example, depict a woman in traditional dress being treated for an enlarged thyroid, surrounded by white men in white coats. Others depict Iranian women in a laboratory setting, conducting scientific work under the tutelage of foreigners, often in IAEA-sponsored training programs in Europe and the United States. Although such photographs were staged, they portrayed real ailments, treatments, and training programs. One of the young women portrayed, Zhila Khalkhali, would become a prominent cancer researcher in the United States after moving there during the Iranian Revolution. She later recalled of a 1960s training program in Denmark, "I want to emphasize the importance of the program and the vast number of people like me (not only in Iran but all over the world) who benefited from participating in it. . . . I worked for many years in Iran trying to employ what I learnt while studying in Denmark."[74]

It was Henry Kissinger who facilitated Iran's transition toward a vision of economic development that included not only agriculture and medicine but also commercial nuclear power. He did so as a strategy to address the global oil crisis. He believed that by working together, the oil consumers could weaken OPEC in the long term, using the promise of nuclear power to do it. Publicly, the United States tried to put on a brave face during the oil crisis, and both Presidents Nixon and Ford urged Americans to conserve fuel while pushing Project Independence, touted as a kind of Manhattan Project for energy self-sufficiency through research on alternative fuel sources.[75] Secretly, the United States' goal was focused on petroleum. As Kissinger put it to Ford in the summer of 1974, "We have to find a way to break the cartel."[76] Nuclear reactors in Iran would play a role.

To "break" the oil cartel, the Nixon and Ford administrations embarked on an ambitious and complex plan to create binding, multi-year projects that would tie oil producers' hands—and prevent any reductions in oil production. Kissinger believed that Middle East oil suppliers like Iran and Saudi Arabia were powerful not just because of their oil but also because of their uninvested capital. Reducing oil production did not pressure them because they were not spending their immense wealth anyway. Kissinger's proposed solution was to identify capital-intensive projects that would give such countries more bills to pay. "What we need to do," Kissinger said privately, "is to preempt the structure of relationships in the area and to develop a flow of benefits which they won't want to lose."[77]

American diplomats worked hard to convince Saudi Arabia and Iran in particular that they needed to invest in high-tech sectors, the key "benefit" Americans possessed. For example, they played up military vulnerabilities and vowed to provide expensive conventional arms, training, and personnel. In addition, they touted the role of technology in modernization, such as fertilizers, even when US experts said that such technologies would be fruitless in the recipient country. Kissinger disliked that American government experts working in bodies such as the US Agency for International Development (AID) often took the target country's needs too seriously. "The problem is that the United States has a missionary streak," he complained in a meeting with some congressmen on foreign economic policy. "Whenever the Saudis have development projects we send six missions over there to explain to them why they don't need them. To explain why they don't need to spend the money."[78] Kissinger explained that the State Department's purpose was to serve US interests, not to promote rational planning. "I need assets in Saudi Arabia," he explained in a cabinet meeting on oil strategy. He needed leverage. "I don't give a damn about a well distributed world fertilizer industry. In fact, a badly distributed industry is probably in our interest." The goal was to establish the means of asserting US influence through trade with expensive long-term projects. "If we can put a nuclear plant into Egypt in eight years and do something in fertilizers in Saudi Arabia, then we have a strategy," he said. "Then we have something they don't want to lose. I want a confrontation, believe me," he said, referring to OPEC. "But I need chips."[79]

The country in the region most vulnerable to this strategy seemed to be Iran. The shah, Mohammad Reza Pahlavi, already had removed Iran from solidarity with the Arabs. "They say we are Moslems, but we are Aryans," he said, noting the difference between religious and ethnic affinity. To Pahlavi, Arab nationalism was not Iran's fight, and he refused to participate in the embargo. But he did believe in ambitious development plans that would make Iran one of the top five developed nations of the world in a short span of time: "What I want for Iran is very simple, very clear, very ambitious and very possible. In 20 or 25 years I want it to be ahead of the greatest nations of the world."[80] The United States and Iran already had a strong relationship, with the Americans facilitating the shah's acquisition of an enormous range of military hardware. Kissinger had little faith in the Saudis, confiding to Ford that they "belong to the most feckless and gutless of the Arabs." More important, Saudi Arabia had only about 5 million people and no industry to speak of. By contrast, Iran had more than 40 million people and ambitions for major industrial development. Its surplus oil was far less than Saudi Arabia's. If Pahlavi could be convinced to spend Iran's money on long-term projects, he would be less able to reduce oil production. Confiding his strategy to select members of Congress, Kissinger was blunt: "Large scale development projects and other projects will put the shah, for example, in a position where he must sell oil in order to sustain the commitments he has made." The projects would need to be big.[81]

It may seem counterintuitive to imagine one of the world's major oil producers being convinced of the need to invest in nuclear power, but that is precisely what occurred. It ticked all the right boxes—expensive, multi-year, and requiring many different kinds of surveying, construction, training, and operating contracts. In early 1974 Kissinger directed the US embassy in Tehran to strengthen ties between the two countries in economic and technological fields. His first two suggestions were explicitly nuclear, one inviting further investment in breeder reactor technology and the other offering to couple nuclear power plants with water desalination facilities.[82] The latter was an idea held over from the Johnson administration's abortive "Water for Peace" project in Israel. When ambassador to Iran Richard Helms met with Pahlavi, the two men talked at length about nuclear power. The shah "wanted to get down to brass tacks on that right away," Helms reported. Iran had committed to creating the Atomic Energy Organization of Iran (AEOI) and putting "a practical man, not just a theoretician," in charge of it. Helms had clearly touched on the right topic, and he reported that the shah's eyes visibly brightened when certain applications, such as using reactor heat to reduce iron ore, were brought up. Given the shah's obvious enthusiasm, Kissinger told Helms that nuclear power was clearly the area to exploit for increasing collaboration and getting Iran to spend its wealth.[83]

In hindsight, it is tempting to frame this relationship in terms of Iran's nascent nuclear weapons program or to imagine that Kissinger was mostly concerned with proliferation. However, while it may be true that the shah had in mind potential weapons programs, or that Kissinger considered non-proliferation dimensions (he did), declassified documents clearly indicate that these efforts were connected to petroleum and that they were part of Kissinger's cartel-breaking strategy.[84] At the 1975 Economic Summit Meeting in Rambouillet (the first Group of 6 summit, which included six of the world's leading oil-consuming nations), Kissinger presented a broad strategy of linking energy discussions with other commodities such as military exports. "It would be suicidal to enter a dialogue without cohesion among the oil importers," he asserted. Although the G6 leaders did not agree on all matters, they were unified in their desire to decrease the power of OPEC. "If our countries run in different directions they will create a crisis in the industrialized West," German chancellor Helmut Schmidt agreed, hoping for solidarity. "Our destiny will lie in the hands of a few OPEC leaders rather than in our hands."[85]

Encouraged by the US government, leading American universities played a part in this strategy in OPEC countries. Jerome Wiesner, president of the Massachusetts Institute of Technology (MIT) and former presidential science advisor, visited Iran in 1974 to follow up on Ambassador Helms's meeting, and he discussed with the shah several ways to bring MIT's expertise to Iranian universities. Wiesner found in the shah and Iranian university administrators a mood of "optimism, expansionism and general ebullience," based on Iran's oil wealth. Wiesner established liaison between MIT and the Aryamehr University of Technology to train the first generation of elite engineers. Wiesner encouraged MIT faculty to write proposals for research centers at MIT to be paid for by

Iran, including a $50 million energy research laboratory. It also offered to bring in thirty new Iranian students a year for training in nuclear physics and engineering in a special master's program for Iran. To make it profitable, MIT would be compensated by Iran for each student.[86] Other universities would follow the same path with oil-producing countries of the Middle East, such as Saudi Arabia and Libya, establishing financial ties across numerous fields. Alvin Weinberg guest-lectured in 1978 to a nuclear engineering class at Oregon State University, for example, and discussed the possibility of Libya acquiring a bomb under its leader Muammar Gaddafi. Weinberg recalled himself saying that if he were in charge of a Libyan bomb, "'he would send 20 bright Libyan engineering students each year to Oregon State University to learn nuclear engineering. After a few years he would have enough experts to build isotope plants and plutonium producing reactors.' The class roared—there actually were in the class twenty young Libyans; Oregon State University was being paid $10,000 in tuition fees and expenses annually for each of the students!"[87]

Similarly, the British Foreign and Commonwealth Office encouraged nuclear deals with Iran. At its urging, theoretical physicist Walter Marshall, director of the Atomic Energy Research Establishment at Harwell, visited Iran, Kuwait, and Algeria in early 1975, and the British thereafter reached out to Egypt, Saudi Arabia, and Libya. He hoped to facilitate deals between Iran and Britain's government-owned company, British Nuclear Fuels Limited (BNFL), and proposed a wide variety of projects to Iran (and to Kuwait). He pitched expensive ideas, ranging from aerial geological surveys to training programs in safety standards. "The basic idea of this seems fairly clear," an official reported, "simply to match up Iranian money with BNFL expertise and management ability."[88]

Iran was prepared to expend extraordinary sums on nuclear development. The new Atomic Energy Organization of Iran, led by Akbar E'temad, sent students to get undergraduate degrees at American, British, French, or German universities. In Britain, Iran offered to pay for Iranians' postgraduate training on a lavish scale, suggesting support for about a hundred Iranians per year at Harwell. Iran was offering more money than Harwell knew what to do with, so Marshall invented projects to utilize the money—including the construction of new buildings on site just to make room for the influx of Iranian trainees. Marshall used words such as "astonished" and "staggered" to describe his reaction to the magnitude of Iran's ambitions. After debriefing with the British embassy in Tehran, he reported, "The embassy were particularly pleased at the whole sense of the discussion which showed that the UK was moving toward the position of being general adviser to the Iranian Government on science and technology—this is something they strongly welcome and keenly encourage."[89]

Though the French government did not wish to be perceived as part of any anti-OPEC consortium, it embraced Kissinger's plan to tempt Iran with nuclear technology. French negotiators offered to build reactors in Iran, but first they requested an enormous sum to build a gaseous diffusion plant (for uranium enrichment) in France. Iran agreed in 1974 to put up the money—some $1 billion US—for the facility, in a complex agreement that gave Iran a partial stake and guaranteed it access to enriched uranium. The deal secured France's own enrichment future because it would be built on French soil, in the southern provincial village of Pierrelatte.

The Iranian government did precisely what American negotiators hoped, by buying reactors and services, and making long-term financial commitments. It had signed the non-proliferation treaty in 1968, ostensibly guaranteeing access to technology and fuel sources. Iran confidently developed a twenty-year plan to have about 24,000 megawatts of electricity capacity in place by 1994, at a pace of two pressurized water reactors to be ordered each year. By early 1975 it had ordered four of these, from German (Kraftwerk Union) and French (Creusot-Loire) companies.[90]

Unlike India and Pakistan, which pursued reactors using natural uranium, Iran focused on pressurized-water reactors (PWRs), which operated on enriched uranium. The United Kingdom's Walter Marshall was candid with E'temad, telling him there was no way Iranians would be allowed to get near the diffusion membranes in a uranium enrichment plant. These were classified secret because of their role in bomb programs. Since Iran had already struck a deal with the French and had paid huge sums to build the gaseous diffusion plant at Pierrelatte, the comment annoyed E'temad. One of Iran's aims in financing it, he protested, was to learn how it worked. Marshall suggested that the French might be pretending to share everything about their gaseous diffusion plant with Iran, but it was highly unlikely that the membrane designs had been revealed. "Faced with this direct comment," a British report noted, "Dr. E'temad simply smiled and said that that indeed was the situation, and it was clear that, whatever he might say in negotiations, he accepted that the French and British were behaving similarly on classified matters."[91] Despite paying huge sums of money for the enrichment facility, Iran would continue to rely on others—in this case, the French—and would not have a truly independent source of fuel.

Ironically, what was touted as the route to resource security turned out to be a relationship that smacked of neocolonialism, with outsiders controlling the crucial technology. The Iranians were not happy with the growing view in the West that some aspects of the nuclear fuel cycle should remain perpetually out of reach. They did not wish to give Americans the right to veto Iranian decisions about what to do with their plutonium. The lack of agreement on that turned into a "serious irritant in our relations with Iran," National Security Advisor Brent Scowcroft wrote to the president in 1976.[92] A similar situation was unfolding in Iran's relations with Europeans. Even in advance of a contract, Kraftwerk Union had created what one German embassy official dubbed "the biggest construction site in Iran," to build two 1,300-megawatt power stations near Bushehr. The work started in 1975, and by early 1976 there were hundreds of Germans and thousands of Iranians working at the site. All this happened on the basis of a letter of intent, not a binding contract, which made the German nuclear businessmen nervous but also put pressure on the Atomic Energy Organization of Iran to finalize the deal.[93]

Some Iranians, E'temad included, worried that Iran was squandering the leverage it enjoyed by having enormous surpluses of petroleum. Were they now investing in an energy technology that was vulnerable to the whims of Americans and Europeans? Especially after India's "Smiling Buddha" explosion, political winds in Europe and North America seemed to be shifting toward strict safeguard agreements and mechanisms of enforcement, even for signers of the non-proliferation treaty. Further, the United States was encouraging numerous countries to participate in multi-national ventures for enriching uranium or reprocessing spent reactor fuel to make plutonium—a move that seemed to indicate that Americans were seeking to maintain leverage over fuel supplies.[94] After speaking to E'temad about securing fuel for the reactors, a British official said "they were almost paranoic [sic] about the supply of uranium to Iran in the future."[95]

Despite new complications arising from the Indian nuclear test, the United States' chief diplomat still was focused on oil. Kissinger reported to Ford in March 1975 that "the Iranian stuff is going very well." Iran had agreed on a $12.5 billion trade package over five years, all in addition to military purchases, and nearly half of it was in nuclear programs (the other half was in port facilities and agricultural projects). Iran agreed to sell the United States 500,000–750,000 barrels of oil per day below OPEC prices, a feat that could be accomplished by tying it to military purchases. Kissinger told the president, "I don't think they realize what they are doing." Ford was delighted. The Americans and Europeans were pushing oil producers into such extensive development programs that they would not be able to reduce production. "We may have broken OPEC," Kissinger said to the president, "or will have if we can make one more deal like this."[96]

Among Americans, the strategy of tethering Middle Eastern countries to the United States with expensive projects, including nuclear reactors, soon became a bipartisan one. The Congressional Research Service was writing a report in 1976 and 1977 about energy demand and explicitly rejected the premise of President Nixon's earlier call for energy independence. The problem with "independence" was that most experts declared it to be impossible. One of the scientists tapped for the study was M. King Hubbert, who had predicted that US annual petroleum output would peak in the early 1970s. He believed strongly that the US reliance on foreign oil would increase every year. He and other participants in the congressional study advised not independence from the Middle East but rather the tightening of international bonds.

The director of the study was Melvin Conant, who knew the strategy well, having been assistant administrator for International Energy Affairs at the US Federal Energy Administration from 1974 to 1976. Referring to Middle East oil producers in general but mentioning Libya's outspoken leader as an example, he and his associate Fern Racine Gold noted that it was essential to make Gaddafi's "threat to merely 'return to the desert' increasingly unpalatable if not impossible" by generating infrastructural expectations among the population, "locking in a level of government expenditure and reducing the capacity of the oil producer to forgo revenue for an extended period of time." Such a strategy could be applied widely to oil producers in the Middle East—certainly Iran, but also Libya, Iraq, and Saudi Arabia.[97]

Conant and Gold stated that the United States had to recognize an unprecedented situation, in which control of energy resources vital to the industrialized countries had passed to a small number of developing countries who were in a position to exercise power. It was a scenario "impossible to imagine in the heyday of colonialism or in a time when recourse to military force was far less risky and more 'legitimate' than it is today." Already the post-1973 consumer unity appeared to be splitting, they warned, because Europeans and Japanese did not wish to be targeted for embargo simply because of their associations with the United States.[98] Conant and Gold argued in favor of a plan similar to that of Henry Kissinger vis-à-vis Iran. The imbalance of dependence "might be transformed, slowly and deliberately, into a condition of mutual dependence." The key elements would be to encourage large capital-intensive projects of modernization, to promote sales of military hardware (especially if American personnel were required to operate them), and to push large-scale investments in the industrialized world.[99]

The United States used the promise of nuclear power to tie Iran's hands, and it planned to do the same with other countries. Often the real target was oil. With OPEC countries sitting on the massive oil deposits driving the economies of the industrial West, they had unprecedented global power in the mid-1970s. The Americans and Europeans had found themselves in a position of resource vulnerability—dependence on the whims of a few countries they likely would have described as "backward." They were determined to swing the pendulum of dependency back in the other direction. Nuclear power was a "carrot" to make this happen, along with other expensive products and services related to high technology such as military aircraft, tanks, and rockets. Ironically, many of these deals failed to materialize in the nuclear programs promised by the givers and imagined by the recipients, leading to an era of immense distrust in the 1980s and beyond.[100] Still, nuclear reactors had become symbols of power in South Asia and the Middle East, and numerous governments financed ambitious nuclear programs—many of them with clandestine bomb programs. Despite the risks of weapons proliferation, it seemed clear to US and European governments that encouraging nuclear infrastructure, by promising a future of abundance, was a clear path forward in regaining control of the world's natural resources and reasserting leverage in a changing geopolitical landscape.

CHAPTER 8
The Era of Distrust

On April 26, 1986, in an obscure nuclear reactor complex near the city of Pripyat in the Ukraine, a series of mishaps led to a reactor meltdown, then to an enormous steam explosion. Nine days of fires followed, lifting radioactive contamination into the atmosphere. Radioactivity from the Chernobyl nuclear complex soon would "fall out" onto the western part of the Union of Soviet Socialist Republics and Europe, turning a local catastrophe into a regional and ultimately global one. Four months after the Chernobyl nuclear accident, scientists and other technical experts gathered in a closed meeting at the IAEA headquarters in Vienna to hear Soviet scientists explain what had gone wrong. Before the Russians spoke, the experts listened to the words of Hans Blix, the IAEA's director-general, who was perhaps the most candid of all.

Blix was certain that much of the future work of nuclear energy would be in public relations, managing attitudes and opinions. The world, he believed, would be tempted to turn away from nuclear power. That could not be allowed to happen, he insisted. Nuclear power was "past the point of no return," he said, and he dismissed the fears of "the many people who worry deeply about the invisible, untouchable—but highly traceable—nuclear radiation." These people would never trust nuclear power, he said, but reasonable and rational people would, if presented with persuasive arguments. And so he made a remarkable statement: "As we are focusing on the contamination caused by an accident in a nuclear plant we might do well, however, to remember that it is as a consequence of the perfectly normal burning of oil and coal to produce energy that our forests are dying."[1] Blix invoked environmental rhetoric, pointing to a catastrophic threat to the earth from a different energy system, at a moment of utter disaster in the nuclear sector. In one breath he pointed to irrational fears of nuclear catastrophe—in the midst of the most serious nuclear debacle yet. In another, he reminded nuclear scientists of the "dying" forests due to fossil fuels.

The post-Chernobyl public relations campaign by the IAEA and its member states would portray nuclear power not only as a technology of abundance but also as an alternative to other energy sources that polluted the atmosphere. Such arguments deflected growing environmental concerns about accidents or radiation exposure by reframing nuclear energy as a solution to impending doom amid catastrophic threats from population growth, disease, and pollution and climate change. These arguments were not a result of Chernobyl but had been percolating for years among nuclear boosters and at the IAEA itself, in the context of the world petroleum crisis, the rise of clandestine weapons programs, and the politics of non-proliferation. They were manifestations of long-standing commitments by numerous governments, including the United States, the Soviet Union, and many others, to protect the image of peaceful nuclear technology from critics.

By the mid-1980s, the state-sponsored positive framing of the peaceful atom served a range of government interests while it masked a great deal. It enabled the United States and European states to use nuclear power as leverage against developing countries in a time when petroleum seemed to swing the pendulum of global resource dominance decisively toward several so-called "backward" countries. It was useful to countries trying to prop up the legitimacy of their nuclear weapons programs while secretly working on bombs, as with Pakistan and Iraq. For many countries, such as France and Sweden, it provided alternative environmental arguments to those whose priority was actually energy security. To the United States, the peaceful atom's bountiful promise and its environmental bona fides helped to maintain a veneer of credibility for the Treaty on the Non-Proliferation of Nuclear Weapons, at a time when the IAEA more than ever seemed to have become the treaty's policing instrument. The more the United States relied on the IAEA, the more it recommitted to making promises of peaceful nuclear technology, especially to the developing world. Yet the widespread endorsement of such a technological future masked the intense distrust within the global nuclear order, offering a unified vision of faith in the atom at a time of disillusionment and acrimony.

***

In a nationwide televised address on April 18, 1977, four months after being inaugurated as president, Jimmy Carter stated that he wished to have an "unpleasant talk" with Americans about the energy problem. Aside from the prevention of war itself, it was the "greatest challenge that our country will face during our lifetime." He added that the effort to control the future, rather than be controlled, would be the "moral equivalent of war." In making the case for extraordinary measures and state-mandated directions in energy development, the president relied on the widespread belief that national and world security was under threat, especially given the US reliance on imported oil. "We will constantly live in fear of embargoes," he said. "We could endanger our freedom as a sovereign nation to act in foreign affairs." Inflation and unemployment would soar, he predicted, and production would fall, and there would be intense competition for the world's oil. "If we fail to act soon, we will face an economic, social, and political crisis that will threaten our free institutions." Carter called for an energy transition that returned the United States to coal and moved toward permanent non-fossil energy such as solar power.[2]

Given the previous decades of promising a future of nuclear abundance, one might have expected Carter to endorse breeder reactors, such as the demonstration plant being designed at the Clinch River site in Tennessee. Its many boosters at the nearby Oak Ridge National Laboratory had long promised that it would help the country achieve energy independence and that breeders would become a virtually inexhaustible source of energy. But in his energy plan, presented to Congress two days later, Carter laid out meager expectations for nuclear power. The US had to use nuclear power as a "last resort" to face the gap between the energy needed and the energy produced and imported. He said there were sixty-three nuclear power plants operating, producing about 3 percent of the nation's total energy, and seventy more were already licensed for production. "There is no need," he said, "to enter the plutonium age by licensing or building a fast breeder reactor such as the proposed demonstration plant at Clinch River." Instead, he favored increasing capacity to produce enriched uranium fuels for light water reactors.[3]

Although Carter took the political heat from it, the idea to turn away from breeders was part of a larger strategy about controlling the nuclear trade, and it did not originate with him. In the last few months of his administration, Gerald Ford had requested a study on the future of nuclear power. Convened by the Henry Ford Foundation and chaired by Spurgeon Keeny of the MITRE Corporation, the report was known as the Ford-MITRE study. Totaling more than 400 pages, it was distilled by *Science* magazine thus: "Nuclear Power Yes, Plutonium No." Two of the participants,

Caltech scientist Harold Brown and Harvard political scientist Joseph Nye joined the government when Jimmy Carter became president in 1977, so the group was influential immediately. It identified chemical reprocessing of spent uranium as a dangerous route to weapons proliferation because the resulting plutonium could be diverted to bomb programs. It also recommended against the development of breeder reactors because these also would be major producers of plutonium.[4]

Although it is tempting to say that weapons proliferation became the United States' primary concern in the 1970s and 1980s, such a conclusion would be misleading. It is more accurate to say that the United States wished to reassert geopolitical leverage, especially over petroleum-producing countries that had once been considered "backward." In this approach the United States enjoyed the support of Europeans, Japan, and the USSR—the other major oil consumers. Nixon and Ford, under Kissinger's influence, had given lip service to non-proliferation while encouraging the sale of reactors as part of a petroleum cartel–breaking strategy. Carter's strategy was not very different, but it would deeply alienate allies because he also characterized "the plutonium economy" as the main culprit in weapons proliferation. Many of the reactors being built in the developing world—by suppliers in France, Britain, and Canada, for example—relied on natural uranium. One of the by-products of fission in such reactors was plutonium, itself a bomb fuel. The United States under Carter advised instead selling reactors using enriched uranium and then taking the spent fuel rods back after their use. From a proliferation perspective, it might have seemed reasonable. But from outside the United States, it seemed a convenient position for the Americans to take, given the existing commitments by the US nuclear industry to light water reactors utilizing enriched uranium rather than designs that used natural uranium.

Even within the United States, some nuclear boosters were devastated by Carter's apparent turn away from atomic energy's most compelling promise, the breeder reactor. The president's background seemed to make him an ally of nuclear power. In the early 1950s, he served under Admiral Hyman Rickover during the navy's first project to put reactors on submarines. Yet more than two decades later he was sounding a note of caution about breeders, after huge investments had been made. The *New York Times* reported that almost $500 million already had been spent on the breeder project from a wide range of sponsors. Residents and workers in Oak Ridge, Tennessee, planned to take their cause to Congress.[5] One particularly vocal opponent was Robert E. Kirby, the chairman of Westinghouse Electric Corporation, which was designing the Clinch River plant. Kirby said that by turning its back on breeders, the United States was "forfeiting tremendous energy resources." He predicted that breeders could eventually provide three times as much energy as the oil from the Middle East.[6]

Such American critics pointed to environmental dangers from the continued reliance on fossil fuels (such as coal) that Carter envisioned. One of the leading voices was Alvin Weinberg. The longtime director of the Oak Ridge National Laboratory had been removed from his position in 1973 largely due to his opposition to the LMFBR design of breeder (he was not against breeders per se; rather, he wanted the United States to put its efforts into molten salt breeder reactors). After a brief stint working in Washington, Weinberg returned to Oak Ridge in 1975 and founded the Institute for Energy Analysis as part of the university consortium there.[7] Weinberg would soon turn to a promising new theory to buffet his arguments in favor of a more robust nuclear power program.

The "global carbon dioxide problem" became a specialty at Oak Ridge in the late 1970s. Scientists at the new energy institute were intrigued by the measurements of carbon dioxide taken in Hawaii since the late 1950s, showing increased concentration of the gas in the atmosphere. In 1976, they articulated their concerns in a technical paper, saying that the concentration of carbon dioxide had increased significantly since 1860. Since data collection began in 1958, the increase had accounted for about half of the carbon dioxide released by the burning of fossil fuels (the rest was taken up by the oceans and by land biota). The Oak Ridge scientists warned that if present trends in the consumption of fossil fuels continued, the resulting atmospheric concentration of carbon dioxide in the next century could reach several times pre-industrial values. That would mean considerable warming of the atmosphere—the so-called greenhouse effect—with increases in average temperatures "that range from possibly acceptable to catastrophic."[8]

Most of the scientists in Weinberg's group were neither environmental activists nor even environmental scientists. There was one meteorologist, Ralph M. Rotty, but the others were nuclear researchers. The lead author of the 1976 study, C. F. Baes, was a chemist whose specialization was molten salt reactor fuels and who had moved to climate research. Another author, Jerry Olsen, was a radiation ecologist at Oak Ridge whose career thus far had focused on the role of radioactive wastes in the natural environment.[9] The final author, Harold E. Goeller, was an Oak Ridge materials engineer and self-described optimist, who thought the environmental doomsayers overstated future resource shortfalls. "Once breeder reactors are perfected," he wrote in 1972, "fuel costs become almost insignificant."[10] By the mid-1970s he and Weinberg were calling themselves cornucopians, pitted against the typically "catastrophist" environmentalists.[11]

The carbon dioxide problem fell into Weinberg's lap just when the nuclear future seemed most bleak. It provided another talking point, showing how atomic energy could provide a future of abundant energy while also preventing catastrophic global effects caused by nuclear power's main competitor, fossil fuels. Scientists working for oil companies interpreted his concerns to be strategic, not genuine. Exxon scientist Henry Shaw observed that Weinberg "was careful to indicate that discussions of the potential CO_2 problems should be led by individuals who are not nuclear advocates, since this problem is associated with fossil fuel burning and could be viewed as a political method to promote nuclear technology."[12] Weinberg could not resist pointing out that nuclear power was a way to avoid carbon catastrophe while also providing energy to power-starved people of the world. In the first issue of the journal *Climatic Change*, begun in 1977, he and Rotty co-authored a piece titled "How Long Is Coal's Future?" "It is inconceivable," they argued, "that the developing countries will remain content with the pittance of energy now allotted them." Instead, "the CO2 Sword of Damocles" compelled serious consideration of non-fossil options, especially in the energy-starved developing world.[13]

The carbon dioxide studies continued in the late 1970s, sponsored by the Department of Energy, a new government body that had taken over many of the functions of the old Atomic Energy Commission after it was dissolved in 1975. The studies were managed by a working group comprised of Weinberg and Rotty, along with an array of like-minded colleagues who hoped to reverse the president's decision to turn away from the atom. Among the working group members, Ruth Patrick was an ecologist and Thomas Malone was a meteorologist. The others were old nuclear hands. Norman Hackerman had worked as a chemist on the Manhattan Project. Wilmot Hess was a former director of the Plowshare program to use peaceful nuclear explosives for earthmoving projects. Melvin Calvin was a scientist at the Lawrence Berkeley Laboratory. The group reported to James L. Liverman, who now held various "environment" administrative positions but who also was a former AEC official. Liverman publicly cast doubt on Carter's energy strategy by noting in congressional testimony that coal contained about three times the amount of carbon as oil or gas—making it a special concern regarding the "greenhouse effect." There was enough economically recoverable coal to raise the global average temperatures to at least five times the present levels, he said.[14]

Just as Carter's energy plan provoked distrust and resistance from nuclear boosters at home, it also courted anger and resentment abroad. By trying to eliminate the "plutonium economy," Carter gave the appearance of making dramatic alterations to the nuclear trade. Congress reinforced that perception by passing amendments to the US Foreign Assistance Act. One of these, introduced by Democratic senator Stuart Symington, had occurred already in 1976, and it banned economic and military assistance to countries that traded in uranium enrichment technology if they did not comply with IAEA safeguards. That amendment had begged the question of whether the United States, as promised by the Treaty on the Non-Proliferation of Nuclear Weapons, would be the "reliable supplier" of enriched fuel that it had promised to be. But in 1977 another amendment, sponsored by Democratic senator (and former astronaut) John Glenn, banned aid to any country trying to acquire chemical reprocessing technology for making plutonium from the spent fuel of uranium reactors, or trying to export it. The Glenn amendment also made any kind of nuclear detonation a deal-breaker for foreign aid. Both plutonium and peaceful nuclear explosives, the United States was saying to the world, were off limits.[15] Among industrialized countries, it smacked of unilateral decision making rather than consultation among key partners. Among developing countries, it looked like the long-feared cartelization of nuclear fuel and technology.[16]

Carter, who tried to project a persona of integrity and fairness, attempted to lead by example. He announced a US moratorium on chemical reprocessing. He also proposed an international group to establish norms regarding the nuclear fuel cycle, known as the International Nuclear Fuel Cycle Evaluation, and several key nations (including France, not a party to the NPT) agreed to take part in it, as long as the results were non-binding. It would hold meetings between 1977 and 1979.[17] In the meantime, the United States continued to act unilaterally to change the rules of the nuclear trade. On March 10, 1978, it passed the Nuclear Non-Proliferation Act. It required renegotiation of existing nuclear trade deals and established the plutonium cycle as the standard benchmark on non-proliferation issues. The legislation instantly banned nuclear transfers to numerous countries: Pakistan, India, Argentina, Brazil, South Africa, Israel, Egypt, and Spain.

Beyond American borders, the new legislation seemed like a heavy-handed attempt by the United States to reassert advantageous control over nuclear commerce, under the guise of non-proliferation. As François Bujon de l'Estang, director of international relations at the French Commisariat à l'Energie Atomique, put it in a 1980 essay in *Commentaire*, the law "marks a break in relation to the concerted approach. . . . [N]ow the United States would define and put its non-proliferation policy into practice unilaterally." He noted that the United States included "a battery of draconian measures," such as embargoes against those refusing to subject themselves to full-scope safeguards, or against those who develop or trade in technologies determined by the United States to be a proliferating technology. France had no plans to reduce dependence on nuclear reactors, and it embraced the cornucopian vision of the peaceful atom more than ever, citing the needs of the most impoverished nations. "France forcefully puts forward the impossibility of solving the world energy problem without a very wide commitment to nuclear energy, not only in the industrialized countries but also in the developing countries, above all if they are energy poor." France would continue to build reactors, to reprocess plutonium, to invest in breeders, and to sell to partners in the developing world.[18]

Bujon de l'Estang observed that an "era of distrust" had begun. The world was in the middle of an energy crisis, with much of its oil in the hands of the formerly colonized. The French state would not just keep its commitments to nuclear power but it would also hold on to the promise of the atom for energy abundance. He complained that environmentalists were unnecessarily complicating matters: "The atmosphere of defiance or of rejection maintained around nuclear energy by minority ecologist activists, skeptics in progress who believe in zero growth, find a supplementary diet" in the risks of proliferation. And yet, the United States had only a fraction of the leverage it once enjoyed in nuclear matters. Carter had tried to lead the way in non-proliferation, but it just emboldened "a common front" of Germany, Japan, France, Great Britain, and the Soviet Union to take the initiative and push hard in the opposite direction. "Labor England itself," the French politician noted, "although it rarely makes choices that are clearly opposed to Washington, has inflicted a veritable rap on the knuckles to American policy by deciding in 1978 to launch the construction of new retreatment [reprocessing] capacities at Windscale . . . and has publicly rejected the American stand." [19]

Global commitments to nuclear power encountered a setback on March 28, 1979, when an American commercial power reactor in Pennsylvania suffered a partial meltdown. The site's name, Three Mile Island, quickly became a household word. The accident was the result of a series of responses to a stuck valve in a filtration system, and engineers would spend months and years debating the extent to which the accident should be blamed on design, operator error, or shortcomings in training. One immediate consequence was the local release of radioactive material into the atmosphere. Fearing a radiological catastrophe, the plant managers declared a state of emergency and evacuated thousands. The accident challenged Americans' commitments to nuclear power, with anti-nuclear activists increasingly identifying commercial reactors with the risk of environmental contamination and public health threats such as thyroid cancer.[20]

Outside the United States, Three Mile Island proved more challenging than Carter's non-proliferation strategy had been. In Sweden, the Liberal and Social Democratic Parties withdrew support from the national nuclear power program and endorsed a new national referendum on the issue.[21] In Italy, politicians in the Communist Party reversed their pro-nuclear stances, requesting a halt to the construction of a high-capacity reactor at Montalto di Castro pending further study by scientists and engineers. As communist politician Armando Cossutta stated, "After the Harrisburg accident, we are not afraid of losing votes, but we are afraid of men and machines. The dramatic episode of the Three Mile Island power station demonstrates, in fact, that even in these very sophisticated machines, breakdowns can occur which can have catastrophic consequences." He argued that the party had to be responsive to the people, and the "people, rightly or wrongly, are afraid of the atom."[22]

Despite stimulating anti-nuclear activism around the world, most governments defended their nuclear commitments by differentiating their designs from the American ones. In Japan, where the designs were similar, savvy pro-nuclear politicians called for Japan to discontinue its reliance on US light-water technology and instead accelerate its own research on different designs.[23] Prime Minister Masayoshi Ōhira dismissed political demands for shutting down power plants all over the country, pointing out that although Japan used pressurized light water reactors, they were of a different design than the American ones. Japan actually had eight operational reactors designed by Westinghouse, though, and decided to close them temporarily to make a slate of new safety inspections.[24]

Unsurprisingly, the Soviet Union and its allies focused on design differences too. The Cuban newspaper *Bohemia* stated that capitalistic greed caused Americans to overlook design flaws and safety shortfalls, whereas Soviet-made reactors had no such problems.[25] The timing of the accident was inauspicious for the Soviet government as it sought to use nuclear technologies to consolidate ties with global partners. Not only was it aiding India's nuclear program, it also in the late 1970s had signed agreements to build Cuba's first nuclear power station and to export reactors to Libya. In Cuba, government officials cast their step toward nuclear power as one of liberation—not only from nature but also from dependence on outsiders.[26] Igor Morokhov, the USSR's first deputy chairman of the State Committee for the Utilization of Atomic Energy, was quick to point out that Soviet safety standards ruled out any possibility of such an accident using Soviet designs. The Soviet Union had ten nuclear power stations, providing only about 3.5 percent of the total power output, but it was constructing seven new plants, enlarging the existing ones, and planning for some seventeen more in the next five years. It was embarking on a major commitment to nuclear power, with the expectation that nuclear energy would meet 20 percent of total demand by the year 2000.[27] In addition to Cuba and Libya, it was exporting reactors to countries in Eastern Europe such Bulgaria, Czechoslovakia, Poland, Hungary, Finland, and the German Democratic Republic.[28]

Soviet claims of safety, while expected, struck most American experts as ridiculous. "The Soviet designers believe they employ a conservative design philosophy, but their safety measures are not as rigorous as those in the US," a top-secret US intelligence briefing stated on April 13, 1979. It added: "An accident at a Soviet nuclear power station would probably have severe results; none of the Soviet reactors now in operation has the secondary containment vessel or emergency core-cooling system included in all US nuclear power stations."[29]

Three Mile Island gave even close allies a tactful way to avoid supporting President Carter's reactor design preferences—using enriched rather than natural uranium. One British official stated that "no government, anywhere in the world, can now lightly approve of nuclear systems of that type." The British had been considering a move away from gas-cooled reactors (using natural uranium) to pressurized light water reactors, but now that idea was dead.[30] In Australia and Canada, politicians saw an opportunity to promote natural rather than enriched uranium—after all, these two countries accounted for about a quarter of the world's total estimated uranium reserves. Some Australian politicians even called for a ban on uranium sales to countries operating pressurized water reactors. Canada had an even greater stake, because it had a significant design competitor, the CANDU reactor, using natural uranium. The US Central Intelligence Agency estimated that there would be pressure in these countries to capitalize on the accident at Three Mile Island.[31]

Three Mile Island played into the hands of those outside the United States who were already annoyed with Carter's anti-plutonium strategy. They saw in the accident a justifiable means of diplomatic retreat from the US vision. One CIA report noted gloomily in late April 1979, that "further impetus will be given to the development and spread of technologies more conducive to the manufacture of nuclear weapons." Few of the other suppliers, that is, Europeans and Japan, "share US views on the degree of risk involved."[32] To the contrary, in one 1979 report, the CIA's National Foreign Assessment Center observed that Western Europeans saw the United States as simply trying to be the "principal architect of the international nuclear system."[33]

With the whole world defecting from American designs and rebelling against the government's unilateral decisions, US nuclear policies were swiftly becoming their own kind of disaster. Gone was the 1950s "Era of Good Feelings," as one CIA report phrased it, when the United States was the main supplier of the world's nuclear fuel and technology. Several European states had become major exporters of nuclear technology—led by France and West Germany, but including Italy, Switzerland, and Sweden. They competed with one another, and with the United States and Soviet Union, for markets. Europeans routinely rejected US attempts to create strict, legally binding safeguard policies, fearing that their hands would be tied when trying to negotiate export contracts. Moreover, Europeans could supply the world's enriched uranium just as well as Americans. The CIA estimated that two Europe-based uranium enrichment consortia, URENCO and Eurodif, were positioned to supply Western Europe with about 70 percent of its enrichment requirements between 1979 and 1985. "These developments have significantly eroded the kind of leverage the United States used in the past to advance its policies in the nuclear field."[34] Bujon de L'Estang seemed to be right—the era of distrust had begun.

Few issues invoked distrust more than the ongoing nuclear trade with countries of the Middle East, particularly Iraq. While the Carter administration was demonizing the "plutonium economy," European nations continued the Kissinger-inspired strategy of promising nuclear reactors to major oil producers. Iraq was one such oil producer, and by the late 1970s it had nuclear ambitions that rivaled Iran's. It had established its own Atomic Energy Commission in 1959, in the wake of the IAEA's founding in 1957 and Iraq's own revolution in 1958. Like other revolutionary governments of the era, Iraq established its nuclear program as an emblem of modernization. Having thrown off the Hashemite monarchy of King Faisal II and his pro-Western Prime Minister Nuri al-Said, the Iraqis left the US-influenced Baghdad Pact and looked primarily to the Soviet Union as a key ally while at home combining Arab nationalism with a commitment to socialism. The Soviet Union agreed to build a small nuclear reactor, the IRT-5000 design, to help the Iraqi Atomic Energy Commission get on its feet. It was a "swimming pool" reactor with the core immersed in water for cooling and radiation shielding. This kind of reactor generated relatively low power (only about 2 megawatts), was ideal for research, and was similar to the experimental reactors offered to other allies such as North Korea and Bulgaria. It would be some years before the reactor could go into operation (1967), but the construction period helped to create a nuclear community at the newly built Nuclear Research Institute in the village of Tuwaitha. To honor the revolution, the Iraqis named the project and reactor "Tammuz," the month of the revolution.[35]

The nuclear landscape in Iraq changed as the Ba'ath Party consolidated its authority after taking power in 1968. Ba'ath ideology focused on Arab unity, freedom from foreign domination, and socialism. One of its major policy moves was to nationalize the oil industry, which not only brought in unprecedented revenue (especially with skyrocketing prices after the 1973 energy crisis), but also gave the Iraqi government an important negotiating tool with other governments. Petroleum gave Iraq far greater freedom in its foreign relations and allowed it to decrease its dependence on others, notably the Soviet Union.

Using oil deals as leverage, the Iraqi government negotiated a series of bilateral agreements to expand its nuclear program. Given Iraq's close proximity and the expressly socialistic, anti-imperialist rhetoric of the Ba'ath Party, the Soviet Union seemed a natural partner in the 1960s. But the Soviets proved to be fickle allies. They did not like to see Iraqi oil being channeled to the West, and in 1975 the Soviet Union began to embargo arms sales to Iraq.[36] Such pressure failed to bring Iraq back into the Soviet orbit. Instead, it drove Iraq even further to the West, where the profits were. Looking for a new arms partner, Ba'ath leader Saddam Hussein traveled to France in 1975 to meet with French prime minister Jacques Chirac. Iraq was France's second-biggest oil supplier, after Saudi Arabia. Although not the president of Iraq, Saddam Hussein was a general in the armed forces and had by then taken over responsibilities for many aspects of government, including military policies and foreign relations. He was the face of Iraq. On that visit to France, Chirac gave Saddam a personal tour of a nuclear plant, enticing him to begin a more robust program. This was at the moment when the United States was encouraging European allies to tie up OPEC oil revenues in expensive long-term projects such as nuclear power and arms deals. With Iraq, France was more than willing to do so, selling nuclear reactors and signing contracts to supply dozens of Mirage F-1 fighter planes.[37]

Iraq did precisely what regional neighbors Israel, Pakistan, and India had done—it joined the IAEA and embraced its cornucopian rhetoric. Unlike these, but like Iran, Iraq also joined the non-proliferation treaty. Iraq publicly painted Baghdad as both a hub of peaceful scientific activities and a beacon of Arab independence from Western domination (and after the 1979 Soviet invasion of Afghanistan, from the USSR as well). Baghdad became the home of the Federation of Arab Scientific Research Councils, founded in 1975. After agreeing to buy reactors and to have Iraqi scientists trained by the French, Iraq positioned them as part of its rising level of scientific expertise in a range of peaceful domains. North American and British diplomats did not trust Iraq's intentions and increasingly viewed its commercial program through the lens of weapons proliferation. One British embassy official reported confidentially that the Iraqis were "paranoiacally secretive," and their partners—the French, Italians, and Brazilians—also were tight-lipped, not wishing to get thrown out of Iraq. "I think that Iraq will make nuclear weapons as soon as it can and with whatever help it can get. It will not be inhibited by the Non-Proliferation Treaty. I have no proof of this, but I should be most surprised if I were wrong."[38]

Most of the outside attention to Iraq's nuclear program focused on its partnership with France and also its trade transactions with Italy. The French deal concerned the purchase of two research reactors, named (after ancient deities) Isis and Osirak and constructed by the firm Technicatome. The Osirak reactor was the larger of the two, designed to generate 40 to 70 megawatts of power, significantly more than the existing Soviet-built one at Tuwaitha. The design for Osirak included the use of larger amounts of highly enriched uranium, material that potentially could be diverted to a weapons program. Italy helped Iraq to build a radioisotope production laboratory, a materials testing laboratory, a chemical engineering laboratory, and a fuel fabrication laboratory. Between them, the French and Italians were helping the Iraqis develop a community of working professionals versed in radiochemistry, nuclear physics, nuclear engineering, and other fields indirectly relevant to the nuclear program.[39]

Concerns about the program only heightened when Italy agreed to sell Iraq a "hot cell." This apparatus was essentially a containment area for highly radioactive material, surrounded by lead shielding and using mechanical arms to manipulate objects. A research laboratory would wish to have such a hot cell for any number of legitimate peaceful experiments, but it also could facilitate the separation of plutonium, a weapon fuel. The Italians dismissed concerns, saying that the laboratory would enable Iraq to use nuclear techniques in agriculture, food preservation, and medicine— the typical showcase projects of the IAEA. To do that, they argued, Iraqis needed a laboratory.[40]

Italy's deal with Iraq made a mockery of the international safeguard system, with both participants exhibiting an egregious degree of bad faith to non-proliferation goals. For Iraq to want, and Italy to supply, a radioisotope production laboratory at such an early stage in Iraq's civil nuclear program seemed a clear marker of a desire for plutonium production capability. The argument for having such a facility in Iraq was paper-thin. It would have been cheaper to purchase radioisotopes from any number of research labs outside Iraq. But with this equipment, British government scientists guessed, Iraq could make enough plutonium for a bomb by the end of the decade.[41]

Although the Italians and French received considerable scorn for their roles, exploiting safeguard rules was widespread. In late 1979, for example, the IAEA discovered a scheme by which a German firm, Nukem, had shipped six tons of depleted uranium and four tons of natural uranium to Iraq. Under the non-proliferation treaty, the IAEA should have been notified. The Germans had not done so because they first shipped it to a private company in Italy, which made it a European shipment, within the bounds of the European Atomic Energy Community (Euratom) and requiring no declaration. The Italian firm exported it to Iraq without notifying anyone. The shipment was discovered only because the driver of the truck carrying it had stopped outside Rome for the night to sleep, and a passing police officer noticed the radioactivity labels on the containers. He ordered the driver into a nearby nuclear facility, which made note of the uranium. An official at the British embassy in Vienna wrote: "The complete story, gleaned from a variety of reliable sources within the IAEA, has all the ring of a Frederick Forsyth novel."[42]

The smuggling of uranium did in fact make for dramatic retelling. A 1979 novel by a different author, Ken Follet, recreated the events of a similar Israeli operation a decade earlier. In his book *Triple*, Follet chose as his setting the nuclear arms race in the Middle East, begun after the Six Day War. Part of the action included the (not fictional) efforts by Israel to bypass nuclear safeguards in Europe during the transportation phase. In the real 1968 scenario, which only became widely known in 1977, Israel illegally intercepted hundreds of tons of uranium ore being shipped by sea between Belgium and Italy. While in the open ocean, the uranium, in canisters labeled "Plumbat," was offloaded into the Israeli-controlled vessel. The writer who publicized the story in the *New York Times*, Paul Leventhal, lamented in 1978 that the same weaknesses that had allowed the Israelis to pluck hundreds of tons of uranium out of the ocean in 1968 still could be exploited a decade later.[43] Similarly, in the mid-1960s, a US nuclear facility discovered that about 100 kilograms of bomb-grade uranium had disappeared, and internal investigations in the 1970s seemed to point to Israel as the uranium's eventual destination.[44]

What was remarkable about the 1979 German incident was not just the transaction itself but the willingness of multiple parties to turn a blind eye to it. It was clear that the German firm was trying to exploit a loophole in the non-proliferation system in order to export material to Iraq. The Italians also played a role. Not only was the export company located in Italy, but the Italian government also waited nearly three months before mentioning the incident to Euratom. Then Euratom was implicated because it did not tell the IAEA. It blamed some sort of computer breakdown. The only ones who seemed to know everything were the Israeli intelligence services, who knew exactly how this could be done—after all, they had done it themselves. They tipped off the German news magazine *Der Spiegel* about the incident. Only when *Der Spiegel* asked the IAEA for more information did the so-called proliferation watchdog finally learn of it.[45]

That particular incident illustrated patent failings in the nuclear safeguard system and an obvious will of parties at every level to exploit them. Euratom, conscious of the possibility of another "Plumbat Affair," played down the incident as being of "rather low importance" because of the small amount involved and that the sale itself was legal.[46] This did miss the point, though. As one British official put it, "It is worrying that the Iraqis did not declare receipt of the material. This creates a presupposition that the loophole was being exploited deliberately and that Iraq was seeking to build up some sort of stockpile in breach of her NPT obligations."[47] Furthermore, Euratom's insistence that the amount was small and thus of negligible importance ignored the possibility that this discovered shipment was just one of many.

German nuclear firms were later found to be even deeper into the illicit trade in nuclear materials than a one-time shipment by truck to Italy. A few years later Nukem got into trouble again because its subsidiary, Transnuklear, was caught transporting radioactive materials across Europe, sending uranium to Belgium's reprocessing facility at Mol and then taking the fuel back again as fissionable material. A government investigation uncovered just how systematic these transactions were. Transnuklear's manager, Hans Holtz, committed suicide in jail after being charged with paying millions of dollars in bribes over years. Nukem suspended several top executives. After that scandal, the German government acknowledged that the transportation scheme may have led to bomb material being sent illegally to Sweden, Libya, and Pakistan. Prosecutors later found evidence that other German firms were the sources of fuel as well as technology, having illegally shipped reactor parts to Pakistan, India, and South Africa.[48]

On September 22, 1979, an event occurred that highlighted the widespread ignorance about the state of the world's bomb programs. An American intelligence satellite detected an intense burst of light in the ocean between the southern tip of Africa and Antarctica, leading to speculation about whether it might have been a nuclear test. If so, by whom? The location seemed to suggest South Africa had done it, but no one could know for sure. Perhaps it had been Israel, or Pakistan, journalists wondered, and locating it off South Africa had been a ruse.[49] Speculation also arose that the blast was part of a joint Israeli and South African undertaking. Guesswork about the mysterious flash certainly strengthened the hand of those wishing to bar South Africa from the IAEA. The truth was that President Carter had no idea whether the flash had been a bomb or not, as the intelligence provided to him was inconclusive.[50]

Amid such uncertainty about the state of weapons proliferation, North Americans and Europeans continued to use nuclear reactors as leverage in negotiations over petroleum in both Iran and Iraq, and by 1980 the stage was set for extraordinary levels of tension. Potential or known nuclear weapons programs existed throughout the region, including Israel, Iraq, and Iran, and extending farther into Pakistan, India, and China. Cases of sabotage of individual nuclear programs were widespread. For example, an Egyptian nuclear engineer working for the Iraqi Atomic Energy Commission was a widely noted case of assassination. When Yahya al-Meshad went to France to work out a deal for acquiring highly enriched uranium, he turned up murdered in a Parisian hotel. A French prostitute who had met him was hit by a car and killed a couple of days later. Most believed that the Israelis were responsible, though others suggested Saddam Hussein may have suspected him as a spy and wanted him dead. Another young engineer, Salman Rashid, had been working on designs for uranium enrichment while on a fellowship in Geneva at the European Center for Nuclear Research. Before returning home, Rashid became ill with what appeared to be a bad case of the flu, and he died about ten days later.[51]

Saddam Hussein saw the opportunity for Iraq to become a regional leader in nuclear development and called for a new Arab-wide organization for the peaceful application of nuclear energy, to be based in Baghdad. It would convene conferences and seminars on desert reclamation, seawater desalination, medicine, electricity, and agriculture—in other words, it would mirror the goals of "Atoms for Peace" and the IAEA exactly.[52] Saddam Hussein's rhetoric, while provocative and always bellicose toward Israel, presented scientific expertise as itself a key to Arab strength, whether with peaceful or military intent. The following cable was passed through several British diplomatic posts after a press conference with Saddam Hussein in July 1980:

> Saddam said that a scientifically weak nation would be more easily defeated than one that was scientifically strong. The Arabs' numerical superiority over Israel had been rendered null and void for this reason. But the Arab nation was undergoing a scientific Renaissance. The Arab people realized that they could preserve their independence, rights and honor in today's world only by achieving

a balanced scientific development in line with other countries, including their enemies and particularly the Zionist entity.[53]

Saddam Hussein went even further to underscore the military and peaceful implications of scientific strength, repeating that Iraq's nuclear program was peaceful but that "Israel should however understand that the Arabs were no longer disunited, without a sense of purpose and scientifically backward. Those wishing to be hostile to the Arabs should realize that in five years time they would no longer face an under-developed nation." He accused Israel of trying to impede scientific development so that it could maintain its lead over the Arabs.[54]

By the time highly enriched fuel began to arrive in Iraq from France in the summer of 1980, the situations in both Iraq and Iran had become even more volatile. The Iranian Revolution of 1979 utterly transformed the diplomatic landscape of the Middle East, turning a country with close ties to Europe and the United States into a Shia Islamist nation that stood in open defiance of the United States and called for new Islamic republican governments throughout the region. The United States found its embassy overrun and its citizens held hostage in Tehran. The country it had spent a decade arming to the teeth and supplying with nuclear infrastructure had become an implacable foe. Meanwhile Iraq seemed ready to take Iran's place as the West's oil supplier and had strong trade relationships with France, Italy, and Japan. By 1980 it was supplying 20 percent of France's petroleum imports (Saudi Arabia accounted for nearly 35 percent), and in return it was getting not only Mirage fighter planes but also rockets, helicopters, and other military equipment.[55]

Israeli experts believed that the Osirak site was already part of a bomb project. The former president of Tel Aviv University, physicist Yuval Ne'eman, routinely pointed out the military threat posed by Iraq's reactor. He warned in the summer of 1980 that Iraq had brought in several Pakistani scientists to help build a bomb. He dismissed the notion of a "research" reactor, totally unjustified in a country without the bare rudiments of a nuclear research community. The reactor's only purpose, he maintained, was an atomic bomb. In a press interview he went so far as to predict that a bomb could be ready in a year, and he warned that the uranium sold to Iraq by France could be used without further processing to construct about eight bombs. And more uranium was being purchased from Africa that could, with the help of the Italian reprocessing facility, be used to make plutonium.[56]

Israel and Iran, strange bedfellows, together scoffed at Saddam's claims of a peaceful atomic energy program, and both nations took dramatic steps to hinder Iraq's nuclear development. Iran did so at the start of a long and bloody war. Iraq had invaded Iran on September 22, 1980, pressing its border disputes at a time when Western countries were still recoiling from the Iranian revolution. Shortly after, on September 30, Iran sent two of its American-made F-4 Phantom jets to bomb the Osirak reactor. Less than a year after that strike, on June 7, Israel conducted another air strike on the facility, using six of its American-made F-16A planes. It did so even though it was not at war with Iraq. The Israelis made no secret of it and took responsibility shortly after the bombing. Prime Minister Menachem Begin justified the strike on the grounds that Saddam Hussein was evil and would have no qualms about dropping atomic bombs on Israeli cities as soon as they were available. The official announcement said that no foreigners at the site had been killed, though the French pointed out that in fact one of their workers had died in the raid.[57]

The Osirak attacks forced a reckoning about US attitudes toward the peaceful atom. Was the United States still committed to promoting peaceful nuclear technologies or had the era of "Atoms for Peace" passed into insignificance? The United States had spent the past decade trying assert leverage over the Middle East, offering expensive technologies such as fighter jets, aerial reconnaissance planes, and nuclear reactors. But the attacks on Osirak indicated that at least two countries—Israel and Iran—considered the peaceful atom to be enough of a sham to justify bombing a reactor site.

The election of Ronald Reagan as US president yielded a dramatic pivot away from Carter's efforts to eliminate the plutonium economy. While on the presidential campaign trail, Reagan had promised to repeal the Nuclear Non-Proliferation Act. Early in the campaign he said of other nations' nuclear programs: "I just don't think it's any of our business." That sent his aides scurrying for a more thoughtful policy, and soon Reagan affirmed that he too was against the spread of nuclear weapons but with a disclaimer that it seemed futile since "we're the only one in the world that's trying to stop it."[58] While campaigning in Tennessee, he appeased pro-nuclear constituents by voicing his support for the breeder reactor at Clinch River, raising hopes that breeders would come alive under a new administration. Reagan dismissed Carter's concern that support of breeders would lead the world toward an increasingly dangerous plutonium economy.[59]

After his inauguration in 1981, Reagan attempted to resuscitate the US nuclear industry. Not only did he endorse the breeder reactor project but he also planned more subsidies for the nuclear sector, despite coming into power on a platform of free enterprise and decreased government spending.[60] Later in the year he went further, saying he wanted to increase the speed of licensing new reactors and to lift the US ban on reprocessing spent reactor fuel.[61] Like many intelligence analysts, diplomats, and others within the Carter administration, Reagan had come to believe that US actions in recent years had done more harm than good, undermining the nation's position as a reliable supplier and diminishing its negotiating leverage. Reagan stated that the United States would increase its support of international inspections and would stop pressuring countries to abandon the plutonium system.[62]

After Israel's raid on Osirak, Reagan faced a dilemma. Should the United States defend the aggressor, simply because it was an ally? Or should it defend the country that had embraced the peaceful atom, its multiple promises, and even the non-proliferation treaty? Opposition to Israel's action was widespread in the United Nations as well as among member states of the International Atomic Energy Agency, many of whom called for stripping Israel of membership. Reagan's diplomats tried to navigate delicately, joining in the UN Security Council condemnation of Israel's attack while also successfully lobbying against the suspension of Israel from the IAEA. They failed to prevent a resolution suspending technical assistance to Israel and condemning the Osirak attack as an act of aggression. The United States also failed to block a UN resolution calling on Israel to put its own nuclear facilities under IAEA safeguards. The vote on that resolution was 107 to 2, with Reagan the only leader willing side with Israel, and 31 countries abstaining.[63]

Lacking a consistent position about nuclear programs in the region, Reagan fell into the practice of seeking leverage in the way his predecessors had, by offering access to American technologies that, once gained, would be hard to give up. In practice, that usually meant military technology. The United States provided tanks, advanced fighter aircraft, air defense missiles, naval patrol crafts, and logistical support not only to Israel but also to the Arab states. The level of military sales credits (large amounts of which would be forgiven) to Egypt, for example, was slated to go up from an already-hefty $900 million in 1982 to $1.3 billion in 1983. Israel got $1.4 billion in 1982, with $1.7 billion planned for 1983.[64]

One reason military assistance was so attractive to the US government was that, like the efforts with nuclear reactors in Iran in the mid-1970s, they were often multi-year commitments that created bonds of dependence. Earlier Kissinger had described the Saudis as "feckless and gutless," and his strategies for securing oil had focused on Iran. With the Islamic Revolution under way in Iran, the United States could not count on Iranian oil. After the outbreak of war between Iran and Iraq, the future of oil supplies rested increasingly on good relations with allies on the Arabian peninsula. The US ambassador to Saudi Arabia, John C. West, cautioned that the use of oil as a weapon was highly likely. "The Saudis are by instinct and heredity traders and survivors," he wrote in a secret report to Washington. "The experience of 3,000 years of swapping camels, trading horses and selling carpets seems to be in their genes. They have a most valuable commodity and we would be making a grave mistake to expect that they will ultimately take less than full value for it." He noted that a cutoff of present supplies, or even a substantial decrease, "will produce an economic disaster."[65] Given Saudi concerns about their own security during the Iran-Iraq conflict, the Carter administration already had begun to talk with them about helping develop an air defense system and expanded ground facilities, with US support.[66]

Military assistance provided the United States with continuing influence, especially when the technology could be tied to large-scale defense systems that required constant refining, training, and engagement by the United States. Saudi Arabia, by the end of 1981, was "by far the largest single purchaser of US military equipment, services, and construction," and that was set to expand with an $8.5 billion air defense enhancement package.[67] That package was designed to help Saudi Arabia protect its oilfields with the most advanced technology, including the latest Sidewinder heat-seeking missiles, refueling tankers for F-15s fighter jets, and an airborne warning and control system (AWACS) to provide a sevenfold increase in range from ground-based radar systems. The AWACS system, based on the distinctive E-3A planes with giant rotodomes housing radar antennas, could detect any incoming attacking aircraft. It accounted for the largest share of the budget, five planes totaling $5.8 billion. According to the arms package description by the United States, "the nature of the AWACS is so complex that US contractor personnel will be required to maintain key elements of the system for its entire life. . . . The withdrawal of US support for the Saudi AWACS would quickly result in the system becoming non-operational." In addition, the air system would necessitate an extensive logistics and supply base using American-made equipment, spare parts, and facilities, "fully compatible with equipment which would be deployed with US forces" should need arise. Implementing these systems, along with their required ground facilities, was planned to take some six years.[68]

Military hardware became the Reagan administration's preferred means of exerting leverage over existing nuclear programs by key regional allies. Some national security advisors thought that supplying surveillance aircraft to Pakistan—like the kind provided to Saudi Arabia—could also maintain American influence over Pakistan's nuclear program. After discovering that Pakistan had an undisclosed uranium enrichment facility near Kahuta, the United States imposed economic and military sanctions starting in 1979.

But in December 1981, Reagan lifted these sanctions, keeping in place only the restriction on nuclear aid. He reasoned that after the Soviet invasion of neighboring Afghanistan, Pakistan needed to be heavily armed. Rather than bring the full force of sanctions to bear on Pakistan, the United States simply got out of the nuclear trade with it and strengthened it in every other way.[69] Indian diplomats later pointed out that the division between nuclear and non-nuclear was not so clear-cut. US-supplied F-16 fighter jets could be interpreted as a delivery vehicle for nuclear bombs. To India, the Americans' two-faced actions with Pakistan, like its dealings with Israel, simply revealed the bankruptcy of American non-proliferation policy.[70]

Cynicism about American actions ran high at IAEA meetings too, especially among the so-called less developed countries (LDCs). Were the Americans shaping the IAEA into a mechanism of technological control akin to the colonial era, while also turning a blind eye to the bomb programs of its military allies? The United States remained a staunch ally and arms supplier of both Israel and Pakistan, both of which belonged to the IAEA but refused to become party to the non-proliferation treaty. Moreover, the United States continued to cozy up to the racist government of South Africa, a key uranium supplier in sub-Saharan Africa—and another non-signer of the treaty. Further, the United States and Europeans seemed to be treating nuclear fuel in the same way that OPEC was treating oil—trying to act like a cartel.

In the early 1980s, the IAEA was nearly torn apart by conflicts on these issues. At one September 1981 meeting of the IAEA board of governors, the US representative, Richard T. Kennedy, found himself trying to block resolutions about IAEA hiring quotas for less developed countries and another resolution suspending Israel from membership in the agency in reprisal for its attack on Iraq's Osirak reactor. Although the United States succeeded in blocking these, it was unable to prevent the board from pledging to cut Israel's annual technical assistance package and from threatening to eject Israel if it did not agree to subject its own nuclear facilities to IAEA safeguards by the next meeting in a year's time. One US official reported, "It was the most politicized, most contentious session I've ever attended. . . . For a while, we really thought that the agency would not survive." [71] US intelligence analysts perceived a "growing disenchantment" with the atom in the developing world as a reaction to the increasingly policeman-like quality of the agency. "Many developing countries view these efforts as an affront to their national sovereignty," one report asserted, "and as another example of attempts by the industrialized countries to hold the developing states in a position of permanent economic, political, and military subordination."[72]

Conflicts about the agency's identity were epitomized by the months-long dispute in 1981 about hiring a new director-general to succeed Sigvard Eklund—who planned to retire after serving for two decades. The two leading candidates highlighted the North-South split within the agency. The one favored by most of the developing nations was Domingo Siazon of the Philippines. Siazon was widely perceived as likely to reaffirm the IAEA's role of making atomic energy widely available rather than using the agency to pursue non-proliferation aims. Favored by industrialized countries was another Swede, Hans Blix. Both men were diplomats, with Siazon having been an ambassador and Blix serving as Sweden's minister for foreign affairs. Siazon had degrees in political science and physics, whereas Blix was a professor of law who came to prominence at the IAEA as a weapons inspector. He had made several inspections of the Osirak reactor in Iraq before it was bombed. Blix was perceived as an experienced arms control specialist who would bend the IAEA toward pursuing non-proliferation goals.[73]

Although Blix was selected, the decision involved a compromise: the IAEA vowed to expand its board of governors to include more members from developing countries, and it endorsed a resolution to consider a representative of less developed countries when the next director-general was chosen in 1985. Journalist Judith Miller wrote: "Many officials interpret this as a signal that Mr. Blix may be a one-term chief." (They were wrong: Blix would remain as head of the IAEA until 1997.)[74] Superficially, the selection of Blix to succeed Eklund as director-general represented continuity in leadership, with similarities ranging from the predictable (both were white men) to the implausible (both were Swedes, and both had studied at Uppsala University). But there were important differences between the two men. Eklund was a nuclear physicist, with experience in bodies promoting peaceful uses of atomic energy, and he had led the efforts to build Sweden's first research reactor in the 1950s. Blix, on the other hand, was a professor of international law and briefly a politician, with no scientific credentials. He had spent the 1970s in Sweden's Ministry of Foreign Affairs, advising on legal matters, and he participated in his nation's delegation to the United Nation's Conference on Disarmament. He then served as Sweden's foreign minister from 1978 to 1979. After the Three Mile Island accident, Blix led the Swedish Liberal Party's efforts to retain the nuclear program amid a national referendum on the future of energy. He was both a staunch promoter of nuclear power and a seasoned veteran of disarmament negotiations.

The political compromise between North and South within the IAEA had immediate consequences that inflamed divisions even further. On

September 24, 1982, the IAEA board of governors—with its newly expanded membership—voted to reject Israel's credentials as a member state at the meeting. It was not the first such move by the board of governors, which had barred South Africa from a meeting in 1979.[75] This time the target was a key US ally. Arab, African, and Soviet bloc nations made up most of those voting for it, and indeed they had tried to expel Israel from the agency permanently, with the accusation that—in addition to building atomic bombs—Israel had committed genocide against the Palestinians. Although that had failed by a vote of 43 to 27, a softer resolution did pass, offered by Iraq, recognizing all states' credentials to be at the meeting except Israel's. It required only a majority to pass, and squeaked by at 41 to 39.[76] Reagan was so outraged at the rejection of Israel that he withdrew the US delegation and suspended participation in the agency's activities. Other nations did the same—Japan, Australia, Canada, and the Europeans on the board. Since the meeting was nearly finished, the "walkout" was not very consequential. However, the United States stated that it was going to reassess its commitments to, and even participation in, the IAEA.[77]

The "walkout" by the countries of the nuclear North provoked a serious policy reconsideration that pushed the agency even further toward a policing role. Within the US government, an inter-agency group began a formal reassessment of the IAEA and carefully redefined its purpose. One revealing State Department analysis drew sharp distinctions between the IAEA's original purpose of assisting developing countries to adopt the "peaceful atom," against its current role as a non-proliferation watchdog. The right balance between these roles was the major source of contention within the agency, and it divided members along North-South lines. More and more, the large budgets from states like the United States were oriented toward policing, not technical assistance.[78] But the United States needed the agency more than it liked to admit. According to the new State Department analysis, the agency had become an indispensable instrument of US policy. "The IAEA plays a vital role in the implementation of our non-proliferation policy which, in turn, provides an essential foundation for our international nuclear commerce," the State Department assessment read. "It is thus an important element in our national security system. No other international organization is relied upon by the U.S. in this manner."[79] No safeguards-only organization could ever hope to attract as many members as the IAEA, since the only reason most members joined was for the technical assistance. "Developing countries view the Agency primarily as a conduit for technical assistance and technology transfer," despite most industrialized countries seeing its purpose as keeping nuclear weapons in the hands of just a few states.[80]

Reagan administration officials reasoned that only through the IAEA could the nuclear North hope to control the nuclear trade without blatantly seeming like a cartel. A CIA report noted that creating a different supplier-based safeguards organization would be asking for trouble, because it would appear to developing countries to be a "nuclear OPEC." Working through the IAEA allowed the United States to avoid that accusation, and it "provides unique intelligence access to the nuclear programs of potential proliferators." Even non-signatories to the NPT still had to be members of the IAEA if they expected to engage in legal nuclear commerce. By participating in the IAEA, the United States obtained intelligence from inspectors while providing the nation with "a convenient and political[ly] acceptable forum for addressing major proliferation problems posed by certain countries."[81] The inter-agency group was unanimous, according to Reagan's ambassador-at-large on non-proliferation Richard Kennedy, "in the belief that the IAEA contributes significantly to US national security interests because of its role in helping to prevent the spread of nuclear weapons."[82]

The 1982 reassessment did not mark a turning point, but the decision affirmed trends that had been under-way for many years. In laying out the reasons for taking part in the IAEA, the group laid to rest any conviction that the agency genuinely played a useful role in promoting effective energy choices or economical solutions to resource shortfalls and environmental problems. None of the rationales provided by any of the members of the working group put even the slightest stock in the positive value of nuclear technology per se. They instead focused on weapons programs and the "attitudinal problem" of the developing world, which seemed obsessed with criticizing Israel and South Africa.[83] Yet the need to advertise such benefits of atomic energy remained as strong as ever. At that time, about $30 million ($8 million paid by the United States) of the agency's overall budget of $91 million ($21 million from the United States) was devoted to non-proliferation safeguards. The IAEA claimed it would need to double its safeguards staff to meet non-proliferation needs. To do so without provoking the ire of the global South, they would need to enhance the "peaceful atom" projects as well and play up the benefits of nuclear technology.[84]

The recommitment of the United States and its allies to the IAEA provided a clear rationale for governments to defend commercial nuclear power against its critics. This was more easily done in Europe, especially where heavy state investments were already under way—like France, for example, where nuclear power supplied most of the nation's electricity. In the United States, Reagan faced opposition from numerous political foes in his efforts to promote nuclear power. Democratic congressman Richard

Ottinger observed, in congressional hearings, that while the Department of Energy had stopped printing fuel economy guides or information about solar energy, federal taxpayer dollars were collaborating in a public relations blitz for the nuclear industry, much of which was geared toward assuaging public concerns about environmental contamination or the public health effects of accidents. "I do think that the Government ought not to be a propaganda organization seeking to indoctrinate the public on policies which it favors," he told Shelby Brewer, Department of Energy assistant secretary. Brewer defended these decisions by saying the general public had become too hysterical, like a madman arguing the world was flat. "And is, in this instance, the assertion that the earth is indeed round not a fact, or is it a political statement?"[85]

Reagan tried to reinvigorate the nuclear industry in the face of repeated failures. He supported the Clinch River Breeder Reactor program, but it had many enemies in Congress who worried about its cost, its contributions to the plutonium economy, or more accidents like the one at Three Mile Island. In December 1982, the General Accounting Office estimated that the project's estimated cost was too low by half and could end up costing some $8.5 billion.[86] The project lost steam in both houses of Congress, and by October 1983 it was virtually dead, with funds voted down by the Senate—after some $1.7 billion had already been spent. Arkansas senator Dale Bumpers, a Democrat, observed, "We put some money down a rat hole and decided not to spend any more."[87] Still, the Reagan administration looked for other pathways to keep the nuclear industry alive, such as an effort to build nuclear reactors on military bases within the United States.[88] Nuclear reactors became crucial features of the imagined space-based missile defense system, the Strategic Defense Initiative.[89] And Reagan negotiated an agreement with China allowing it to purchase American reactors, to make US suppliers more competitive against French and German ones.[90]

Nuclear energy advocates tried to be responsive to the perceived attack on commercial nuclear power by environmentalists by turning increasingly toward environmental arguments of their own. They saw opportunity not only in climate change but also in acid rain. One of the key environmental disputes in 1982 and 1983 was on the effects of sulfur dioxide pollution from burning coal—the "acid rain" that garnered headlines all over the United States and Canada. Scientists pointed out the stresses of such pollution on forest ecosystems over huge swaths of territory.[91] Many of those who promoted nuclear energy in the early 1980s agreed with physicist Bernard L. Cohen's 1983 book *Before It's Too Late*, which pointed out that nuclear energy was virtually harmless compared to burning oil or coal.[92]

Such arguments comparing nuclear power favorably to other forms of atmospheric pollution would come into widespread use at the IAEA as well. When Hans Blix became director-general of the IAEA, he wrote an essay on the agency's relevance, and at that time he drew mainly on familiar arguments for nuclear technologies—its role in food and agriculture, in medicine, and in energy production. Blix also discussed nuclear proliferation at length.[93] Yet in the next few years, as nuclear power came under increased scrutiny throughout Europe and as the United States appeared to be walking away from it altogether, he and others at the IAEA adopted arguments that attempted to play up the environmental threats from existing energy sources such as oil and coal, and to describe nuclear power as environmentally benign in comparison. Blix's IAEA would adopt this approach intensively in the wake of the Chernobyl disaster of 1986.

Because the Chernobyl nuclear accident occurred in Ukraine, one of the Soviet Socialist Republics, there was precious little public information about what happened there. We now know that the accident involved a reactor meltdown, chemical explosions, and the release of an enormous amount of radioactive debris into the atmosphere. As an ecological and public health disaster it was more serious than the one at Three Mile Island had been. It involved numerous deaths onsite among operators as they attempted to control the problem, among workers cleaning up debris, and among helicopter pilots attempting to drop materials onto the reactor to suffocate it. The nearby village of Pripyat was evacuated, and scientists continue to debate the extent, and consequences, of exposure to humans in the vicinity, to neighboring countries, and beyond.[94]

At the IAEA, Blix and his colleagues knew few of the details about the accident, but that did not prevent them from attempting to do public relations damage control for nuclear power. Blix visited Moscow in early May 1986 shortly after the accident and, in a joint communiqué, he and a Soviet government official stated that the USSR would provide as soon as possible some information about the accident to be discussed by nuclear safety experts. Prior to that, in a Chernobyl-themed issue of the *IAEA Bulletin* shortly after the accident, Blix acknowledged that large accidents were capable of inflicting damage. But he urged a comparative approach, taking into account the risks of dams bursting, gas explosions, and the like. "We must be equally aware how much sulphur dioxide, nitrogen oxide, and carbon dioxide are produced by power stations generating electricity by coal or oil. To the concern we feel about their contribution to dead forests, acid lakes, and cancer we must now add anxiety about possible greenhouse effect of the carbon dioxide generation that is inevitably linked with the burning of fossil fuel." He then reminded his readers that providing nuclear technology was essential for controlling the spread of nuclear weapons, noting that the "basic approach during 30 years of effort has been to make nuclear material and technology available in return for non-proliferation commitments and the verification of compliance with those commitments." Saying that this had been the approach of the previous three decades was, to say the least, an over-generalization. He observed, "It is fair to say that this 'Atoms for Peace' approach has been reasonably successful—at least if we compare the situation now with what many people once feared."[95]

The Soviets made good on their promise and sent experts to Vienna in August 1986 to provide a detailed report of the accident at the IAEA headquarters. Things had gone terribly wrong, they acknowledged, though they laid blame on the operators of the plant (some of whom would go to prison). The Soviets emphasized that at each decision point in the test, the operators broke procedural rules or made poor judgments. For example, because the test itself was going to disturb water levels, and this would have initiated automatic emergency cooling water injection, the operators disabled that safety feature. In fact, several automatic shut-down features were disabled during the overnight test of April 25 and 26, but the operators assumed they would be able to assert manual control if things went awry. They were wrong, and when the reactor overheated, their many efforts to shut it down failed. Not only did the reaction continue, but the increased heat led to a non-nuclear explosion that destroyed the reactor and much of the building. Chemical reactions produced hydrogen gas that "was able to escape through the breach and to mix with air providing an explosive mixture," one British digest of the Soviet report noted. "This reaction was observed as fireworks of flying hot and glowing fragments."[96]

The human cost of Chernobyl, even in the short term, was high. In addition to the fireworks display, the air was filled with radionuclides. The Soviets reported that in the first thirty-six hours, about 350 people showed signs of radiation sickness and were evacuated to a hospital in Moscow. Some had thermal burns, and most had skin burns from beta irradiation up to 100 percent of their body surface. Twenty-one of twenty-two patients who received doses greater than 6 Gy (Gy is shorthand for Gray, a unit measuring radiation absorption) died within a month. Seven of twenty-three people who received 4–6 Gy died, and one of ninety-eight people receiving less than 4 Gy died in that period. Russian doctors attempted skin grafting, bone marrow grafting, and even transplants of human embryo liver cells in their efforts to save patients. Some died from complications of such procedures, but most deaths were due to overwhelming skin damage from the first exposure to beta irradiation. Despite such a grave report, the Soviets insisted that no member of the public suffered acute radiation sickness. The population in a 30 km zone was evacuated, they said, and was being thoroughly monitored through studies of blood, thyroid, and often total body gamma counting.[97]

Like Blix, head of the Soviet delegation Valerii Legasov stated that it was important to prevent Chernobyl from hindering nuclear development. Without nuclear plants, he said, the USSR would be "unable to master" the next development stage in Soviet society. He amplified the message of the written report that the fault lay in operator error, but in person he was more expansive in his criticism. The designers of the RBMK reactor made a "tremendous psychological mistake" in relying on humans to make intelligent choices and to obey rules. Legasov lamented that the reactor designers had relied on safety rules rather than engineered safety mechanisms. "We have started later than other specialists to think about the need to protect against this kind of human stupidity and it is our fault."[98] Legasov's criticism of Soviet reactor designers, and implicitly of the Soviet government, surprised some of the participants. He would pay a high price when he returned, as Soviet officials interpreted it as a betrayal. While applauded in the West, he sank into a deep depression, attempted suicide in 1987, and finally ended his own life the following year.[99]

To those at the IAEA meeting, Legasov's report seemed to be a remarkable product of the policy of glasnost ("openness"), promoted by Soviet leader Mikhael Gorbachev. Legasov had begun his presentation for two hours before lunch, then continued again for three hours in the afternoon. He had been candid in attitude, had walked the participants through the accident step by step, with visual aids and with a video, and had taken time to discuss steps being taken to achieve greater automation. He discussed the delayed evacuation of the town of Pripyat and the efforts to stifle the fire. He guessed that 3.5 percent of the radioactivity of the reactor core was released before being contained on May 6—some 50 million curies into the atmosphere. When he finished speaking that evening, he clearly had impressed his audience. "The presentation ended to loud and prolonged applause," a British participant noted. "It had been a marathon performance, both open and frank."[100]

In his remarks at the meeting, IAEA director-general Hans Blix said that one of the most important impacts of the Chernobyl accident was the "strong impact on public opinion on nuclear power in several countries." Such public opinions would require careful shaping in the aftermath of Chernobyl. It was a serious accident, he acknowledged, but he played down the accident's significance when compared to other forms of energy. "As we are focusing on the contamination caused by an accident in a nuclear plant we might do well, however, to remember that it is as a consequence of the perfectly normal burning of oil and coal to produce energy that our forests are dying," he said. "Regrettably, few industrial activities are without risk and all forms of energy production are connected with some hazards." Some countries would undoubtedly see declines in enthusiasm after Chernobyl. The task of the assembled experts, he claimed, was to help restore confidence. "It is hard to conceive of any major industry prospering or, indeed, surviving without public confidence in it," Blix warned.[101]

The technical discussions were closed to the public, an ironic decision given Blix's claim at the start of the meeting that "to regain public confidence will also require an openness by nuclear operators, regulators and governments about all uses of nuclear energy and about the management and disposal of radioactive waste." The truth was that neither Blix nor many other participants trusted public participation. "I am not certain," he stated, "that the many people who worry deeply about the invisible, untouchable—but highly traceable—nuclear radiation will be calmed by any amount of information and rational explanation." Instead they needed to arrive at common positions before letting the general public in on the discussion. As the experts discussed these technical matters during a week in Vienna learning about the Chernobyl accident, Blix encouraged them to "make use of it to enlighten others, including the media. If we do not allow them into the technical working groups it is not because the discussions of the groups are secret, but because it is difficult to attain the right atmosphere for an expert discussion if every word, every phrase is recorded."[102]

While the Soviet government worked to contain the Chernobyl disaster physically and politically, Western governments ramped up public relations for nuclear power. By 1987, a CIA analysis noted that the accident had had a serious impact on the Soviet regime's credibility, and this did not bode well for other countries. The Soviet government's handling of the accident—initially playing it down, the sluggish response—made Gorbachev's glasnost policy appear to be insincere. Fears of contaminated water and food continued long after the incident. The government's claim, that radiation fallout from Chernobyl would not add significantly to the cancer risk facing society, simply were not believed by large portions of the population.[103]

In the West, politicians moved quickly to shore up the arguments for a commercial nuclear sector. In the United States, Congress passed a resolution to officially honor a "national nuclear medicine week," and President Reagan issued a proclamation designating it as the week of July 27, in a symbolic gesture of support for the ambitions of peaceful atomic energy.[104] In Europe, Chernobyl halted some countries' purchases of new reactors and energized anti-nuclear activism, consolidating it further with environmental activism generally. Greenpeace most notably focused on both, and many European "Green" parties stridently opposed nuclear power. Yet governments remained committed to the nuclear sector. In 1987 nuclear energy accounted for about a third of the electricity consumption in the European Community, with some nations much higher—France, for example, generated 70 percent of its electricity from nuclear power, and in Sweden, nuclear power accounted for more than 40 percent. Chancellor Helmut Kohl of West Germany tried to placate political opponents by creating a new Environment Ministry and by convening an international conference on nuclear safety under the auspices of the IAEA. One CIA report pointed out that Western governments routinely used the reassuring statements of the IAEA "to mollify their publics somewhat," evidently because of the agency's reputation as objective and unbiased.[105]

The IAEA was not unbiased, however, and was explicitly trying to manage public opinion. Its publicity experts gathered their arguments into a 1987 themed issue of the *IAEA Bulletin* called "Progress," on the occasion of the agency's thirty-year anniversary. It featured essays from numerous scientists and officials and included images of nuclear-themed commemorative stamps from several different countries, artistic depictions of the atom, the phrase "Atoms for Peace," and the word "Progress" in five different languages. The issue began with a ringing endorsement from the UN Secretary General Javier Pérez de Cuéllar pointing out how much the world benefited from the IAEA's efforts to facilitate the spread of nuclear technologies. De Cuellar also pointed out that the agency contributed to non-proliferation. But in a swipe at nuclear weapons states, he noted: "Here I must stress that non-proliferation means not only preventing the horizontal spread of nuclear weapons, but also curbing the growth of the nuclear arsenals that already exist." In the latter, he said, the world had yet to be successful.[106] The bulletin quoted from a variety of anodyne congratulatory diplomatic messages on the occasion of the agency's birthday, including quotes from Reagan describing the IAEA as a "model of effective international cooperation" and an "organization of singular importance to the United States"—ironic given Reagan's threat to abandon the agency just a few years earlier.[107]

A further irony in that commemorative issue of the *IAEA Bulletin* was that Hans Blix's essay sat next to one by Munir Ahmad Khan, chairman of the IAEA's board of governors, who for years headed the IAEA's reactor division and was also the head of Pakistan's Atomic Energy Commission—and director of its secret bomb program. Both men were eager to put Chernobyl behind them, to prevent it from interrupting the forward march of nuclear power. Both Blix and Khan gave lip service to the idea of the peaceful atom, particularly its potential to liberate developing countries from the constraints of nature and its comparatively clean environmental record in terms of atmospheric pollution. But both perceived the IAEA as a vehicle for other ends—either policing the world's nuclear programs (Blix) or providing justifications for building up nuclear infrastructure (Khan). Both were at the forefront of discourse about atomic energy's connection to lifting up the world, but both had already long since begun to think primarily about bombs.

Unsurprisingly, Khan's view of the evolution of the IAEA differed from Blix's. For Khan, the weapons safeguards programs that developed in the 1960s had not been universally endorsed by members, and he pointed out that strict guidelines for technical assistance was a relatively recent phenomenon coming from "a group of advanced states" in the aftermath of the 1974 nuclear explosion by a "non-nuclear-weapon State." Khan was still optimistic about help for the developing world, pointing to the cooperative training courses since the 1960s, the widening of membership in the board of governors to include more countries from the developing world, and the rise in IAEA budgets for technical assistance in the 1980s. Such programs—in agriculture, medicine, and electricity generation—should be expanded further, he said. "Only then would the tighter controls and ever-widening scope of safeguards be acceptable to Members States in the Third World."[108]

By contrast, Blix reaffirmed the role of the IAEA in overseeing safeguard agreements, not just for the Treaty on the Non-Proliferation of Nuclear Weapons but also for regional "nuclear free zone" agreements such as the Tlatelolco Treaty in Latin America.[109] He feared that the IAEA's role would be impossible to achieve without expanding its budget substantially. As the Americans determined in their reassessment of the IAEA, Blix believed that shoring up the credibility of peaceful technologies—especially for the developing world—would be essential for securing cooperation in weapons inspections. That meant that, especially in the post-Chernobyl world, the nuclear sector would need better public relations. He credited Chernobyl with the rise in skepticism about food irradiation, for example. In all nuclear domains, that confidence had to be won back. One strategy for doing so was to promote nuclear power as "an environmentally benign energy option for the future," one that could be bent to address environmental and health crises.[110]

Looking back at the previous thirty years, none of these commentators could ignore the dramatic change in the promise of "Atoms for Peace." As Blix himself mentioned, there were many circumstances that no one could have predicted, and he hesitated to "gaze into the crystal ball," as he put it. While he and Khan may have disagreed sharply on matters of policy—after all,

Blix routinely voiced frustrations at Pakistan's secretive nuclear program—they agreed that the IAEA needed to exist, that all nations should increase its funding, and that it ought to be promoting nuclear technologies in the so-called developing world. For Khan, the IAEA was a source of training and a path to technological acquisition. Even leaving aside the cover the IAEA provided for clandestine bomb programs, access to such technologies was perceived as the right of any member state. Governments had determined that they needed nuclear power—for energy security in part, but also for nuclear weapons security. For a future reliant on monitoring the uses of dangerous technologies in the developing world, government actions to play up the positive benefits of nuclear technologies—whether based on reality or not—would be essential.

Conclusion

The Cornucopian Illusion

In the twenty-first century, the promise of a nuclear cornucopia is alive and well, as we are confronted with enormous natural crises, ranging from food and water security, to population growth, energy shortfalls, and most pressing of all—the existential threat of a changing climate due to the accumulation of carbon dioxide in the earth's atmosphere. Nuclear power can save the world, as a benign form of energy production, leading scholars argued in the *New York Times* in 2019.[1] It is a promise that not only is dangled in front of the poorest countries of the world but is put before us all. Perhaps if we just believe a little and have a bit of faith, nuclear technologies will pull us out of the mess we are in. We can rebuild nature, find a future of abundance, and outrun the environmental hellhounds on our trail. So the argument goes.

If these claims seem familiar, it is because they have been deployed routinely over the past seven decades, not simply by the nuclear industry but also by governments using the many promises of nuclear technology to achieve strategic goals. While we debate whether nuclear reactors are capable of mitigating climate change, we should not lose sight of the historical reasons nuclear technologies were promoted in the first place, and why they continue to be endorsed by governments around the world. In our zeal to cast nuclear power as merely a technological option to address energy needs—one that must be balanced against its risks and social costs—we wrongly disconnect it from global issues of geopolitical influence, colonialism and neocolonialism, racial divisiveness, the spread of arms, and war. We also wrongly understate the role of governments in framing such decisions, due to their own preferences and strategic investments. Just as the United States used the promise of the atom as an integral part of its nuclear weapons posture and its non-proliferation goals, so too did countries such as Japan, France, and Sweden because of their deep commitments to nuclear power in the pursuit of energy security. And so too did countries such as Israel, India, and other states that have long-standing multi-purpose nuclear programs. Of course, every single emergent nuclear weapons state has deployed the rhetoric of lifting themselves out of poverty, reshaping nature, and providing abundant energy. It is both a time-honored promise and an environmental illusion. The question must be asked: Where has it led the world?

In the decades since Chernobyl, atomic promises have continued to be formidable: providing plentiful food and water despite population rise, controlling diseases without pesticides, mitigating climate change, and even curing diseases such as cancer. Those promises have animated conversations in Europe and North America, but more important, they have continued to be at the center of the tensions between the so-called global North and global South. The United States and Europeans in particular have relied on these promises to increase their policing power over smaller countries' nuclear programs. Events at the close of the century amplified this trend. For example, the dissolution of the USSR in 1991 strengthened the ability of the United States and Western Europeans to focus on non-proliferation and weapons inspections, with the fate of the Soviet Union's weapons in question and with no meaningful opposition to US political hegemony worldwide. The first Gulf War also strengthened the role of the IAEA as an inspections and policing body, particularly of developing countries' nuclear programs. When in 1990 Saddam Hussein's Iraq invaded Kuwait—a crucial source of petroleum for the United States and Europe—the United States and its allies reacted swiftly to push back Saddam's forces militarily. In the aftermath, inspections of Iraq's facilities revealed that Iraq had been able to conceal a nuclear weapons program, and the cease-fire with Iraq included provisions for inspections by the IAEA.

One symbolic victory for the developing world on nuclear issues was the 1997 election of an Egyptian, Mohamed ElBaradei, to succeed Hans Blix as director-general of the IAEA. While ElBaradei continued to focus on non-proliferation issues, he clashed with the Americans repeatedly. For example, the United States heightened its political and military involvement in the Middle East after the September 11, 2001, terrorist attacks on US soil, and the George W. Bush administration identified an "axis of evil" in the world—Iraq, Iran, and North Korea. What united these countries was their pursuit of weapons of mass destruction behind veils of purportedly peaceful nuclear programs. But ElBaradei's IAEA did not take a similarly oppositional stance to these countries. In 2003, for example, ElBaradei pleaded for more time to make inspections of nuclear sites, while the US military prepared to invade Saddam Hussein's Iraq—which it did in 2003. And in 2005, the United States pressured ElBaradei in vain to declare Iran to be in violation of the Treaty on the Nonproliferation of Nuclear Weapons.[2]

Though unpopular in the US administration, ElBaradei did maintain the agency's identity as a non-proliferation watchdog. The IAEA and ElBaradei shared the Nobel Prize for Peace in 2005 "for their efforts to prevent nuclear energy from being used for military purposes and to ensure that nuclear energy for peaceful purposes is used in the safest possible way." In speaking with a journalist about the prize, ElBaradei observed that "we are facing unprecedented challenges in the last few years, since Iraq, the Iraq '91 war, and there's been no let-go since that time. After Iraq there was Korea, there was Libya, there was Iran, 9/11. . . . So this is not just recognition of achievement. To me, I read that to mean: 'Keep doing what you are doing, and more.' And that's the message I get from this Prize today."[3] The term "watchdog" would become ubiquitous in the media. The *New York Times* called ElBaradei the UN's Geiger Counter, suggesting he was on a vigilant watch.[4]

Bush's view of the IAEA in the 2000s was not unlike Reagan's in the early 1980s. Bush disliked the occurrence of political fights within the agency and the outsized presence of the poorer and less-developed countries. The agency was not as easy to handle as an instrument of US policy as it was supposed to be. For a while, Bush administration officials forgot about nuclear technology's rhetoric of peace and plenty and how useful it had been to all of Bush's predecessors. Just as Reagan threatened to abandon it altogether—before concluding that it was indispensable as a means of propaganda and surveillance—the Bush administration and US allies also scrutinized their commitments to the IAEA. One particularly strange budgetary item they sought to cut, to undermine ElBaradei, was the huge budget for projects unrelated to weapons inspections, such as the agency's collaboration with the Food and Agriculture Organization (FAO). Skeptical of the IAEA's claims of having saved billions of dollars for the developing world through its agricultural program, in 2008 several countries attempted to shut down the joint program. They may have been right to be skeptical, but they also had lost historical memories of the role those programs played in propping up the peaceful atom's utopian story. Now, FAO's "token" contribution just seemed like a puzzle and the program "did not necessarily make fiscal sense." But the confusion did not last long. According to one American diplomatic cable, US officials backtracked when they remembered that such programs were symbolic of the IAEA's commitment to the developing world. The survival of these programs, as one American diplomat wrote, "became a litmus test for the many developing countries that complain of U.S. and developed country efforts to play up the IAEA's 'watch dog' status at the expense of its promotional role." So, the IAEA would need to continue to produce "glossy pamphlets" that "tout the accomplishments" of the joint FAO-IAEA program. The US government would remain a "skeptical supporter" of it, "recognizing this as part of the overall bargain that makes the IAEA's enforcement/verification role stronger." The nuclear weapons states needed such programs. It was all part of paying the piper, to be able to use the IAEA as its watchdog.[5]

The supposed "solutions" offered by nuclear technologies were so deeply embedded into US global strategy that it did not matter whether they were real or not. Over time, that has rarely if ever mattered. Bush's successor Barack Obama, like past US presidents, also embraced the multiple promises of the atom as a price to pay for promoting American security interests. He campaigned on the idea that there ought to be a nuclear renaissance, as a suite of technologies that were relatively benign environmentally, explicitly linking nuclear power to forestalling climate change from carbon emissions.[6] And President Obama's diplomats worked well with IAEA director-general Yukiya Amano, who replaced ElBaradei in 2009. A Japanese diplomat by profession, Amano had spent years working in the realm of nuclear and biological weapons proliferation. The election had been close, with many countries of the global South voting instead for Abdul Minty, a South African diplomat with strong anti-racist credentials. At the end of Amano's first day on the job, American diplomat Esther Brimmer assured him of the Obama administration's full support and expressed some dissatisfaction at ElBaradei's independent spirit. Amano was grateful for the support and assured Brimmer of his total agreement that his job was not to play politics. As one diplomatic cable put it, "Amano was acutely conscious of staying in his technical lane as IAEA Director General."

The agency under Amano focused on reinforcing and refining atomic energy's narrative of abundance. He hoped to achieve more "buy-in" by other countries, particularly those of the developing world, and to deemphasize the agency's image as a security watchdog, portraying it instead as offering helpful applications. He had in mind a number of specifics, such as cancer control and programs to promote water and food access. Amano looked once again into the unknown future, confident that nuclear technologies would provide solutions. Together, Brimmer and Amano agreed that nuclear technology was an ideal way to ease the divisions between the industrialized North and the impoverished South.[7] Amano and the Obama administration provided a unified message, that nuclear power should undergo a renaissance—to mitigate climate change but also to put nuclear technologies to work in numerous other fields. Amano openly criticized the characterization of the IAEA as simply a watchdog. He started a cancer awareness campaign. He started an initiative to convince countries to adopt nuclear power. He urged insurance companies to back power plants and banks to lend money.[8]

Such promises of future environmental paradise were perturbed but not truly shaken by a real environmental disaster. On March 11, 2011, a magnitude 9.0 earthquake rocked Japan, and the resultant tsunami flooded the Fukushima nuclear power plant. The site was prepared for seismic activity but far less prepared for the tsunami, which disabled backup generators and other equipment needed to keep the reactors cooled. In short order, the plant operators had multiple nuclear meltdowns to contend with. As the disaster mounted, the IAEA upgraded its status from one with only "local consequences" to a "major accident" comparable in magnitude to Chernobyl. Amano may have sensed the weight of nuclear history descending on Japan: two atomic bombs in 1945, the first major fallout controversy in 1954 (afflicting Japanese fishermen aboard the *Daigo Fukuryu Maru*), a robust nuclear power industry, and now the worst nuclear disaster in decades. Some countries, notably Germany, were pledging to abandon nuclear power altogether. Others, such as France and Sweden, were too deeply committed to it to imagine doing the same. The United States was unwavering after Fukushima: Barack Obama's energy secretary Steven Chu reaffirmed that mitigating climate change would continue to be a compelling reason to hold on to nuclear power. It must have been a delicate task for Amano, balancing his agency responsibilities with the expectations of his government, the political pressures in Japan to downplay the accident, and his own personal feelings as a Japanese citizen. But in the end, he was still the IAEA director-general. Amano stated confidently that Fukushima would slow the expansion of nuclear power, but it would not stop it. The IAEA maintained the same outlook as it always had: the future was to be nuclear.[9]

***

The story of Ronald Silow, who in the 1960s had a total career meltdown, transforming himself from a respected international bureaucrat into a professional pariah, appeared earlier in this book. I discovered his story while conducting research in the archives of the Food and Agriculture Organization (FAO), in Rome. The helpful archivist noted, as an aside, that there might be some information in "Dr. Silow's files." When he brought them to me, I was astonished at their volume—thick folders filled to the brim—but even more stunned by what I found inside. Instead of the staid formal correspondence and project reports typical of FAO material, I found Silow's handwritten letters, poorly edited, sometimes with entire paragraphs crossed out. His letters were extremely long, often twenty to forty pages in length, written to the directors-general of both FAO and the IAEA. Their contents were filled with accusations of corruption, incompetence, and unethical practices.

The gist of Silow's critique was that development projects in the poorest countries of the world had been hijacked by the International Atomic Energy Agency and its richest sponsors, which made false claims about the role of atomic energy in helping to increase food supplies. Silow believed his own organization was a sham, run by ideologues more interested in identifying success stories in the nuclear realm than trying to find the most promising ways to help countries solve their very real problems. Although Silow's story did not persuade me that the IAEA was a wholly corrupt organization, it did compel me to rethink the importance of atomic energy's cornucopian message and to ask how it touched broader themes of history, such as Cold War geopolitics or the post-colonial world order. Was there something to learn about the way atomic energy was presented to those countries with natural resource shortfalls, or that were constantly threatened by population pressures, famine, or disease? And how did those countries—some emerging from recent defeat, like Japan, or from years of colonial rule, like India or Ghana—themselves use the promise of atomic energy? Previously, I thought about atomic energy as primarily an issue about electricity, environmental issues, and social justice. Separately, I thought of nuclear weapons and proliferation in terms of diplomacy, statecraft, and arms control. Like many people, I understood that there were stark differences in the ways that pro- or anti-nuclear energy advocates cast environmental and natural resource questions. But I had not considered how deeply embedded such ideas were in the policies and actions of governments as they pursued strategic goals around the world.

Frantz Fanon warned in the 1960s that the "wretched" or "damned" of the earth would be offered dreams of rapid advance and of economic miracles. That surely has been true of the atom. The promise of plenty was not only tempting to poorer countries, but it was also at the core of the atom's appeal as an instrument of geopolitical influence and power. In highlighting this point, this book has emphasized four interrelated themes.

One is that atomic energy's future has been a pliable idea. Governments reshaped it according to their strategic needs, often in pursuit of controlling the earth's natural resources. The United States did it when urging governments to adopt radioisotopes in the 1950s or nuclear reactors in the 1970s—at one turn protecting access to uranium for the US nuclear arsenal and at another trying to "break" some developing countries' dominance of the world's oil supplies. Another theme is that the so-called peaceful atom relied on a constructive, bountiful vision that called for reshaping nature according to human needs, in opposition to one emphasizing harm from environmental contamination. These were both environmental narratives but they collided repeatedly. Time and again, only the cornucopian narrative proved itself a reliable instrument of governments.

A third theme is that promises of plenty often had political value out of proportion to their economic worth or technical feasibility; indeed, sometimes the latter two never materialized at all. "Atoms for Peace" began purely as propaganda, and the purported peaceful applications of atomic energy were based on aspirations. Many of the projects discussed here—miracle grains in India, transformation of desert landscapes in Israel, just to mention two—were not based on proven techniques and they turned out to be mirages. They existed for other purposes, such as prestige, geopolitical leverage, distraction from bomb tests or even concealment of new bomb programs. They were not necessarily, and indeed never needed to be, based on reality.

Perhaps most important of all the themes is the evolution of international bodies and treaties into instruments of manipulation and control reminiscent of the colonial era. At the close of the century, the world's nuclear order still divided the global North from the global South. Cooperation in the nuclear field that drew in developing countries—the Asian Nuclear Center, the CENTO Nuclear Institute, and the IAEA, to provide a few examples—were designed by Europeans and North Americans. Racial politics permeated the IAEA from the start, despite its reputation as being purely technical, and the most acrimonious disputes were not between East and West but between the predominantly white countries and those of the so-called developing world. In the case of the IAEA, what began as a promise of sharing peaceful atomic energy—to remake nature, to outrun natural pressures, and to escape environmental threats—served as an instrument for concentrating power in the hands of Europeans and North Americans. That was the "wretched" atom—the continued consolidation of geopolitical power and influence, clothed as a utopian future.

What can we conclude from this history of atomic energy "solutions" in the developing world, promoted by the United States, its political allies, and international agencies? By reframing our understanding of nuclear issues, we can see more clearly the intersection of the so-called peaceful atom with seemingly disconnected topics, including racism, colonialism and neo-colonialism, propaganda, surveillance and control, weapons programs, and war. When we acknowledge these connections, the centrality of a narrative of plenty emerges—one that counts on remaking nature, quickening its pulse, or avoiding environmental dangers—as an unmistakable feature of atomic energy when pursued by governments. If that is the case, we must begin to acknowledge that these particular ideas are deeply embedded in the same range of difficult and ugly questions. The cornucopian promise of the atom has been an extraordinarily useful instrument of power. It was not a marginal issue in the global nuclear order. Instead, it has been the one indispensable piece of it.

NOTES

INTRODUCTION
1. Memorandum of Conversation, 2 November 1974, *Foreign Relations of the United States*, 1969–1976, vol. 27, ed. Monica L. Belmonte (Washington, DC: US Government Printing Office, 2012), Document 88.
2. Memorandum of Conversation, 4 March 1975, *Foreign Relations of the United States*, 1969–1976, vol. 27, ed. Monica L. Belmonte (Washington, DC: US Government Printing Office, 2012), Document 110.
3. Memorandum of Conversation, 4 March 1975, *Foreign Relations of the United States*, 1969-1976, vol. 27, ed. Monica L. Belmonte (Washington, DC: US Government Printing Office, 2012), Document 110.
4. Memorandum of Conversation, 4 March 1975, 9:55–10:33 a.m., *Foreign Relations of the United States*, 1969–1976, vol. 27, ed. Monica L. Belmonte (Washington, DC: US Government Printing Office, 2012), Document 109.
5. Memorandum of Conversation, 4 March 1975, *Foreign Relations of the United States*, 1969–1976, vol. 27, ed. Monica L. Belmonte (Washington, DC: US Government Printing Office, 2012), Document 110.
6. Remarks prepared by Lewis L. Strauss, Chairman, United States Atomic Energy Commission, for Delivery at the Founders' Day Dinner, National Association of Science Writers, 16 September 1954, https://www.nrc.gov/docs/ML1613/ML16131A120.pdf [accessed 26 June 2020].
7. Harland Manchester, "The New Age of Atomic Crops," *Popular Mechanics*, October 1958, 106–110, 282–288, quote on pp. 288 and 284.
8. Harland Manchester, "The New Age of Atomic Crops," *Popular Mechanics* (October 1958), 106–110, 282–288, quote on p. 108. On plant breeding, see Helen Anne Curry, *Evolution Made to Order: Plant Breeding and Technological Innovation in Twentieth-Century America* (Chicago: University of Chicago Press, 2016). For a thoughtful exploration of some potential atomic energy applications, see Paul Boyer, *By the Bomb's Early Light: American Thought and Culture at the Dawn of the Atomic Age* (Chapel Hill: University of North Carolina Press, 1985).
9. Literature on the IAEA will be cited throughout the present work. The official history (now seriously out of date) was authored by long-term IAEA official David Fischer. The companion volume to that history included personal reminiscences by other long-term employees of the agency. Recent scholarship on the history of the agency has moved into critical analysis using multiple archives and sources. Some such work is emerging due to the efforts of the

University of Vienna's IAEA History Project, led by Elisabeth Roehrlich. For an example of this new history, see her essay "The Cold War, the Developing World, and the Creation of the International Atomic Energy Agency (IAEA), 1953–1957," *Cold War History* 16:2 (2016), 195–212. The older volumes are David Fischer, *History of the International Atomic Energy Agency: The First Forty Years* (Vienna: IAEA, 1997); International Atomic Energy Agency, *International Atomic Energy Agency: Personal Reflections* (Vienna: IAEA, 1997).

10. On the role of nuclear issues in environmental activism, see Frank Zelko, *Make It a Green Peace! The Rise of a Countercultural Environmentalism* (Oxford: Oxford University Press, 2013). On nuclear accidents and radiation exposure, see Kate Brown, *Manual for Survival: A Chernobyl Guide to the Future* (New York: Norton, 2019); Natasha Zaretsky, *Radiation Nation: Three Mile Island and the Political Transformation of the 1970s* (New York: Columbia University Press, 2018). On the politics of radioactive waste at the front and back end of the fuel cycle, see Gabrielle Hecht, *Being Nuclear: Africans and the Global Uranium Trade* (Cambridge, MA: MIT Press, 2014); Jacob Darwin Hamblin, *Poison in the Well: Radioactive Waste in the Oceans at the Dawn of the Nuclear Age* (New Brunswick, NJ: Rutgers University Press, 2008); J. Samuel Walker, *The Road to Yucca Mountain: The Development of Radioactive Waste Policy in the United States* (Berkeley: University of California Press, 2009). On the evolution of public trust, see Kate Brown, *Plutopia: Nuclear Families, Atomic Cities, and the Great Soviet and American Plutonium Disasters* (Oxford: Oxford University Press, 2013); Brian Balogh, *Chain Reaction: Expert Debate and Public Participation in American Commercial Nuclear Power, 1945–1975* (New York: Cambridge University Press, 1991); J. Samuel Walker, "The Atomic Energy Commission and the Politics of Radiation Protection, 1967–1971," *Isis* 85:1 (1994), 57–78; Ioanna Semendeferi, "Legitimating a Nuclear Critic: John Gofman, Radiation Safety, and Cancer Risks," *Historical Studies in the Natural Sciences* 38:2 (2008), 259–301.

11. For a range of interpretations on the history of nuclear proliferation, see Francis J. Gavin, *Nuclear Statecraft: History and Strategy in America's Atomic Age* (Ithaca, NY: Cornell University Press, 2012); Shane J Maddock, *Nuclear Apartheid: The Quest for American Atomic Supremacy from World War II to the Present* (Chapel Hill: University of North Carolina Press, 2010); Jayita Sarkar, "India's Nuclear Limbo and the Fatalism of the Nuclear Non-Proliferation Regime, 1974–1983," *Strategic Analysis* 37:3 (2013), 322–337. An edited volume on the origins of the Treaty on the Non-Proliferation of Nuclear Weapons (including an essay by the author) is Roland Popp, Liviu Horovitz, and Andreas Wenger, eds., *Negotiating the Nuclear Non-Proliferation Treaty: Origins of the Nuclear Order* (New York: Routledge, 2017). Numerous excellent case studies of nuclear proliferation have emerged from the Wilson Center's Nuclear Proliferation International History Project, https://www.wilsoncenter.org/program/nuclear-proliferation-international-history-project [accessed 26 June 2020].

12. Itty Abraham articulated this limitation in Itty Abraham, "The Ambivalence of Nuclear Histories," *Osiris* 21:1 (2006), 49–65. On state-building and nuclear programs, see Jahnavi Phalkey, *Atomic State: Big Science in Twentieth-Century India* (Ranikhet: Permanent Black, 2013); M. V. Ramana, *The Power of Promise: Examining Nuclear Energy in India* (New Delhi: Penguin, 2012); Itty Abraham, ed., *South Asian Cultures of the Bomb: Atomic Publics and the State in India and Pakistan* (Hyderabad: Orient Blackswan, 2010); Gabrielle Hecht, *The Radiance of France: Nuclear Power and National Identity after World War II*

(Cambridge, MA: MIT Press, 2009); Sara B. Pritchard, *Confluence: The Nature of Technology and the Remaking of the Rhône* (Cambridge, MA: Harvard University Press, 2011); Mara Drogan, "The Nuclear Nation and the German Question: An American Reactor in West Berlin," *Cold War History* 15:3 (2015), 301–319; Sheila Jasanoff and Sang-Hyun Kim, "Containing the Atom: Sociotechnical Imaginaries and Nuclear Power in the United States and South Korea," *Minerva* 47:119 (2009).

13. Nick Cullather, *The Hungry World: America's Cold War Battle against Poverty in Asia* (Cambridge, MA: Harvard University Press, 2013). On technology and propaganda, see Kenneth Osgood, *Total Cold War: Eisenhower's Secret Propaganda Battle at Home and Abroad* (Lawrence: University Press of Kansas, 2006). On the deployment of science and technology for state aims, see Audra J. Wolfe, *Competing with the Soviets: Science, Technology, and the State in Cold War America* (Baltimore: Johns Hopkins University Press, 2013). On the use of science for ideological purposes by the United States and its allies, see Audra J. Wolfe, *Freedom's Laboratory: The Cold War Struggle for the Soul of Science* (Baltimore: Johns Hopkins University Press, 2018). On modernization, see Nils Gilman, *Mandarins of the Future: Modernization Theory in Cold War America* (Baltimore: Johns Hopkins University Press, 2007).

14. John Krige and Jayita Sarkar, "US Technological Collaboration for Nonproliferation: Key Evidence from the Cold War," *Nonproliferation Review* 25:3–4 (2018), 249–262; Mara Drogan, "The Nuclear Imperative: Atoms for Peace and the Development of US Policy on Exporting Nuclear Power, 1953–1955," *Diplomatic History* 40:5 (2016), 948–974; John Krige, "The Peaceful Atom as Political Weapon: Euratom and American Foreign Policy in the Late 1950s," *Historical Studies in the Natural Sciences* 38:1 (2008): 5–44; John Krige, "Atoms for Peace, Scientific Internationalism, and Scientific Intelligence," *Osiris* 21:1 (2006), 161–181; Ira Chernus, *Eisenhower's Atoms for Peace* (College Station: Texas A&M University Press, 2002).

15. The edition of Fanon cited here is Frantz Fanon, *The Wretched of the Earth*, trans. Richard Philcox (New York: Grove Press, 2004), quote on p. 41.

16. The positionality of the IAEA as a non-political and technical body is emphasized in much of Gabrielle Hecht's work. See especially her *Being Nuclear*.

CHAPTER 1

1. On Boris Davidovitch and monazite sands, see Agrisson Lopes and Natália Bourguignon, "A Guerra de Guarapari," *Gazeta Online*, http://especiais.gazetaonline.com.br/bomba/ [accessed 18 July 2016].
2. *Executive Sessions of the Senate Foreign Relations Committee* (Historical Series), vol. 3, part 1, *82nd Congress, First Session, 1951* (Washington, DC: US Government Printing Office, 1976), document 420.
3. Statement by the Under Secretary of State (Acheson) to an Executive Session of the Joint Congressional Committee on Atomic Energy, Washington, May 12, 1947. *Foreign Relations of the United States*, 1947, General; The United Nations, vol. 1, ed. Ralph E. Goodwin, Neal H. Petersen, Marvin W. Kranz, and William Slany (Washington, DC: US Government Printing Office, 1973), document 412.
4. Memorandum by the Under Secretary of State (Lovett) to the Secretary of State, 11 August 1947. *Foreign Relations of the United States*, 1947, General; The United Nations, vol. 1, ed. Ralph E. Goodwin, Neal H. Petersen, Marvin W. Kranz,

and William Slany (Washington, DC: US Government Printing Office, 1973), document 425.
5. The United States Embassy to the Brazilian Foreign Office, 15 December 1949. *Foreign Relations of the United States*, 1949, National Security Affairs, Foreign Economic Policy, vol. 1, ed. Neal H. Petersen, Ralph R. Goodwin, William Z. Slany, and Marvin W. Kranz (Washington, DC: US Government Printing Office, 1976), document 222.
6. Angela N. H. Creager, *Life Atomic: A History of Radioisotopes in Science and Medicine* (Chicago: University of Chicago Press, 2013), 86.
7. Néstor Herran, "Spreading Nucleonics: The Isotope School at the Atomic Energy Research Establishment, 1951–67," *British Journal for the History of Science* 39:4 (2006), 569–586.
8. Creager, *Life Atomic*, 93, 116–117.
9. Creager, *Life Atomic*, 121–132.
10. Gerson Moura, *Brazilian Foreign Relations, 1939–1950: The Changing Nature of Brazil-United States Relations during and after the Second World War* (Brasília: Fundação de Gusmão, 2013), 257–259.
11. Creager, *Life Atomic*, 7, 123.
12. Nathaniel C. Nash, "Argentine Files Show Huge Effort to Harbor Nazis," *New York Times* (14 December 1993), A10.
13. The Secretary of State to the Chargé in Argentina (Cabot), 26 January 1946. *Foreign Relations of the United States*, 1946. The American Republics, vol. 11, ed. Velma Hastings Cassidy and Almon H. Wright (Washington, DC: US Government Printing Office, 1969), document 155. Oscar Ibarra García was a "German agent" according to Byrnes.
14. United States Government, *Blue Book on Argentina: Consultation among the American Republics with Respect to the Argentine Situation* (New York: Greenberg, 1946), 38.
15. Diego Hurtado de Mendoza, "Autonomy, even Regional Hegemony: Argentina and the 'Hard Way' toward Its First Research Reactor," *Science in Context* 18:2 (2005), 285–308, quote on p. 288.
16. "Soviet Said to 'Buy' German Atom Men," *New York Times* (24 February 1947), 1.
17. Daniel K. Lewis, *The History of Argentina* (New York: St. Martin's Press, 2003), p. 85
18. Quoted in Hurtado de Mendoza, "Autonomy," 289.
19. Jonathan Hagood, "Bottling Atomic Energy: Technology, Politics, and the State in Peronist Argentina," in *Beyond Imported Magic: Essays on Science, Technology, and Society in Latin America*, ed. Eden Medina, Ivan da Costa Marques, and Christina Holmes (Cambridge, MA: MIT Press, 2014), 267–285. See also Hurtado de Mendoza, "Autonomy." Argentina's post-Richter nuclear programs would be marked by an unapologetic alliance between scientists and military (usually naval) officers.
20. *History of the S.I.S. Division*, vol. 2, *Accompaniment, Argentina-Japan* (Washington, DC: Federal Bureau of Investigation, 1947), part 5, pp. 22–23.
21. Secretary of State to Embassy in Argentina, 5 August 1948. *Foreign Relations of the United States*, 1948, The Western Hemisphere, vol. 9, ed. Almon R. Wright, Velma Hastings Cassidy, and David H. Stauffer (Washington, DC: US Government Printing Office, 1972), document 237.
22. *History of the S.I.S. Division*, vol. 2, *Accompaniment, Argentina-Japan* (Washington, DC: Federal Bureau of Investigation, 1947), part 5, pp. 22–23.

23. Jack DeMent and H. C. Drake, *Handbook of Uranium Minerals* (Portland, OR: Mineralogist Publishing, 1947), quotes on p. 5.
24. Discussed in Secretary of State to the Diplomatic Representatives in the American Republics, 10 August 1948. *Foreign Relations of the United States, 1948, The Western Hemisphere*, vol. 9, ed. Almon R. Wright, Velma Hastings Cassidy, and David H. Stauffer (Washington, DC: US Government Printing Office, 1972), document 238.
25. "Argentina Report Uranium Find," *New York Times*, 2 December 1946, 4.
26. Meeting of Ambassador Nufer with President Perón, 3 September 1953. *Foreign Relations of the United States, 1952–1954, The American Republics*, vol. 4, ed. N. Stephen Kane and William J. Sanford Jr. (Washington, DC: US Government Printing Office, 1983), document 119.
27. East Asian names are rendered in this book with surnames last except in cases when other renderings are widely used, such as Mao Zedong, Chiang Kai-shek, and Zhou Enlai. The Ambassador in China (Stuart) to the Secretary of State, 26 July 1948. *Foreign Relations of the United States, 1948, The Far East: China*, vol. 8, ed. E. Ralph Perkins, Fredrick Aandahl, Francis C. Prescott, Herbert A. Fine, and Velma Hastings Cassidy (Washington, DC: US Government Printing Office, 1973), document 634.
28. The Secretary of State to the Ambassador in China (Stuart), 24 March 1948. *Foreign Relations of the United States, 1948, The Far East: China*, vol. 8, ed. E. Ralph Perkins, Fredrick Aandahl, Francis C. Prescott, Herbert A. Fine, and Velma Hastings Cassidy (Washington, DC: US Government Printing Office, 1973), document 630.
29. The Ambassador in China (Stuart) to the Secretary of State, 26 November 1948, *Foreign Relations of the United States, 1948*, vol. 8, *The Far East: China*, ed. E. Ralph Perkins, Fredrick Aandahl, Francis C. Prescott, Herbert A. Fine, and Velma Hastings Cassidy (Washington, DC: US Government Printing Office, 1973), document 640.
30. Memorandum of Conversation, by Mr. R. Gordon Arneson, Special Assistant to the Under Secretary of State (Lovett), 25 August 1948, *Foreign Relations of the United States, 1948*, vol. 1, part 2, *General: The United Nations*, ed. Neal H. Petersen, Ralph R. Goodwin, Marvin W. Kranz, and William Z. Slany (Washington, DC: US Government Printing Office, 1976), document 96.
31. Memorandum of Convsersation, by Mr. David H. McKillop of the Office of the Special Assistant to the Secretary of State (Arneson), 12 March 1951, *Foreign Relations of the United States, 1951, National Security Affairs: Foreign Economic Policy*, vol. 1, ed. Neal H. Petersen, Harriet D. Schwar, Carl N. Raether, John A. Bernbaum, and Ralph R. Goodwin (Washington, DC: US Government Printing Office, 1979), document 236.
32. Memorandum by Mr. Thomas E. Murray, Member of the United States Atomic Energy Commission, to the Ambassador in Spain (Griffis), 19 October 1951, *Foreign Relations of the United States, 1951*, vol. 1, *National Security Affairs: Foreign Economic Policy*, ed. Neal H. Petersen, Harriet D. Schwar, Carl N. Raether, John A. Bernbaum, and Ralph R. Goodwin (Washington, DC: US Government Printing Office, 1979), document 266.
33. Laurel Sefton MacDowell, "The Elliot Lake Uranium Miners' Battle to Gain Occupational Health and Safety Improvements, 1950–1980," *Labour / Le Travail* 69 (2012): 91–118; Ian Bellany, *Australia in the Nuclear Age: National Defence and National Development* (Sydney: Sydney University Press, 1972); Gabrielle

Hecht, *Being Nuclear: Africans and the Global Uranium Trade* (Cambridge, MA: MIT Press, 2012); Doug Brugge, *The Navajo People and Uranium Mining* (Albuquerque: University of New Mexico Press, 2009).

34. Norman M. Naimark, *The Russians in Germany: A History of the Soviet Zone of Occupation, 1945–1949* (Cambridge, MA: Belknap Press, 2001); Robynne N. Mellor, "The Cold War Underground: An Environmental History of Uranium Mining in the United States, Canada, and the Soviet Union, 1945–1991," PhD dissertation, Georgetown University, 2018.

35. Memorandum for the Files by Mr. J. Bruce Hamilton of the Office of the Special Assistant to the Secretary of State (Arneson), 8 August 1951. *Foreign Relations of the United States, 1951*, vol. 1, *National Security Affairs: Foreign Economic Policy*, ed. Neal H. Petersen, Harriet D. Schwar, Carl N. Raether, John A. Bernbaum, and Ralph R. Goodwin (Washington, DC: US Government Printing Office, 1979), document 253. On the politics of uranium in Africa, see Gabrielle Hecht, *Being Nuclear*.

36. "Truman's Inaugural Address, January 20, 1949," Harry S. Truman Presidential Library and Museum, https://www.trumanlibrary.gov/library/public-papers/19/inaugural-address [accessed 26 June 2020].

37. Robert Bendider, "Point Four—Still the Great Basic Hope," *New York Times*, 1 April 1951, 171.

38. Address before the Annual Convention of the American Newspaper Guild, Public Papers of the Presidents: Harry S. Truman, 1945–1953, https://www.trumanlibrary.gov/library/public-papers/177/address-annual-convention-american-newspaper-guild [accessed 26 June 2020].

39. Address before the Annual Convention of the American Newspaper Guild, Public Papers of the Presidents: Harry S. Truman, 1945–1953, https://www.trumanlibrary.gov/library/public-papers/177/address-annual-convention-american-newspaper-guild [accessed 26 June 2020].

40. Sydney Gruson, "Belgium Has Plan to Develop Congo," *New York Times*, 17 October 1949, 9. On the Shinkolobwe mines, see Johathan E. Helmreich, *Gathering Rare Ores: The Diplomacy of Uranium Acquisition, 1943–1954* (Princeton, NJ: Princeton University Press, 1986), 207–208.

41. "Belgium Plans Aid to African Territories to Develop Resources for Mutual Benefit," *New York Times*, 4 January 1950, 67.

42. William S. White, "Malanism Absent in Belgian Congo," *New York Times*, 12 May 1952, 3.

43. Paper Prepared in the Office of the Special Assistant to the Secretary of State (Arneson), 6 July 1951. *Foreign Relations of the United States*, 1951, National Security Affairs: Foreign Economic Policy, vol. 1, ed. Neal H. Petersen, Harriet D. Schwar, Carl N. Raether, John A. Bernbaum, and Ralph R. Goodwin (Washington, DC: US Government Printing Office, 1979), document 249.

44. Bidyut Chakrabarty, "Jawaharlal Nehru and Planning, 1938–41: India at the Crossroads," *Modern Asian Studies* 26:2 (1992), 275–287.

45. The Ambassador in Brazil (Johnson) to the Secretary of State, 8 October 1948. *Foreign Relations of the United States, 1948*, vol. 9, *The Western Hemisphere*, ed. Almon R. Wright, Velma Hastings Cassidy, and David H. Stauffer (Washington, DC: US Government Printing Office, 1972), document 266.

46. Carlo Patti, "The Origins of the Brazilian Nuclear Programme, 1951–1955," *Cold War History* 15: 3 (2014), 1–21.

47. P. M. S. Blackett, *Fear, War, and the Bomb* (New York: Whittlesey House, 1949).

48. Assar Lindbeck, ed., *Nobel Lectures, Economics 1969–1980* (Singapore: World Scientific, 1992), http://www.nobelprize.org/nobel_prizes/economic-sciences/laureates/1978/simon-bio.html [accessed 26 June 2020].
49. Sam H. Schurr and Jacob Marschak, *Economic Aspects of Atomic Power* (Princeton, NJ: Princeton University Press, 1950). The authors ostensibly were economists Marschak (former director of the Cowles Commission) and Sam Schurr, though individual chapters were contributed by a range of scholars.
50. Kingsley Davis, "Population and the Further Spread of Industrial Society," *Proceedings of the American Philosophical Society* 95:1 (1951), 8–19, quotes on p. 8 and p. 16.
51. Schurr and Marschak, "Population and the Further Spread of Industrial Society," 254, 273.
52. Vincent Heath Whitney, "Resistance to Innovation: The Case of Atomic Power," *American Journal of Sociology* 56:3 (1950), 247–254.
53. Walter Isard and Vincent Whitney, *Atomic Power: An Economic and Social Analysis* (New York: Blakiston, 1952), 141–143.
54. Isard and Whitney, *Atomic Power*, 143–144, 218, 212.
55. Helmreich, *Gathering Rare Ores*, 168–171. See also "M. Khurshed Lal Expose au 'Monde' les Projets du Gouvernement Indien," *Le Monde*, 15 June 1949.
56. The Special Assistant to the Secretary of State (Arneson) to the First Secretary of the British Embassy (Marten), 9 March 1951, *Foreign Relations of the United States, 1951*, vol. 1, *National Security Affairs: Foreign Economic Policy*, ed. Neal H. Petersen, Harriet D. Schwar, Carl N. Raether, John A. Bernbaum, and Ralph R. Goodwin (Washington, DC: US Government Printing Office, 1979), document 235.
57. *India Emergency Assistance Act of 1951*, Hearings before the Committee on Foreign Affairs House of Representatives, Eighty-Second Congress, First Session, February 1951 (Washington, DC: US Government Printing Office, 1951), 211–212.
58. Helmreich, *Gathering Rare Ores*, 170.
59. *Executive Sessions of the Senate Foreign Relations Committee* (Historical Series), vol. 3, part 1, *82nd Congress, First Session, 1951* (Washington, DC: US Government Printing Office, 1976), 420. For more on the anxieties generated by the Franco-Indian collaboration, see Jayita Sarkar, "'Wean Them Away from French Tutelage': Franco-Indian Nuclear Relations and Anglo-American Anxieties during the Early Cold War, 1948–1952," *Cold War History* 15, no. 3 (2015): 375–394.
60. *Executive Sessions of the Senate Foreign Relations Committee* (Historical Series), vol. 3, part 1, *82nd Congress, First Session, 1951* (Washington, DC: US Government Printing Office, 1976), 424–425.
61. *India Emergency Assistance Act of 1951*, Hearings before the Committee on Foreign Affairs House of Representatives, Eighty-Second Congress, First Session, February 1951 (Washington, DC: US Government Printing Office, 1951), 212. The reference is to H. V. Kaltenborn's Broadcast, 19 February 1951.
62. The United States Atomic Energy Commission to the Secretary of State, 19 February 1951, *Foreign Relations of the United States, 1951*, vol. 1, *National Security Affairs: Foreign Economic Policy*, ed. Neal H. Petersen, Harriet D. Schwar, Carl N. Raether, John A. Bernbaum, and Ralph R. Goodwin (Washington, DC: US Government Printing Office, 1979), document 233.
63. Helmreich, *Gathering Rare Ores*, 172.

64. *Executive Sessions of the Senate Foreign Relations Committee* (Historical Series), vol. 3, part 1, *82nd Congress, First Session, 1951* (Washington, DC: US Government Printing Office, 1976), 361.
65. *Executive Sessions of the Senate Foreign Relations Committee* (Historical Series), vol. 3, part 1, *82nd Congress, First Session, 1951* (Washington, DC: US Government Printing Office, 1976), 364–365.
66. Thomas Robertson, *The Malthusian Moment: Global Population Growth and the Birth of American Environmentalism* (New Brunswick, NJ: Rutgers University Press, 2012).
67. *Executive Sessions of the Senate Foreign Relations Committee* (Historical Series), vol. 3, part 1, *82nd Congress, First Session, 1951* (Washington, DC: US Government Printing Office, 1976), 374, 391.
68. *Executive Sessions of the Senate Foreign Relations Committee* (Historical Series), vol. 3, part 1, *82nd Congress, First Session, 1951* (Washington, DC: US Government Printing Office, 1976), 385.
69. *Executive Sessions of the Senate Foreign Relations* Committee (Historical Series), vol. 3, part 1, *82nd Congress, First Session, 1951* (Washington, DC: US Government Printing Office, 1976), 498.
70. *Executive Sessions of the Senate Foreign Relations Committee* (Historical Series), vol. 3, part 1, *82nd Congress, First Session, 1951* (Washington, DC: US Government Printing Office, 1976), 420–421.
71. *Public Papers of the Presidents of the United States: Harry S. Truman, 1951* (Washington, DC: US Government Printing Office, 1965), 123
72. Agreement between the United States, United Kingdom, and Belgium, 13 July 1951. *Foreign Relations of the United States, 1951*, vol. 1, *National Security Affairs: Foreign Economic Policy*, ed. Neal H. Petersen, Harriet D. Schwar, Carl N. Raether, John A. Bernbaum, and Ralph R. Goodwin (Washington, DC: US Government Printing Office, 1979), document 250.
73. The Acting Secretary of State to the Embassy in Brazil, 6 December 1951, *Foreign Relations of the United States, 1951*, vol. 1, *National Security Affairs: Foreign Economic Policy*, ed. Neal H. Petersen, Harriet D. Schwar, Carl N. Raether, John A. Bernbaum, and Ralph R. Goodwin (Washington, DC: US Government Printing Office, 1979), document 273.
74. The importance of the cyclotron to Brazil is emphasized in Carlo Patti, "The Origins of the Brazilian Nuclear Programme, 1951–1955." The source quoted here is the Ambassador in Brazil (Johnson) to the Special Assistant to the Secretary of State (Arneson), 11 December 1951. *Foreign Relations of the United States, 1951*, vol. 1, *National Security Affairs: Foreign Economic Policy*, ed. Neal H. Petersen, Harriet D. Schwar, Carl N. Raether, John A. Bernbaum, and Ralph R. Goodwin (Washington, DC: US Government Printing Office, 1979), document 274.
75. The Deputy Counselor of the Embassy in France (Terrill) to the Department of State, 28 March 1951. *Foreign Relations of the United States, 1951*, vol. 1, *National Security Affairs: Foreign Economic Policy*, ed. Neal H. Petersen, Harriet D. Schwar, Carl N. Raether, John A. Bernbaum, and Ralph R. Goodwin (Washington, DC: US Government Printing Office, 1979), document 239.
76. Raye C. Ringholz, *Uranium Frenzy: Boom and Bust on the Colorado Plateau* (New York: Norton, 1989); Traci Brynne Voyles, *Wastelanding: Legacies of Uranium Mining in Navajo Country* (Minneapolis: University of Minnesota Press, 2015).

77. Robert J. Roscoe, James A. Deddens, Alberto Salvan, and Teresa M. Schnorr, "Mortality among Navajo Uranium Miners," *American Journal of Public Health* 85:4 (1995), 535–540.
78. Linda M. Richards, "Rocks and Reactors: An Atomic Interpretation of Human Rights," PhD dissertation, Oregon State University, 2014.
79. Mitchell R. Zavon, letter to the editor, "Navajo Uranium Miners in Utah, 1951," *American Journal of Public Health* 93:3 (2003), 362.
80. Doug Brugge and Rob Goble, "The History of Uranium Mining and the Navajo People," *American Journal of Public Health* 92:9 (2002), 1410–1419.

CHAPTER 2
1. Walters minutes, Bermuda, 4 December 1953, *Foreign Relations of the United States*, 1952–1954, vol. 5, part 2, *Western European Security*, ed. John A. Bernbaum, Lisle A. Rose, and Charles S. Sampson (Washington, DC: US Government Printing Office, 1983), document 340.
2. Memorandum Prepared in the Department of State, 1 December 1945, *Foreign Relations of the United States, 1946*, vol. 1, *General: The United Nations*, ed. Ralph R. Goodwin, Neal H. Petersen, Marvin W. Kranz, and William Slany (Washington, DC: US Government Printing Office, 1972), document 395.
3. Richard G. Hewlett and Oscar E. Anderson, *A History of the United States Atomic Energy Commission*, vol. 1, *The New World* (University Park: Pennsylvania State University Press, 1962). See pp. 554–576.
4. "The Baruch Plan," presented to the United Nations Atomic Energy Commission, 14 June 1946, http://www.atomicarchive.com/Docs/Deterrence/BaruchPlan.shtml [accessed 26 June 2020].
5. Vice Admiral W. H. P. Blandy, USN Commander Joint Task Force One, "Blandy: Report on Bikini," *All Hands: The Bureau of Naval Personnel Information Bulletin* 355 (September 1946), 2–9, quote on p. 2.
6. "Observers of U.N. Little Impressed," *New York Times*, 1 July 1946, 3.
7. Blandy, USN Commander Joint Task Force One, "Blandy: Report on Bikini," quote on p. 8.
8. These figures reflect details as reported by William Penney, in W. G. Penney, "A Preliminary High-Light Summary of Able and Baker," 11 August 1946, Chadwick Papers, Churchill College Archives, Cambridge, England, Chadwick IV, 5/24B.
9. William Penney to James Chadwick, 31 July 1946, Chadwick Papers, Churchill College Archives, Cambridge, England, Chadwick IV, 5/24B.
10. Stafford L. Warren, "Conclusions: Tests Proved Irresistible Spread of Radioactivity," Life, 11 August 1947, 86, 88.
11. "Radium girls" refers to women who worked in watch dial factories in the 1920s, many of whom became ill or died of cancer due to radium exposure. Luis Campos, *Radium and the Secret of Life* (Chicago: University of Chicago Press, 2015), 66–67; Kate Moore, *The Radium Girls: The Dark Story of America's Shining Women* (Naperville, IL: Sourcebooks, 2017); Matthew Lavine, *The First Atomic Age: Scientists, Radiations, and the American Public, 189–1945* (New York: Palgrave Macmillan, 2013).
12. Lawrence Badash, *Radioactivity in America: Growth and Decay of a Science* (Baltimore: Johns Hopkins University Press, 1979), 152–153, 190–191.
13. Gennady Gorelik with Antonina W. Bouis, *The World of Andrei Sakharov: A Russian Physicist's Path to Freedom* (New York: Oxford University Press, 2005), 77.

14. Muller himself wrote tantalizingly that the time was not yet ripe to discuss the ramifications of this research for the human species. H. J. Muller, "Artificial Transmutation of the Gene," *Science* 66:1699, New Series (22 July 1927), 84–87.
15. L. J. Stadler, "Mutations in Barley Induced by X-Rays and Radium," *Science* 68:1756, New Series (1928), 186–187.
16. Genetic work in corn (maize) in the 1930s that made scientists such as Barbara McClintock and George Beadle world famous was deeply informed by induced mutation from X-rays or from chemicals such as colchicine. See Helen Anne Curry, *Evolution Made to Order: Plant Breeding and Technological Innovation in Twentieth-Century America* (Chicago: University of Chicago Press, 2016).
17. Stadler, "Mutations in Barley,"186–187.
18. On Stadler's work with X-rays, and his views on deleterious effects, see Curry, *Evolution Made to Order*, 30–74, especially p. 44.
19. Hermann J. Muller, "Banquet Speech," 10 December 1946, https://www.nobelprize.org/prizes/medicine/1946/muller/speech/ [accessed 26 June 2020].
20. On Brown's (and others') work with Patterson, see the essays in "Studies in the Genetics of Drosophila directed by J. T. Patterson," in *The University of Texas Publication* 4032 (22 August 1940).
21. "Atom Alters Heredity," *Science News Letter*, 16 September 1950, 188.
22. "Radiation Dwarfs Cotton," *Science News Letter*, 7 February 1948, 87.
23. J. B. Hutchinson, R. A. Silow, and S. G. Stephens, *The Evolution of Gossypium and the Differentiation of the Cultivated Cottons* (London: Oxford University Press, 1947). See also M. H. Arnold, "Joseph Burtt Hutchinson, 21 March 1902–16 January 1988," *Biographical Memoirs of Fellows of the Royal Society* 37 (November 1991), 278–297.
24. Luther Smith, "Cytology and Genetics of Barley," *Botanical Review* 17:1 (1951), 1–51, quote on p. 25. See also Luther Smith, "Effects of Atomic Bomb Radiations and X-Rays on Seeds of Cereals," *Journal of Heredity* 41 (1950), 125–130; and L. F. Randolph, A. E. Longley, and Ching Hsiung Li, "Cytogenetic Effects in Corn Exposed to Atomic Bomb Ionizing Radiation at Bikini," *Science* 108:2792 (1948), 13–15.
25. Karl Sax, "The Effect of Ionizing Radiation on Plant Growth," *American Journal of Botany* 42:4 (1955), 360–364.
26. Alan D. Conger, "Arnold Hicks Sparrow (1914–1976), *Radiation Research* 69:1 (1977), 194–196.
27. Harland Manchester, "The New Age of Atomic Crops," *Popular Mechanics* (October 1958): 106–110, 282–288, quote p. 108.
28. For a discussion of the creation of gamma gardens at Brookhaven, see Curry, *Evolution Made to Order*, 148–155. Arnold H. Sparrow and W. Ralph Singleton, "The Use of Radiocobalt as a Source of Gamma Rays and Some Effects of Chronic Irradiation on Growing Plants," *American Naturalist* 87:832 (1953), 29–48.
29. Sparrow and Singleton, "The Use of Radiocobalt as a Source of Gamma Rays."
30. Brien McMahon, "A New Bid for Atomic Peace," *Bulletin of the Atomic Scientists* (March 1950), 80–82.
31. McMahon, "A New Bid for Atomic Peace."
32. William S. White, "McMahon Proposes 50 Billion Crusade to Halt Atom," *New York Times*, 3 February 1950, 1.
33. "McMahon Proposal Held 'Peace Weapon,'" *New York Times*, 12 February 1950, 4.
34. McMahon, "A New Bid for Atomic Peace."

35. "Soviet Union Using Atomic Energy to Move Mountains, Vishinsky Tells UN Group," *Schenectady Gazette*, 11 November 1949, 1, 8.
36. McMahon, "A New Bid for Atomic Peace."
37. Greg Barnhisel, "Encounter Magazine and the Twilight of Modernism," *ELH* 81:1 (2014), 381–416. See also Frances Stonor Saunders, *The Cultural Cold War: The CIA and the World of Arts and Letters* (New York: New Press, 2000).
38. Audra J. Wolfe, *Freedom's Laboratory: The Cold War Struggle for the Soul of Science* (Baltimore: Johns Hopkins University Press, 2018), 80.
39. Elof Axel Carlson, *Genes, Radiation, and Society: The Life and Work of H. J. Muller* (Ithaca, NY: Cornell University Press, 1981).
40. David E. Lilienthal, "The 4th R is for Radiation," *Phi Delta Kappan* 33:2 (1951), 79.
41. Brien McMahon, "Survival—the Real Issue of Our Times," *Bulletin of the Atomic Scientists* 8:6 (August 1952), 173–175.
42. Roger Dingman, "Atomic Diplomacy during the Korean War," *International Security* 13, no. 3 (1988), 50–91.
43. Memorandum of Discussion at a Special Meeting of the National Security Council on Tuesday, 31 March 1953. *Foreign Relations of the United States, 1952–1954*, vol. 15, part 1, *Korea*, ed. Edward C. Keefer (Washington: Government Printing Office, 1984), document 427.
44. "For Eisenhower, 2 Goals if Bomb Was to Be Used," *New York Times*, 8 June 1984, 8.
45. Robynne N. Mellor, "The Cold War Underground: An Environmental History of Uranium Mining in the United States, Canada, and the Soviet Union, 1945–1991," PhD dissertation, Georgetown University, 2018.
46. Report to the National Security Council by the Atomic Energy Commission, 6 March 1953, *Foreign Relations of the United States, 1952–1954*, vol. 2, part 2, *National Security Affairs*, ed. Lisle A. Rose and Neal H. Petersen (Washington, DC: US Government Printing Office, 1984), document 76.
47. Chairman of the United States Atomic Energy Commission (Dean) to Robert Cutler, Special Assistant to the President, 30 March 1953, *Foreign Relations of the United States*, 1952–1954, vol. 2, part 2, *National Security Affairs*, ed. Lisle A. Rose and Neal H. Petersen (Washington, DC: US Government Printing Office, 1984), document 81.
48. Memorandum of Discussion at the 143rd Meeting of the National Security Council, 6 May 1953, *Foreign Relations of the United States, 1952–1954*, vol. 2, part 2, *National Security Affairs*, ed. Lisle A. Rose and Neal H. Petersen (Washington, DC: US Government Printing Office, 1984), document 87.
49. Memorandum by R. Gordon Arneson to the Secretary of State, 10 March 1953, *Foreign Relations of the United States, 1952–1954*, vol. 2, part 2, *National Security Affairs*, ed. Lisle A. Rose and Neal H. Petersen (Washington, DC: US Government Printing Office, 1984), document 77.
50. Memorandum of Discussion at the 136th Meeting of the National Security Council 11 March 1953, *Foreign Relations of the United States, 1952–1954*, vol. 2, part 2, *National Security Affairs*, ed. Lisle A. Rose and Neal H. Petersen (Washington, DC: US Government Printing Office, 1984), document 78.
51. Oral History Interview with Gordon Arneson, 21 June 1989, by Niel M. Johnson, Harry S. Truman Presidential Library and Museum, https://www.trumanlibrary.org/oralhist/arneson.htm [accessed 26 June 2020].
52. Chairman of the Joint Congressional Committee on Atomic Energy (Cole) to the President, 21 August 1953, *Foreign Relations of the United States, 1952–1954*,

vol. 2, part 2, *National Security Affairs*, ed. Lisle A. Rose and Neal H. Petersen (Washington, DC: US Government Printing Office, 1984), document 98.

53. See editorial footnote, Chairman of the Joint Congressional Committee on Atomic Energy (Cole) to the President, 21 August 1953, *Foreign Relations of the United States, 1952–1954*, vol. 2, part 2, *National Security Affairs*, ed. Lisle A. Rose and Neal H. Petersen (Washington, DC: US Government Printing Office, 1984), document 98.

54. Report to the National Security Council by the NSC Planning Board, 1 September 1953, *Foreign Relations of the United States, 1952–1954*, vol. 2, part 2, *National Security Affairs*, ed. Lisle A. Rose and Neal H. Petersen (Washington, DC: US Government Printing Office, 1984), document 101.

55. Memorandum of discussion at the 161st Meeting of the National Security Council, 9 September 1953, *Foreign Relations of the United States, 1952–1954*, vol. 2, part 2, *National Security Affairs*, ed. Lisle A. Rose and Neal H. Petersen (Washington, DC: US Government Printing Office, 1984), document 103.

56. Report to the National Security Council by the NSC Planning Board, 1 September 1953, *Foreign Relations of the United States, 1952–1954*, vol. 2, part 2, *National Security Affairs*, ed. Lisle A. Rose and Neal H. Petersen (Washington, DC: US Government Printing Office, 1984), document 101.

57. Memorandum by Robert Cutler, Special Assistant to the President for National Security Affairs, 10 September 1953, *Foreign Relations of the United States, 1952–1954*, vol. 2, part 2, *National Security Affairs*, ed. Lisle A. Rose and Neal H. Petersen (Washington, DC: US Government Printing Office, 1984), document 104.

58. Memorandum of discussion at the 162nd Meeting of the National Security Council, 17 September 1953, *Foreign Relations of the United States, 1952–1954*, vol. 2, part 2, *National Security Affairs*, ed. Lisle A. Rose and Neal H. Petersen (Washington, DC: US Government Printing Office, 1984), document 108.

59. Memorandum by Charles C. Stelle to the Director of the Policy Planning Staff (Bowie), 23 September 1953, *Foreign Relations of the United States, 1952–1954*, vol. 2, part 2, *National Security Affairs*, ed. Lisle A. Rose and Neal H. Petersen (Washington, DC: US Government Printing Office, 1984), document 110. See also Ira Chernus, "Operation Candor: Fear, Faith, and Flexibility," *Diplomatic History* 29:5 (1 November 2005), 779–809; and Kenneth A. Osgood, *Total Cold War: Eisenhower's Secret Propaganda Battle at Home and Abroad* (Lawrence: University of Kansas Press, 2008).

60. Special Assistant to the President (Jackson) to Under Secretary of State (Smith), 25 September 1953, *Foreign Relations of the United States, 1952–1954*, vol. 2, part 2, *National Security Affairs*, ed. Lisle A. Rose and Neal H. Petersen (Washington, DC: US Government Printing Office, 1984), document 111.

61. Memorandum of conversation, by the Secretary of State, Bermuda, 4 December 1953, *Foreign Relations of the United States, 1952–1954*, vol. 2, part 2, *Western European Security*, ed. John A. Bernbaum, Lisle A. Rose, and Charles S. Sampson (Washington, DC: US Government Printing Office, 1983), document 335.

62. On the Bermuda meeting, see Fredrik Logevall, *Embers of War: The Fall of an Empire and the Making of America's Vietnam* (New York: Random House, 2014).

63. Walters minutes, Bermuda, 4 December 1953, *Foreign Relations of the United States, 1952–1954*, vol. 2, part 2, *Western European Security*, ed. John A. Bernbaum, Lisle A. Rose, and Charles S. Sampson (Washington. DC: US Government Printing Office, 1983), document 340.

64. Walters minutes, Bermuda, 4 December 1953, *Foreign Relations of the United States, 1952–1954*, vol. 2, part 2, *Western European Security*, ed. John A. Bernbaum, Lisle A. Rose, and Charles S. Sampson (Washington, DC: US Government Printing Office, 1983), document 340.
65. Notes prepared by Admiral Strauss, Bermuda, 5 December 1953, *Foreign Relations of the United States, 1952–1954*, vol. 5, part 2, *Western European Security*, ed. John A. Bernbaum, Lisle A. Rose, and Charles S. Sampson (Washington, DC: US Government Printing Office, 1983), document 344.
66. Atoms for Peace Draft, [C.D. Jackson Papers, box 30, "Atoms for Peace—Evolution (5)"], Eisenhower Presidential Library, https://www.eisenhowerlibrary.gov/research/online-documents/atoms-peace [accessed 26 June 2020].
67. Text of the speech by Dwight D. Eisenhower, delivered on December 8, 1953, can be found at http://voicesofdemocracy.umd.edu/eisenhower-atoms-for-peace-speech-text/ [accessed 26 June 2020].
68. Paul R. Josephson, *Red Atom: Russia's Nuclear Power Program from Stalin to Today* (Pittsburgh: University of Pittsburgh Press, 2005), 27.
69. "Revue de la Presse," *Le Monde* (10 December 1953), https://www.lemonde.fr/archives/article/1953/12/10/revue-de-la-presse_1978013_1819218.html [accessed 26 June 2020].

CHAPTER 3

1. Arthur Herman, *Freedom's Forge: How American Business Produced Victory in World War II* (New York: Random House, 2013). On the *Barb*, see Naval History and Heritage Command, "Barb 1," https://www.history.navy.mil/research/histories/ship-histories/danfs/b/barb-i.html [accessed 27 June 2020].
2. Chief of [deleted] Base to Chief, FE, 5 July 1955, CIA Electronic Reading Room, Special Collection, Nazi War Crimes Disclosure Act, "Shoriki, Matsutaro," vol. 2:13.
3. Beverly Ann Deepe Keever, *News Zero: The New York Times and the Bomb* (Monroe, ME: Common Courage Press, 2004). For thoughtful commentary on Laurence's role, see Amy Goodman and David Goodman, "Hiroshima Cover-Up: How the War Department's Timesman Won a Pulitzer," Common Dreams, http://www.commondreams.org/views/2004/08/10/hiroshima-cover-how-war-departments-timesman-won-pulitzer [accessed 26 June 2020].
4. William L. Laurence, "Atomic Power Being Tamed to Turn Industry's Wheels," *New York Times*, 4 January 1954, 49.
5. Laurence, "Atomic Power Being Tamed," 49.
6. William L. Laurence, "Electricity Is Made from Atomic Waste," *New York Times*, 27 January 1954, 1.
7. Elizabeth Walker Mechling and Jay Mechling, "The Atom According to Disney," *Quarterly Journal of Speech* 81:4 (1995), 436–453, 444.
8. See, for example, Michael Amrine, "Atoms for Peace—by Way of War: A Projected Sub Becomes Our First Attempt to Convert Nuclear Fission into Practical Power," *New York Times*, 2 September 1951, 101.
9. Official Program by General Dynamics Corp., for the launching of the USS Nautilus, 1954, https://www.eisenhowerlibrary.gov/research/online-documents/uss-nautilus [accessed 26 June 2020].
10. Steven Heller, "Erik Nitsche: The Reluctant Modernist," *Typotheque*, 29 November 200, https://www.typotheque.com/articles/erik_nitsche_the_reluctant_modernist [accessed 26 June 2020].

11. SAC, Los Angeles, to Director, FBI, Attn: Assistant to Director Louis B. Nichols and Assistant Director Donald J. Parsons, 1 March 1957, in "Walter Elias Disney Part 01 of 03," https://vault.fbi.gov/walter-elias-disney/walter-elias-disney-part-01-of-03/view [accessed 26 June 2020].
12. SAC, Los Angeles to Director, FBI, Attn: Training and Inspection Division, 16 December 1954, in "Walter Elias Disney Part 01 of 03," https://vault.fbi.gov/walter-elias-disney/walter-elias-disney-part-01-of-03/view [accessed 26 June 2020].
13. Mike Wright, "The Disney-Von Braun Collaboration and Its Influence on Space Exploration," 1993, https://www.nasa.gov/centers/marshall/history/vonbraun/disney_article.html [accessed 26 June 2020].
14. Mechling and Mechling, "The Atom According to Disney," 443.
15. Mechling and Mechling, "The Atom According to Disney," 441.
16. *Walker Lee Cisler, Twenty-Third Hoover Medalist* (New York: Hoover Medal Board of Award, 1962).
17. Joseph D. Martin, "Nuclear Optimism and the Michigan Memorial-Phoenix Project," *Historical Studies in the Natural Sciences* (in press).
18. *Walker Lee Cisler, Twenty-Third Hoover Medalist*, 9.
19. *Development, Growth, and the State of the Atomic Energy Industry*, Hearings before the Joint Committee on Atomic Energy, Congress of the United States, February 7, 8, 9, and 10, 1955 (Washington, DC: US Government Printing Office, 1955), 238.
20. Alvin Weinberg, "Chapters from the Life of a Technological Fixer," *Minerva* 31:4 (1993), 379–454. In subsequent years, this choice was reinforced further when the head of the AEC's Division of Reactor Development, Ken Davis, insisted that the United States had to commit to one kind of reactor rather than divide its efforts.
21. On FPAD and US diplomatic goals, see Gisela Mateos and Edna Suárez-Díaz, "'The Door to the Promised Land of Atomic Peace and Plenty': Mexican Students and the Phoenix Memorial Project," *Historical Studies in the Natural Sciences* (in press).
22. Frances Stonor Saunders, *The Cultural Cold War: The CIA and the World of Arts and Letters* (New York: New Press, 2000).
23. Harold E. Stassen to Allen Dulles, 29 September 1955, Central Intelligence Agency FOIA Electronic Reading Room, document CIA-RDP80B01676R004200110041-1.
24. *World Development of Atomic Energy: A Forum Survey* (New York: Atomic Industrial Forum, 1955), 17–18.
25. *Peaceful Uses of Atomic Energy, Background Material for the Report of the Panel on the Impact of the Peaceful Uses of Atomic Energy to the Joint Committee on Atomic Energy* (Washington, DC: US Government Printing Office, 1956), 381–382.
26. *World Development of Atomic Energy.*
27. On the promotion of agricultural techniques, see Neil Oatsvall, "Atomic Agriculture: Policymaking, Food Production, and Nuclear Technologies in the United States, 1945–1960," *Agricultural History* 88:3 (2014), 368–387. For the survey of the world's atomic energy programs, see *World Development of Atomic Energy*, 27.
28. *World Development of Atomic Energy*, 17–18, 64.
29. Christopher Hinton, "Atomic Power in Britain," *Scientific American* 198:3 (1958), 29–35. For more on Britain's early nuclear program, see Margaret

Gowing, *Independence and Deterrence: Britain and Atomic Energy, 1945–1952* (London: Macmillan, 1974).
30. Paul R. Josephson, *Red Atom: Russia's Nuclear Power Program from Stalin to Today* (Pittsburgh, PA: University of Pittsburgh Press, 2005), 10, 27, 56.
31. *Development, Growth, and the State of the Atomic Energy Industry*, Hearings before the Joint Committee on Atomic Energy, Congress of the United States, February 7, 8, 9, and 10, 1955 (Washington, DC: US Government Printing Office, 1955).
32. On the Shippingport reactor, see Richard G. Hewlett and Jack M. Holl, *Atoms for Peace and War, 1953–1961: Eisenhower and the Atomic Energy Commission*, California Studies in the History of Science (Berkeley: University of California Press, 1989).
33. Alvin Weinberg, "Chapters from the Life of a Technological Fixer," *Minerva* 31:4 (1993), 379–454. In subsequent years, this choice was reinforced further when the head of the AEC's Division of Reactor Development, Ken Davis, insisted that the United States had to commit to one kind of reactor rather than divide its efforts.
34. On the ambitions of the TRIGA reactor, see Edward Teller with Judith L. Schoolery, *Memoirs: A Twentieth-Century Journey in Science and Politics* (Cambridge, MA: Perseus, 2001).
35. John DiMoia, "Atoms for Sale? Cold War Institution-Building and the South Korean Atomic Energy Project, 1945–1965," *Technology and Culture* 51:3 (2010), 589–618.
36. DiMoia, "Atoms for Sale?," 598.
37. DiMoia, "Atoms for Sale?," 599–601.
38. DiMoia, "Atoms for Sale?," 599–601.
39. DiMoia, "Atoms for Sale?," 611–-613.
40. CIA Office of National Estimates, Draft Memorandum for the Director of Central Intelligence, Subject: Political and Psychological Effects of a US Program for Cooperation with Other Nations in the Peaceful Uses of Atomic Energy, 9 August 1954, CIA-RDP79R00904A000500020132-1.
41. Yoshio Nishina, "A Japanese Scientist Describes the Destruction of His Cyclotrons," *Bulletin of the Atomic Scientists*, 1 June 1947, 145, 167.
42. *World Development of Atomic Energy*, 34. On Japan's wartime work and the state of atomic research in the immediate postwar years, see Walter E. Grunden, Mark Walker, and Masakatsu Yamazaki, "Wartime Nuclear Weapons Research in Germany and Japan," *Osiris* 20 (2005), 107–130.
43. O. O., "Japan's Economic Recovery," *The World Today* 8:9 (September 1952), 392–404.
44. These events are related in much of the extant literature. For an account from the perspective of Japanese scholarship, see Masakatsu Yamazaki and Kenzo Okuda, "Pacifying Anti-American Sentiments: Introducing Nuclear Reactors into Japan after the Bikini Incident," *Journal of History of Science, Japan* 43:230 (2004), 83–93.
45. Extracts from Statement made by the Prime Minister of India in the House of the People on 2 April 1954 on the Subject of the Hydrogen Bomb. Central Intelligence Agency FOIA Electronic Reading Room, document CIA-RDP86T00268R000800100021-2.
46. Summary of Developments in Japan Arising from Bikini Incident, 9 June 1954. Central Intelligence Agency FOIA Electronic Reading Room, document CIA-RDP80R01731R003000130003-6.

47. Morris Low, *Japan on Display: Photography and the Emperor* (New York: Routledge, 2006), 124–126. For perspective on Japanese scientists after the 1954 incident, see Toshihiro Higuchi, "The Strange Career of Dr. Fish: Yoshio Hiyama, Radioactive Fallout, and Nuclear Fear Management in Japan, 1954–1958,"*Historia Scientiarum* 25:1(2015), 57–77.
48. On the role of Nakasone and other conservative Japanese politicians in early atomic energy, see Yoshimi Shun'ya, "Radioactive Rain and the American Umbrella," *Journal of Asian Studies* 71:2 (2012), 319–331, translated by Shi-Lin Loh; and Dominic Kelly, "Ideology, Society, and the Origins of Nuclear Power in Japan," *East Asian Science, Technology and Society: An International Journal* 9:1 (2015), 47–64.
49. One prominent Japanese-language account of Shōriki's role in atomic energy, including his collaboration with the CIA, is Tetsuo Arima, *Genpatsu, Shoriki, CIA* (Tokyo: Shinchosha, 2008). For an English-language discussion, see Yamazaki and Okuda, "Pacifying Anti-American Sentiments."
50. Low, *Japan on Display*, 116.
51. "Biographical Data: Leaders in Japanese Television Industry," n.d., CIA Electronic Reading Room, Special Collection, Nazi War Crimes Disclosure Act, "Shoriki, Matsutaro," vol. 1:3. For a summary of the case against Shōriki and the American estimation of them, see Memorandum for the Record, 27 January 1953, CIA Electronic Reading Room, Special Collection, Nazi War Crimes Disclosure Act, "Shoriki, Matsutaro," vol. 1:14.
52. *Political Reorientation of Japan, September 1945 to September 1948*, Report of Government Section, Supreme Commander for the Allied Powers (Washington, DC: US Government Printing Office, 1948), 58.
53. For Shōriki's role in Japanese baseball, see Sayuri Guthrie-Shimizu, *Transpacific Field of Dreams: How Baseball Linked the United States and Japan in Peace and War* (Chapel Hill: University of North Carolina Press, 2012).
54. "Controversies in Japanese Telecommunications Field," dated 1952–53, CIA Electronic Reading Room, Special Collection, Nazi War Crimes Disclosure Act, "Shoriki, Matsutaro," vol. 1:12.
55. More detailed analysis of these meetings and their relationship to the creation of Nippon TV can be found in Simon Partner, *Assembled in Japan: Electrical Goods and the Making of the Japanese Consumer* (Berkeley: University of California Press, 2000), 74–82.
56. On Holthusen and UNITEL in Japan, see James Schwoch, *Global TV: New Media and the Cold War, 1946–69* (Urbana: University of Illinois Press, 2009), 87–89.
57. "Biographical Data: Leaders in Japanese Television Industry," n.d., CIA Electronic Reading Room, Special Collection, Nazi War Crimes Disclosure Act, "Shoriki, Matsutaro," vol. 1:3.
58. Untitled document providing biographical detail (and using the name POJackpot/1), CIA Electronic Reading Room, Special Collection, Nazi War Crimes Disclosure Act, "Shoriki, Matsutaro," vol. 1:9. See also "Personal Record Questionnaire," n.d., noting Shōriki's cryptonym as PODAM, same collection, vol. 1:11.
59. Untitled memorandum, 30 November 1953 regarding PODAM, CIA Electronic Reading Room, Special Collection, Nazi War Crimes Disclosure Act, "Shoriki, Matsutaro," vol. 1:22.
60. James Schwoch, *Global TV: New Media and the Cold War, 1946–69* (Urbana: University of Illinois Press, 2009), 88–89.

61. William L. Laurence, "Atomic-Submarine Builder Urges Nuclear Marshall Plan by Industry," *New York Times*, 2 December 1954, 1, 34.
62. Unsigned letter to Director of Central Intelligence, 31 December 1954, CIA Electronic Reading Room, Special Collection, Nazi War Crimes Disclosure Act, "Shoriki, Matsutaro," vol. 1:27. For detailed discussion of Shibata's role in facilitating contacts between the Americans and Shōriki, see Yamazaki and Okuda, "Pacifying Anti-American Sentiments."
63. Information report, 10 March 1955, CIA Electronic Reading Room, Special Collection, Nazi War Crimes Disclosure Act, "Shoriki, Matsutaro," vol. 1:36.
64. Central Intelligence Agency Information Report, No. CS-61948, distribution date 22 April 1955, CIA Electronic Reading Room, Special Collection, Nazi War Crimes Disclosure Act, "Shoriki, Matsutaro," vol. 2:3. For more detailed discussion drawn in part from Shibata's recollections, see Yamazaki and Okuda, "Pacifying Anti-American Sentiments," 83–93.
65. Director to Chief, [redacted] Mission, [redacted], 16 May 1955, CIA Electronic Reading Room, Special Collection, Nazi War Crimes Disclosure Act, "Shoriki, Matsutaro," vol. 2:4.
66. Matsutaro Shōriki and eighteen other Japanese signatories (all members of the Organizing Committee for Japan Atoms-for-Peace Council) to John Jay Hopkins, 26 May 1955, CIA Electronic Reading Room, Special Collection, Nazi War Crimes Disclosure Act, "Shoriki, Matsutaro," vol. 2:7. More details from the CIA's point of view are at Chief of [deleted] Base to Chief, FE, 5 July 1955, Special Collection, Nazi War Crimes Disclosure Act, "Shoriki, Matsutaro," vol. 2:13.
67. Matsutaro Shōriki and eighteen other Japanese signatories, "Shoriki, Matsutaro," vol. 2:7. More details from the CIA's point of view are at Chief of [deleted] Base to Chief, FE, 5 July 1955, Special Collection, Nazi War Crimes Disclosure Act, "Shoriki, Matsutaro," vol. 2:13.
68. Chief of [deleted] Base to Chief, FE, 5 July 1955, CIA Electronic Reading Room, Special Collection, Nazi War Crimes Disclosure Act, "Shoriki, Matsutaro," vol. 2:13.
69. Matsutaro Shōriki and eighteen other Japanese signatories, "Shoriki, Matsutaro," vol. 2:7.
70. Matsutaro Shōriki and eighteen other Japanese signatories, "Shoriki, Matsutaro," vol. 2:7.
71. Matsutaro Shōriki and eighteen other Japanese signatories, "Shoriki, Matsutaro," vol. 2:7.
72. Unsigned classified message to Director of Central Intelligence, 20 May 1955, CIA Electronic Reading Room, Special Collection, Nazi War Crimes Disclosure Act, "Shoriki, Matsutaro," vol. 2:6.
73. On public opinion about civilian nuclear energy in Japan and a detailed analysis of the exhibit in Hiroshima, see Ran Zwigenberg, "'The Coming of a Second Sun': The 1956 Atoms for Peace Exhibit in Hiroshima and Japan's Embrace of Nuclear Power," *Asia-Pacific Journal* 10:6 (2012), https://apjjf.org/2012/10/6/Ran-Zwigenberg/3685/article.html [accessed 27 June 2020].
74. Memorandum for Chief, Information Coordination Division, 28 January 1955, CIA Electronic Reading Room, Special Collection, Nazi War Crimes Disclosure Act, "Shoriki, Matsutaro," vol. 1:35.

75. Acting KUCAGE [Psychological Warfare] Operations Officer to Chief, FE, 5 July 1955, CIA Electronic Reading Room, Special Collection, Nazi War Crimes Disclosure Act, "Shoriki, Matsutaro," vol. 2:38.
76. Matsutaro Shōriki to President Dwight D. Eisenhower, 17 November 1955. Foreign Service Despatch from US Embassy, Tokyo, to Department of State, Washington, 10 July 1956, CIA Electronic Reading Room, Special Collection, Nazi War Crimes Disclosure Act, "Shoriki, Matsutaro," vol. 2:38.
77. The change in public opinion is discussed in Yuki Tanaka and Peter J. Kuznick, "Japan, the Atomic Bomb, and the 'Peaceful Uses of Nuclear Power,'" *Asia-Pacific Journal* 9:18 (2011), https://apjjf.org/2011/9/18/Yuki-Tanaka/3521/article.html [accessed 26 June 2020].
78. Chief, [deleted] Base, [deleted], to Chief, FE, Subject Psych Operational, PODAM/ [deleted] Progress Report, 9 December 1955. CIA Electronic Reading Room, Special Collection, Nazi War Crimes Disclosure Act, "Shoriki, Matsutaro," vol. 2:43.
79. [Author redacted] to Director, 30 April 1956. CIA Electronic Reading Room, Special Collection, Nazi War Crimes Disclosure Act, "Shoriki, Matsutaro," vol. 3:3.
80. [Redacted] to Director, 20 July 1955. CIA Electronic Reading Room, Special Collection, Nazi War Crimes Disclosure Act, "Shoriki, Matsutaro," vol. 2:17.
81. [Redacted] to Director, 13 December 1955. CIA Electronic Reading Room, Special Collection, Nazi War Crimes Disclosure Act, "Shoriki, Matsutaro," vol. 2:46
82. "A Talk to People in the Inner Circle of Atomic Energy in Japan," April 1956, Papers of Sir Christopher Hinton, Churchill College Archives, Cambridge University, United Kingdom, folder 3/4.
83. "A Talk to People in the Inner Circle of Atomic Energy in Japan."
84. "A Talk to People in the Inner Circle of Atomic Energy in Japan."
85. "A Talk to People in the Inner Circle of Atomic Energy in Japan."
86. Foreign Service Despatch from US Embassy, Tokyo to Department of State, Washington, 3 August 1956, CIA Electronic Reading Room, Special Collection, Nazi War Crimes Disclosure Act, "Shoriki, Matsutaro," vol. 3:19.
87. "Scientists Studying H-Bomb Blast Data," *New York Times*, 22 May 1956, 1.
88. Chief, FE to Chief of [redacted] Station, [redacted], 26 June 1956. CIA Electronic Reading Room, Special Collection, Nazi War Crimes Disclosure Act, "Shoriki, Matsutaro," vol. 3:14
89. Chief, FE to Chief of [redacted] Station, [redacted], 26 June 1956.
90. Correspondence between Chief, FE and Acting Chief [redacted] Station, [redacted], 6 July 1956, CIA Electronic Reading Room, Special Collection, Nazi War Crimes Disclosure Act, "Shoriki, Matsutaro," vol. 3:15.
91. Foreign Service Despatch from US Embassy, Tokyo, to Department of State, Washington, 10 July 1956, CIA Electronic Reading Room, Special Collection, Nazi War Crimes Disclosure Act, "Shoriki, Matsutaro," vol. 3:17.
92. Foreign Service Despatch from US Embassy, Tokyo, to Department of State, Washington.
93. Early information about the Tokai reactor is in E. R. Appleby, *Review of Power and Heat Reactor Designs, Domestic and Foreign*, report HW-66666, vol. 1 (Richland, WA: Hanford Atomic Products Operation, 1961), 143.
94. The Japanese government's focus on positive aspects of atomic power and its alliance with national media is discussed in Christopher F. Jones, Shi-Lin Loh,

and Kyoko Satō, "Narrating Fukushima: Scales of a Nuclear Meltdown," *East Asian Science, Technology and Society: An International Journal* 7 (2013), 601–623.

CHAPTER 4

1. On the connection between racial politics and Cold War diplomacy in the 1950s and 1960s, see Mary L. Dudziak, *Cold War Civil Rights: Race and the Image of American Democracy* (Princeton, NJ: Princeton University Press, 2000); and Thomas Borstelmann, *The Cold War and the Color Line: American Race Relations in the Global Arena* (Cambridge, MA: Harvard University Press, 2003). On neutralism, see H. W. Brands, *The Specter of Neutralism: The United States and the Emergence of the Third World* (New York: Columbia University Press, 1989).
2. Mark Vallen, "A New Look at Rivera's 'Gloriosa Victoria,'" 8 February 2016, http://art-for-a-change.com/blog/2016/02/a-new-look-at-riveras-gloriosa-victoria.html [accessed 26 June 2020].
3. Original Spanish, along with English translations (used here) can be found in William Pitt Root, trans., *Sublime Blue: Selected Early Odes by Pablo Neruda* (San Antonio, TX: Wings Press, 2013), 23–31.
4. National Security Council Report NSC 5507/2, 12 March 1955, *Foreign Relations of the United States, 1955–1957*, vol. 20, *Regulation of Armaments; Atomic Energy*, ed. David S. Patterson (Washington, DC: US Government Printing Office, 1990), document 14.
5. *Meeting the Human Problems of the Nuclear Age, Address by President Eisenhower, June 11, 1955* (Washington, DC: US Government Printing Office, 1955).
6. Memorandum of Discussion at the 251st Meeting of the National Security Council, 9 June 1955, *Foreign Relations of the United States, 1955–1957*, vol. 20, *Regulation of Armaments; Atomic Energy*, ed. David S. Patterson (Washington, DC: US Government Printing Office, 1990), document 35.
7. Letter from the Secretary of State to the President's Special Assistant, 2 May 1955, *Foreign Relations of the United States, 1955–1957*, vol. 20, *Regulation of Armaments; Atomic Energy*, ed. David S. Patterson (Washington, DC: US Government Printing Office, 1990), document 21.
8. Memorandum of Discussion at the 240th Meeting of the National Security Council, 10 March 1955, *Foreign Relations of the United States, 1955–1957*, vol. 20, *Regulation of Armaments; Atomic Energy*, ed. David S. Patterson (Washington, DC: US Government Printing Office, 1990), document 13.
9. Jahnavi Phalkey, *Atomic State: Big Science in Twentieth-Century India* (New Delhi: Permanent Black, 2013).
10. Memorandum from the Deputy Assistant Secretary of State for International Organization Affairs (Wainhouse) and the Secretary of State's Assistant for Atomic Energy Affairs (Smith) to the Under Secretary of State (Hooever), 19 January 1955, *Foreign Relations of the United States, 1955–1957*, vol. 20, *Regulation of Armaments; Atomic Energy*, ed. David S. Patterson (Washington, DC: US Government Printing Office, 1990), document 3.
11. Memorandum of Discussion at the 240th Meeting of the National Security Council, 10 March 1955, *Foreign Relations of the United States, 1955–1957*, vol. 20, *Regulation of Armaments; Atomic Energy*, ed. David S. Patterson (Washington, DC: US Government Printing Office, 1990), document 13.
12. Cindy Ewing, "The Colombo Powers: Crafting Diplomacy in the Third World and Launching Afro-Asia at Bandung," *Cold War History* 19:1 (2019), 1–19.

13. The communiqué is quoted in full in Jack A. Homer, *Bandung: An On-the-Spot Description of the Asian-African Conference, Bandung, Indonesia, April, 1955* (Chicago: Toward Freedom, 1956), 17–29.
14. Editorial Note, *Foreign Relations of the United States, 1955–1957*, vol. 20, *Regulation of Armaments; Atomic Energy*, ed. David S. Patterson (Washington, DC: US Government Printing Office, 1990), document 48.
15. Memorandum of Discussion at the 261st Meeting of the National Security Council, Washington, 13 October 1955, *Foreign Relations of the United States, 1955–1957*, vol. 20, *Regulation of Armaments; Atomic Energy*, ed. David S. Patterson (Washington, DC: US Government Printing Office, 1990), document 77.
16. Memorandum of Discussion at the 261st Meeting of the National Security Council, Washington, 13 October 1955, *Foreign Relations of the United States, 1955–1957*, vol. 20, *Regulation of Armaments; Atomic Energy*, ed. David S. Patterson (Washington, DC: US Government Printing Office, 1990), document 77.
17. Paul R. Josephson, *Red Atom: Russia's Nuclear Power Program from Stalin to Today* (Pittsburgh, PA: University of Pittsburgh Press, 2005), 174–175.
18. Memorandum of a Conversation, Department of State, 8 April 1955 (subject: Asian African Conference), *Foreign Relations of the United States, 1955–1957*, vol. 2, *China*, ed. Harriet D. Schwar (Washington, DC: US Government Printing Office, 1986), document 195; Memorandum of a Conversation, Department of State, Washington, 24 May 1955 (subject: Bandung conference), *Foreign Relations of the United States, 1955–1957*, vol. 21, *East Asian Security; Cambodia; Laos*, ed. Edward C. Keefer and David W. Mabon (Washington, DC: US Government Printing Office, 1990), document 54.
19. F. M. Serrano, *Atoms for Peace in the Philippines: Official Report of the Philippine Delegation to the International Conference on the Peaceful Uses of Atomic Energy* (New York: Philippine Mission to the United Nations, 1955).
20. Confidential cable from British Embassy, Washington, DC, to Foreign Office, 21 December 1955, DO 35/5779, UK National Archives, Kew, England.
21. British Chancery, Manila, to South East Asian Department, Foreign Office, 31 December 1955, DO 35/5779, UK National Archives, Kew, England.
22. N. E. Costar to J. Thomson, 4 April 1956, DO 35/5779, UK National Archives, Kew, England.
23. J. C. A. Roper, British Embassy, Washington, to I. F. Porter, Foreign Office, 2 April 1956, DO 35/5779, UK National Archives, Kew, England.
24. Brookhaven National Laboratory, *Annual Report, July 1, 1956* (Upton, NY: Associated Universities, 1957), xv–xvi.
25. G. J. Madison, note 23 April 1956, DO 35/5779, UK National Archives, Kew, England.
26. J. Thomson (Commonwealth Relations Office) to S. T. Charles, 29 February 1956, DO 35/5779, UK National Archives, Kew, England.
27. G. J. Madison, note, 23 April 1956, DO 35/5779, UK National Archives, Kew, England.
28. Chancery (British Embassy, Rangoon) to South-East Asia Department, Foreign Office, 12 May 1956, DO 35/5779, UK National Archives, Kew, England.
29. G. J. Madison, note, 23 April 1956, DO 35/5779, UK National Archives, Kew, England.

30. O. L. Williams (UK High Commission, Karachi) to James Thomson (Commonwealth Relations Office), 17 March 1956, DO 35/5779, UK National Archives, Kew, England.
31. These views are based on reflections from British diplomats in Washington. J. C. A. Roper, British Embassy, Washington, to I. F. Porter, Foreign Office, 16 October 1956, DO 35/5780, UK National Archives, Kew, England.
32. Chancery (British Embassy, Rangoon) to South-East Asia Department, Foreign Office, 12 May 1956, DO 35/5779, UK National Archives, Kew, England.
33. J. C. A. Roper (British Embassy, Washington) to I. F. Porter (Foreign Office), 11 October 1956, DO 35/5779, UK National Archives, Kew, England.
34. See, for example, R. A. Thompson to A. E. Parsons, 4 July 1956 (and indeed see the whole folder for variants of these views), DO 35/5779, UK National Archives, Kew, England.
35. Chancery, British Embassy, Rangoon, to Southeast Asia Dept, Foreign Office, 21 September 1956, DO 35/5780, UK National Archives, Kew, England.
36. Memorandum from the Secretary of State to the President, 19 August 1955. *Foreign Relations of the United States, 1955–1957,* vol. 20, *Regulation of Armaments; Atomic Energy,* ed. David S. Patterson (Washington, DC: US Government Printing Office, 1990), document 57.
37. See Phalkey, *Atomic State*.
38. J. C. A. Roper (British Embassy, Washington) to D. V. Bendall (Foreign Office), 1 August 1956, DO 35/5779, UK National Archives, Kew, England.
39. These reflections on the Bombay meeting are in K. A. East (Office of the High Commissioner for the United Kingdom, Colombo, Ceylon) to T. W. Aston (Commonwealth Relations Office), 11 September 1956, DO 35/5779, UK National Archives, Kew, England.
40. On the role of the IAEA Board of Governors, see David Fischer, *History of the International Atomic Energy Agency: The First Forty Years* (Vienna: IAEA, 1997), 38.
41. Memorandum for the Files, by William O. Hall of the United States Mission to the United Nations, 13 May 1955, *Foreign Relations of the United States, 1955–1957,* vol. 20, *Regulation of Armaments; Atomic Energy,* ed. David S. Patterson (Washington, DC: US Government Printing Office, 1990), document 29.
42. Memorandum for the Files, by William O. Hall of the United States Mission to the United Nations, 13 May 1955, *Foreign Relations of the United States, 1955–1957,* vol. 20, *Regulation of Armaments; Atomic Energy,* ed. David S. Patterson (Washington, DC: US Government Printing Office, 1990), document 29, https://history.state.gov/historicaldocuments/frus1955-57v20/d29.
43. Fischer, *History of the International Atomic Energy Agency,* 38–39.
44. Holmes Alexander, "Atoms-for-India," *Independent Record* [Helena, Montana], 18 October 1957, 4.
45. Gérard De Boe, "Lovanium" (Productions GDB, 1959), available at https://www.youtube.com/watch?v=nz0sw11yYps [accessed 26 June 2020].
46. "South African Atomic Energy Program," 1963, Paul Aebersold Papers, folder "General Correspondence-May-December-1963," Texas A&M Archives and Special Collections, https://www.osti.gov/opennet/servlets/purl/905939.pdf [accessed 26 June 2020].
47. Clyde Farnsworth, "Africa Gets New Atomic Witchcraft," *Chicago Tribune,* 10 March 1963, 1.

48. An overview of Ghanaian nuclear experiences is in M. V. Ramana and Priscilla Agyapong, "Thinking Big? Ghana, Small Reactors, and Nuclear Power," *Energy Research and Social Science* 21 (2016), 101–113. For a discussion of nuclear power in Africa, with Ghana's role at the center, see Abena Dove Osseo-Asare, *Atomic Junction: Nuclear Power in Africa after Independence* (New York: Cambridge University Press, 2019).
49. Paul Hoffman, "Bunche Says '60 Is Year of Africa," *New York Times*, 17 February 1960, 15.
50. "Dr. Verwoerd Makes a Statement as South Africa Becomes a Republic," British Pathé Archive, Film ID 2932.17, https://www.britishpathe.com/video/dr-verwoerd-makes-a-statement-as-south-africa-beco [accessed 26 June 2020].
51. Leonard Ingalls, "Verwoerd Dooms Apartheid Shift," *New York Times*, January 29, 1961, 29.
52. "African A-Bomb Ability Seen," *New York Times*, 18 December 1961, 3.
53. "African Summit Urged," *New York Times*, 17 June 1960, 2.
54. "Nouvelles Protestations contre l'Explosion de Reggane," *Le Monde*, 30 December 1960, https://www.lemonde.fr/archives/article/1960/12/30/nouvelles-protestations-contre-l-explosion-de-reggane_2104033_1819218.html [accessed 26 June 2020]; Samuel Obeng, ed., *Selected Speeches of Kwame Nkrumah*, vol. 1 (Accra, Ghana: Afram Publications, 1979), 25.
55. Frantz Fanon, *The Wretched of the Earth*, trans. Richard Philcox (New York: Grove Press, 2004), 100, 228.
56. Obeng, *Selected Speeches of Kwame Nkrumah*, vol. 1, 48, 114.
57. Obeng, *Selected Speeches of Kwame Nkrumah*, vol. 1, 131.
58. Special National Intelligence Estimate, 10 January 1961, *Foreign Relations of the United States, 1961–1963*, vol. 20, *Congo Crisis*, ed. Harriet Dashiell Schwar (Washington, DC: US Government Printing Office, 1994), document 2.
59. For an analysis of the Eisenhower administration's changing attitudes toward Nkrumah during the Congo crisis, see Ebere Nwaubani, "Eisenhower, Nkrumah and the Congo Crisis," *Journal of Contemporary History* 36:4 (2001), 599–622.
60. Editorial note, *Foreign Relations of the United States, 1961–1963*, vol. 20, *Congo Crisis*, ed. Harriet Dashiell Schwar (Washington, DC: US Government Printing Office, 1994), document 4.
61. On the many interpretations of the Lumumba assassination, see Emmanuel Gerard and Bruce Kuklick, *Death in the Congo: Murdering Patrice Lumumba* (Cambridge, MA: Harvard University Press, 2015). See also Editorial note, *Foreign Relations of the United States, 1961–1963*, vol. 20, *Congo Crisis*, ed. Harriet Dashiell Schwar (Washington. DC: US Government Printing Office, 1994), document 6.
62. Memorandum from Secretary of Defense McNamara to the President's Special Assistant for National Security Affairs (Bundy), 21 February 1961, *Foreign Relations of the United States, 1961–1963*, vol. 9, *Foreign Economic Policy*, ed. Evans Gerakas, David S. Patterson, William F. Sanford Jr., and Carolyn B. Yee (Washington, DC: US Government Printing Office, 1995), document 338.
63. Memorandum by the Deputy Representative-Designate to the United Nations Security Council (Yost), 17 February 1961, *Foreign Relations of the United States, 1961–1963*, vol. 20, *Congo Crisis*, ed. Harriet Dashiell Schwar (Washington, DC: US Government Printing Office, 1994), document 32.

64. Memorandum of Conversation, 28 April 1962, *Foreign Relations of the United States, 1961–1963*, vol. 20, *Congo Crisis*, ed. Harriet Dashiell Schwar (Washington, DC: US Government Printing Office, 1994), document 224.
65. IAEA Board of Governors, Official Record of the One Hundred and Fifty-Ninth Meeting, 2 July 1959, GOV/OR.159, 12 September 1959, p. 3, SAC 1958-1960 Meetings nos. 1–5, IAEA Archives, Vienna, Austria.
66. Gabrielle Hecht, *Being Nuclear: Africans and the Global Uranium Trade* (Cambridge, MA: MIT Press, 2012), 28.
67. Nathaniel T. Coleman (IAEA) to Dr. P. G. Marais, 21 December 1960, SC/822 PT I, IAEA Archives, Vienna, Austria.
68. On Fried's work, see Maurice Fried and Hans Broeshart, *The Soil-Plant System in Relation to Inorganic Nutrition* (New York: Academic Press, 1967).
69. Pieter Marais to Mr. N. T. Coleman, 13 January 1961, SC/822 PT I, IAEA Archives, Vienna, Austria.
70. Alternate Governor, South African Legation (to the IAEA) to Dr. M. Fried (IAEA), 19 July 1961, SC/822 PT I, IAEA Archives, Vienna, Austria.
71. "South African Atomic Energy Program," 1963, Paul Aebersold Papers, folder "General Correspondence-May-December-1963," Texas A&M Archives and Special Collections, https://www.osti.gov/opennet/servlets/purl/905939.pdf [accessed 26 June 2020].
72. A. H. Ward (Radio-isotope Unit, University College, Legon, Ghana) to Dr. Fried and Dr. Broeshart (IAEA), 28 December 1961, S/289-6 PT II, IAEA Archives, Vienna, Austria.
73. M. E. Jefferson (US Department of Agriculture) to Dr. Maurice Fried (IAEA), SC/731 PT I, IAEA Archives, Vienna, Austria.
74. R. Scott Russell (UK Agricultural Research Council) to Dr. M. Fried, 4 December 1964, SC/822 (5) PT I, IAEA Archives, Vienna, Austria.
75. See United Nations Resolution 1881 (1963), https://digitallibrary.un.org/record/540387 [accessed 26 June 2020].
76. See United Nations Security Council Resolution 182 (1963), https://digitallibrary.un.org/record/112182 [accessed 26 June 2020].
77. Memorandum from William H. Brubeck of the National Security Council Staff to the President's Special Assistant for National Security Affairs (Bundy), 17 August 1964, *Foreign Relations of the United States 1964–1968*, vol. 24, *Africa*, ed. Nina Davis Howland (Washington, DC: US Government Printing Office, 1999), document 594.
78. See M. S. van Wyk, "Ally or Critic? The United States' Response to South African Nuclear Development, 1949–1980," *Cold War History* 7:2 (2007), 195–225.
79. Joseph Lelyveld, "Reactor Started in South Africa: Verwoerd Says Black States Can Share Atomic Gains," *New York Times*, August 6, 1965, 7.
80. Joseph Lelyveld, "Reactor Started in South Africa." On South Africa's diplomatic strategy of making itself indispensable to Western nations in the 1960s, see Jamie Miller, *An African Volk: The Apartheid Regime and Its Search for Survival* (New York: Oxford University Press, 2016).
81. "Alan Nunn May," *Times*, 24 January 2003, https://www.thetimes.co.uk/article/alan-nunn-may-sl9rx6xf709 [accessed 26 June 2020].
82. Robert C. Ruark, "Dr. May a Symbol of Times," *Lawrence Journal-World*, 24 January 1962, 3.
83. On the visits of Rustin and others to Africa in the late 1950s and early 1960s, see Vincent J. Intondi, *African Americans against the Bomb: Nuclear Weapons,*

Colonialism, and the Black Freedom Movement (Stanford, CA: Stanford University Press, 2015), chapter 3.
84. W. E. B. Du Bois, *The Souls of Black Folk* (New York: Cosimo, 2007), 9.
85. On Du Bois in Ghana, see Correspondence between FBI Director and SAC New York, 20 July 1960, Federal Bureau of Investigation, William E. B. Du Bois, File # 100-99729, part 5 of 5, p. 57, available at https://vault.fbi.gov. On Robeson, see Federal Bureau of Investigation, Paul Robeson Sr., File # 100-12304, Section 17 [part 22 of 31], p. 12.
86. Federal Bureau of Investigation, "Malcolm X Little," File #: 100-399321, file 24 of 27, available at https://vault.fbi.gov, p. 114. On the US government's reactions to the analogy of civil rights to colonialism, see Borstelmann, *The Cold War and the Color Line*, 205–207.
87. Obeng, *Selected Speeches of Kwame Nkrumah*, vol. 1, 33, 29.
88. Obeng, *Selected Speeches of Kwame Nkrumah*, vol. 1, 152–154.
89. Obeng, *Selected Speeches of Kwame Nkrumah*, vol. 1, 155.
90. *Yearbook of the United Nations* (New York: UN Office of Public Information, 1964), 569.
91. For an analysis of how the IAEA projects in Ghana fit into conceptions of the cocoa sector in Ghana, see Lukas Bretwieser and Karin Zachmann, "Biofakte des Atomszeitalters: Strahlende Entwicklungen in Ghanas Landwirtschaft," *Technikgeschichte* 84:2 (2017), 107–133.
92. IAEA, Request from the Government of Ghana, Job Description IAEA-GHANA-2, 22 January 1962, TA/GHA-3, IAEA Archives, Vienna, Austria.
93. Osseo-Asare, *Atomic Junction*, 60–68.
94. J. C. Webb (Acting Director, Division of Economic and Technical Assistance, IAEA) to His Excellency Ako Adjei, Minister for Foreign Affairs (Ghana), 4 July 1962, TA/GHA-3, IAEA Archives, Vienna, Austria.
95. Undated and unsigned handwritten message in TA/GHA-3, IAEA Archives, Vienna, Austria.
96. Dr. V. A. Golikov, "About Some Measures on the Development of Agricultural Investigations with the Application of Radioisotopes," n.d. TA/GHA-3, IAEA Archives, Vienna, Austria.
97. Harold Miller to F. A. Medine (IAEA), 1 June 1965, TA/GHA-5, IAEA Archives, Vienna, Austria.
98. Memorandum of Conversation, 12 February 1964, *Foreign Relations of the United States, 1964–1968*, vol. 24, *Africa*, ed. Nina Davis Howland (Washington, DC: US Government Printing Office, 1999), document 238.
99. Letter from President Nkrumah to President Johnson, 26 February 1964, *Foreign Relations of the United States, 1964–1968*, vol. 24, *Africa*, ed. Nina Davis Howland (Washington, DC: US Government Printing Office, 1999), document 243.
100. Memorandum from Robert W. Komer of the National Security Council Staff to the President's Special Assistant for National Security Affairs (Bundy), 27 May 1965, *Foreign Relations of the United States, 1964–1968*, vol. 24, *Africa*, ed. Nina Davis Howland (Washington, DC: US Government Printing Office, 1999), document 253.
101. A CIA internal summary of Nkrumah's 1965 book can be found in Walter Pforzheimer to Deputy Director of Central Intelligence, 8 November 1965, https://www.cia.gov/library/readingroom/docs/CIA-RDP75-00149R000600010011-6.pdf [accessed 26 June 2020].

102. Circular Telegram from the Department of State to Embassies in Africa, 23 November 1965, *Foreign Relations of the United States, 1964–1968* vol. 24, *Africa*, ed. Nina Davis Howland (Washington, DC: US Government Printing Office, 1999), document 256.
103. Telegram from the Embassy in Ghana to the Department of State, 3 March 1966, *Foreign Relations of the United States, 1964–1968*, vol. 24, *Africa*, ed. Nina Davis Howland (Washington, DC: US Government Printing Office, 1999), document 259.
104. Memorandum from the President's Acting Special Assistant for National Security Affairs (Komer) to President Johnson, 12 March 1966, *Foreign Relations of the United States, 1964–1968*, vol. 24, *Africa*, ed. Nina Davis Howland (Washington, DC: US Government Printing Office, 1999), document 260.
105. Memorandum from the President's Special Assistant (Rostow) to President Johnson, 9 October 1967, *Foreign Relations of the United States, 1964–1968*, vol. 24, *Africa*, ed. Nina Davis Howland (Washington, DC: US Government Printing Office, 1999), document 271.
106. Osseo-Asare, *Atomic Junction*, 99.
107. Jo-Ansie van Wyk, "Atoms, Apartheid, and the Agency: South Africa's Relations with the IAEA, 1957–1995," *Cold War History* 15:3 (2015), 395–416.
108. As quoted in Matthew Jones, *After Hiroshima: The United States, Race, and Nuclear Weapons in Asia, 1945–1965* (New York: Cambridge University Press, 2010), 461.
109. See David Levering Lewis, *W. E. B. Du Bois: A Biography* (New York: Henry Holt, 2009).
110. "China as a Nuclear Power," document I-29442/64, 7 October 1964. See "The United States, China, and the Bomb," National Security Archive Electronic Briefing Book No. 1, ed. William Burr, http://nsarchive.gwu.edu/NSAEBB/NSAEBB1.
111. "Le Ghana 'Regrette' que la Chine ait fait Exploser une Bombe Atomique," *Le Monde*, 27 October 1964, https://www.lemonde.fr/archives/article/1964/10/27/le-ghana-regrette-que-la-chine-ait-fait-exploser-une-bombe-atomique_2132934_1819218.html [accessed 26 June 2020].
112. Federal Bureau of Investigation, "Malcolm X Little," File #: 105-8999, file 39 of 41, available at https://vault.fbi.gov, 107.
113. Federal Bureau of Investigation, "Malcolm X Little," File #: 105-8999, file 39 of 41, available at https://vault.fbi.gov, 107.

CHAPTER 5

1. "Atomic Needler, William Sterling Cole," *New York Times*, 8 October 1957, 10.
2. "Atomic Needler."
3. On British and Soviet perspectives, see Stephen Twigge, "The Atomic Marshall Plan: Atoms for Peace, British Diplomacy and Civil Nuclear Power," *Cold War History* 16:2 (2016), 213–230; David Holloway, "The Soviet Union and the Creation of the International Atomic Energy Agency," *Cold War History* 16:2 (2016), 177–193.
4. David Fischer, *History of the International Atomic Energy Agency: The First Forty Years* (Vienna: IAEA, 1997), 76.
5. Fischer, *History of the International Atomic Energy Agency*, 77.
6. Paul R. Josephson, *Red Atom: Russia's Nuclear Power Program from Stalin to Today* (Pittsburgh, PA: University of Pittsburgh Press, 2005), 148–150.

7. P. Dorolle to A. J. Cipriani, 4 March 1955, A14/373/2 J.1, WHO Archives, Geneva, Switzerland.
8. P. Dorolle to A. J. Cipriani, 4 March 1955.
9. A. J. Cipriani to P. Dorolle, 24 March 1955, A14/373/2 J.1, WHO Archives, Geneva, Switzerland.
10. Extract from letter of 28 May 1955 from Professor Tubiana, A14/373/2 J.1, WHO Archives, Geneva, Switzerland.
11. Extract from letter of 28 May 1955 from Professor Tubiana, A14/373/2 J.1, WHO Archives, Geneva, Switzerland.
12. "Activities of the World Health Organization in Connection with the Peaceful Uses of Atomic Energy," 21 January 1958, O/320-2 PT I, IAEA Archives, Vienna, Austria.
13. I. S. Eve (WHO) to Dr. A. H. Tait (Director, Health and Safety Division, IAEA), 27 March 1958, O/320-2 PT I, IAEA Archives, Vienna, Austria.
14. M. G. Candau to Sterling Cole, 9 May 1958, O/320-2 PT I, IAEA Archives, Vienna, Austria.
15. Sterling Cole (IAEA) to Dr. M. G. Candau (WHO), 15 May 1958, O/320-2 PT I, IAEA Archives, Vienna, Austria.
16. V. Migulin (Acting Director-General, IAEA) to Dr. M. G. Candau, 15 July 1958, O/320-2 PT IV, IAEA Archives, Vienna, Austria.
17. Bo Lindell and R. Lowry Dobson, *Ionizing Radiation and Health* (Geneva: World Health Organization, 1961), 65.
18. IAEA Press Release PR 59/70, "Watching Radioactivity of Man's Surroundings: IAEA Panel to Recommend Best Methods," 4 September 1959, A14/372/4(a) J.1, WHO Archives, Geneva, Switzerland.
19. Lowry Dobson, memorandum to Deputy Director-General, "IAEA Meeting on Radioactivity Measurements," 6 November 1959, A14/372/4(a) J.1, WHO Archives, Geneva, Switzerland.
20. Lowry Dobson (WHO) to H. T. Daw (IAEA), 28 July 1961, A14/372/4(a) J.1, WHO Archives, Geneva, Switzerland.
21. "IAEA Notes," *Bulletin of the Atomic Scientists* 17:9 (1961), 399.
22. Fischer, *History of the International Atomic Energy Agency*, 74.
23. "Meeting with Dr. Candau, Geneva, February 1963, Draft Briefing for the Director General," n.d., O/320-2 PT IV, IAEA Archives, Vienna, Austria.
24. "Meeting with Dr. Candau, Geneva, February 1963, Draft Briefing for the Director General," n.d., O/320-2 PT IV, IAEA Archives, Vienna, Austria.
25. Gisela Mateos and Edna Suárez-Díaz, *Radioisótopos Itinerantes en América Latina* (México, D. F.: Universidad Nacional Autónoma de México, 2015).
26. On Seibersdorf's origins and early work, see Otto Suschny, "The Agency's Laboratories at Seibersdorf and Vienna," in *International Atomic Energy Agency: Personal Reflections* (Vienna: IAEA, 1997), 211–219.
27. M. Fried, "Application of Radioisotopes and Radiation Sources in Agriculture, Food Production and the Food Industry with Special Reference to IAEA's Work," 19 April 1963, box 10ADG351, folder Dr. Fischnich/Dr. Silow 1963/1967, FAO Archives, Rome, Italy.
28. A. W. Lindquist (USDA) to Johan Halverstadt (IAEA), 14 May 1959, SC/822 PT I, IAEA Archives, Vienna, Austria.
29. Helen Anne Curry, *Evolution Made to Order: Plant Breeding and Technological Innovation in Twentieth-Century America* (Chicago: University of Chicago Press, 2016), 165.

30. Perry R. Stout (University of California) to Harold H. Smith (IAEA), 31 December 1958, SC/822 PT I, IAEA Archives, Vienna, Austria.
31. R. Scott Russell (Agricultural Research Council, Radiobiological Laboratory, Wantage) to K. C. Tsien (Department of Research and Isotopes, IAEA), 12 January 1960, SC/735-1, IAEA Archives, Vienna, Austria.
32. G. D. H. Bell (Cambridge University) to K. C. Tsien (Department of Research and Isotopes, IAEA), 12 January 1960, SC/735-1, IAEA Archives, Vienna, Austria.
33. Harold H. Smith (Brookhaven National Laboratory, USA) to K. C. Tsien (Department of Research and Isotopes, IAEA), 27 January 1960, SC/735-1, IAEA Archives, Vienna, Austria.
34. Kiyoshi Kawara, "Introduction of a Gamma Field in Japan," *Radiation Botany* 3 (1963), 175–177.
35. The "cost-free" concept is in Björn Sigurbjörnsson to Arne Hagberg, (EUCARPIA, Sweden), 20 October 1974, SC/822 (5) PT I, IAEA Archives, Vienna, Austria.
36. Björn Sigurbjörnsson to R. S. Caldecott (University of Minnesota), 3 December 1964, SC/822 (5) PT I, IAEA Archives, Vienna, Austria.
37. T. Kawai to Björn Sigurbjörnsson, 16 March 1966, SC/822 (5) PT II, IAEA Archives, Vienna, Austria.
38. Interview with Peter Jennings, conducted by Gene Hettel, 20 July 2007, http://archive.irri.org/publications/today/Jennings.asp [accessed 3 November 2010].
39. Björn Sigurbjörnsson, "Quickening the Pulse of Nature," *IAEA Bulletin* 13:4 (1971), 20–27.
40. Björn Sigurbjörnsson to Henry Seligman, 2 May 1967, SC/822 (5) PT IV, IAEA Archives, Vienna, Austria.
41. R. A. Silow to B. Sigurbjörnsson, 18 July 1967, O/251 PT II, IAEA Archives, Vienna, Austria.
42. B. Sigurbjörnsson, "Conception, Birth and Growth of the Joint FAO/IAEA Division," in *International Atomic Energy Agency: Personal Reflections* (Vienna: IAEA, 1997), 195–209, quote on p. 199.
43. R. A. Silow, "Appraisal of the Programme of Work of Atomic Energy in Agriculture," interoffice memorandum, 20 January 1966, folder "Dr. Fischnich/Dr. Silow 1963/1967," box 10ADG351, FAO Archives, Rome, Italy.
44. R. A. Silow, "Appraisal of the Programme of Work of Atomic Energy in Agriculture," interoffice memorandum, 20 January 1966.
45. Sigvard Eklund to Orvis V. Wells, 5 February 1966, folder "Dr. Fischnich/Dr. Silow 1963/1967," box 10ADG351, FAO Archives, Rome, Italy.
46. R. A. Silow to B. R. Sen, 15 August 1966, folder "Dr. Fischnich/Dr. Silow 1963/1967," box 10ADG351, FAO Archives, Rome, Italy.
47. R. A. Silow to Sigvard Eklund and B. R. Sen, 14 March 1967, folder "Dr. Fischnich/Dr. Silow 1963/1967," box 10ADG351, FAO Archives, Rome, Italy.
48. R. A. Silow to Sigvard Eklund and B. R. Sen, 14 March 1967.
49. On this controversy, see James Spiller, "Radiant Cuisine: The Commercial Fate of Food Irradiation in the United States," *Technology and Culture* 45:4 (2004), 740–763.
50. R. A. Silow to Sigvard Eklund and B. R. Sen, 14 March 1967.
51. R. A. Silow to Sigvard Eklund and B. R. Sen, 14 March 1967.
52. Fischer, *History of the International Atomic Energy Agency* 132.
53. R. A. Silow to S. Eklund, B. R. Sen, and O. E. Fischnich, 14 April 1967, "The Joint FAO/IAEA Programme in Food Irradiation," folder "Dr. Fischnich/Dr. Silow 1963/1967," box 10ADG351, FAO Archives, Rome, Italy.

54. "Comments on 'The Joint FAO/IAEA Programme in Food Irradiation,' by R. A. Silow," unnamed author, August 1967, folder "Dr. Fischnich/Dr. Silow 1963/1967," box 10ADG351, FAO Archives, Rome, Italy.
55. R. A. Silow to S. Eklund, B. R. Sen, and O. E. Fischnich, 14 April 1967, "The Joint FAO/IAEA Programme in Food Irradiation."
56. "Comments on 'The Joint FAO/IAEA Programme in Food Irradiation,' by R. A. Silow," unnamed author, August 1967.
57. Spiller, "Radiant Cuisine."
58. "Comments on 'The Joint FAO/IAEA Programme in Food Irradiation,' by R. A. Silow," unnamed author, August 1967.
59. S. Eklund to B. R. Sen, 15 September 1967, folder "Dr. Fischnich/Dr. Silow 1963/1967," box 10ADG351, FAO Archives, Rome, Italy.
60. See Amy L. S. Staples, *The Birth of Development: How the World Bank, Food and Agriculture Organization, and World Health Organization Changed the World, 1945–1965* (Kent, OH: Kent State University Press, 2006), 121.
61. "Comments on the memorandum of 11 September 1967 by Dr. Silow," n.d., unnamed author, folder "Dr. Fischnich/Dr. Silow 1963/1967," box 10ADG351, FAO Archives, Rome, Italy.
62. "The Green Revolution," *New York Times*, 21 May 1968, 46.
63. William C. Paddock, "How Green Is the Green Revolution?" *BioScience* 20:16 (1970), 897–902.
64. See C. Subramaniam to Binay Ranjan Sen, 18 October 1966, folder "Dr. Fischnich/Dr. Silow 1968/1973," box 10ADG351, FAO Archives, Rome, Italy.
65. The importance of Mexican wheat to Indian national security is emphasized in John H. Perkins, *Geopolitics and the Green Revolution: Wheat, Genes, and the Cold War* (New York: Oxford University Press, 1997), 242.
66. Joseph Hanlon, "Top Food Scientist Published False Data," *New Scientist* (7 November 1974), 436–437.
67. R. O. Whyte to Robert A. Luse (Plant Breeding and Genetics Section, Joint FAO/IAEA Division), 3 October 1968, SC/822 (5) PT V, IAEA Archives, Vienna, Austria.
68. Robert A. Luse to R. O. Whyte (Hongkong and Shanghai Banking Corporation, Ltd.), 24 October 1968, SC/822 (5) PT V, IAEA Archives, Vienna, Austria.
69. Robert A. Luse, "Plant Protein Improvement: A Partial Solution to the Problem of Protein Malnutrition," *Kalamazoo College Review* 35:3 (1973), 3–6.
70. Robert Rabson (Assistant Chief, Biology Branch, Division of Biology and Medicine, AEC) to Maurice Fried (Director, FAO/IAEA Joint Division), 25 April 1969, SC/822 (4), IAEA Archives, Vienna, Austria.
71. Björn Sigurbjörnsson to O. E. Fischnich, 2 April 1969, folder "Dr. Fischnich/Dr. Silow 1968/1973," box 10ADG351, FAO Archives, Rome, Italy.
72. James F. Crow and Jerry Kermicle, "Oliver Nelson and Quality Protein Maize," *Genetics* 160:3 (2002), 819–821.
73. The details of Swaminathan's protein data, and Shah's suicide, are reported in Hanlon, "Top Food Scientist Published False Data."
74. R. A. Silow to O. E. Fischnich, 21 March 1969, folder "Dr. Fischnich/Dr. Silow 1968/1973," box 10ADG351, FAO Archives, Rome, Italy.
75. R. A. Silow to T. E. Ritchie, 30 April 1969, folder "Dr. Fischnich/Dr. Silow 1968/1973," box 10ADG351, FAO Archives, Rome, Italy.
76. R. A. Silow to O. E. Fischnich, 19 September 1969, folder "Dr. Fischnich/Dr. Silow 1968/1973," box 10ADG351, FAO Archives, Rome, Italy.

77. Maurice Fried to O. E. Fischnich, n.d., folder "Dr. Fischnich/Dr. Silow 1968/1973," box 10ADG351, FAO Archives, Rome, Italy.
78. Maurice Fried to O. E. Fischnich, 25 September 1969, folder "Dr. Fischnich/Dr. Silow 1968/1973, box 10ADG351, FAO Archives, Rome, Italy.
79. The handwritten comment to Otto Fischnich, signed but not decipherable, is next to a typed letter from O. E. Fischnich to A. H. Boerma, 19 November 1969, folder "Dr. Fischnich/Dr. Silow 1968/1973," box 10ADG351, FAO Archives, Rome, Italy.
80. Arne Lachen to A. H. Boerma, 5 January 1970, folder "Jt FAO/IAEA Division," box 10ADG351, FAO Archives, Rome, Italy.
81. Aresvik, draft book manuscript, attached to Arne Lachen to A. H. Boerma, 5 January 1970, folder "Jt FAO/IAEA Division," box 10ADG351, FAO Archives, Rome, Italy.
82. Maurice Fried to O. E. Fischnich, 16 January 1970, folder "Jt FAO/IAEA Division," box 10ADG351, FAO Archives, Rome, Italy.
83. R. A. Silow to O. E. Fischnich, 29 January 1970, folder "Dr. Fischnich/Dr. Silow 1968/1973," box 10ADG351, FAO Archives, Rome, Italy.
84. Oddvar Aresvik, *The Agricultural Development of Turkey* (New York: Praeger, 1975).
85. International Labor Organization, Administrative Tribunal, Thirteenth Ordinary Session, In re Silow (No. 5), Judgment No. 205, 14 May 1973, https://www.ilo.org/dyn/triblex/triblexmain.detail?p_judgment_no=205 [accessed 26 June 2020].
86. Unauthored, n.d., folder "Dr. Fischnich/Dr. Silow 1968/1973," box 10ADG351, FAO Archives, Rome, Italy.
87. Hanlon, "Top Food Scientist Published False Data."
88. Robert D. Havener, "Scientists: Their Rewards and Humanity," *Science* 237:4820 (1987), 1281. "A Guru of the Green Revolution Reflects on Borlaug's Legacy," *Science* 326:5951 (2009), 361.
89. Björn Sigurbjörnsson, "Conception, Birth and Growth of the Joint FAO/IAEA Division," in *International Atomic Energy Agency: Personal Reflections* (Vienna: IAEA, 1997), 195–209, quote on pp. 198–199.
90. Norman Borlaug, "The Green Revolution, Peace, and Humanity," Nobel Lecture, 11 December 1970, http://nobelprize.org/nobel_prizes/peace/laureates/1970/borlaug-lecture.html [accessed 26 June 2020].
91. Maurice Fried (Director, FAO/IAEA Joint Division) to E. J. Wellhausen (Director-General, International Maize and Wheat Improvement Center), 23 December 1968, SC/822 (4), IAEA Archives, Vienna, Austria.
92. "Radiation and the Green Revolution," *IAEA Bulletin* 11:5 (1969), 16–27.
93. Björn Sigurbjörnsson, "Quickening the Pulse of Nature," *IAEA Bulletin* 13:4 (1971), 20–27.

CHAPTER 6

1. On the Chinese bomb, see John Wilson Lewis and Xue Litai, *China Builds the Bomb* (Stanford, CA: Stanford University Press, 1991).
2. Memorandum from the Assistant Director for Scientific Intelligence of the Central Intelligence Agency (Chamberlain) to the Deputy Director of Central Intelligence (Carter), 15 October 1964, *Foreign Relations of the United States, 1964–1968*, vol. 30, *China*, ed. Harriet Dashiell Schwar (Washington, DC: US Government Printing Office, 1998), document 56.

3. Report of Meetings, Tapei, 23–24 October 1964, *Foreign Relations of the United States, 1964–1968*, vol. 30, *China*, ed. Harriet Dashiell Schwar (Washington, DC: US Government Printing Office, 1998), document 62.
4. McGeorge Bundy, Memorandum for the Record, 19 October 1964, *Foreign Relations of the United States, 1964–1968*, vol. 30, *China*, ed. Harriet Dashiell Schwar (Washington, DC: US Government Printing Office, 1998), document 60.
5. Memorandum from the Joint Chiefs of Staff to Secretary of Defense McNamara, 16 January 1965, *Foreign Relations of the United States, 1964–1968*, vol. 30, *China*, ed. Harriet Dashiell Schwar (Washington, DC: US Government Printing Office, 1998), document 76.
6. Memorandum of Conversation, 23 November 1964, *Foreign Relations of the United States, 1964–1968*, vol. 11, *Arms Control and Disarmament*, ed. Evans Gerakas, David S. Patterson, and Carolyn B. Yee (Washington, DC: US Government Printing Office, 1997), document 50.
7. Memorandum of Conversation, 9 December 1964, *Foreign Relations of the United States, 1964–1968*, vol. 11, *Arms Control and Disarmament*, ed. Evans Gerakas, David S. Patterson, and Carolyn B. Yee (Washington, DC: US Government Printing Office, 1997), document 54. For a discussion of these events after the Chinese atomic bomb test, see Francis J. Gavin, "Blasts from the Past: Proliferation Lessons from the 1960s," *International Security* 29:3 (2004/2005), 100–135.
8. Minutes of Discussion, Committee on Nuclear Proliferation, 7–8 January 1965, *Foreign Relations of the United States, 1964–1968*, vol. 11, *Arms Control and Disarmament*, ed. Evans Gerakas, David S. Patterson, and Carolyn B. Yee (Washington, DC: US Government Printing Office, 1997), document 60.
9. Report by the Committee on Nuclear Proliferation, 21 January 1965, *Foreign Relations of the United States, 1964–1968*, vol. 11, *Arms Control and Disarmament*, ed. Evans Gerakas, David S. Patterson, and Carolyn B. Yee (Washington, DC: US Government Printing Office, 1997), document 64.
10. Memorandum of Conversation (William C. Foster and Lord Chalfont, UK), 1 August 1965, *Foreign Relations of the United States, 1964–1968*, vol. 11, *Arms Control and Disarmament*, ed. Evans Gerakas, David S. Patterson, and Carolyn B. Yee (Washington, DC: US Government Printing Office, 1997), document 91.
11. IAEA Board of Governors, Official Record of the Three Hundred and Fifty-Sixth Meeting, 25 February 1965 (dated 13 May 1965), EG 8/2, UK National Archives, Kew, England.
12. American Embassy, Buenos Aires, to US Department of State, 3 February 1965 (and enclosures), NARA 59, 1964–1966 Inco-Uranium, http://digitalarchive.wilsoncenter.org/document/117168 [accessed 26 June 2020].
13. IAEA Board of Governors, Official Record of the Three Hundred and Fifty-Sixth Meeting, 25 February 1965 (dated 13 May 1965), EG 8/2, UK National Archives, Kew, England.
14. IAEA Board of Governors, Official Record of the Three Hundred and Fifty-Sixth Meeting, 25 February 1965 (dated 13 May 1965).
15. IAEA Board of Governors, Official Record of the Three Hundred and Fifty-Sixth Meeting, 25 February 1965 (dated 13 May 1965).
16. Bhumitra Chakma, "Toward Pokhran II: Explaining India's Nuclearisation Process," *Modern Asian Studies* (2005), 189–236.
17. Jayita Sarkar, "The Making of a Non-Aligned Nuclear Power: India's Proliferation Drift, 1964–8," *International History Review* 37:5 (2015), 933–950.

18. Jayita Sarkar, "Sino-Indian Nuclear Rivalry: Glacially Declassified," *The Diplomat*, 2 June 2017, https://thediplomat.com/2017/06/sino-indian-nuclear-rivalry-glacially-declassified/ [accessed 26 June 2020].
19. On Plowshare projects, see Scott Kirsch, *Proving Grounds: Project Plowshare and the Unrealized Dream of Nuclear Earthmoving* (New Brunswick, NJ: Rutgers University Press, 2005); and Scott Kaufman, *Project Plowshare: The Peaceful Use of Nuclear Explosives in Cold War America* (Ithaca, NY: Cornell University Press, 2013).
20. Christine Keiner, *Deep Cut: Science, Power, and the Unbuilt Interoceanic Canal* (Athens: University of Georgia Press, 2020).
21. Jayita Sarkar, "The Making of a Non-Aligned Nuclear Power."
22. Avner Cohen, *Israel and the Bomb* (New York: Columbia University Press, 1998). See also Binyamin Pinkus and Moshe Tlamim, "Atomic Power to Israel's Rescue: French-Israeli Nuclear Cooperation, 1949–1957," *Israel Studies* 7:1 (2002), 104–138; and Guy Ziv, "Shimon Peres and the French-Israeli Alliance, 1954–9," *Journal of Contemporary History* 45:2 (2010), 406–429.
23. On US attitudes toward Israel's nuclear program circa 1960, see Matteo Gerlini, "Waiting for Dimona: The United States and Israel's Development of Nuclear Capability," *Cold War History* 10:2 (2010), 143–161.
24. Circular Airgram from Department of State to Certain Posts, 31 October 1962, *Foreign Relations of the United States, 1961–63*, vol. 18, *Near East, 1962–1963*, ed. Nina J. Noring (Washington, DC: US Government Printing Office, 1995), document 87.
25. Avner Cohen and Marvin Miller, phone interview with Edwin E. Kinter (undated, 1993 or 1994), Nuclear Proliferation International History Project, record ID 116880, http://digitalarchive.wilsoncenter.org/document/116880 [accessed 26 June 2020].
26. Sherman Kent, Memorandum from the Board of National Estimates, Central Intelligence Agency, to Director of Central Intelligence McCone, 6 March 1963, *Foreign Relations of the United States, 1961–63*, vol. 18, *Near East, 1962–1963*, ed. Nina J. Noring (Washington, DC: US Government Printing Office, 1995), document 179.
27. Telegram from the Department of State to the Embassy in the United Arab Republic, 7 July 1963, *Foreign Relations of the United States, 1961–63*, vol. 18, *Near East, 1962–1963*, ed. Nina J. Noring (Washington, DC: US Government Printing Office, 1995), document 292.
28. Memorandum of Conversation [Golda Meier, Dean Rusk, and others], 30 September 1963, *Foreign Relations of the United States, 1961–63*, vol. 18, *Near East, 1962–1963*, ed. Nina J. Noring (Washington, DC: US Government Printing Office, 1995), document 331.
29. Dany Shoham, "The Evolution of Chemical and Biological Weapons in Egypt," Ariel Center for Policy Research Policy Paper 46 (1998), http://www.acpr.org.il/pp/pp046-shohame.pdf [accessed 26 June 2020].
30. Lyndon B. Johnson, "Remarks in New York City at the Dinner of the Weizmann Institute of Science," 6 February 1964, http://www.presidency.ucsb.edu/ws/index.php?pid=26060 [accessed 26 June 2020].
31. Lyndon B. Johnson, "Toasts of the President and Prime Minister Eshkol," 1 June 1964, http://www.presidency.ucsb.edu/ws/index.php?pid=26285 [accessed 26 June 2020].

32. Seth M. Siegel, *Let There Be Water: Israel's Solution for a Water-Starved World* (New York: Thomas Dunne, 2015).
33. Alexander Zucker, "Alvin M. Weinberg, 20 April 1915–18 October 2006," *Proceedings of the American Philosophical Society* 152:4 (2008), 571–576.
34. Stewart L. Udall, *The Quiet Crisis* (New York: Avon, 1963).
35. L. Boyd Finch, *Legacies of Camelot: Stewart and Lee Udall, American Culture, and the Arts* (Norman: University of Oklahoma Press, 2008), 135.
36. Jacob Darwin Hamblin, *Poison in the Well: Radioactive Waste in the Oceans at the Dawn of the Nuclear Age* (New Brunswick, NJ: Rutgers University Press, 2008).
37. On Project Plowshare, see Scott Kirsch, *Proving Grounds: Project Plowshare and the Unrealized Dream of Nuclear Earthmoving* (New Brunswick, NJ: Rutgers University Press, 2005); on Seaborg's continued hope to return to peaceful nuclear explosions, see Scott Kaufman, *Project Plowshare: The Peaceful Use of Nuclear Explosions* (Ithaca, NY: Cornell University Press, 2012).
38. Alvin M. Weinberg, *The First Nuclear Era: The Life and Times of a Technological Fixer* (New York: American Institute of Physics, 1994), 144.
39. Donald F. Hornig, Memorandum for the Record, 9 July 1964, *Foreign Relations of the United States, 1964–1968*, vol. 34, *Energy Diplomacy and Global Issues*, ed. Susan K. Holly (Washington, DC: US Government Printing Office, 1999), document 133.
40. The American attitude can be found in a telegram from the Consulate General at Jerusalem to the Department of State, 14 October 1955, *Foreign Relations of the United States, 1955–1957*, vol. 14, *Arab-Israeli Dispute, 1955*, ed. Carl N. Raether (Washington, DC: US Government Printing Office, 1989), document 336.
41. Memorandum from the Assistant Secretary of State for Near Eastern and South Asian Affairs (Talbot) to Secretary of State Rusk, 18 November 1963, *Foreign Relations of the United States, 1961–1963*, vol. 18, *Near East, 1962–1963*, ed. Nina J. Noring (Washington, DC: US Government Printing Office, 1995), document 364.
42. Itay Fischhendler, "When Ambiguity in Treaty Design Becomes Destructive: A Study in Transboundary Water," *Global Environmental Politics* 8:1 (2008), 111–136. See also Yoram Nimrod, *Angry Waters: Controversy over the Jordan River* (Givat Haviva, Israel: Center for Arabic and Afro Asian Studies, 1966). For an overview of the conflict over the Jordan River basin, see Miriam R. Lowi, *Water and Power: The Politics of a Scarce Resource in the Jordan River Basin* (New York: Cambridge University Press, 1993).
43. Zaki Shalom, *Israel's Nuclear Option: Behind the Scenes Diplomacy between Dimona and Washington* (Brighton, UK: Sussex Academic Press, 2005), 73.
44. A. Giambusso, "Trip Report—Catalytic Construction Company, Philadelphia, Pennsylvania—July 19–21, 1965 (U.S.-Israel Study)," n. d., US Atomic Energy Commission, Files of the Former Reactor Division, box 19, National Archives and Records Administration, Southeast Region, Atlanta, Georgia.
45. On Israel's plutonium separation program in the 1960s, see Cohen, *Israel and the Bomb*.
46. A. Giambusso, "Trip Report—Catalytic Construction Company, Philadelphia, Pennsylvania—July 19–21, 1965 (U.S.-Israel Study)," n. d., US Atomic Energy Commission, Files of the Former Reactor Division, box 19, National Archives and Records Administration, Southeast Region, Atlanta, Georgia.
47. A. Giambusso, "Trip Report—Catalytic Construction Company, Philadelphia, Pennsylvania—July 19–21, 1965 (U.S.-Israel Study),"

48. Memorandum of conversation, 2 November 1964, *Foreign Relations of the United States, 1964–1968*, vol. 34, *Energy Diplomacy and Global Issues*, ed. Susan K. Holly (Washington, DC: US Government Printing Office, 1999), document 134.
49. Memorandum from the President's Special Assistant (Johnson) to the President's Special Assistant for National Security Affairs (Bundy), 30 August 1965, *Foreign Relations of the United States, 1964–1968*, vol. 34, *Energy Diplomacy and Global Issues*, ed. Susan K. Holly (Washington, DC: US Government Printing Office, 1999), document 138.
50. Memorandum from the President's Special Assistant for Science and Technology (Hornig) to the President's Special Assistant (Valenti), 14 September 1965, *Foreign Relations of the United States, 1964–1968*, vol. 34, *Energy Diplomacy and Global Issues*, ed. Susan K. Holly (Washington, DC: US Government Printing Office, 1999), document 140.
51. Information Memorandum from the Director of the Office of International Scientific Affairs (Pollack) to Secretary of State Rusk, 20 October 1965, *Foreign Relations of the United States, 1964–1968*, vol. 34, *Energy Diplomacy and Global Issues*, ed. Susan K. Holly (Washington, DC: US Government Printing Office, 1999), document144.
52. Peveril Meigs, "Coastal Deserts: Prime Customers of Desalination," paper for First International Symposium on Water Desalination, October 3–9, 1965, Washington, DC, US Atomic Energy Commission, Files of the Former Reactor Division, box 20, National Archives and Records Administration, Southeast Region, Atlanta, Georgia.
53. See Sean F. Johnston, "Alvin Weinberg and the Promotion of the Technological Fix," *Technology and Culture* 59:3 (2018), 620–651.
54. Alvin M. Weinberg, "Can Technology Replace Social Engineering?" *Bulletin of the Atomic Scientists*, December 1966, 4–8.
55. Richard Philippone, Reactor Projects Branch, "Visit of Joseph Adar of Israel to ORNL," 21 December 1965, US Atomic Energy Commission, Files of the Former Reactor Division, box 19, National Archives and Records Administration, Southeast Region, Atlanta, Georgia.
56. Letter from Jerome Wiesner of the Massachusetts Institute of Technology to President Johnson, 28 February 1966, *Foreign Relations of the United States, 1964–1968*, vol. 34, *Energy Diplomacy and Global Issues*, ed. Susan K. Holly (Washington, DC: US Government Printing Office, 1999), document 146.
57. Letter from Jerome Wiesner of the Massachusetts Institute of Technology to President Johnson, 28 February 1966, *Foreign Relations of the United States, 1964–1968*, vol. 34, *Energy Diplomacy and Global Issues*, ed. Susan K. Holly (Washington, DC: US Government Printing Office, 1999), document 146.
58. Memorandum from the President's Special Assistant (Rostow) to President Johnson, 30 May 1966, *Foreign Relations of the United States, 1964–1968*, vol. 34, *Energy Diplomacy and Global Issues*, ed. Susan K. Holly (Washington, DC: US Government Printing Office, 1999), document 148.
59. Memorandum from the President's Special Assistant (Rostow) to President Johnson, 14 June 1966, *Foreign Relations of the United States, 1964–1968*, vol. 18, *Arab-Israeli Dispute, 1964–67*, ed. Harriet Dashiell Schwar (Washington, DC: US Government Printing Office, 2000), document 299.
60. For a conversation covering military aircraft as well as desalting, see Memorandum for the Record, 3 May 1966 [between Rostow and Ambassador Harman], *Foreign Relations of the United States, 1964–1968*, vol. 18, *Arab-Israeli*

Dispute, 1964–67, ed. Harriet Dashiell Schwar (Washington, DC: US Government Printing Office, 2000), document 288.

61. Memorandum from the Under Secretary of State (Katzenbach) to President Johnson, 1 May 1967, *Foreign Relations of the United States, 1964–1968*, vol. 18, *Arab-Israeli Dispute, 1964–67*, ed. Harriet Dashiell Schwar (Washington, DC: US Government Printing Office, 2000), document 415.
62. See editorial note, *Foreign Relations of the United States, 1964–1968*, vol. 34, *Energy Diplomacy and Global Issues*, ed. Susan K. Holly (Washington, DC: US Government Printing Office, 1999), document 151.
63. Memorandum from the President's Special Assistant (Rostow) to President Johnson, 12 August 1966, *Foreign Relations of the United States, 1964–1968*, vol. 34, *Energy Diplomacy and Global Issues*, ed. Susan K. Holly (Washington, DC: US Government Printing Office, 1999), document 152.
64. Memorandum from the President's Special Assistant (Rostow) to President Johnson, 19 September 1966, *Foreign Relations of the United States, 1964–1968*, vol. 34, *Energy Diplomacy and Global Issues*, ed. Susan K. Holly (Washington, DC: US Government Printing Office, 1999), document 155.
65. See editorial note, *Foreign Relations of the United States, 1964–1968*, vol. 34, *Energy Diplomacy and Global Issues*, ed. Susan K. Holly (Washington, DC: US Government Printing Office, 1999), document 161.
66. On Tzvi Tzur (or Zvi Tsur)'s appointments, see https://www.knesset.gov.il/mk/eng/mk_eng.asp?mk_individual_id_t=588 [accessed 26 June 2020].
67. The current text of the Treaty on the Non-Proliferation of Nuclear Weapons can be found here at https://www.un.org/disarmament/wmd/nuclear/npt/text [accessed 26 June 2020].
68. Memorandum from the Chairman of the Atomic Energy Commission (Seaborg) to Secretary of State Rusk, 13 June 1967, *Foreign Relations of the United States, 1964–1968*, vol. 34, *Energy Diplomacy and Global Issues*, ed. Susan K. Holly (Washington, DC: US Government Printing Office, 1999), document 163.
69. Memorandum from the President's Special Assistant (Rostow) to President Johnson, 19 July 1967, *Foreign Relations of the United States, 1964–1968*, vol. 34, *Energy Diplomacy and Global Issues*, ed. Susan K. Holly (Washington, DC: US Government Printing Office, 1999), document 164.
70. Memorandum from the President's Special Assistant for Science and Technology (Hornig) to President Johnson, 26 July 1967, *Foreign Relations of the United States, 1964–1968*, vol. 34, *Energy Diplomacy and Global Issues*, ed. Susan K. Holly (Washington, DC: US Government Printing Office, 1999), document 165.
71. "A Proposal for Our Time," memorandum from Admiral Lewis J. Strauss to Former President Eisenhower, undated, *Foreign Relations of the United States, 1964–1968*, vol. 34, *Energy Diplomacy and Global Issues*, ed. Susan K. Holly (Washington, DC: US Government Printing Office, 1999), document 166.
72. C. L. Sulzberger, "Foreign Affairs: Water and Work I," *New York Times*, 14 July 1967, 26; C. L. Sulzberger, "Foreign Affairs: Water and Work II," *New York Times*, 16 July 1967, 142; C. L. Sulzberger, "Foreign Affairs: Water and Work III," *New York Times*, 19 July 1967, 38.
73. "G.O.P. Pushes Plan on Mideast Water," *New York Times*, 20 October 1967, 24.
74. Editorial note, *Foreign Relations of the United States, 1964–1968*, vol. 34, *Energy Diplomacy and Global Issues*, ed. Susan K. Holly (Washington, DC: US Government Printing Office, 1999), document 168.

75. Aaron Wolfe, audio interview with Alvin Weinberg and Calvin Burwell, 1991, courtesy of Aaron Wolfe.
76. Memorandum from the President's Special Assistant (Rostow) to President Johnson, 9 March 1968, *Foreign Relations of the United States, 1964–1968*, vol. 34, *Energy Diplomacy and Global Issues*, ed. Susan K. Holly (Washington, DC: US Government Printing Office, 1999), document 170.
77. Letter from the Coordinator of the Israeli Power and Desalting Project (Woods) to the President's Special Assistant (Rostow), 28 August 1968, *Foreign Relations of the United States, 1964–1968*, vol. 34, *Energy Diplomacy and Global Issues*, ed. Susan K. Holly (Washington, DC: US Government Printing Office, 1999), document 172.
78. Memorandum from Harold Saunders of the National Security Council Staff to President Johnson, 18 December 1968, *Foreign Relations of the United States, 1964–1968*, vol. 34, *Energy Diplomacy and Global Issues*, ed. Susan K. Holly (Washington, DC: US Government Printing Office, 1999), document 174.
79. Minutes of a Review Group Meeting, 23 September 1969, *Foreign Relations of the United States, 1969–1976*, vol. 24, *Middle East Region and Arabian Peninsula, 1969–1972; Jordan, September 1970*, ed. Linda W. Qaimmaqami and Adam M. Howard (Washington, DC: US Government Printing Office, 2008), document 9.

CHAPTER 7
1. On Canada's nuclear aid to India and reactions to the explosion, see Duane Bratt, *The Politics of CANDU Exports* (Toronto: University of Toronto Press, 2006).
2. Memorandum of conversation, Washington, 2 August 1974, 11am, Review of Indo-American Relations, *Foreign Relations of the United States, 1969–1976*, vol. E-8, *Documents on South Asia, 1973–1976*, ed. Paul J. Hibbeln and Peter A. Kraemer (Washington, DC: US Government Printing Office, 2007), document 171.
3. "India, Uninvited, Joins the Nuclear Club," *New York Times*, 19 May 1974, 206.
4. For a critical analysis of the Indian bomb, with an emphasis on its destabilizing effects, see Itty Abraham, *The Making of the Indian Atomic Bomb: Science, Secrecy, and the Postcolonial State* (London: Zed Books, 1998). On the importance of control and sovereignty in nuclear development, see also Feroz Hassan Khan, *Eating Grass: The Making of the Pakistani Bomb* (Stanford, CA: Stanford University Press, 2012).
5. Airgram from the Embassy in Iran to the Department of State, 9 January 1973, *Foreign Relations of the United States, 1969–1976*, vol. 27, *Iran; Iraq, 1973–1976*, ed. Monica L. Belmonte (Washington, DC: US Government Printing Office, 2012), document 1.
6. John Cockcroft, "The Baghdad Pact Nuclear Training Centre," *Nature* 179 (11 May 1957), 936.
7. On British efforts to control Iraq, see Matthew Elliot, *"Independent Iraq": British Influence from 1941–1958* (London: Tauris, 1996).
8. "CENTO Institute of Nuclear Science, Biennial Report for 1959/61 (Second Draft)," n.d., FO 371/157486, UK National Archives, Kew, England.
9. C. R. A. Rae to Sir William Slater, 30 May 1962, FO 371/164058, UK National Archives, Kew, England.
10. Michael J. Cohen, *Strategy and Politics in the Middle East, 1954–1960: Defending the Northern Tier* (London: Frank Cass, 2005), 205–206.
11. C. R. A. Rae to Sir William Slater, 30 May 1962, FO 371/164058, UK National Archives, Kew, England.

12. "Future of the CENTO Institute of Nuclear Science, Tehran," n. d., FO 371/157484, UK National Archives, Kew, England.
13. F. J. Leishman to S. J. Whitwell, 9 February 1961, FO 371/157484, UK National Archives, Kew, England.
14. F. J. Leishman to S. J. Whitwell, 9 February 1961, FO 371/157484, UK National Archives, Kew, England. Material about American participation is located in FO 371/170247, UK National Archives, Kew, England.
15. W. J. A. Wilberforce to C. R. A. Rae, 23 September 1963, FO 371/170247, UK National Archives, Kew, England.
16. C. R. A. Rae to W. Morris (Foreign Office), 12 June 1964, FO 371/175630, UK National Archives, Kew, England.
17. Zia Mian, "Fevered with Dreams of the Future: The Coming of the Atomic Age to Pakistan," in *South Asian Cultures of the Bomb*, ed. Itty Abraham (Bloomington: Indiana University Press, 2009), 20–40.
18. Alexis de Greiff, "The Tale of Two Peripheries: The Creation of the International Centre for Theoretical Physics in Trieste," *Historical Studies in the Natural Sciences* 33:1 (2002), 33–60.
19. I. H. Usmani, "Working Paper on The Future of the CENTO Institute of Nuclear Science, Tehran," for discussion at the Ninth Session of the Scientific Council of CENTO, to be held in May 1961, n.d., FO 371/157485, UK National Archives, Kew, England.
20. See Sankaran Krishna, "The Social Life of a Bomb: India and the Ontology of an 'Overpopulated' Society," in *South Asian Cultures of the Bomb*, ed. Itty Abraham (Bloomington: Indiana University Press, 2009), 68–88.
21. On the importance of nuclear programs in Indian's state-building projects, see Jahnavi Phalkey, *Atomic State: Big Science in Twentieth-Century India* (Ranikhet: Permanent Black, 2013). On the architecture of nuclear institutes, see Stuart W. Leslie, "Atomic Structures: The Architecture of Nuclear Nationalism in India and Pakistan," *History and Technology* 31:3 (2015), 220–242, quote on p. 222.
22. S. A. Hasnain, "Dr. I. H. Usmani and the Early Days of the PAEC," *The Nucleus* 42 (2005), 13–20, quotes on p. 17.
23. Hasnain, "Dr. I. H. Usmani and the Early Days of the PAEC," 13–20.
24. A description of Cameron can be found in J. Kuba (IAEA Department of Technical Assistance) to the Governor from the United Arab Rebublic to the IAEA, 23 December 1965, folder TA/EGY-26 Prospection Geology, IAEA Archives, Vienna, Austria.
25. "Request from the Government of Pakistan, Pakistan Atomic Energy Commission, for United Nations Development Programme Special Fund Assistance in 'The Development of Uranium Resources of Pakistan (West),'" n.d., folder "TA/PAK-53, vol. 5, Exploration of Uranium Resources," IAEA Archives, Vienna, Austria.
26. United Nations Development Programme and International Atomic Energy Agency, "Exploration for Uranium in the Siwalik Sandstones, Dera Ghazi Khan District, PAK-70-553/PAK-74-002, Pakistan, Project Findings and Recommendations," 1976, folder "TA/PAK-53, vol. 5, Exploration of Uranium Resources," IAEA Archives, Vienna, Austria.
27. J. W. Hoadley, "Project Manager's Final Report on UNDP-IAEA Project PAK/70/553, Detailed Exploration of Uranium and Other Radioactive Occurences in the Siwalik Sandstones in the Dera Ghazi District," 21 June 1974, folder "TA/

PAK-53, vol. 5, Exploration of Uranium Resources," IAEA Archives, Vienna, Austria.
28. "Request from the Government of Pakistan, Pakistan Atomic Energy Commission, for United Nations Development Programme Special Fund Assistance in 'The Development of Uranium Resources of Pakistan (West),'" n.d., folder "TA/PAK-53, vol. 5, Exploration of Uranium Resources," IAEA Archives, Vienna, Austria.
29. Richard Sisson and Leo E. Rose, *War and Secession: Pakistan, India, and the Creation of Bangladesh* (Berkeley: University of California Press, 1990).
30. On the Multan meeting, Usmani's ouster, and Khan's appointment, see Khan, *Eating Grass*, 87–92. Rabia Akhtar has suggested that Pakistan's commitment to its bomb was related to American non-proliferation policies after the Indian nuclear test. See Rabia Akhtar, "Making of the Seventh NWS: Historiography of the Beginning of the Nuclear Disorder in South Asia," *International History Review* 40 (2018), 1115–1133.
31. Bhutto's 1972 remarks are quoted in Statement by the Leader of Pakistan Delegation, Munir A. Khan, Chairman, Pakistan Atomic Energy Commission, 17 September 1974, FCO 66/607, UK National Archives, Kew, England.
32. P. H. Grattan, "Pakistan Nuclear Power Plant," 21 November 1972, FCO 55/937 Nuclear UK Pakistan, UK National Archives, Kew, England.
33. G. P. C. Macartney, "Reprocessing Plan for Pakistan Atomic Energy Commission," 14 August 1972, FCO 55/937 Nuclear UK Pakistan, UK National Archives, Kew, England.
34. Akhtar Mahmud Faruqui, "A Review of the AEC in Pakistan," *IAEA Bulletin* 14–5 (1972), 2–8, quote on p. 8.
35. United Nations Development Programme and International Atomic Energy Agency, "Exploration for Uranium in the Siwalik Sandstones, Dera Ghazi Khan District, PAK-70-553/PAK-74-002, Pakistan, Project Findings and Recommendations," 1976, folder "TA/PAK-53, vol. 5, *Exploration of Uranium Resources*," IAEA Archives, Vienna, Austria.
36. G. Woite, "The Potential Role of Nuclear Power in Developing Countries," *IAEA Bulletin* 17:3 (1975), 21–32.
37. For an overview of Canada's reactor strategies, see Duane Bratt, "CANDU or CANDON'T: Competing Values behind Canada's Nuclear Sales," *Nonproliferation Review* 5:3 (1998), 1–16.
38. D. J. Cahill, "Exploration for Uranium in the Siwalik Sandstones, Dera Ghazi Khan District, Pakistan," May 1978, folder "TA/PAK-53, vol. 5, Exploration of Uranium Resources," IAEA Archives, Vienna, Austria.
39. South Asia Department, Foreign and Commonwealth Office, "Call by the Indian High Commissioner, 2 May 1974," 30 April 1974, FCO 66/604, UK National Archives, Kew, England.
40. Telegram 6591 from the US Embassy in India to the Department of State and the Embassy in the United Kingdom, May 18, 1974, 0600Z, *Foreign Relations of the United States, 1969–1976*, vol. E-8, *Documents on South Asia, 1973–1976*, ed. Paul J. Hibbeln and Peter A. Kraemer (Washington, DC: US Government Printing Office, 2007), document 161.
41. For historical perspectives on the Indian nuclear program, see Itty Abraham, *The Making of the Indian Atomic Bomb*, and George Perkovich, *India's Nuclear Bomb: The Impact on Global Proliferation* (Berkely: University of California Press, 1999).

42. P. H. Roberts (Information Research Department), memo on "India and the NPT," 6 June 1974, FCO 66/604, UK National Archives, Kew, England.
43. Telegram TOSEC 794/104621, from the Department of State to the Mission to the International Atomic Energy Agency, 18 May 1974, 2238Z, *Foreign Relations of the United States, 1969–1976*, vol. E-8, *Documents on South Asia, 1973–1976*, ed. Paul J. Hibbeln and Peter A. Kraemer (Washington, DC: US Government Printing Office, 2007), document 162.
44. Kapor's presentation is discussed in A. E. Montgomery to Mr. Summerhayes, "Indian Nuclear Test," 1 July 1974, FCO 66/604, UK National Archives, Kew, England.
45. J. J. Taylor (British High Commission, Ottawa), to L. V. Appleyard (New Delhi), memorandum regarding Indo/Canadian Bilateral Talks, 6 August 1974, FCO 82/367, UK National Archives, Kew, England.
46. J. J. Taylor (British High Commission, Ottawa), to L. V. Appleyard (New Delhi), memorandum regarding Indo/Canadian Bilateral Talks, 6 August 1974.
47. A. F. Maddock to Mr. Taylor, memorandum regarding India and Canada, 9 August 1974, FCO 82/367, UK National Archives, Kew, England.
48. Paul R. Josephson, *Red Atom: Russia's Nuclear Power Program from Stalin to Today* (Pittsburgh, PA: University of Pittsburgh Press, 2005), 246–248.
49. William C. Potter, "The Soviet Union and Nuclear Proliferation," *Slavic Review* 44:3 (1985), 468–488, esp. p. 474.
50. G. B. Chalmers (South Asian Department, FCO), memo, "Training in Nuclear Research for India," 26 June 1974, FCO 66/604, UK National Archives, Kew, England.
51. J. A. Thomson to Mr. Coles, 20 June 1974, FCO 66/606, UK National Archives, Kew, England.
52. Bernard Weintraub, "India Is Angered by A-Test Critics," *New York Times*, 26 May 1974, 15.
53. Telegram TOSEC 794/104621 From the Department of State to the Mission to the International Atomic Energy Agency, 18 May 1974, 2238Z, *Foreign Relations of the United States, 1969–1976*, vol. E-8, *Documents on South Asia, 1973–1976*, ed. Paul J. Hibbeln and Peter A. Kraemer (Washington, DC: US Government Printing Office, 2007), document 162.
54. W. V. Fell to D. M. Summerhayes, 20 June 1974, FCO 66/604, UK National Archives, Kew, England.
55. James Callaghan, 11 June 1974, "Aid to India and the Recent Indian Nuclear Explosion," FCO 37/1465, UK National Archives, Kew, England.
56. Statement by the Leader of Pakistan Delegation, Munir A. Khan, Chairman, Pakistan Atomic Energy Commission, 17 September 1974, FCO 66/607, UK National Archives, Kew, England.
57. Memorandum of conversation, Washington, August 2, 1974, 11am, Review of Indo-American Relations, *Foreign Relations of the United States, 1969–1976*, vol. E-8, *Documents on South Asia, 1973–1976*, ed. Paul J. Hibbeln and Peter A. Kraemer (Washington, DC: US Government Printing Office, 2007), document 171.
58. Memorandum of conversation, Washington, August 2, 1974, 11am, Review of Indo-American Relations.
59. See, for example, discussions in 1971 about Gandhi, conversation among President Nixon, the President's Assistant for National Security Affairs (Kissinger), and the President's Assistant (Haldeman), Washington, 5 November

1971, *Foreign Relations of the United States, 1969–1975*, vol. E-7, *Documents on South Asia, 1969–1972*, ed. Louis J. Smith (Washington, DC: US Government Printing Office, 2005), document 150.
60. Memorandum from the President's Deputy Assistant for National Security Affairs (Scowcroft) to President Ford, 28 October 1974, *Foreign Relations of the United States, 1969–1976*, vol. E-8, *Documents on South Asia, 1973–1976*, ed. Paul J. Hibbeln and Peter A. Kraemer (Washington. DC: US Government Printing Office, 2007), document 179.
61. Isabelle Anstey, "Negotiating Nuclear Control:The Zangger Committee and the Nuclear Suppliers' Group in the 1970s, *International History Review* 40 (2018), 975–995; Yogesh Joshi, "Between Principles and Pragmatism: India and the Nuclear Non-Proliferation Regime in the Post-PNE Era, 1974–1980," *International History Review* 40 (2018), 1073–1093.
62. An overview of the oil crisis, including a discussion of nuclear power, is in Francisco Parra, *Oil Politics: A Modern History of Petroleum* (London: I. B. Tauris, 2004).
63. Memorandum of conversation, Washington, 2 August 1974, 11am, Review of Indo-American Relations, *Foreign Relations of the United States, 1969–1976*, vol. E-8, *Documents on South Asia, 1973–1976*, ed. Paul J. Hibbeln and Peter A. Kraemer (Washington, DC: US Government Printing Office, 2007), document 171.
64. Sigvard Eklund, "Advance Draft Statement by the Director General to the 18th Session of the General Conference," received in registry 6 September 1974, FCO 66/607, UK National Archives, Kew, England.
65. Kenneth S. Deffeyes, *Hubbert's Peak: The Impending World Oil Shortage* (Princeton, NJ: Princeton University Press, 2001).
66. Edward Cowan, "Expert Doubts U.S. Can Substantially Cut Oil Imports by 1985," *New York Times*, 8 July 1975, 53.
67. Cowan, "Expert Doubts U.S. Can Substantially Cut Oil Imports by 1985," 53.
68. On nuclear fracking and other projects with nuclear detonations, see Scott Kaufman, *Project Plowshare: The Peaceful Use of Nuclear Explosives in Cold War America* (Ithaca, NY: Cornell University Press, 2013).
69. Scientists' Institute for Public Information, Inc., Appellant, v. Atomic Energy Commission et al., No. 72-1331, United States Court of Appeals, District of Columbia Circuit, argued 8 September 1972, decided 12 June 1973, http://openjurist.org/481/f2d/1079/scientists-institute-for-public-information-inc-v-atomic-energy-commission [accessed 26 June 2020].
70. Cowan, "Expert Doubts U.S. Can Substantially Cut Oil Imports by 1985," 53.
71. Gary Snyder, *Turtle Island* (New York: New Directions, 1974), 67.
72. Yossi Melman and Meir Javedanfar, *The Nuclear Sphinx of Iran: Mahmoud Ahmadinejad and the State of Iran* (New York: Carroll and Graf, 2007), 85.
73. Atomic Energy Organization of Iran, Nuclear Research Center, "Progress Report, July—September 1976," October 1976, AEOI-68, NRC-76-41, AB 48/1530, UK National Archives, Kew, England.
74. Zhila Khalkhali-Ellis, personal email communication with the author (Hamblin), 24 October 2018.
75. For an overview of Project Independence and an analysis of the oil embargo's impact on the United States, see Federal Energy Administration, *Project Independence: A Summary* (Washington, DC: US Government Printing Office, 1974).

76. Memorandum of Conversation, 17 August 1974, *Foreign Relations of the United States, 1969–1976*, vol. 37, *Energy Crisis 1974–1980*, ed. Steven G. Galpern (Washington, DC: US Government Printing Office, 2012), document 2.
77. Memorandum of Conversation, 13 August 1974, *Foreign Relations of the United States, 1969–1976*, vol. 37, *Energy Crisis 1974–1980*, ed. Steven G. Galpern (Washington, DC: US Government Printing Office, 2012), document 1. On Kissinger's strategies, particularly of linkage, see John Lewis Gaddis, *Strategies of Containment* (New York: Oxford University Press, 1982); on Kissinger's penchant for realism in diplomacy, see Jeremi Suri, *Henry Kissinger and the American Century* (Cambridge, MA: Harvard University Press, 2007).
78. Memorandum of conversation, 10 June 1975, *Foreign Relations of the United States, 1969–1976*, vol. 37, *Energy Crisis 1974–1980*, ed. Steven G. Galpern (Washington, DC: US Government Printing Office, 2012), document 65.
79. Memorandum of Conversation, 13 August 1974, *Foreign Relations of the United States, 1969–1976*, vol. 37, *Energy Crisis 1974–1980*, ed. Steven G. Galpern (Washington, DC: US Government Printing Office, 2012), document 1.
80. Bernard Weintraub, "Shah of Iran Urges End of Oil Embargo," *New York Times*, 22 December 1973, 6, 51.
81. Memorandum of conversation, 10 June 1975, *Foreign Relations of the United States, 1969–1976*, vol. 37, *Energy Crisis 1974–1980*, ed. Steven G. Galpern (Washington, DC: US Government Printing Office, 2012), document 65.
82. Telegram from the Department of State to the Embassy in Iran, 11 March 1974, *Foreign Relations of the United States, 1969–1976*, vol. 27, *Iran; Iraq, 1973–1976*, ed. Monica L. Belmonte (Washington, DC: US Government Printing Office, 2012), document 55.
83. Telegram from the Embassy in Iran to the Department of State, 15 March 1974; Kissinger's response is in Telegram from the Department of State to the Embassy in Iran, 11 April 1974, *Foreign Relations of the United States, 1969–1976*, vol. 27, *Iran; Iraq, 1973–1976*, ed. Monica L. Belmonte (Washington, DC: US Government Printing Office, 2012), documents 56 and 58.
84. For more detailed discussion of Kissinger's non-proliferation aims as Iran invested heavily in nuclear programs in the 1970s, see Roham Alvandi, *Nixon, Kissinger, and the Shah: The United States and Iran in the Cold War* (New York: Oxford University Press, 2014).
85. Minutes of the Rambouillet Economic Summit Meeting, 16 November 1975, Memorandum of conversation, 10 June 1975, *Foreign Relations of the United States, 1969–1976*, vol. 37, *Energy Crisis 1974–1980*, ed. Steven G. Galpern (Washington, DC: US Government Printing Office, 2012), document 88.
86. Stuart W. Leslie and Robert Kargon, "Exporting MIT: Science, Technology, and Nation-Building in India and Iran," *Osiris* 21 (2006), 110–130, quote p. 125. An exploration of MIT's internal discussions about accommodating such Iranian students is in Juana C. Becerra, "Herman Feshbach: What It Meant to be a Physicist in the Twentieth Century," unpublished senior thesis, Massachusetts Institute of Technology, 2015.
87. Alvin M. Weinberg, "Chapters from the Life of a Technological Fixer," *Minerva* 31:4 (1993), 379–454, 411.
88. W. Marshall, Note for the Record of a Visit to Iran from 4th–6th February, 1975, AB 65/1066, UK National Archives, Kew, England.
89. W. Marshall, Note for the Record of a Visit to Iran from 4th–6th February, 1975.

90. W. Marshall, Note for the Record of a Visit to Iran from 4th–6th February, 1975.
91. Note for the Record of a visit to Iran by Dr. Marshall, Mr. Plail and Mrs. Hutchins, 9th–12th July 1976, AB 65/1066, UK National Archives, Kew, England.
92. Memorandum from the President's Assistant for National Security Affairs (Scowcroft) to President Ford, 19 April 1976, *Foreign Relations of the United States, 1969–1976*, vol. 27, *Iran; Iraq, 1973–1976*, ed. Monica L. Belmonte (Washington, DC: US Government Printing Office, 2012), document 172.
93. P. J. Westmacott [British Embassy, Tehran] to M. J. Wilmshurst [Energy Department, FCO], 24 March 1976, AB 65/1066, UK National Archives, Kew, England.
94. On attempts at multi-national fuel fabrication, see Shinsuke Tomotsugu, "After the Hegemony of the 'Atoms for Peace' Program: Multinational Nonproliferation Policy under the Nixon and Ford Administrations," *Japanese Journal of American Studies* 27 (2016), 167–188.
95. W. Marshall, Note for the Record of a Visit to Iran from 4th–6th February, 1975, UK National Archives, Kew, England, AB 65/1066. On E'temad's perspectives, and his relations with the British during this period, see Ali M. Ansari, "The Curious Case of the Nuclear Company of Britain and Iran," *Journal of the British Institute of Persian Studies* 55:1 (2017), 73–86.
96. Memorandum of Conversation, 4 March 1975, *Foreign Relations of the United States, 1969–1976*, vol. 27, *Iran; Iraq, 1973–1976*, ed. Monica L. Belmonte (Washington, DC: US Government Printing Office, 2012), document 109.
97. Congressional Research Service, *Project Interdependence: U.S. and World Energy Outlook through 1990* (Washington, DC: US Government Printing Office, 1977), 697.
98. Congressional Research Service, *Project Interdependence: U.S. and World Energy Outlook through 1990*, 690.
99. Congressional Research Service, *Project Interdependence: U.S. and World Energy Outlook through 1990*, 690–693.
100. A discussion of several deals that never came to pass is Or Rabinowitz and Jayita Sarkar, "'It Isn't over until the Fuel Cell Sings': A Reassessment of the US and French Pledges of Nuclear Assistance in the 1970s," *Journal of Strategic Studies* 41:1–2 (2018), 275–300.

CHAPTER 8

1. Introductory Statement by Director General Dr. Hans Blix at the Post-Accident Review Meeting on the Chernobyl Accident, Vienna, 25 August 1986, AB 38/2164, UK National Archives, Kew, England.
2. Transcript, Jimmy Carter, Address to the Nation on Energy (18 April 1977), https://millercenter.org/the-presidency/presidential-speeches/april-18-1977-address-nation-energy [accessed 26 June 2020].
3. "Transcript of Speech by Carter on Energy Program at Joint Session of Congress," *New York Times*, 21 April 1977, 34.
4. William D. Metz, "Ford-MITRE Study: Nuclear Power Yes, Plutonium No," *Science* 196:4285 (1977), 41.
5. "Backers of Tennessee Breeder Reactor Hope for Funds from Congress: 450 Affected in Oak Ridge," *New York Times*, 24 April 1977, 26.
6. "Westinghouse Chief Opposes Curb on Breeder Reactor as 'Unwise,'" *New York Times*, 28 April 1977, 95.

7. On Weinberg's activities during this period, see Alvin M. Weinberg, *The First Nuclear Era: The Life and Times of a Technological Fixer* (New York: AIP Press, 1994).
8. C. F. Baes Jr., H. E. Goeller, J. S. Olsen, and R. M. Rotty, *The Global Carbon Dioxide Problem*, ORNL-5194 (Oak Ridge, TN: Oak Ridge National Laboratory, 1976).
9. "World of BNL," *Brookhaven Bulletin* 26:21 (25 May 1972), 2.
10. H. E. Goeller, "The Ultimate Mineral Resource Situation—An Optimistic View," *Proceedings of the National Academy of Sciences of the United States of America* 69:10 (1972), 2991–2992.
11. H. E. Goeller and Alvin M. Weinberg, "The Age of Substitutability," *Science* 191:4228 (1976), 683–689.
12. Henry Shaw to John W. Harrison, 31 October 1977, reference 77GR 961, available at https://insideclimatenews.org/sites/default/files/documents/Government%20Meeting%20Memo%20%281977%29.pdf [accessed 26 June 2020].
13. Ralph M. Rotty and Alvin M. Weinberg, "How Long Is Coal's Future?" *Climatic Change* 1:1 (1977), 45–58, quote on p. 56.
14. *Constraints on Coal Development*, Oversight Hearing before the Subcommittee on Energy and the Environment of the Committee on Interior and Insular Affairs, House of Representatives, 9 June 1977 (Washington, DC: US Government Printing Office, 1977), quote on p. 24.
15. For an analysis of the Glenn and Symington amendments, see Jayita Sarkar, "US Policy to Curb West European Nuclear Exports, 1974–1978," *Journal of Cold War Studies* 21:2 (2019), 110–149.
16. Such concerns were a theme of a nuclear conference in Iran in 1977. See Farzan Sabet, "The April 1977 Persepolis Conference on the Transfer of Nuclear Technology: A Third World Revolt against US Non-Proliferation Policy?" *International History Review* 40 (2018), 1134–1151.
17. R. Skjöldebrand, "The International Fuel Cycle Evaluation—INFCE," *IAEA Bulletin* 22:2 (1980), 30–33.
18. The essay appeared in *Commentaire* (Spring 1980), 91–104 and a translated excerpt for the CIA is in CIA-RDP82-00850R000200080011-9, US National Archives and Records Administration, College Park, MD. On the rise of France and West Germany as nuclear suppliers, see Sarkar, "US Policy to Curb West European Nuclear Exports, 1974–1978."
19. The essay appeared in *Commentaire* (Spring 1980), 91–104, and a translated excerpt for the CIA is in CIA-RDP82-00850R000200080011-9, US National Archives and Records Administration, College Park, MD.
20. Gayle Greene, *The Woman Who Knew Too Much: Alice Stewart and the Secrets of Radiation* (Ann Arbor: University of Michigan Press, 2017); J. Samuel Walker, *Three Mile Island: A Nuclear Crisis in Historical Perspective* (Berkeley: University of California Press, 2004).
21. National Intelligence Cable, 6 April 1979, CIA-RDP79T00975A031300050001-8, US National Archives and Records Administration, College Park, MD.
22. Translated excerpt for CIA, "Harrisburg Accident Provokes PCI Nuclear Policy Reversal," Milan *Corriere Della Serra* (26 April 1979), 9, CIA-RDP82-00850R000100060052-7, US National Archives and Records Administration, College Park, MD.

23. Central Intelligence Agency, East Asia Review, 10 April 1979, CIA-RDP79T00912A002200010021-2, US National Archives and Records Administration, College Park, MD.
24. Central Intelligence Agency, International Issues Review, 30 April 1979, CIA-RDP80T00942A000500010001-8, US National Archives and Records Administration, College Park, MD.
25. Translated excerpt for CIA, "'Bohemia' Sees Capitalist Greed Causing Nuclear Reactor Accident," Havana *Prela*, 12 April 1979, CIA-RDP82-00850R000100050023-0, US National Archives and Records Administration, College Park, MD.
26. On Cuba's nuclear efforts, see Jonathan Benjamin-Alvarado, *Power to the People: Energy and the Cuban Nuclear Program* (New York: Routledge, 2000); and Gustav Cederlöf, "The Revolutionary City: Socialist Urbanisation and Nuclear Modernity in Cienfuegos, Cuba," *Journal of Latin American Studies* (2019), 1–24. On Soviet exports generally, see William C. Potter, "The Soviet Union and Nuclear Proliferation," *Slavic Review* 44:3 (1985), 468–488.
27. National Intelligence Daily, Cable, 13 April 1979, CIA-RDP79T00975A031300110001-1, US National Archives and Records Administration, College Park, MD.
28. Potter, "The Soviet Union and Nuclear Proliferation," 472.
29. National Intelligence Daily, Cable, 13 April 1979, CIA-RDP79T00975A031300110001-1, US National Archives and Records Administration, College Park, MD.
30. National Issues Review, 30 April 1979, CIA-RDP80T00942A000500010001-8, US National Archives and Records Administration, College Park, MD.
31. National Issues Review, 30 April 1979.
32. National Issues Review, 30 April 1979.
33. International Issues Review, 31 October 1979, CIA-RDP80T00942A000500010011-7, US National Archives and Records Administration, College Park, MD.
34. International Issues Review, 31 October 1979.
35. "The Iraqi Nuclear Program: Progress Despite Setbacks," Central Intelligence Agency, June 1983. Declassified version available at www.gwu.edu/%7Ensarchiv/NSAEBB/NSAEBB82/iraq19.pdf [accessed 26 June 2020].
36. Francis Fukuyama, "The Soviet Union and Iraq since 1968," Rand Note N-1524-AF, July 1980.
37. "Le Second Fournisseur de Pétrole de la France," *Le Monde*, 3 August 1978, https://www.lemonde.fr/archives/article/1978/08/03/le-second-fournisseur-de-petrole-de-la-france_2994415_1819218.html [accessed 26 June 2020].
38. A. J. D. Stirling (British embassy, Baghdad) to R. J. Alston (Joint Nuclear Unit, Foreign and Commonwealth Office, UK), March 1980, FCO 8/3723, UK National Archives, Kew, England.
39. An overview of Iraq's nuclear program can be found in Khidhir Hamza with Jeff Stein, *Saddam's Bombmaker* (New York: Scribner, 2001).
40. Discussion of American and British discussions with the Italians is in A. C. Galsworthy (British Embassy, Rome) to R. J. Alston (Joint Nuclear Unit, FCO), 20 March 1980, UK National Archives, Kew, England, FCO 8/3723. Other details are in Joint Nuclear Unit (Foreign and Commonwealth Office), "Sale of 'Hot Cell' by Italy to Iraq," 19 October 1980, FCO 8/3723, UK National Archives, Kew, England.

41. The connection between the French and Italian deals and proliferation is reflected in comments made in briefs for Parliamentary questions. See Joint Nuclear Unit, Notes for Supplementaries, 22 October 1980, GCO 8/3724, UK National Archives, Kew, England.
42. Frederick Forsyth published several popular espionage novels in the 1970s, including *Day of the Jackal* and *The Odessa File*. K. R. Gosling (British Embassy, Vienna) to Dr. F. Brown (AE Division, Department of Energy), 23 April 1980, FCO 8/3723, UK National Archives, Kew, England.
43. Paul L. Leventhal, "The Plumbat Affair," *New York Times*, 30 April 1978, E19.
44. Victor Gilinsky and Roger J. Mattson, "Did Israel Steal Bomb-Grade Uranium from the United States?" *Bulletin of the Atomic Scientists* 17 April 2014, https://thebulletin.org/2014/04/did-israel-steal-bomb-grade-uranium-from-the-united-states/ [accessed 26 June 2020].
45. K. R. Gosling (British Embassy, Vienna) to Dr. F. Brown (AE Division, Department of Energy), 23 April 1980, FCO 8/3723, UK National Archives, Kew, England.
46. S. Thorstensen (Euratom Section) to Mr. O'Neal, 14 April1980, FCO 8/3723, UK National Archives, Kew, England.
47. R. J. Alston (Joint Nuclear Unit), "Transfer of Unsafeguarded Material to Iraq," 1 May 1980, FCO 8/3723, UK National Archives, Kew, England.
48. Serge Schemann, "Bonn Inquiry Hints Pakistan and Libya Got Atom Material," *New York Times*, 15 January 1988, A9. The other firms implicated were Neue Technologien and Physikalisch Technische Beratung. See "German Prosecutors Say 2 Nuclear Firms Illegally Sold Parts," *Wall Street Journal*, 22 December 1988, 1.
49. Richard Burt, "Burst of Light Led to Speculation South Africa Exploded A-Bomb," *New York Times*, 27 October 1979, 5.
50. For discussion of the event in the context of South Africa's overall nuclear program, see M. S. van Wyk, "Ally or Critic? The United States' Response to South African Nuclear Development, 1949–1980," *Cold War History* 7: 2 (2007), 195–225. On the official findings by the United States, see "Possible Nuclear Explosion Panel: Findings and Conclusions," Office of Science and Technology Policy, 7 January 1980. Attached to Memorandum from President's Assistant for National Security Affairs (Brzezinski) to President Carter, 9 January 1980, *Foreign Relations of the United States, 1977–1980*, vol. 16, *Southern Africa*, ed. Myra F. Burton (Washington, DC: US Government Printing Office, 2016), document 368.
51. Khidhir Hamza with Jeff Stein, *Saddam's Bombmaker* (New York: Scribner, 2001), 134.
52. D. F. Richmond (Bagdad) to Foreign and Commonwealth Office, 24 August 1980, FCO 8/3723, UK National Archives, Kew, England.
53. D. F. Richmond [cable to various diplomatic posts], "Iraq Nuclear," 24 July 1980, FCO 8/3723, UK National Archives, Kew, England.
54. Richmond [cable to various diplomatic posts], "Iraq Nuclear," 24 July 1980.
55. Jean-Michel Quatrepoint, "L'Irak a Pris la Place qu'Occupait l'Iran dans le Commerce extérieur de l'Europe et du Japon," *Le Monde*, 30 April 1980, https://www.lemonde.fr/archives/article/1980/04/30/l-irak-a-pris-la-place-qu-occupait-l-iran-dans-le-commerce-exterieur-de-l-europe-et-du-japon_2803708_1819218.html [accessed 26 June 2020].

56. Ne'eman's views are summarized in an intelligence report for Britain's Foreign and Commonwealth Office, A. J. Colquhoun, "Iraqi Nuclear Programme," 18 July 1980, FCO 8/3723, UK National Archives, Kew, England.
57. Amos Perlmutter, Michael Handel, and Uri Bar-Joseph, *Two Minutes over Baghdad* (New York: Routledge, 2004).
58. Robert Lindsey, "Reagan Says America Should Not Bar Others from A-Bomb Output," *New York Times*, 1 February 1980, A12.
59. "Breeder Reactor Officials Expect Clinch River Project to Be Built," *New York Times*, 16 November 1980, 62.
60. "Reagan Said to Support Tennessee Nuclear Plant," *New York Times*, 26 February 1981, B15.
61. "Reagan Nuclear Policy Is Called Irresponsible," *New York Times*, 10 October 1981, 9.
62. Judith Miller, "Reagan Announces a Policy to Curb the Spread of Nuclear Weapons," *New York Times*, 17 July 1981, A4.
63. "Middle East Nuclear Weapon Free Zone and Other Middle East Arms Control Issues," no author, no date. [This is a response to the president's memorandum of 22 December 1981], CIA-RDP83M00914R002100110033-5, US National Archives and Records Administration, College Park, MD.
64. "Middle East Nuclear Weapon Free Zone and Other Middle East Arms Control Issues," no author, no date. [This is a response to the president's memorandum of 22 December 1981], CIA-RDP83M00914R002100110033-5. US National Archives and Records Administration, College Park, MD.
65. "Saudi Arabia: An Assessment as of October 1980," document no. NLC-15-47-1-9-4, Jimmy Carter Presidential Library, Atlanta, Georgia.
66. Zbigniew Brzezinski to the President, 3 October 1980, document no. NLC-128-10-4-9-5, Jimmy Carter Presidential Library, Atlanta, Georgia.
67. "Middle East Nuclear Weapon Free Zone and Other Middle East Arms Control Issues," no author, no date. [This is a response to the president's memorandum of December 22, 1981], CIA-RDP83M00914R002100110033-5, US National Archives and Records Administration, College Park, MD.
68. "The Air Defense Enhancement Package for Saudi Arabia," no author, no date, Carnegie Mellon University, H. John Heinz III collection, John Heinz Files, 1977–1991, http://doi.library.cmu.edu/10.1184/pmc/heinz/box00246/fld00018/bdl0032/doc0002, [accessed 9 December 2016].
69. Director of Global Issues to Director of Soviet Analysis, 29 October 1982, CIA-RDP08S01350R000200470001-4, US National Archives and Records Administration, College Park, MD.
70. AMEMBASSY NEW DELHI to NUERC/SECSTATE WASHDC, 19 March 1987, document no. NLC-131-5-7-6-7, Jimmy Carter Presidential Library, Atlanta, Georgia.
71. Judith Miller, "Disputes Growing in U.N. Atom Panel," *New York Times*, 1 November 1981, 14.
72. International Issues, Regional and Political Analysis, RP AII 77-002, 16 February 1977, CIA-RDP79T00912A002300010010-3, US National Archives and Records Administration, College Park, MD.
73. Miller, "Disputes Growing in U.N. Atom Panel."
74. Miller, "Disputes Growing in U.N. Atom Panel."
75. Martha van Wyk, "Sunset over Atomic Apartheid: United States-South African Nuclear Relations, 1981–93," *Cold War History* 10:1 (2010), 51–79.

76. Judith Miller, "U.S. Walks Out as Atom Parley Bars the Israelis," *New York Times*, 25 September 1982, 1.
77. Miller, "U.S. Walks Out as Atom Parley Bars the Israelis."
78. OES/NTS (Allen L. Sessoms, Acting, Department of State) to IAEA IG, 12 October 1982, with paper "IAEA Reassessment—Long Term Issues," CIA-RDP85M00364R000801330032-5, US National Archives and Records Administration, College Park, MD.
79. OES/NTS (Allen L. Sessoms, Acting, Department of State) to IAEA IG, 12 October 1982.
80. OES/NTS (Allen L. Sessoms, Acting, Department of State) to IAEA IG, 12 October 1982.
81. [Redacted], Weapons Proliferation/ISID/OGI, memorandum for National Intelligence Officer, Nuclear Proliferation, 12 October 1982, CIA-RDP85M00364R000801330030-7, US National Archives and Records Administration, College Park, MD.
82. S/NP (Mr. Richard Kennedy) to The Secretary (of State), n.d., (subject: IAEA Reassessment), CIA-RDP85M00364R000801330013-6, US National Archives and Records Administration, College Park, MD.
83. S/NP (Mr. Richard Kennedy) to The Secretary (of State), n.d., (subject: IAEA Reassessment).
84. L. Paul Bremer III, to various (Interagency Group No. 32), 17 November 1982, with draft strategy paper on IAEA Reassessment, CIA-RDP84B00049R000501260009-4, US National Archives and Records Administration, College Park, MD.
85. *Nuclear Public Relations Campaign*, Hearings before the Subcommittee on Energy Conservation and Power of the Committee on Energy and Commerce, House of Representatives, 23 May and 30 June, 1983 (Washington, DC: US Government Printing Office, 1983), 12, 220.
86. Judith Miller, "Breeder Reactor Faulted on Cost," *New York Times*, 12 December 1982, 43.
87. Martin Tolchin, "Senate Vote Virtually Kills Clinch River Atom Reactor," *New York Times*, 27 October 1983, 24. For a fuller discussion, see Michael Camp, "'Wandering in the Desert': The Clinch River Breeder Reactor Debate in the US Congress, 1972–1983," *Technology and Culture* 59:1 (2018), 26–47.
88. Mark Kirk, "Atomizing Bases," *New York Times*, 30 August 1984, 23.
89. "US Resumes Plan for Space Reactor," *New York Times*, 23 November 1985, 6.
90. Lester Berstein, "A Different Kind of China Syndrome," *New York Times*, 22 August 1985, 23.
91. F. H. Bormann, "Air Pollution and Forests: An Ecosystem Perspective," *BioScience* 35:7 (1985), 434–441.
92. Bernard L. Cohen, *Before It's Too Late: A Scientist's Case for Nuclear Energy* (New York: Plenum, 1983).
93. Hans Blix, "The Relevance of the IAEA," *IAEA Bulletin Supplement* 24 (1982), 3–5.
94. On the Chernobyl accident, see Serhii Plokhy, *Chernobyl: The History of a Nuclear Catastrophe* (New York: Basic Books, 2018), and Kate Brown, *Manual for Survival: A Chernobyl Guide to the Future* (New York: Norton, 2019).
95. Hans Blix, "The Post-Chernobyl Outlook for Nuclear Power," *IAEA Bulletin* 28:3 (Autumn 1986), 9–12.
96. K. G. Steele, Nuclear Operations Support Group, to Dr. J. H. Gittus, Atomic Energy Authority, 21 August 1986, with attached report "Chernobyl

Accident—Simplified Interpretation of Soviet's Reported Accident Sequence," AB 38/2164, UK National Archives, Kew, England.
97. "Medical Aspects," n.d. (part of materials related to August 1986 meeting in Vienna about Chernobyl) AB 38/2164, UK National Archives, Kew, England.
98. John H. Gittus, "IAEA Post Accident Review Meeting on the Chernobyl Accident, 25–29 August 1986," AB 38/2164, UK National Archives, Kew, England.
99. On Legasov, see Plokhy, *Chernobyl*.
100. A curie is a unit of measuring radioactivity. John H. Gittus, "Accident, 25–29 August 1986," AB 38/2164, UK National Archives, Kew, England.
101. "Introductory Statement by Director General Dr. Hans Blix at the Post-Accident Review Meeting on the Chernobyl Accident, Vienna, 25 August 1986," AB 38/2164, UK National Archives, Kew, England.
102. "Introductory Statement by Director General Dr. Hans Blix."
103. Directorate of Intelligence, Central Intelligence Agency, "The Chernobyl Accident: Social and Political Implications," December 1987, CIA-RDP08S01350R000300900002-4, National Archives and Records Administration, College Park, MD.
104. Ronald Reagan, Presidential Proclamation 5514, 100 Stat. 4478, 29 July 1986.
105. Chernobyl Task Force, Office of Soviet Analysis et al., Central Intelligence Agency, "Chernobyl: A Year Later," SOV 87-10047, August 1987, Central Intelligence Agency Freedom of Information Act Reading Room, document number CIA-RDP08S01350R000401290002-0, quote on pp. 23–24.
106. Javier Pérez de Cuéllar, "Nations of the World Have Greatly Benefited from the IAEA," *IAEA Bulletin* 29:3 (1987), 5–7.
107. "Congratulatory Messages on IAEA's 30th Birthday," *IAEA Bulletin* 29:3 (1987), 6.
108. Munir Ahmad Khan, "1957–87: Development through Global Co-operation," *IAEA Bulletin* 29:3 (1987), 7–10.
109. On the nuclear free zone treaty, see Jonathan Hunt, "Mexican Nuclear Diplomacy, the Latin American Nuclear-Weapon-Free Zone, and the NPT Grand Bargain, 1962–1968," in *Negotiating the Nuclear Non-Proliferation Treaty: The Making of a Nuclear Order*, ed. Roland Popp, Liviu Horovitz, and Andreas Wenger (New York: Routledge, 2016), 179–202.
110. Hans Blix, "The Next 10 Years: Major Challenges Shaping the IAEA's Future," *IAEA Bulletin* 29:3 (1987), 11–13.

CONCLUSION

1. Joshua S. Goldstein, Staffan A. Qvist, and Steven Pinker, "Nuclear Power Can Save the World," *New York Times*, 19 April 2019, SR, 4. An example of such appeals also appears in Jeff W. Eerkens, *The Nuclear Imperative: A Critical Look at the Approaching Energy Crisis* (Dordrecht: Springer, 2006).
2. Mohamed ElBaradei, *The Age of Deception: Nuclear Diplomacy in Treacherous Times* (New York: Metropolitan, 2011).
3. Interview with Mohamed ElBaradei by freelance journalist Marika Griehsel, 7 October 2005, https://www.nobelprize.org/prizes/peace/2005/elbaradei/26135-interview-with-mohamed-elbaradei/ [accessed 26 June 2020].
4. Mark Landler, "Man in the News: The UN's Geiger Counter," *New York Times*, 8 October 2005, 10.
5. In this book I have occasionally used documents that were part of the 2010 release of US diplomatic cables by Wikileaks. I have adopted the same stance on the use of such documents as that adopted by the editorial team

of the *New York Times*. See "A Note to Readers: The Decision to Publish Diplomatic Documents," *New York Times*, 28 November 2010, A10. The cable referenced here is "IAEA: What Is Being Done in Food Security," 9 July 2009, ID: 09UNVIEVIENNA327, https://search.wikileaks.org/plusd/cables/09UNVIEVIENNA327_a.html [accessed 26 June 2020].

6. For perspective on nuclear technology in the Obama years, see Gregory B. Jaczko, *Confessions of a Rogue Nuclear Regulator* (New York: Simon and Schuster, 2019).

7. Brimmer was the US assistant secretary of state for International Organization Affairs; "IO A/S Brimmer's First Call on DG Amano and Meetings with IAEA Reps," 4 December 2009, http://wikileaks.org/cable/2009/12/09UNVIEVIENNA545.html [accessed 26 June 2020].

8. Sasha Henriques (IAEAS Division of Public Information), "More than a Watchdog," 20 September 2010, https://www.iaea.org/newscenter/news/more-watchdog [accessed 26 June 2020].

9. Fredrik Dahl, "Analysis: Fukushima to Slow, Not Stop, Nuclear Growth," *Reuters World News*, 22 September 2011, https://in.reuters.com/article/idINIndia-59491320110922 [accessed 26 June 2020].

INDEX

For the benefit of digital users, indexed terms that span two pages (e.g., 52–53) may, on occasion, appear on only one of those pages.

Abbink, John, 26–27
Acheson-Lilienthal Report, 14
Acheson, Dean, 15, 32
acid rain, 241–43
Aebersold, Paul, 16–17, 114
Agency for International Development (United States), 138, 209–10
agriculture, 6–9, 18–19, 24–29, 43, 46–55, 58–59, 92–94, 99–100, 112–44, 182–85, 251–54
airborne warning and control system (AWACS), 236
Ako Adjei, Ebenezer, 108–9
al-Meshad, Yahya, 232
Alberto a Mota e Silva, Álvaro, 34–35
Alexander, Holmes, 105
Alexandrov, Simon, 42
Algeria, 107–10
Amano, Yukiya, 252–53
Ankrah, Joseph Arthur, 121
Ansari, Hushang, 1–4
Arab nationalism. *See* pan-Arabism
Aresvik, Oddvar, 111–12
Argentina, 18–21, 169–72, 182, 184, 203–4
Arneson, Gordon, 22, 53–54
Asian Nuclear Center, 87, 89–90, 97–103
Asian-African Conference. *See* Bandung Conference (1955)
Atomic Energy Act of 1946 (United States), 22, 51, 70
Atomic Energy Act of 1954 (United States), 70, 123

Atomic Energy Authority (Turkey), 193
Atomic Energy Board (South Africa), 108, 112–13
Atomic Energy Commission (Argentina), 169–70
Atomic Energy Commission (Ghana), 118
Atomic Energy Commission (India), 194
Atomic Energy Commission (Iraq), 227–28, 232
Atomic Energy Commission (Israel), 177
Atomic Energy Commission (Japan), 87
Atomic Energy Commission (Pakistan), 69–70, 101–2, 193–94, 246–47
Atomic Energy Commission (United States), 17–18, 22–23, 32, 36, 52–53, 70, 136–37, 139–40, 171–87, 196, 207, 222
Atomic Energy of Canada, 126, 135, 199
Atomic Energy Organization of Iran, 210–14
Atomic Energy Research Establishment (United Kingdom), 16–17, 98, 194–95, 212
Atomic Industrial Forum, 70–71
Atoms for Peace, 3, 9, 38–40, 55–59, 63–124, 168–69, 185, 193–94, 232, 234, 242–43, 246–48, 255
Australia, 18, 23–24, 105, 226, 238–39

Baes, C. F., 221
Baffour, Robert P., 118
Baghdad Pact. *See* Central Treaty Organization

Baker, Howard, Jr., 185–86
Ball, George, 111–12
Bandung Conference (1955),
    96–99, 104–5
Bangladesh, 130, 197–99
Baruch Plan, 40–43, 51, 54, 59, 166
Batur, Mehmet, 193
Beck, Guido, 19
Begin, Menachem, 233–34
Belgium, 15, 22–27, 96–97,
    103–12, 230–31
Bell, G. D. H., 130–31
Berkner, Lloyd, 2–3, 46
Bermuda Conference of 1953, 38–39,
    56–58, 92–93
beryl, 21–32, 71–72
Bhabha, Homi, 95–104, 170–71, 194
Bhutto, Zulfikar Ali, 197–200
Bikini, 39–48, 89, 94
Blackett, Patrick, 27, 29, 193–94, 195
Blandy, William H. P., 41–43
Blix, Hans, 217–18, 238, 242–48, 250–51
Boerma, Addeke Hendrik, 137–38, 141
boiling water reactors, 73–74
Borlaug, Norman, 143–44
Bowman, J. L., 196
Bravo shot, 77–78, 85, 89. *See also*
    United States nuclear tests
Brazil, 13–31, 34–36, 71–72, 104–5
breeder reactors, 65–66, 70–75, 81, 206–
    11, 219–21, 223–24, 234–35, 241.
    See also liquid metal fast breeder
    reactors *and* molten salt breeder
    reactors
Brewer, Shelby, 240–41
Brimmer, Esther, 252–53
Britain. *See* United Kingdom
British Nuclear Fuels Limited (BNFL),
    198, 212
Brookhaven National Laboratory, 46–47,
    65–66, 89–90, 100–3, 130–31
Brown, Meta Suche, 45
Bujon de l'Estang, François, 223–24, 227
Bumpers, Dale, 241
Bunche, Ralph J., 107
Bundy, McGeorge, 120
Bunker, Ellsworth, 182, 187
Burke, John Butler, 43
Bush, George W., 250–51
Byrnes, James, 18–19

Calder Hall reactor, 72–73, 87–89
Calvin, Melvin, 222
Cameron, James, 195–96
Canada, 36, 52–53, 111–12, 135, 166,
    189–90, 196–202, 226
cancer, 16, 17, 36–37, 43, 208–9, 224,
    250, 252–53
Candau, Marcolino, 127–29
CANDU reactors, 226
carbon dioxide. *See* climate change
carbon-14, 15–16, 118
Carrillo Flores, Nabor, 94
Carter, Jimmy, 219–28, 231–36
Castle series, 77–78. *See also* United
    States nuclear tests
Cats, Chaim, 177
Central Intelligence Agency (United
    States), 8–9, 26, 49–50, 63–64, 71,
    80–90, 119–20, 167–68, 173, 226–
    27, 240, 245–46
Central Treaty Organization, 140–41,
    191–94, 208, 255
cesium-137, 125–26
Ceylon, 99–103
Chadwick, James, 42–43
Chase, G. W., 196
chemical reprocessing. *See* nuclear
    reprocessing facilities
Chernobyl, 7–8, 217–18, 242–47. *See also*
    nuclear accidents
Cherokee test, 89
Chiang Kai-shek, 21–22, 168
China, 4, 9, 21–22, 52, 96–97, 121–22,
    165–66, 168–71, 201–2, 241
Chinese nuclear test, 121–22,
    165–66, 168–71
Chirac, Jacques, 228
Chu, Steven, 253
Churchill, Winston, 38–39, 56–57, 72
Cipriani, André, 126–27
CIRUS reactor, 194, 196–97, 201
Cisler, Walker, 70–77
civil rights, 111–12, 114–16,
    121–22, 175–76
Civil Rights Act, 122
climate change, 7–8, 221–41, 249–53
Clinch River Breeder Reactor Project,
    219–21, 234, 241
coal, 28–29, 69–70, 88, 117–18, 196,
    217–22, 241–43, 244–45

cobalt-60, 46–47, 121, 125–26, 131, 208
Cockcroft, John, 16–17, 191–92
Cohen, Bernard L., 241
Cole, W. Sterling, 54–55, 123–29
Coleman, Nathaniel, 112–13
Colombo Plan, 98–104, 191–92, 203
colonialism, 4–9, 14–15, 19, 23–28, 33, 36, 92–122, 165–71, 190–94, 213–14, 215, 237. *See also* neocolonialism
Colorado Plateau, 36, 52–53
Combined Development Trust, 23
Comisión Nacional de Energía Atómica (Argentina), 20
Commissariat à l'Énergie Atomique (France), 17–18, 35
Conant, Melvin, 215
Congo, 15, 22–26, 105–13
Congress for Cultural Freedom, 50
Cossutta, Armando, 225
Cottrell, Alan, 198
Cowles Commission, 27–28
Cuba, 225–26
Curman, Sigurd, 45
Cutler, Robert, 55
cyclotrons, 15–17, 34–35, 76–77

Daigo Fukuryū Maru (Japanese vessel), 77–79, 90–91
Davidovitch, David, 13, 21
Davis, Kingsley, 28
Dean, Gordon, 24, 32, 53
Department of Agriculture (United States), 46, 112–13, 130, 136–37
Department of Energy (United States), 240–41, 255
Department of State (United States), 14–15, 18, 21–23, 53, 85, 87, 90–91, 95–96, 98–103, 178–79, 181–82, 189–90, 201, 209–10, 239
desalination, 174–87, 197–98, 210–11
desalting. *See* desalination
Dimona nuclear site, 172–74, 177, 180–82
Diné, 36–37
Disney, Walt, 64, 68–69
Dixon, Pierson, 72
Dobson, R. Lowry, 127–28
Dorolle, Pierre, 126, 127–28
Du Bois, W. E. B., 116, 121–22, 165
Dulles, Allen, 26, 71, 85
Dulles, John Foster, 56, 95, 99

Durham, Carl T., 73
durum wheat trials, 132–33, 143–44
Duschinsky, Walter, 80

E'temad, Akbar, 212–14
East Germany, 225–26
East Pakistan, 130, 196–97
Egypt, 106–7, 111, 119, 121, 133, 170, 173–74, 180–81, 183, 190–91, 192, 209–10, 235, 250–51
Eisenhower, Dwight, 3–4, 9, 37, 38–40, 51–59, 63–91, 92–107, 111, 123–25, 184–88
Eklund, Sigvard, 123–24, 128–29, 134, 137, 206, 238
ElBaradei, Mohamed, 250–52
Emelyanov, Vasily, 128–29
energy crisis, 10, 190–91, 205–16, 217–28
enriched uranium, 72–74, 84, 87–88, 113, 196–97, 213, 219–20, 226–32
Eshkol, Levi, 174, 181
Eurodif, 227
European Atomic Energy Community (Euratom), 230–31

Faisal II (King of Iraq), 192, 227–28
fallout. *See* nuclear fallout
Fanon, Frantz, 5–6, 109–10, 254–55
FAO/IAEA Joint Division for Atomic Energy in Agriculture, 133–44, 251–52, 253–54
Faruqui, Akhtar Mahmud, 198
Federal Bureau of Investigation (United States), 20–21, 68, 116
Federation of Arab Scientific Research Councils, 228–29
Feldman, Myer, 178–79, 180–81
Fischnich, Otto E., 137–38
Food and Agriculture Organization, 8, 124, 132–44, 251–52, 253–54
food and grain irradiation, 124, 130, 134–37, 140–43
food security. *See* water and food security
Ford-MITRE study, 219–20
Ford, Gerald, 1, 205, 206–7, 209–10, 214, 219–20
Foreign and Commonwealth Office (United Kingdom), 198, 203, 212

Foreign Assistance Act (United States), 222–23
Fox, Marvin, 89–90, 100–1
fracking, 206–7
France, 4, 17–18, 23, 35, 38, 56–57, 72–73, 107, 108–10, 120, 172, 184, 199, 213, 218, 223–24, 227–29, 233, 240–41, 245–46, 253
Francis, Sharon, 175
Franco, Francisco, 22–23
French nuclear tests, 108–9
Fried, Maurice, 112–94, 130, 133–43
Fukushima, 253. *See also* nuclear accidents
Fulbright, J. William, 32–33
Fulford, Dwight, 202

Gaddafi, Muammar, 211–12, 215
gamma fields. *See* gamma gardens
gamma gardens, 46–47, 59, 65–66, 89–90, 130–31
Gandhi, Indira, 172, 194, 197, 200–5
Gandhi, Mohandas, 26–27, 28
gas-cooled reactors, 72, 90, 226
Gaud, William, 138
Gaul, Horst, 132
Gaviola, Enrique, 19–20
General Atomics, 67–68, 74, 75–76
General Dynamics, 63–68, 74, 81–88, 94
Germany. *See* Nazi Germany, West Germany, *and* East Germany
Ghana, 5–6, 9, 92, 93–94, 106–22
Gilpatric, Roswell, 168–69
Glenn Amendment, 222–23
global warming. *See* climate change
Goeller, Harold E., 221
Gold, Fern Racine, 215
Golikov, Vladimir Alexseevich, 118–19
González, Juan Loyo, 42
Gorbachev, Mikhael, 244, 245
Great Society, 114–15, 122, 174–88
Green Revolution, 138–44, 200
greenhouse effect. *See* climate change
Greenpeace, 245–46
Gromyko, Andrei, 168
Gruson, Sydney, 25–26

Haber, Heinz, 68–70
Hackerman, Norman, 222
Hafstad, Lawrence, 83

Halstead, William S., 80–82
Hammond, R. Philip, 182–83, 184–85
Harrar, J. George, 182–83
Hatoyama, Ichirō, 82–83, 84
Heisenberg, Werner, 19–20
Helms, Richard, 211–12
Hess, Wilmot, 222
Hickenlooper, Bourke, 32–33
Hinton, Christopher, 87–90
Hoadley, J. W., 196
Hollister, John, 98–102
Holthusen, Henry, 80
Holtz, Hans, 231
Hopkins, John Jay, 63–68, 81–89
Hornig, Donald, 176–81
Hubbert, M. King, 206–8, 214–15

India Emergency Food Aid Act of 1951 (United States), 34
India, 1–2, 4–7, 13–15, 26–37, 71–72, 78, 92–105, 125, 138–43, 165–74, 189–91, 194, 196–206, 214, 225–26, 236–37
Indian nuclear test, 189–90, 205–6, 214
Indo-Pakistani War of 1965, 138–39, 197, 201–2
Indo-Pakistani War of 1971, 197, 200, 202–3
Information Agency (United States), 83, 85–86, 120
insect control, 2–3, 6–8, 124–26, 130, 192–93
International Atomic Energy Agency, 3–9, 38, 58–59, 103–8, 112–19, 123–44, 166–82, 189, 193–200, 206–9, 217–18, 222–48, 250–55
International Conference on the Peaceful Uses of Atomic Energy (First, 1955), 67–68, 95–98
International Conference on the Peaceful Uses of Atomic Energy (Fourth, 1971), 196–97
International Conference on the Peaceful Uses of Atomic Energy (Second, 1958), 106–7
International Cooperation Administration (United States), 98, 100
International Maize and Wheat Improvement Center, 139–40

International Nuclear Fuel Cycle Evaluation, 223
International Rice Research Institute, 132, 143
iodine-131, 15–16
Iran-Iraq War, 233–35
Iran, 1–4, 133, 140–41, 190–93, 208–16, 227–36, 250–51
Iranian Revolution (1979), 233–36
Iraq Revolution (1958), 227–28
Iraq, 3–4, 191–92, 215, 218, 227–39, 250–51
IRT-5000 reactor, 227–28
Irwin, Rodney, 202
Isard, Walter, 29–30
Isis reactor, 229
Isochem, 135
Israel, 5–6, 8, 166, 170–88, 203, 205, 230, 240

Jackson, C. D., 56
Japan, 5–6, 34–35, 41–42, 63–65, 76–91, 92, 94, 99, 104–5, 131, 132, 143–44, 167, 168, 205, 215, 220, 225, 252–53
Jefferson, M. E., 113–14
Johnson, Charles, 179
Johnson, Herschel, 34–35
Johnson, Lyndon, 8, 114–15, 119–22, 168–88, 210–11
Joint Chiefs of Staff (United States), 26, 168
Joint Committee on Atomic Energy (United States Congress), 15, 51, 54–55, 73, 136–37
Joliot-Curie, Frédéric, 17–18, 35, 49–50
Jordan, 177, 180–81, 183–85
Jordan waters dispute, 177, 180–81, 183

Kaempffert, Waldemar, 65
Kaiser Aluminum, 116–20
Kaiser, Edgar, Jr., 119–20
Kaltenborn, H. V., 31–32
Kapor, Ashok, 201–2
Karachi Nuclear Power Project (KANUPP), 196–99
Katanga, 110–12
Kaul, Triloki Nath, 204–5
Kawai, Takeshi, 132
Kawara, Kiyoshi, 131–32

Keeny, Spurgeon, 219–20
Kennedy, John F., 111–12, 128–29, 171, 176–77, 178–79
Kennedy, Richard T., 237, 240
Khalkhali, Zhila, 208–9
Khan, Muhammad Ayub, 171
Khan, Munir Ahmad, 193–94, 195, 196–97, 204, 246–47
Khrushchev, Nikita, 72–73, 98, 125–26
Kirby, Robert E., 220–21
Kissinger, Henry, 1–2, 188, 189–90, 204–6, 209–15, 220, 227–28, 235–36
Knipling, Edward, 130
Kohl, Helmut, 245–46
Komer, Robert, 120–21, 180–81
Korea. See North Korea and South Korea
Korean War, 52, 54, 56, 64–65, 74–75
Kraftwerk Union, 213–14

Laniel, Joseph, 38, 57, 92–93
Laurence, William, 65–66
Lawrence, Ernest, 83
Legasov, Valerii, 244
less developed countries (LDCs), 3–4, 130, 237–38, 247
Leventhal, Paul, 230
Libya, 196–226, 231, 251
Lilienthal, David, 14, 17–18, 20–21, 50
Limited Test Ban Treaty, 174–76, 204
Lindell, Bo, 128
Lindquist, A. W., 130
Lindsay Light and Chemical Company, 13–14, 30–31
Lindsay, Charles R., 30–31
liquid metal fast breeder reactors, 207–8, 221
Liverman, James L., 222
Lodge, Henry Cabot, Jr., 33, 104
Long Amendment, 204–5
Lovanium University, 106
Lucky Dragon. See *Daigo Fukuryū Maru*
Lumumba, Patrice, 108–9, 110–11
Luse, Robert A., 139

Macmillan, Harold, 107, 111–12
Malcolm X, 116, 122
Malone, Thomas, 222
Malthus, Thomas, 2–3, 7–8, 29–30, 33, 43–44, 143–44, 175
Mao Zedong, 21–22

Marais, Pieter, 112–13
Marshall Islands, 39–43, 54, 77–78
Marshall Plan, 17, 24, 33, 39–40, 47–48, 51–52, 54–55, 81
Marshall, George, 15, 20–22
Marshall, Walter, 212–13
Massachusetts Institute of Technology, 211–12
McCone, John, 119–20
McMahon, Brien, 22, 31, 33–34, 47–55
McNamara, Robert, 168–69
medicine, 14–17, 36–37, 39, 59, 85, 89–90, 92, 94, 119, 127–28. *See also* cancer
Meigs, Peveril, 179
Meir, Golda, 173–74
Mertz, Edwin, 140
Mexico, 29, 71, 94, 129–30, 139–40, 178–79
Michigan Memorial Phoenix Project, 70, 75–76
Miller, Harold, 119
Miller, Judith, 238
Minty, Abdul, 252
Mobile Radioisotope Laboratory, 129–30
molten salt breeder reactors, 221
Monazita Ilmenita do Brasil (MIBRA), 13–14, 21
monazite, 6–7, 9, 13–16, 21, 23–24, 30–35
Montalto di Castro nuclear site, 225
Morokhov, Igor, 225–26
Muller, Hermann J., 44–45, 50
Mundt, Karl, 80
Murray, Thomas, 23

Nakasone, Yasuhiro, 78–79
Nasser, Gamal, 107, 172–74, 180–81, 192
National Security Council (United States), 52, 55, 94, 96, 111
natural uranium, 72, 87–88, 90, 196–200, 213, 220, 226
Nautilus, USS, 65–68, 73–74,
Navajo. *See* Diné
Navy, United States, 41–43, 53–54, 66–67, 70–74, 220–21
Nazi Germany, 13–14, 18–21, 68–69
Ne'eman, Yuval, 233
Nehru, Jawaharlal, 26–27, 31, 78, 138–39, 170–71

Nelson, Oliver, 140
neocolonialism, 5–6, 109–10, 120, 170–71, 190, 213–14, 249–50
Neves da Fontoura, João, 30
Nippon TV, 80–81, 85–86, 90–91
Nitsche, Erik, 67–68
Nixon, Richard, 55, 188, 189, 204–9, 214–15, 220
Nkrumah, Kwame, 106–22, 192
Non-proliferation Treaty. *See* Treaty on the Non-Proliferation of Nuclear Weapons
North Korea, 4, 52, 74–75, 227–28, 250–51
nuclear accidents, 4, 217–18, 224–26, 238, 240–45, 253. *See also* Three Mile Island, Chernobyl, *and* Fukushima
nuclear energy. *See* nuclear power reactors
nuclear fallout, 77–78, 89, 128–30, 144, 175–76, 245, 253
nuclear power reactors, 1, 6–7, 15–16, 18, 33–34, 52–55, 59, 64–76, 81–82, 84–85, 87–91, 92–95, 98–103, 106, 113–21, 165–88, 191, 193–202, 206–16, 217–47, 249–50, 254–55. *See also* boiling water reactors, breeder reactors, CANDU reactors, gas-cooled reactors, nuclear accidents, nuclear power reactors, pressurized water reactors, RBMK reactors, TRIGA reactors, *and* research reactors
nuclear reprocessing facilities, 72, 172–73, 198–200, 214, 220, 222–24, 231–35
nuclear safeguards, 4, 90, 165–70, 181–84, 187, 199, 202, 214, 222–24, 227–30, 235, 237, 239–40, 247
nuclear waste. *See* radioactive waste
nuclear weapons proliferation, 2–5, 8–10, 57, 64, 165–72, 180–82, 184, 190, 199–216, 217–48, 249–52, 254
nuclear weapons tests, 9, 14, 36, 38–49, 54, 64–65, 77–78, 85, 89, 108–10, 121–22, 167–71, 174–76, 190, 199–206, 214, 231–32. *See also* United States nuclear tests, Soviet nuclear tests, French nuclear tests,

Chinese nuclear test, peaceful nuclear explosion (PNE), *and* Indian nuclear test
Nukem, 230–31
Nunn May, Alan, 115–16, 118–19
Nuri al-Said, 227–28

Oak Ridge National Laboratory, 16–17, 70–71, 93, 114–15, 175, 180, 193–94, 219–21
Obama, Barack, 252–53
Obninsk, 59, 72–73, 98. *See also* nuclear power reactors
Ōhira, Masayoshi, 225
oil crisis. *See* energy crisis
oil. *See* petroleum
Olsen, Jerry, 221
Open Skies proposal, 97
Operation Crossroads, 41–45
Operation Redwing, 89
Operation Wigwam, 85
Organization of African Unity, 119–20
Organization of Petroleum-Exporting Countries (OPEC), 2, 190–91, 205, 209–16, 228, 237, 240
Osirak nuclear reactor, 229, 233–38
Ottinger, Richard, 240–41
Our Friend the Atom, 68–69

Pahlavi, Mohammad Reza (Shah of Iran), 192, 208–12
Pakistan Institute of Nuclear Science and Technology, 194–95, 198
Pakistan, 8–9, 99–104, 139, 170–71, 190–204, 213, 231, 233, 236–37, 246–48. *See also* East Pakistan
pan-Africanism, 9–10, 113, 116–18, 121, 192
pan-Arabism, 9–10, 107, 173–74
Panama, 171–72
Pao Tou nuclear reactor, 167–68
Park, Chul-Jae, 75
Pastore, John O., 73
Patrick, Ruth, 222
Patterson, J. T., 45
Patterson, Morehead, 103–4
Pawley, William D., 31
peaceful nuclear explosion (PNE), 48–49, 171–72, 175–76, 190, 200–4, 206–7

Penney, William, 42–43
Pérez de Cuéllar, Javier, 246
Perkins, James A., 168–69
Perón, Juan, 18–21
petroleum, 1–2, 4–5, 6–7, 9, 65–66, 69–70, 76, 88, 117–18, 190–91, 200, 202–3, 205–16, 217–28, 233–43, 244–45, 255
Philippines, 87, 92–93, 99–104, 191–92
phosphorus-32, 113, 118
plant breeding, 2–3, 6–7, 44–46, 59, 92, 95, 124, 130–33, 138–40, 143–44, 167, 189
plowshare projects, 66, 99, 171, 175–76, 222. *See also* peaceful nuclear explosion (PNE)
Plumbat affair, 230–31
plutonium, 16–17, 21, 34–35, 39, 70–71, 72, 171–74, 177, 182, 198–99, 207–8, 211–14, 219–35, 241
plutonium production. *See* nuclear reprocessing facilities
Point Four programs, 24–26, 34, 47–51, 55
population growth, 2–3, 7–8, 28–30, 32–33, 43–44, 79, 93, 124, 126–27, 138–39, 143–44, 194, 198–200, 218, 249–50
Porter, William J., 203–4
Portugal, 22–23, 103
President's Science Advisory Committee (United States), 136–37
pressurized water reactors, 70–71, 73–74, 213, 225–26
Price, Gwilym, 66–67
Project Independence, 209
proliferation. *See* nuclear weapons proliferation
propaganda, 9, 37, 38–39, 49–50, 51–59, 64, 72–73, 78–91, 94–98, 114, 124, 240–41, 251–52, 255–56
public health, 6–9, 16–17, 124–30, 140–41, 224, 241–42

Quarshie, Richard, 106–7
Quihillalt, Oscar, 169–70

Rabin, Yitzhak, 186
Rabinowitch, Eugene, 50
Rabson, Robert, 139–40

race and racism, 6, 8–9, 25–26, 95–97, 104–9, 114–19, 168, 237, 252
radioactive waste, 14–15, 16–17, 37, 127, 135, 175–76, 245
radioisotopes, 2–3, 6–7, 15–23, 37, 39–40, 46–47, 59, 71, 76–77, 94, 106, 112–13, 118, 129–30, 135, 165–66, 167, 191–94, 198, 229, 254–55. *See also* phosphorus-32, cobalt-60, strontium-90, iodine-131, *and* cesium-137
radium, 23–24, 43–45
Rae, Angus, 193
Rajasthan-1 reactor, 196–97
Raman, C. V., 100
Rangel, Orlando, 42
Rashid, Salman, 232
RBMK reactors, 244
Reagan, Ronald, 234–46, 251–52
Réard, Louis, 41
Reed, Philip, 83
Reimei rice, 143–44
research reactors, 21–22, 67–68, 70–71, 74–76, 81–82, 87–88, 90, 92, 94–95, 103, 113, 142, 172–73, 194–97, 201, 208, 227–29. *See also* TRIGA reactors
Revelle, Roger, 175
Rhee, Syngman, 75
Richter, Ronald, 20
Rickover, Hyman, 220–21
Robeson, Paul, 116
Romulo, Carlos P., 99
Rooppur Nuclear Power Project, 196
Rostow, Walt, 181–82, 186–87
Rothschild, Edmond de, 184
Rotty, Ralph M., 221–22
Roux, Abraham J. A., 108
Rush, Kenneth, 201, 203–4
Rusk, Dean, 168, 172–73, 181
Russell, Scott, 113–14, 130–31
Russell, William F., 98–99
Rutherford, Ernest, 43–44
Ryckmans, Pierre, 22

Saddam Hussein, 228, 232–34, 250–51
safeguards. *See* nuclear safeguards
Salam, Abdus, 193–94
Salvetti, Carlo, 135–36
Sarnoff, David, 66

Sashichirō, Matsui, 90
Saudi Arabia, 2, 209–12, 215, 228, 233–37
Schaetzel, Robert, 102, 103
Schmidt, Helmut, 211
Science Council of Japan, 77–78, 83
Scowcroft, Brent, 213–14
Seaborg, Glenn T., 137, 175–88, 203–4
Seibersdorf Laboratory, 129–30, 135–36
Seligman, Henry, 16–17, 135–36
Sen, Binay Ranjan, 134, 137–39
Serrano, Felixberto M., 99
Shah, Vinod, 140, 143
Sharbati Sonora, 139–40, 143–44
Shastri, Lal Bahadur, 138–39, 170–72
Shaw, Henry, 222
Shibata, Hidetoshi, 80–82, 85–86
Shinkolobwe mine (Congo), 26, 108–9, 110
Shippingport reactor, 73, 95
Shōriki, Matsutarō, 63–64, 78–91, 99
Siazon, Domingo, 238
Sigurbjörnsson, Björn, 131–38, 140–44
Silow, Ronald, 133–43, 253–54
Simon, Herbert A., 27–29
Singh, Kewal, 189–90, 200–6
Singleton, W. Ralph, 46–47
Sino-Indian War, 165, 170–71
Six Day War, 183–86, 190–91, 230
Smiling Buddha. *See* Indian nuclear test
Smith, Luther, 46
Smyth, Henry DeWolf, 18
Snyder, Gary, 207–8
Soddy, Frederick, 43–44
solar power, 117–18, 206–7, 219, 240–41
Sole, Donald B., 112
Sonora-64 wheat, 139–40, 143–44
South Africa, 8–9, 18, 24, 103, 105–19, 121, 167, 170, 184, 223, 231–32, 237, 238–39
South Korea, 64–65, 74–76, 81
Soviet nuclear tests, 48–49, 54
Soviet Union. *See* Union of Soviet Socialist Republics
Spain, 22–23, 223
Sparrow, Arnold, 46–47, 130–31
Stadler, Lewis, 44–45
Stalin, Joseph, 43–44, 50, 72–73
Stassen, Harold, 71
sterile male insect technique, 2–3, 130

Stone, Edward Durell, 194–95, 198
Stout, Perry R., 130–31
Strauss, Lewis, 2–3, 17–18, 53–54, 55–56, 94–98, 102, 184–88
strontium-90, 66
Subrahmanyam, Krishnaswamy, 201
Subramaniam, Chidambaram, 138–39
Suez crisis, 172, 192, 205
Sulzberger, C. L., 185–86
Swaminathan, Mankombu S., 132, 138–43
Sweden, 102, 218, 225, 231, 238, 245–46, 249–50, 253
Symington Amendment, 222–23
Syria, 177, 183, 190–91

Tammuz nuclear reactor, 227–28
Tanzania, 135
Tarapur nuclear site, 172
Taylor, J. J., 202
Technicatome, 229
Thomson, J. A., 203
thorium, 13–16, 21–23, 30–34, 36, 40, 71, 95–96
Three Mile Island, 7–8, 224–26, 238, 241–42. *See also* nuclear accidents
Tlatelolco Treaty, 247
Tohamy, Hassan M., 170
Tomonaga, Sin-itirō, 78
Transnuklear, 231
Treaty on the Non-Proliferation of Nuclear Weapons (NPT), 8–10, 165–66, 168–72, 184, 199–205, 208–9, 213, 214, 218, 222–24, 228–31, 235, 237, 247, 250–51
TRIGA reactors, 74, 75–76, 87, 106, 113
Truman, Harry, 17, 20–21, 24–25, 34, 39–41, 47–49, 54, 55
Tshombe, Moïse, 110–11
Tubiana, Maurice, 126–27
Turkey, 71, 96–97, 133, 191–92, 193
Tuwaitha nuclear site, 227–29

Udall, Stewart, 175–81, 186
Union of Soviet Socialist Republics, 3, 4, 14–15, 17–18, 20–21, 23–24, 27, 31, 37, 40–41, 43–44, 47–49, 51, 53, 54, 55, 56–57, 58, 59, 72–73, 95–96, 98, 113, 115–16, 118–20, 121, 125–26, 128–29, 144, 165, 168, 178–79, 200, 202–3, 205, 217–18, 225–29, 237, 242–45, 250
United Arab Republic. *See* Egypt
United Kingdom, 13–14, 16–20, 23, 34, 35, 38–39, 57, 72, 73, 75, 87–89, 90–91, 94–95, 98, 100–5, 125, 136, 169, 193–94, 200,
United Nations, 38, 40, 48–49, 51, 55–57, 58, 97, 104, 107, 111, 114, 124, 134–35, 165, 235
United Nations Development Program, 195, 200
United Nations Special Fund, 97
United States nuclear tests, 14, 38–39, 41–45, 54, 77–79, 85, 89, 94, 95–96
Unitel, 80, 81
uranium isotope separation facilities, 16, 196–97, 200, 213, 222–23, 227, 236–37
uranium, 3, 6–9, 19–26, 32, 35–37, 38–39, 40, 43–44, 52–53, 66, 69, 70–74, 84, 87–88, 96–97, 103, 105–6, 108–9, 110, 111–12, 113, 114–15, 118–19, 125, 170, 172, 182, 195–97, 198, 199–200, 213, 214, 219–20, 222–23, 226, 227, 229, 230–32, 233, 236–37, 254–55. *See also* natural uranium *and* enriched uranium
URENCO, 227
Usmani, Ishrat Hussain, 193–97

Vanunu, Mordechai, 172–73
Vargas, Getúlio Dornelles, 26–27
Vernadsky, Vladimir, 43–44
Verwoerd, Hendrik, 107–8, 115
Vishinsky, Andrei, 48–49
Voice of America, 49, 80, 81
Volta dam project, 116–17, 119
von Braun, Werner, 68–69
von Wettstein, Diter, 2–3
Voting Rights Act, 114–15

Wantage Radiation Laboratory (United Kingdom), 135–36
Warburg, James P., 48
Ward, Alan H., 106–7, 113, 118–19
Warren, Stafford, 42–43
water and food security, 7–8, 138–39, 172, 174–84, 249
Water for Peace, 8, 174–88, 196, 210–11

Weinberg, Alvin, 70–71, 73–74, 114–15, 175, 176, 180, 182–83, 184–85, 186–87, 211–12, 221–22
Welsh, Vernon, 81–82, 83, 87
West Germany, 168, 169, 205, 211, 213–14, 227, 230–31, 241, 245–46
West, John C., 235–36
Westinghouse, 23, 66–68, 73–74, 220–21, 225
white supremacy, 26, 96–97, 105. *See also* race and racism
White, William S., 26
Whitman, Walter, 95–96
Whitney, Courtney, 79–80
Whitney, Vincent, 29–30
Whyte, R. O., 139
Wiesner, Jerome, 175, 180–81, 211–12
Wigny, Pierre, 25–26

Wiley, Alexander, 33–34
Windscale nuclear site, 72, 224
Wong, Wen-hao, 21–22
Woods, George D., 187
World Health Organization, 8, 124–30, 134, 144, 192–93

X-Rays, 44–45, 143–44

Yiftah, Shimon, 177–78
Yom Kippur War, 190–91, 205
Yomiuri Shimbun, 79, 84, 85–86, 89
Younkin, Stuart G., 136–37

Zhou Enlai, 96–97
Zia ul-Haq, Muhammad, 199–200
Zinn, Walter, 70–71, 73–74
Zur, Zvi, 177–78, 183–84